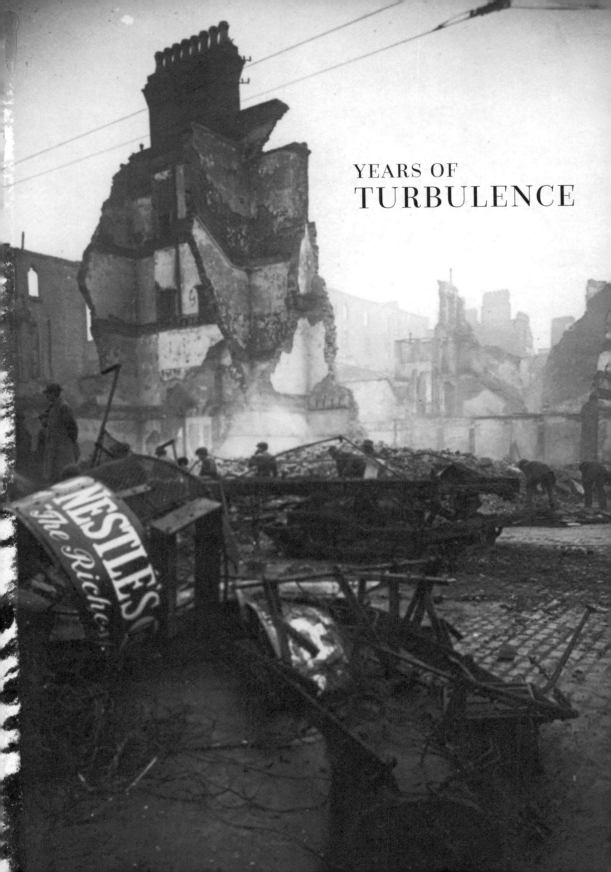

YEARS OF
TURBULENCE

YEARS OF
TURBULENCE

The Irish Revolution and Its Aftermath

In Honour of Michael Laffan

Editors DIARMAID FERRITER & SUSANNAH RIORDAN

UNIVERSITY COLLEGE DUBLIN PRESS
PREAS CHOLÁISTE OLLSCOILE BHAILE ÁTHA CLIATH
2015

First published 2015 by
UNIVERSITY COLLEGE DUBLIN PRESS
UCD Humanities Institute
Belfield
Dublin 4
Ireland
www.ucdpress.ie

ISBN 978-1-910820-07-0 hb

CIP data available from the British Library

Text design and layout by Lyn Davies Design
Typeset in Arnhem and Questa
Printed in England on acid-free paper
by CPI Antony Rowe, Chippenham, Wiltshire.

CONTENTS

ACKNOWLEDGEMENTS

We would like to acknowledge the generous support of the National University of Ireland and the School of History, University College Dublin, towards the publication of this volume. Sincere thanks are also due to our colleagues in the School of History for their interest in the project and their help in bringing it to fruition.

A collection of this kind accrues a great debt of gratitude to archivists and librarians. We would like to thank the staffs of: the GAA Museum and Archives; Galway City Council Archives; Galway County Council Archives; Galway Diocesan Archives; the Historical Library of the Religious Society of Friends in Ireland; the Irish Jesuit Archives; Military Archives, Cathal Brugha Barracks; Monaghan County Museum; The National Archives, London; the National Archives of Ireland; the National Library of Ireland; Trinity College Dublin Department of Early Printed Books and Special Collections; Trinity College Dublin Manuscripts and Archive Research Library; the Parliamentary Archives, London; University College Dublin Archives; and University College Dublin Library Special Collections.

Noelle Moran and Damien Lynam at UCD Press were a pleasure to work with. We are grateful for their commitment and professionalism and in particular for their determination to ensure that this would be a beautiful book. We would like to thank the GAA Museum and Archives, the National Archives of Ireland, the National Library of Ireland, RTÉ Stills Library, UCD Archives and UCD Library Special Collections for their permission to reproduce the images which illustrate it. We are particularly grateful to Kate Manning in UCD Archives for her invaluable help in sourcing images. We also wish to express gratitude to Lyn Davies Design for typesetting, Origin Design for the cover design, and the anonymous readers whose constructive criticism made an important contribution to the quality of the collection.

Finally, and most importantly, we want to thank the contributors. Their enthusiasm for this project was evident from their great patience, willing responses to suggestions, and exemplary adherence to deadlines.

ABBREVIATIONS

BMH	Bureau of Military History
BMH WS	Bureau of Military History Witness Statement
CDH	Combined Departments of History, University College Dublin
CO	Colonial Office
DMP	Dublin Metropolitan Police
DT	Department of the Taoiseach
EEC	European Economic Community
EPB	Department of Early Printed Books and Special Collections, Trinity College, Dublin
GAA	Gaelic Athletic Association
GHQ	General Headquarters
GPO	General Post Office
HLRSFI	Historical Library of the Religious Society of Friends in Ireland
IAWGCG	Irish Association of Women Graduates and Candidate Graduates
IJA	Irish Jesuit Archives
INTO	Irish National Teachers' Organisation
IRA	Irish Republican Army
IRB	Irish Republican Brotherhood
IWFL	Irish Women's Franchise League
IWSLGA	Irish Women's Suffrage and Local Government Association
IWSS	Irish Women's Suffrage Society
MA	Military Archives, Cathal Brugha Barracks
MP	Member of Parliament
MSPC	Military Service Pensions Collection
MWFL	Munster Women's Franchise League
NAI	National Archives of Ireland
NLI	National Library of Ireland
Parl. Arch.	Parliamentary Archives, London
RIC	Royal Irish Constabulary
RTÉ	Raidió Teilifís Éireann
TCD	Trinity College Dublin

TD	Teachta Dála
TNA	The National Archives, Kew, London
UCD	University College Dublin
UCDA	University College Dublin Archives
UEA	University of East Anglia
UVF	Ulster Volunteer Force
WFL	Women's Freedom League
WILPF	Women's International League for Peace and Freedom
WO	War Office
WSPU	Women's Social and Political Union

CONTRIBUTORS

MARIE COLEMAN

A lecturer in Irish history at Queen's University Belfast, she did her PhD in UCD in 1998 under Michael Laffan's supervision and it was subsequently published as *County Longford and the Irish Revolution, 1910–1923* (2003). Her other publications include *The Irish Sweep: A History of the Irish Hospitals Sweepstake, 1930–1987* (2009) and *The Irish Revolution, 1916–1923* (2013). She is currently working on the experience of veterans after the revolution, with particular emphasis on military service pensions.

CLARA CULLEN

A former academic librarian and an Associate of UCD Humanities Institute, her research focuses on various aspects of Dublin's cultural institutions and on Irish women in nineteenth- and twentieth-century Ireland. She co-edited *The Building of the State* (2011) with Orla Feely and *His Grace is Displeased: Selected Correspondence of John Charles McQuaid* (2012) with Margaret Ó hÓgartaigh. Clara also edited *The World Upturning: Elsie Henry's Irish Wartime Diaries, 1913–1919* (2013) and has contributed to a wide range of academic publications. Her forthcoming publications include *Jones 125: A Dublin Engineering Company since 1890* and *'A Veritable Genius': Sir Robert John Kane in Nineteenth-Century Ireland* (2016).

ANNE DOLAN

A lecturer in modern Irish history at TCD, she is author of *Commemorating the Irish Civil War: History and Memory, 1922–2000* (2003), and, with Cormac O'Malley, is co-editor of *'No Surrender Here!': The Civil War Papers of Ernie O'Malley* (2008). She is currently working on a book on violence in post-war Ireland.

DIARMAID FERRITER

One of Ireland's best-known historians, he is Professor of Modern Irish History at UCD. His books include *The Transformation of Ireland 1900–2000* (2004),

Judging Dev: A Reassessment of the Life and Legacy of Éamon de Valera (2007), *Occasions of Sin: Sex and Society in Modern Ireland* (2009), and *Ambiguous Republic: Ireland in the 1970s* (2012). His most recent book is *A Nation and Not a Rabble: The Irish Revolution 1913–23* (2015). He is a regular broadcaster on television and radio and a weekly columnist with the *Irish Times*.

TOM GARVIN

Emeritus Professor of Politics at UCD, he is also an alumnus of Woodrow Wilson International Center for Scholars, Washington DC, and the author of many books and articles. His books include *The Evolution of Irish Nationalist Politics* (1981); *1922: The Birth of Irish Democracy* (1996); *Judging Lemass* (2009); and *News from a New Republic* (2010). He has taught extensively at UCD and several American universities. His topics have included Irish politics, nationalism, the Constitution of the United States and comparative politics. His biography of Daniel Binchy, Irish scholar, diplomat and anti-Nazi, is to be published in early 2016.

SHAUNA GILLIGAN

She completed her MA in History in UCD under the supervision of Michael Laffan and has since completed a PhD (Creative Writing) at the University of South Wales. Her debut novel *Happiness Comes from Nowhere* was published in 2012.

MARNIE HAY

A lecturer in history at St Patrick's Campus, Dublin City University, she is the author of a monograph entitled *Bulmer Hobson and the Nationalist Movement in Twentieth-Century Ireland* (2009), as well as many articles in journals and edited collections. Her current research focuses on Na Fianna Éireann and other aspects of Irish nationalist youth culture in the early twentieth century.

KATIE LINGARD

Her study of the Irish revolutionary period began with her MA thesis on Michael Collins's military strategy, through Waikato University in New Zealand. This research sparked an abiding interest in the role of GHQ, leading to further study under the supervision of Michael Laffan at UCD. As a lecturer with King's College London, Katie taught insurgency for three years at the Royal Air Force College, Cranwell in the UK. She has lived in Australia since 2013, and is currently completing her research on the role of GHQ in the Irish War of Independence.

BRIAN MAYE

A teacher, journalist and historian, his books include *Fine Gael 1923–1987* (1993), *Arthur Griffith* (1997), *With Casement's Irish Brigade* (ed., 2010) and *The Search for*

Justice: Trócaire, a History (2010). He is currently researching how the Irish independence struggle was reflected visually, especially in painting, from 1798 to 1922. He lectures in Griffith College Dublin.

CONOR MULVAGH

A lecturer in Irish history at UCD with special responsibility for the 'decade of centenaries', his research focuses on late nineteenth- and early twentieth-century Irish history, especially Home Rule and the Irish revolution. His forthcoming monograph explores the work of Irish Nationalist MPs at Westminster, 1900–18. He first worked with Michael Laffan on a thesis entitled 'The road to Woodenbridge, tension and disunity in the Irish Volunteers, 1914' (2007). Michael Laffan subsequently became his doctoral thesis supervisor. Conor is a member of the UCD Centre for War Studies and an editor on HistoryHub.ie, UCD's public history website.

WILLIAM MURPHY

Author of *Political Imprisonment and the Irish, 1912–1921* (2014) and co-editor of *The Gaelic Athletic Association, 1884–2009* (2009), he edited and introduced Darrell Figgis, *A Chronicle of Jails* (2010). He is a lecturer in history and Irish studies at Dublin City University.

ÚNA NEWELL

Watson Semantic Specialist at ORRECO, she is a graduate of the National University of Ireland, Galway (BA) and UCD (MA, PhD). She is an Irish Research Council Fellow and a Research Associate of the UCD Humanities Institute. Her most recent publications include *The West Must Wait: County Galway and the Irish Free State 1922–32* (2015).

ROSS O'CARROLL

A history teacher at St Mark's Community College, Tallaght, Dublin, he graduated with a First Class Honours MA in History from UCD in 2010. His MA thesis was entitled 'The Gaelic Athletic Association 1914–1918'.

EAMON O'FLAHERTY

He studied at UCD and Cambridge and is Senior Lecturer in the UCD School of History. Most recently he has published on Irish urban history and twentieth-century French historiography, and is currently working on a study of urbanism in Restoration and Hanoverian Ireland.

SUSANNAH RIORDAN

A lecturer in the School of History, UCD, her main research interests lie in the fields of Irish and British social, religious and intellectual history and in the history of sexuality. She has published numerous articles on these topics and is the co-editor, with Catherine Cox, of *Adolescence in Modern Irish History* (2015).

PAUL ROUSE

A lecturer in the School of History, UCD, he has written extensively on the history of Irish sport and his book *Sport and Ireland: A History* was published in 2015.

LIST OF ILLUSTRATIONS

INTRODUCTION

DIARMAID FERRITER AND SUSANNAH RIORDAN

W e both first experienced Michael Laffan lecture as First Year history students in the 1980s in Theatre L, University College Dublin's largest theatre, which seats 500. It was often apparent to students in Theatre L that some academics were better suited to it than others. Michael, it was clear, thrived in it. Lecturing in that environment suited him for different reasons; his big personality, his sense of drama and because he was a powerful and natural communicator with a fluent command over the intricacies of modern Irish history. Michael was what would be considered today, in an era of PowerPoint, multiple screens and appliances, an old-fashioned lecturer, but in a good way; he relied on erudite oratory rather than visuals to command attention.

Throughout his career at UCD from 1976 to 2010, the intellectual development of students and their welfare were central to Michael's career. He was firm when he had to be, but also humorous, hospitable, loyal, fully engaged and, thankfully, often completely indiscreet. He taught a number of courses in modern Irish and European history but former UCD history students will associate him particularly with a third-year course entitled 'The Irish Revolution 1910–23'. This was consistently the most popular course at that level, not alone because it was an opportunity to study a fascinating period with one of its most accomplished and entertaining historians but because tutorial discussions were famously lively. Michael encouraged students to question their own and each other's preconceptions and to enjoy, and understand the value of, informed historical debate. In the preface to his *The Resurrection of Ireland: The Sinn Féin Party, 1916–1923* (1999) he paid his own tribute to many of these undergraduate students: 'I have been stimulated by some of the questions which they raised in tutorial discussions and (although they might be surprised to learn of it) also by some of the arguments in essays they wrote.' In turn, the course was instrumental in inspiring many students, including both editors of and several of the contributors to this volume, to undertake graduate research.

As Eamon O'Flaherty observes in the portrait which opens the collection, Michael has often made reference to the far-too-frequent absences of the supervisor of his MA dissertation. As a supervisor of graduate research, Michael was anything but an absentee: he was attentive, fair, encouraging and focused but also spiky when necessary. He was concerned that the system of supervised research should not produce scholars whose subjects and approaches were identical to their supervisors' and actively encouraged his graduate students to develop their own research interests and methodologies. He set few limits for the historians he trained, other than that their research be extensive, their arguments evidence-based, their analysis rigorous, and their writing both polished and accessible. As a teacher on UCD's MA in Modern Irish History programme, he gave valuable insights into historiography but also very practical advice on the nuts and bolts of recording and organising archival research, and proudly displayed his beloved file cards in their shoe boxes. The roll call of those who benefited from his expertise and guidance is impressive and a number of them illuminate the pages of this book, having had their appetite first whetted and their research plans solidified by Michael.

Focusing on the subject with which Michael is most familiarly associated, the Irish revolutionary period and its aftermath, this collection contains – in addition to Eamon O'Flaherty's portrait and a select bibliography of Michael's published works by Clara Cullen – 12 chapters by established and emerging scholars, most of whom share the experience of having undertaken graduate research under Michael's supervision. These chapters are arranged chronologically and the collection does not pretend to offer a comprehensive treatment of the Irish revolution or any aspect of it; rather it highlights some of the themes and approaches currently engaging historians of the period.

In his contribution to a collection of essays published in 2002 under the title *The Irish Revolution, 1913–23*, historian Peter Hart declared that the revolution 'needs to be re-conceptualised and to have all the myriad assumptions underlying its standard narratives interrogated'. Such a process, he elaborated, would need to include examinations of 'gender, class, community, elites and masses, religion and ethnicity, the nature of violence and power'.[1] Hart's observation was a call to scholars to recognise that, to do justice to the revolutionary period, it was necessary to see it as one that was, while propelled by much idealism and courage, also multi-layered, complicated, brutal and sometimes compromised. Generalising about the period was coming under increased critical scrutiny as evolving historiography revealed numerous competing impulses, tensions, and the use of the revolution as a cloak to try and settle grievances over land, class, the distribution of power and status.

One of the advantages we now have is the variety of source material available to do justice to that complexity and to approach the revolutionary generation through the prism of their era. Hart's observations were made in the context of the expanded range of source material relating to the revolution then available, but, in the 15 years since, the amount of new source material has substantially increased again. Much of it is available digitally, most notably the census returns of 1901 and 1911, the witness statements collected by the Bureau of Military History from War of Independence veterans in the 1940s and 1950s, released to the public in 2003, and the voluminous archive of the Military Service Pension files, detailing the applications of those who applied for pensions and compensation based on service and suffering during the revolutionary period, which began to be released on a phased basis in 2013.

The scale and accessibility of such valuable primary sources means that historians of this period can do much regarding its re-conceptualising, without moralising or avoiding the reality of traumatic experiences, ambiguities, and conservative as well as radical impulses, reflected in the recent observation of Roy Foster that 'we search now ... to find clarification through terms of paradox and nuance; we have become interested in what does not change during revolutions as much as what does.'[2] This is a process which has been ongoing throughout Michael's career. From the 1960s onwards, an abundance of new archival material, including British and Irish state papers and the private collections of British and Irish veterans of the revolutionary period began to become available making it possible to establish new frameworks for interpreting the Irish revolutionary period and to offer new perspectives on the key events and personalities, a process that was accompanied by intense debates about the legacy of that era. Michael played an important role in those debates, while keeping a focus on the importance of evidence and a genuine historical revisionism based on the new sources, an approach which also informed his teaching. He demonstrated a learned scepticism about simplistic narratives and explored the nature of revolution and all the contradictions it incorporated by delineating the politics of that revolution, analysing the interactions of unionists, moderate and radical republicans and nationalists, Anglo-Irish relations, and patterns of continuity and discontinuity.

Very much an exponent of the public communication of history beyond the university, Michael contributed to newspapers, radio and television, and was responsible for many informative and fluent history broadcasts. By the end of his teaching career in UCD in 2010, Michael was engaged in researching the politics of commemoration, at a time when there was much focus on the 'decade of centenaries' of the events of 1912–23. Many of those that Michael taught and supervised, including the contributors to this book, will be centrally involved in the historical debates about these events, bringing their own new perspectives and research to illuminate the decade and complicate the narrative, but there is also little doubt that Michael's work, which provided such solid and sophisticated foundations, will remain for them an essential point of reference, and that his positive influence and example will endure.

This collection showcases many new perspectives, with the authors focusing on new angles, or revisiting traditional assumptions, and elaborating on some of the central, current debates in the historiography of the revolutionary period. They cover such themes as the experience of violence in its various forms, the specific circumstances of individual counties, tensions between constitutional-ism and radicalism, between elites and the grassroots, and the extent to which the IRA's campaign was effectively co-ordinated and controlled. They also dem-onstrate a determination to uncover personal experiences and protests that until now have remained relatively undocumented, as well as the wider backdrop, including the sporting one and the challenge of writing about women and what they experienced. This collection also recognises the need to address, not just events of the revolutionary period, but its afterlife, assessing what the revolution and its leaders came to symbolise and the extent to which a hierarchy of benefit existed in its aftermath and what the implications were for survivors.

William Murphy's chapter provides an excellent example of the possibilities for research created by new sources, in this case the searchable, online, 1911 census returns. Held at a time of radicalisation for both British and Irish suffra-gists, the census offered women a means of protesting against their votelessness either by refusing to participate or by using the return to send a message to government. British suffragettes organised a very public boycott; in Ireland suf-fragist societies were divided on the advisability of boycotting and their members were more dispersed. A limited boycott occurred, but, as Murphy demonstrates, there were other ways, many of them highly imaginative, in which women could use the census form as a means of expressing a suffragist identity.

In their chapter on the 1915 All-Ireland hurling championship, Paul Rouse and Ross O'Carroll examine the well-financed training regime which contributed to Leix's surprise victory over Cork in that year's final, arguing that the adoption of these methods, together with many of the rituals surrounding training, playing, spectating and reporting, set the Gaelic Athletic Association firmly within the sporting revolution then being experienced in Britain and elsewhere. Taking place against the backdrop of war and the renewed militarisation of politics, the 1915 championship also offers Rouse and O'Carroll an exceptional opportunity to explore how the tensions between the GAA's twin sporting and political functions played themselves out in practice.

In 1915 Michael Keogh was a prisoner of war in Germany, where he became involved with Roger Casement's efforts to recruit an Irish brigade. Keogh's colourful memoir of his life, which had been thought lost since his death in 1964, was uncovered in University College Dublin Archives in 2005. It was edited by Brian Maye and published as *With Casement's Irish Brigade* in 2009. In his chapter for this volume, Maye revisits Keogh's memoir to develop such topics as Casement's charisma and the loyalty he inspired; the profile and motivations of the men who joined the Irish Brigade; and the reasons for the failure of Casement's mission.

Conor Mulvagh's chapter provides an in-depth analysis of the leadership crisis in the Irish Parliamentary Party in the aftermath of the 1916 Rising, demonstrating that the Rising did not so much create as reveal fissures in the relationship between John Redmond, John Dillon, T. P. O'Connor and Joseph Devlin. As is well known, Dillon was the only one of the four to witness events in Dublin during and after Easter Week and afterwards rejected the Redmondite politics of conciliation. However, as Mulvagh shows, the London-based Redmond and O'Connor had become increasingly disconnected from the realities of politics in Ireland since the outbreak of war. Dillon and Devlin, meanwhile, had gained a freer hand in Ireland – and Dillon's scepticism about conciliation was already well established.

Shauna Gilligan also reflects on the legacy of the Rising, though from a very different perspective. Her subject is the scholarly, popular and political representation of P. H. Pearse in the decade after his execution, when he truly became 'all things to all men'. For many early historians and biographers, Pearse embodied both the insurrection and the nation and his significance lay not in who he had been but in what his life and death could be shown to say about Irish identity. His life's work was viewed primarily as a prelude to his death and his educational and political writings neglected as scholars sought to explain him through his fiction and poetry.

Chapters by Katie Lingard, Marie Coleman and Anne Dolan all explore facets of violence during the War of Independence. Lingard analyses Volunteer/IRA GHQ strategy during the conflict, and suggests that GHQ, and in particular Chief of Staff Richard Mulcahy, developed a policy of discriminate violence, restraining as well as ordering operations. Intended to create and sustain national and international support, this strategy promoted an image of the Volunteers/IRA as a legitimate army engaged in defending a democratically elected civil authority. This was a perspective which was not entirely appreciated either by the Dáil, which was slow to take responsibility for military actions, or by frustrated local commanders. However, its relative autonomy allowed GHQ to organise effectively and successfully to implement a strategy that was more political than military.

As Marie Coleman notes, the role played by women in the Irish revolution is in the process of receiving much more focused attention from historians due to the release of the Bureau of Military History and Military Service Pensions Collections. Here, however, she considers women as the victims of violence – fatal and non-fatal, sexual and non-sexual. It remains difficult to estimate the extent of sexual violence during the War of Independence but the recently released sources tend to confirm the view that incidences were rare and that rape was not used as a weapon of war by any of the combatant forces. Situating her analysis within the historiography of sexual violence in nationalist conflicts, Coleman assesses the factors which may have contributed to containing it in the Irish case.

If sexual violence was uncommon, IRA executions were sufficiently frequent for the practices surrounding them to become familiar. Victims were usually taken from their homes at night, bound, shot, labelled 'spy' or 'informer', and their bodies left to act as warnings to their neighbours. The executed were, Anne Dolan points out, a limited number of the dead of the War of Independence but their deaths were crucial in creating an atmosphere of fear in local communities with wavering loyalties. Dolan's chapter is not concerned with the reasons or justifications for the executions but with the nature of such intimate killings, the humanity of the dead and their executioners, and the impression these deaths made on those who inflicted, witnessed or were bereaved by them.

The complexities of political life during the revolutionary period are often best illuminated by local studies. In her chapter, Úna Newell discusses Co. Galway between the signing of the Anglo-Irish Treaty and the end of the Civil War. She focuses on the general election of June 1922, contested under an electoral pact agreed by Michael Collins and Éamon de Valera, when Galway voters ousted sitting Republican TD Liam Mellows in favour of Labour candidate T. J. O'Connell. Her detailed analysis of voting and transfers offers insights into the political and economic priorities of the Galway electorate but also demonstrates how, despite the pact, voters used proportional representation to distinguish between supporters and opponents of the Treaty and between different shades of republicanism.

The final three chapters in this collection explore the post-revolutionary lives of prominent and less well-known individuals. The importance of the Military Service Pensions Collection for historians of the 1916 Rising, War of Independence and Civil War has already been mentioned, but in his chapter for this volume, Diarmaid Ferriter assesses the collection from a different angle, exploring what the files reveal about the personal and financial circumstances which impelled applicants to make a claim. For some, the pension was of symbolic value, but for others, it meant the possibility of escaping destitution caused by disability or the death of a breadwinner. Their correspondence provides a unique perspective on the human cost of the revolution, and on the social and economic history of the independent state.

Bulmer Hobson was one of the most prominent organisers of, and propagandists for, advanced nationalism prior to 1916. However, his opposition to an insurrection without the possibility of military success caused him to be held captive by his erstwhile colleagues in the Irish Republican Brotherhood for the duration of Easter Week. Thereafter, he was effectively excluded from both political life and popular history. However, Hobson's subsequent career, the subject of Marnie Hay's chapter, was energetic and productive. Embracing the sometimes incompatible roles of civil servant and propagandist for economic reconstruction, the older Hobson continued to be a maverick in the cause of advancing what he believed to be Ireland's best economic and cultural interests.

In the final chapter in this collection, Tom Garvin draws some parallels between the early life and later career of his subject, Seán Lemass. Here Garvin describes how, when writing his biography, *Judging Lemass: The Measure of the Man* (2009), he revisited the ideas about the social origins of revolutionary elites which he had originally developed in *Nationalist Revolutionaries in Ireland 1858–1928* (1987). He noted that Lemass fitted well with the stereotype, being from a lower-middle-class family with a history of agrarian agitation and some claim to ethnic marginality. Garvin explores how this heritage influenced aspects of Lemass's career from his youthful political influences, through his involvement in the fighting of 1916–23, to the economic policies he embraced as Taoiseach.

The contributors to *Years of Turbulence* reveal a fascinating web of different experiences during and after the revolutionary era. Their work is not only a fitting tribute to the pioneering scholarship of Michael Laffan but a significant contribution to the historiography of a much debated revolution.

MICHAEL LAFFAN

Portrait of a historian[1]

EAMON O'FLAHERTY

Michael Laffan was a war baby, being born in Dublin on 13 August 1945, the day before the Japanese surrender. His father, Joseph Laffan, was an Irish army doctor who had spent his early years in Australia, returning to Ireland at the age of 16. Laffan's was a comfortable middle-class upbringing in Rathmines and Rathgar. Joseph Laffan studied medicine at UCD and joined the army during the Emergency, becoming director of the Army Medical Corps. He married Maureen O'Gorman in 1943.[2] Laffan's father was always interested in science and science fiction, writing an astronomy column in one of the daily newspapers for many years and keen on predicting future developments such as space travel which were regarded as belonging in the realms of science fiction for many years. The young Laffan did not share his father's scientific bent, however, and showed an early interest in literature and history, his youthful imagination caught by illustrated historical romances based on the works of writers like Alexandre Dumas and G. A. Henty, with stirring titles such as *Under the Red Dragon*, *In the Reign of Terror* and *To Sweep the Spanish Main*.[3] This delight in the colourful sweep of history was accompanied by the familiar schoolboy interest in geography and exotic places.

His interest in history and literature was also nourished at school. Between the ages of eight and 18 he was educated at Gonzaga College in Ranelagh, which the Jesuits had established in 1950, just three years before he started there. There were not many in the older streams by this stage, but Laffan was impressed by the example of some of his older contemporaries such as Charles Lysaght, Brendan Walsh and Anthony Clare. Gonzaga was somewhat different to most schools of that time in that the boys did not sit the state examinations, but were prepared for National University of Ireland Matriculation, an exam which the boys sat at the end of the fifth year, leaving the sixth year free to develop the school's own policy of reviving the Jesuit *Ratio Studiorum*: 'There would be a great emphasis on languages and on rhetoric. Greek and Latin would have an honoured place. But English and, hopefully Irish, would be equally important. The sciences would not feature on the curriculum.'[4] Laffan particularly enjoyed the discovery of English literature at school and enjoyed learning by heart passages from Shakespeare, Yeats and the speeches of Pearse and Lincoln. Hating games, he asked the rector if he could be excused and was given permission to be absent from games on condition he read books in the school library, which led to pleasant afternoons spent there. From this time comes his remarkable memory for detail, including an ability to remember telephone numbers by associating them with historical dates. Although he was surrounded by the typically conservative influences prevalent in Irish society in the 1950s, he was reading widely and exposed to a more cosmopolitan world before he left school to go to university in 1963.

Going on to University College Dublin was the logical progression for someone of Laffan's background in the early 1960s, long before the ban on Dublin Catholics attending Trinity College was lifted in the following decade. UCD still contained a large number of Jesuit professors and lecturers in the early 1960s, and the transition between school and college was quite seamless under these conditions. In a pattern common in Dublin at the time, Laffan had attended lectures and debates at UCD while he was still at school. But history and literature were not inevitable choices despite his own inclinations. His parents wanted him to study economics in First Arts and commence a parallel law degree in his second year. Although slightly concerned at his preference for history over the more solid career choice, his parents accepted and encouraged his interests. A key moment at the end of First Year was an interview with Paddy Lynch of the Department of Economics. Lynch saw that Laffan was clearly more interested in history than in economics and sent him to talk to T. Desmond Williams in the Department of Modern History, one of four theoretically autonomous history departments in UCD at this period (the others were Early Irish, Modern Irish and Medieval History). From this point Laffan's career was influenced and guided by Williams's magnetic powers of attracting and inspiring young historians. Law was forgotten and he concentrated on history and politics from Second Year on.

The college was a very small place at this period, although it was in the throes of an enormous expansion in student numbers which placed huge pressure on space in its buildings on Earlsfort Terrace and St Stephen's Green. The politics department had only three members at this point, Conor Martin, Fergal O'Connor and John Whyte, the only layman. Politics was to expand greatly in the following decade but at this stage could only be taken as a second and third year subject. Donal McCartney described Martin as a 'cautious progressive', while O'Connor was seen as a radical in the 1960s.[5] Whyte, as the first layman in the department, was to arouse clerical concern by his research into church–state relations in twentieth-century Ireland and eventually left UCD to go to Queen's University Belfast, but his lectures on political institutions were appreciated by Laffan, as were O'Connor's lectures on the history of political thought. It was impossible to avoid the shadow of clerical influence in UCD in the 1960s, but there were signs of change while Laffan was a student. Indeed he himself was one of the minority who ignored the custom whereby students reading in the college library would get up from their seats to say the Angelus at the appointed time, a custom which is almost unimaginable now.

Tom Garvin has remarked that the subjects which had broken free of clerical control, such as economics and history, were among the most dynamic in UCD at this stage.[6] This was very much the case with the modern history departments, which had always had lay professors since the National University of Ireland charter of 1908 and which were dominated by the colourful and formidable personalities of Desmond Williams and R. Dudley Edwards. Laffan had first encountered Williams as a lecturer when he arrived unexpectedly one day in First Year to announce that the lecturer on British history, David Steele, had suddenly resigned. Laffan was delighted to find the focus switch from municipal socialism to high politics and diplomatic history. He was to learn the story behind Steele's departure (a complicated mixture of the personal and the philosophical) the following year, when he became part of a group of history students who were almost as fascinated by the affairs of the department as by history itself, helped no doubt by having access to inside information from fellow students such as Dudley Edwards's daughter Ruth. Recent historiography, largely written by English historians exploring the links between UCD and Cambridge in this period, has produced a caricatural image of Edwards and Williams which is sorely in need of a corrective account. Williams's contribution to opening the college to a wider world, his role in professionalising Irish history, his literary journalism and the ambitious research projects at which he worked, though not to completion, need to be understood as the basis for his intriguing personality. From the students' perspective, at any rate, there is no doubt that both men were inspiring if erratic teachers, who succeeded in producing a gifted generation of students until the 1970s.

Laffan benefited from the creative tension which existed between Edwards and Williams, and a less creative tension between them and the newly appointed professor of medieval history, F. X. Martin. Kevin B. Nowlan, Donal McCartney, Margaret McCurtain, Peter Butterfield and Hilary Jenkins were lecturers at this time, all of whom were to be his colleagues at a later stage. Maureen Wall he found very impressive, if somewhat intimidating and Peter King an inspirational teacher of medieval history. Joe Lee gave a course on European economic history as a very young research student. An important figure in Laffan's undergraduate career was his second year tutor Patrick Cosgrave, then a research student.

Cosgrave, who later married Ruth Dudley Edwards, was an unusual figure who wore a poppy in early November which few dared to do in those days. He taught the largely medieval second year syllabus, but came into his own when giving tutorials on Williams's optional course on the balance of power. Cosgrave, who went on to Peterhouse, Cambridge to do a PhD, encouraged Laffan and others to take the same course. That so many of the brightest historians did so was a testimony to Williams's charismatic influence as well as to the almost complete absence of any funding for research students in the Republic of Ireland at this period.

The prospect of funded study in Cambridge and other universities was an essential component of the rapid development of Irish history in the 1960s and 1970s. It also points to limitations on academic life in UCD, and elsewhere in Ireland, in this period. Nothing written by Williams and Edwards was comparable to their conversation and lectures. Nor was there a culture of research in the college comparable to the present. The weight of teaching was heavy and the weight of examining punishing at this period. Many of the younger members of the academic staff resented the lack of interest shown in their research, which was very much regarded as secondary to their main duties of teaching and examining undergraduates. A very hierarchical structure militated against academic productivity and was sometimes demoralising, but this did little to affect the enthusiasm of the students. On graduation, Laffan embarked on what was for some time a standard course of research in UCD, consisting of a two-year research MA at UCD, which acted as a thorough training in research methods and writing, followed by a PhD, sometimes on a very different subject, at Cambridge or elsewhere.

Laffan began his MA on Sinn Féin under the supervision of Williams, who was then going through a particularly bad phase of absenteeism, often disappearing for long periods and often keeping his students waiting. When he did appear, his charm and stimulating company made up for the disappointments, but the department decided that Dudley Edwards should take over as Laffan's supervisor. Laffan had not had much to do with Dudley before this and found his first supervision rather disconcerting as Edwards spoke to him from behind, addressing the back of his head. On another occasion Laffan was taken aback to be told that Edwards had been dreaming about him and his thesis. Apart from these mild eccentricities, supervision by Dudley was an intense experience as a slightly indirect and even gnomic style of utterance combined with an astonishing range of knowledge. To the young researcher it sometimes seemed as if Dudley knew everything and this too could be inspiring. Dudley was also to have a very important influence on the future of Laffan's career. The thesis itself was also the foundation for Laffan's later work on Sinn Féin.

In 1968 Laffan left Dublin to take up a studentship at Trinity Hall, Cambridge. The original intention was to study British policy towards Ireland after the First

World War under the supervision of Nicholas Mansergh, then Smuts Professor of Commonwealth History and soon to be master of St John's College. But Williams had planted the seeds of a different project in Laffan's mind, suggesting that he might work on Anglo-German relations instead. At his first interview with Mansergh, Laffan informed him of his change of direction, whereupon Mansergh lifted the telephone and arranged a meeting with Harry Hinsley, the leading Cambridge historian of international relations and later author of a monumental history of British intelligence.[7] Hinsley was a kind and generous man with a large and devoted group of research students who congregated at his Thursday afternoon seminars. Laffan also met Herbert Butterfield on one occasion and Butterfield warned him that his subject was too wide, but for a time it became even wider. Gradually the work came to focus on the role of the question of French security in Anglo-German relations in the years after the Treaty of Versailles, 'the road to Locarno' as the work might be usefully re-titled.[8]

Williams's influence continued remotely from Dublin, leading to a research trip to Germany based in the Institute for European History at Mainz. This was initially for a six-month period, but Laffan spent 15 months in Germany in all, where he learned German from scratch and worked in the Foreign Ministry Archives in Bonn, the Federal Archives, then in Coblenz, and the Gustav Stresemann papers on microfilm in the Institute. He benefitted from the cosmopolitan atmosphere of the Institute, meeting students from Eastern Europe for the first time and gaining a valuable central European perspective on international relations at the height of the Cold War. These years also saw him continue his practice of travelling widely in Europe, something which had started in 1964 when he travelled to Greece via France and Italy. Laffan's generation grew up at a time when Ireland was attempting to forge closer links with Europe. He had been an avid listener to Garret FitzGerald's broadcasts on the Irish economy and was dismayed by Charles de Gaulle's veto on British entry to the EEC in 1963, which inevitably prevented Irish membership, although he was later aware of the value of the interval thus obtained as it enabled Ireland to prepare for entry when it came in 1973.

Laffan completed his PhD in 1973, at a time when the first oil crisis delivered a shock to the world economy and halted the academic expansion of the previous decade. He took an editorial job on a current affairs paper, *The European Review*, based in Norwich and then a one-year post, which was renewed, lecturing in European and German political history at the University of East Anglia (UEA). At this period he also got a grant to spend some time in Paris working in the recently opened French foreign office archives. This expanded the range of his archival work and confirmed his love of the city of Paris. Although fond of Norwich and the East Anglian countryside, he was less comfortable in the History Sector of UEA, which at that time was riven with factional disputes leading to frequent purges and a decision to concentrate on social history to the exclusion of political and diplomatic history. Laffan was persuaded to apply for two lectureships in history at UCD at this stage and, though they were not in his field, he was deemed appointable after interview, so that when a one-year vacancy closer to his research areas came up in 1976, he was appointed. In the absence of any permanent positions, his appointment was extended annually for five years until he was made permanent in 1981. This long and sometimes frustrating experience of insecurity gave him a sympathy for and readiness to support colleagues in similar circumstances throughout his career. While not exactly a Gaullean *traversée du désert*, the experience of the 70s is one that many academics will understand very well.

Laffan's return to UCD in 1976 was to a very different place. The college had largely moved to Belfield in 1970, to a new site which was under construction, and which was treeless and bleak in its physical aspect by comparison with the old site on St Stephen's Green. The aftermath of the student unrest of 1969–70, which had also involved many of the lecturers, was still present, but the university and the country had experienced rapid changes in the period 1968–76. Many of those who had been Laffan's teachers were now his colleagues, as were a number of near-contemporaries from UCD such as Fergus D'Arcy, Charlie Doherty, Ronan Fanning and James McGuire. There was also a new generation of non-Irish historians who had arrived in the interval such as Howard Clarke, Hugh Gough, Albert Lovett, Seymour Phillips and Michael Richter. More than most departments, history was highly collegial, rather like an extended family, Laffan recalls. Colourful, lively, sometimes argumentative but never boring. The almost-weekly Friday departmental meetings contributed to this sense of community, as did the creation of a federal structure of the four separate history departments in the 1970s. The Combined Departments of History (CDH) brought the historians closer together and reinforced the collegial atmosphere of UCD history. The four professors continued to exercise authority through the Board of History, but the regular meetings of the CDH created a lively and vigorous forum for debate, brilliantly captured in its early years in the minutes taken by Denis Bethell of the medieval department. The conditions of his appointment meant that Laffan taught a wide range of subjects both in modern European and modern Irish history, but the return to Dublin also shifted the focus of his research back to Irish history, as Dudley Edwards intended when he appointed him. The result was that his very extensive work in continental archives did not lead to continued work in this area, as would almost certainly have been the case had he remained in England. He now resumed his work on the Sinn Féin party and the Irish revolution at a time when the subject was enjoying a considerable expansion, not least because of the gradual opening up of government archives and private political papers from the 1960s onwards.

Laffan's return to Irish history in the late 1970s, marked by the publication in 1983 of *The Partition of Ireland*, coincided with a period of intense debate about Irish nationalism and political violence in the wake of the eruption of violence in Northern Ireland after 1968. He had left Ireland for Cambridge just days before the Civil Rights March in Derry, often seen as the beginning of the first phase of the Troubles. As violence in Northern Ireland became more serious and destabilised the Northern Ireland state, historians and public intellectuals addressed the crisis by revisiting the historical roots of the conflict. By the late 1970s and early 1980s there was a fully fledged debate in full swing on the theme of historical revisionism which raged far beyond the confines of academic history. History became part of a national conversation in which a wide range of commentators – including journalists, cultural critics, politicians and academic historians – placed recent accounts of the Irish past under sometimes uncomfortable scrutiny.[9] When lecturing in London in the early 1980s Laffan was criticised, fairly he thought, when the point was made that it was much easier to be critical of Irish nationalism in Dublin than in Northern Ireland or as an Irish person living in Britain. But he rejected as absurd the accusation that his historical practice was giving aid and comfort to Margaret Thatcher. Surely, he argued, if Mrs Thatcher did not mean well for Ireland she would be pleased to see a simplistic and one-sided view of Irish history embraced by Irish nationalists. These debates moved far beyond the confines of the universities and became a common focus of media discussion during the 1980s and 1990s, intensified by the various phases of the unfolding crisis in Northern Ireland.

The negative effects of the Ulster crisis on the morale of historians was exemplified by the pessimism of F. S. L. Lyons's *Culture and Anarchy in Ireland* published in 1979. What gave the whole debate such momentum was that it tended to stray far beyond the realm of academic history and overlapped into areas of contemporary politics and ideology. The stresses of the continuing violence in the north, particularly the deaths of the IRA hunger strikers in 1981 which polarised Irish opinion and led to a deterioration in Anglo-Irish relations, all combined with unstable government and an economic recession in the south to give these debates a sense of urgency. History was only one part of a complex of issues which were at stake in these culture wars, and historians found themselves grouped together with others whose role in the debate was much more clearly political. The most important case in point was Conor Cruise O'Brien, whose evolution to an overtly unionist position in politics by the early 1990s seemed to bear out the fears of those for whom a critical approach to the Irish past was tantamount to a repudiation of Irish nationalism.

History was also drawn into what was essentially a contemporary debate about the morality of political violence which had little to do with historical writing but everything to do with the uses of the past to legitimise or condemn the IRA's armed struggle. Historians were well aware of the dangers posed by the heated and occasionally bitter tone of the exchanges around the topic. A collection of some of the major contributions to the debate edited by Ciaran Brady in 1994 (*Interpreting Irish History: The Debate on Historical Revisionism*) gives some sense of the intensity of the engagement during the 1980s and 1990s, though much of the discussion in the mass media was conducted at a much more polemical level. In 1984 members of the UCD Arts faculty broadcast a series of lectures on television which were published as a special issue of *The Crane Bag*, a journal of contemporary cultural criticism, entitled *Ireland: Dependence and Independence*. These lectures were delivered in the shadow of worsening violence in the north, economic crisis in the south and the aftermath of a hotly contested constitutional referendum on abortion which had been a triumph for Catholic conservatism over the forces of secularism in the Republic. Laffan's lecture, 'Two Irish states', arose out of *The Partition of Ireland*, which he had recently published, but also caught the mood of the time:

> All countries are products of their past, but in Ireland we often seem to be prisoners of our past, unable to escape from old problems and condemned to re-fight old battles. The decade of the 1960s, the age of Seán Lemass in the south and Terence O'Neill in the north, an age of optimism, of confidence, of new beginnings, seems far away. We have retreated to the mood of earlier, gloomier, bloodier years. Questions such as the border, re-unification, the role of the IRA and the Catholic nature of the Republic are as immediate to us now as they were to our grandparents.[10]

Laffan argued that the partition of Ireland and the subsequent polarisation of the two states that resulted were unintended consequences, the result of the triumph of extremist parties in different parts of the country – Sinn Féin and the Ulster Unionists. The failure of moderate nationalism had led to the emergence of two states which were hostile to each other and which developed into opposite varieties of intolerance. The Ulster Unionist leadership, accepting a degree of Home Rule which it had never asked for, demanded and got an area which contained a nationalist minority too large for its own long-term stability, and proceeded to discriminate against them, in time provoking the crisis which had recently erupted. The south, once it had achieved limited independence, proceeded to forget the inclusive and pluralist elements in Irish nationalism and construct a narrowly Catholic and avowedly Gaelic state which took no heed of the beliefs and values of the Ulster Protestants. The result was an insular society which had failed to take up the opportunities for greater engagement with the rest of the world offered by independence from Britain and which had, indeed, been content to remain economically dependent in some key areas.

Laffan also argued that the inward-looking southern political elites had nurtured

self-serving myths which tended to reinforce their grip on the minds of the population while at the same time distorting the past. One such myth concerned partition
itself, pretending that the Civil War had been fought on this issue, when in fact
the Ulster question had been practically ignored by Sinn Féin during the War of
Independence and the oath of allegiance to the king, not partition, was the issue on
which people had fought the Civil War. Laffan argued that while Irish nationalism
before independence had cultivated images of the past and future, successive
governments since 1922 had cultivated and imposed myths of the past:

> The successful rebels glorified rebellion – in the past, not in the present; successive
> governments and establishments viewed the role of physical force with ambiguity
> and ambivalence. Irish history and Irish historical characters were forced to undergo
> strange contortions to fit into the image which was deemed appropriate by the
> successful ex-revolutionaries. The claim in the 1916 proclamation that six times during
> the past three hundred years the Irish people had asserted in arms their right to
> national freedom was nonsense, but it was sacred nonsense. It, and the mentality
> which it represented, helped give Irishmen a distorted view of their history.[11]

Statements like these were simply too much for many who had been brought
up with the traditional version of Irish history, and led to accusations that historians
like Laffan were antipathetic to Irish nationalism and, therefore, to the Irish
people. But criticism ranged even more widely against what was percieved to be a
'revisionist school', whose approach to Irish history was characterised by Brendan
Bradshaw, in an influential article published in 1989, as the product of a corrosive
scepticism which prevented Irish historians from having empathy with the Irish
historical experience.[12] Laffan's younger colleague Kevin Whelan expressed these
criticisms more trenchantly in the *UCD History Review* in 1991, accusing the revisionists of a narrowness of vision which led to a partisan history written from the
perspective of the powerful against the powerless, 'a conservative tendency ...
exacerbated by an exaggerated sense of the centrality of political history, a position
inherited from a document-based and constitutionally obsessed Oxbridge
tradition.'[13] The most cogent and subtle of these critics was Seamus Deane,
Professor of Modern English and American Literature at UCD, who published a
series of reflections on the subject in the 1980s, including a contribution to the 1984
Crane Bag collection. Deane very skilfully examined rhetorical practices in contemporary historical writing which he believed concealed a politically motivated
rewriting of history under the guise of objectivity or rationality as opposed to the
irrational rhetoric of Irish nationalism. This 'partitionist rhetoric' was accused of
philosophical naivety and provincialism, but also of concealing what was essentially
a response to the Northern Ireland crisis rather than a dispassionate account of
modern Irish history.[14]

Fear of the close link between the memory of the nationalist revolution and contemporary politics lay behind the Fianna Fáil government's reluctance to sponsor any major commemoration of the 75th anniversary of the 1916 Rising in 1991. This was in marked contrast to their predecessors' response to the 50th anniversary commemoration in 1966. Laffan contributed to a collection of essays bringing together a number of historical and critical responses to the anniversary, *Revising the Rising*. These essays revealed the debate to be as lively as ever, but was not as marked by pessimism and foreboding as those of seven years earlier. In his contribution, 'Insular attitudes: the revisionists and their critics', Laffan sought to defend the historians against some of their critics. He traced the development of historical writing on the 1916 Rising from a long phase when it was 'sacrosanct, immune to criticism or even to serious examination, a model of pure heroism in a world of good and evil'.[15] He rejected the argument that revisionist history was a response to the crisis, pointing out that the key initial developments in the academic writing of Irish history had come in the 1960s, following the opening of the British official archives in 1966. He also pointed to the work done by Irish historians such as F. X. Martin and Maureen Wall in unearthing documentary evidence which shed a new light on Eoin MacNeill's role in the Easter Rising and the manipulation of the IRB Supreme Council by Thomas Clarke and Seán MacDiarmada on the eve of 1916.

Although he was occasionally singled out as a leading revisionist, and although he certainly seemed to enjoy exposing the inconsistencies and absurdities of his opponents, Laffan was not really happy with the label. Indeed most of those who were called revisionists were too individualistic to enjoy being coralled into membership of a school. Laffan felt that he was a member of a generation which had benefitted from the professionalisation of history carried out by Edwards, Williams and their contemporaries in other Irish universities. He had been trained to be suspicious of the nationalist version of Irish history, just as he had been trained to be suspicious of the unionist version. But in Ireland the nationalist version was more powerful and more ingrained, not necessarily among historians, but in the wider public culture, where deeply rooted sensitivities were held in some quarters to be sufficient to debar historians from writing in certain ways. In adopting new perspectives on such fundamental parts of modern Irish history as the Rising, historians were simply being true to their professional responsibilities, doing no more for Irish history than American and French scholars when they revised long-standing accounts of the revolutions which had transformed their own societies. Not to do this would be the real betrayal, and would lead to a closed insularity which was inimical to the search for historical truth. Revisionism was thus a normal historical practice rather than a school of thought with a pre-ordained or agreed agenda. Laffan echoed Herbert Butterfield's classic rejection of the Whig interpretation of history, with its background in the English revolution of 1688, as a retrospective history, written from the perspective of the present rather than the past.[16]

In some ways these debates were distractions from Laffan's main project after the partition book, which was to write a monograph on the rise of Sinn Féin, though the two things were in many ways complementary. He also briefly returned to continental history in the 1980s when he edited a volume of essays on *The Burden of German History 1919–45* (1988), to which he contributed 'Weimar and Versailles: German foreign policy, 1919–33'. His main research activity in this period was gathering materials for his book on Sinn Féin. In 1992, 16 years after joining the history department, he obtained a year's study leave. He chose to rent a house in rural Provence for the winter of 1992–3 to isolate himself with his notes and concentrate on writing. Provence in the winter months had very few distractions and he grew to hate the mistral, while getting used to and even growing to like his monastic life in the village. Living in France was in any case something he had always enjoyed, despite the contrast between his busy social life in Dublin and the isolation of rural life. By the end of the sabbatical he had created a draft of the book and returned to Dublin where he embarked on another period of archival research, extending the range of sources used considerably. This added to the book, which grew substantially in size and which also changed to reflect his own changing views as, for example, in his growing sense of the elitism of the Sinn Féin leadership.

When the book, *The Resurrection of Ireland: The Sinn Féin Party, 1916–1923*, appeared in 1999 it was well received both by academic reviewers and journalists in publications such as the *English Historical Review*, *The Journal of Modern History*, *Irish Historical Studies* and the *Irish Times*. One reviewer, perhaps reviewing the author as much as the book, claimed that Laffan's perspective was that of a moderate, liberal nationalist surveying a period dominated by opposing varieties of extremists. In response to this comment, Laffan acknowledged that he might well be seen as a man of conservative character and liberal inclinations, although those observing his profile in UCD over the last ten years might have disagreed. But though a moderate himself with a feeling for historical characters who were moderate, the people he chose to study were extremists, whom he sought to understand in line with the view that the historian must try to see the world through the eyes of his subjects. Perhaps when dealing with the relations between Sinn Féin politicians and the IRA his sympathies may have leaned towards the politicians, but the politicians were the subject of the book.

In his analysis of the Irish revolution, Laffan focused on the transformation of public opinion by a self-consciously revolutionary elite, but went on to show the limits to revolutionary change in Irish society after the end of British rule. Until well after 1916 the majority of Irish nationalists were prepared to accept a very limited grant of Home Rule which offered few powers to an Irish parliament within the United Kingdom. By 1922 this situation had been transformed. The Anglo-Irish Treaty represented an extraordinary advance on the 1912 Home Rule settlement and the future of Irish politics belonged to the two rival wings of the Sinn Féin party, with an even more revolutionary third Sinn Féin in the offing, repudiating all politics in favour of the IRA. Yet Laffan emphasised the degree to which there were limits on the revolutionary potential of Sinn Féin. The evolution of Sinn Féin into a mass party after 1916 involved the recruitment of very large numbers of converts from the Irish Parliamentary Party many of whom retained their earlier views. External pressures prevented this party from splitting during the period 1917–21, but in 1922–3 deep divisions, which had always existed, split the party. Both the electorate and elements within the party were able to stop in its tracks a more radical revolution after 1922. This was a revolution which few people wanted. The 1922 settlement offered far more than had been available in 1912 and a majority were prepared to accept it. The social revolution that had already occurred with the Land Acts of the nineteenth and early twentieth centuries had anticipated and, for a majority, satisfied the demand for radical social change.

In the desire for a restoration of stability, as Oliver MacDonagh remarked, the people were prepared to accept levels of ruthlessness from an Irish government which they weren't prepared to accept from the British.[17] The inherent contradictions between the revolutionary elite and the more limited desires of the majority of the population were mirrored in the tension between the IRA leadership and the Provisional Government in 1922. IRA leaders like Liam Lynch had no illusions about their lack of popularity. As Laffan put it:

> From the standpoint of some radicals, the island suffered from an inadequate burden of grievances, and the people were too easily satisfied. But Ireland before 1921 was not a conventionally oppressed colonial society … Even the discontented had limited ambitions, and for many of them the republican cure was often worse than the British or the unionist disease. Despite intermittent upsurges of excitement and indignation, particularly in the decade after 1913 and the years after 1968, most nationalists remained ploddingly, selfishly moderate.[18]

Laffan's interest in the internal cultural dynamics of Irish nationalism was increasingly occupying his attention after the publication of *The Resurrection of Ireland*. He had signalled this in 1995 when he delivered a paper on 'The sacred memory: religion, revisionists and the Easter Rising', in which he moved away from political history to look at the complex of religious and political attitudes present in the evolution of Irish nationalism.[19] This has grown into a study of the central place of political funerals in the development of Irish nationalism from the nineteenth century, a very rich field of study which involves Laffan in the growing area of research on the construction of historical memory in

Ireland. This work in progress was accompanied by other work, on Roger Casement, on the historiography of 1916, and on a number of entries for the *Dictionary of Irish Biography*, including those on Casement, Arthur Griffith, John Redmond and Desmond Williams.[20] This expansion of the thematic and chronological scope of his research continues to occupy Laffan's time, but was overshadowed by a commission to write a study of W. T. Cosgrave as part of a series of reassessments of Taoisigh published by the Royal Irish Academy. The book took up most of Laffan's time after his retirement in 2010. He was given access to the surviving Cosgrave papers by Liam Cosgrave, and based the biography on an extensive range of primary sources, including the extensive collections of papers of twentieth-century politicians in the UCD Archives.[21] The Cosgrave book was in many ways a logical extension of Laffan's work on partition and on Sinn Féin, and brought his analysis of the politics of the revolutionary period into a new light as he examined the successor governments of the 1920s. He sought to rescue Cosgrave from historical neglect and the overshadowing effect of more charismatic figures like Collins and de Valera. Ultimately, the book is a sympathetic but not uncritical assessment of a conservative revolutionary who was primarily responsible for the creation of the Irish Free State as a parliamentary democracy in the aftermath of the revolution and Civil War.

There has always been much more to the picture than research and writing, of course. Laffan was a gifted and committed university teacher. At undergraduate level his course on the Irish revolution was hugely popular and always oversubscribed. He also taught European history, notably the 'World at War' course, which ran for many years, and his seminar on diplomatic history after the First World War, remembered by several generations of Mode I (Single Honours History) undergraduates. His fluent lecturing style was unencumbered by PowerPoint presentations, and he was a frequent speaker at the Literary and Historical and History Societies. He was also a dedicated research supervisor at MA and PhD level. Many of the current generation of modern Irish historians were influenced by his supervision of their research. He was always available to students and took great pains to support them in the development of their work.

For many years Laffan was a mainstay of the UCD common room, developing a huge circle of friends and acquaintances across the university, sought out for his engaging company as well as for his well-informed and sensible views about the university. He served as head of the School of History, later History and Archives, between 2003 and 2006, at a time of unprecedented reform in the running of UCD. The School of History was a new arrangement, whereby the traditional control of the discipline by four subject professors, each head of a separate department, was finally replaced by an integrated structure. Laffan was the unanimous choice as the first elected head of the new school. He provided a valuable element of continuity at a time when UCD was undergoing radical change in its organisation and structures. He was, like many of his colleagues, concerned about the pace of change and the danger that some traditional strengths of the university could suffer in the sweeping reforms which were introduced with sometimes bewildering speed. He was much more optimistic by the time he retired in 2010, but still protective of the things he cherished most about the university – collegiality, a strong commitment to undergraduate teaching and academic freedom. Like many of his contemporaries, Laffan continues to contribute to the life and reputation of UCD in retirement.

Laffan's contacts with college have not diminished since retirement, and his return to UCD as a guest lecturer in the history of the Irish revolution five years after his retirement continues the pattern of engagement. He always enjoyed teaching and the company of students and colleagues, his lectures were popular and his courses always over-subscribed, but he has appreciated the opportunity to devote more time to research and writing as well as to foreign travel and to spending more time in his flat in Paris, which has been a favourite retreat for over 15 years. An interesting part of his legacy, which may yet become much more widely known, is the existence of diaries which he has kept for over 50 years and which will be deposited with UCD Archives. Laffan always recorded events with his camera and his photographs are a vivid record of the changing face of UCD and Irish history over five decades. The diaries have not been seen, but will no doubt be a fascinating insight into the times they cover, and some of them will be accessible in 10 years' time when they may become the basis for another phase of historical understanding. Their release will be eagerly awaited in many circles of Irish academic life.

1

'VOTELESS ALAS'

Suffragist protest and the census of Ireland in 1911[1]

WILLIAM MURPHY

On 24 April 1911 Patrick Smith, officer in the Dublin Metropolitan Police and census enumerator, made his way to Hollybank Avenue in the Dublin suburb of Ranelagh. His purpose was to collect the census forms that he had delivered to the 60 houses on that road several weeks earlier. Hollybank Avenue was home to accountants, commercial travellers, civil service clerks, widows, engineers, solicitors, bank officials, insurance agents, Catholics and Protestants. Generally, these were biddable subjects who took their census duty seriously and completed their forms on 2 April, census night. If there was one household that concerned Smith it was surely that of Maude Townshend and Karolina Bart at number 32. Townshend and Bart were committed to the cause of female suffrage and suffragist groups had called on such women to evade the census as a protest against their continuing exclusion from the parliamentary franchise. If Townshend and Bart had responded to this call, then Smith was facing a minor confrontation. The choice before Townshend and Bart and the task before Smith were shared by suffragists and enumerators across Ireland that April. This chapter explores the response.

In recent decades, the Irish suffragist movement and, in particular, militant suffragism of the years before the Great War has received considerable scholarly attention, but the census boycott has not. This is not because scholars have thought it unimportant. Cliona Murphy has argued that the 'census evasion was not just an exercise in undermining the machinery of the state but was also of profound psychological and symbolic importance to the women involved.'[2] Study of the census boycott had foundered, however, on a mundane impediment: a lack of relevant, useable sources. In early 1911 the Irish suffrage movement did not have a newspaper with which to promote a census boycott: the establishment of the *Irish Citizen* was still more than a year away. At the time, that hampered the potential of the evasion campaign. Today, it ensures that the historian of Ireland will not find an opening onto contemporary public debate of the boycott that is as convenient as *Votes for Women* or *The Vote* in the case of Great Britain. Secondly, until recently it was very difficult to trace the actions of Irish suffragists systematically. The key evidence – the census returns – was available on microfilm, but that format meant that if one wanted to examine an individual's census return one had to know their address or at the very least have sufficient information to narrow a search to a manageable cluster of streets or townlands. This has changed because the digitisation of the census has transformed it into a much more flexible research tool, searchable under a range of additional fields including name, profession, religion, age, or a series of specified illnesses. With this development, suddenly, charting the responses of individual suffragists has become comparatively easy. Although it is not the primary purpose of this chapter to highlight this, the chapter does illustrate that the digitisation of historical sources can make certain projects possible by transforming the questions that scholars can ask of the source material.[3] Consequently, having explored the origins of the census boycott and the build up to it in Ireland, this chapter will analyse suffragists' varying reactions, place these within the history and the historiography of the Irish suffrage movement, and compare the Irish boycott to the simultaneous boycott in England. The evidence of the census returns will be parsed so as to offer a taxonomy of protest while these actions – and the debates around the protest – will be probed for what they tell us about Irish suffragists, their organisations, and the attitude of the state at the moment when militant suffragism emerged as an active force in Ireland.

I

In the early years of the twentieth century in Britain, and in Ireland, an element within the campaign for female suffrage, dissatisfied by the limited progress achieved through 40 years of temperate campaigning, was radicalised. A new phenomenon emerged: militant suffrage groups whose members came to be referred to as suffragettes. In Britain, the most famous of these organisations was the Women's Social and Political Union (WSPU), led by the Pankhursts, Emmeline and her daughters. From 1905 the WSPU was at the forefront of a steadily escalating campaign of militancy in which the disruption of political meetings and public protests gave way to the breaking of windows in public buildings, politicians' homes and shops. These actions led to the imprisonment of suffragettes and, beginning in 1909, these women embarked upon a campaign of hunger strike, demanding treatment as political prisoners.[4] Initially, Irish suffragism did not respond to this development, continuing to be comparatively moderate. The most important organisation remained the 'long established, constitutional, law-abiding' Irish Women's Suffrage and Local Government Association (IWSLGA).[5] In November 1908, however, the Dublin-centred Irish Women's Franchise League (IWFL) emerged to pursue a more assertive suffrage policy. It was led by two former members of the IWSLGA, Hanna Sheehy Skeffington and Margaret Cousins. In Belfast too, in 1909, a group containing moderates and more militantly minded women split from the IWSLGA, establishing the Irish Women's Suffrage Society (IWSS).[6]

The IWFL and IWSS did not embark immediately upon militant activity. Instead, gradually a small vanguard of committed activists cohered under their banners. For most of 1910 militant activity in Britain was suspended in reaction to an initiative which held out the prospect of the enactment of a limited female franchise through a bill which became known as the Conciliation Bill. In November, hostilities resumed when it became evident that parliament would dissolve without passing that bill. Then, six IWFL members, including Margaret Cousins, were imprisoned when they participated in resultant protests in London organised by the WSPU.[7] Soon after, the census of April 1911 provided an occasion for the as yet tentatively militant suffragists of the IWFL and IWSS to press their case through a concerted protest which was a significant, yet genteel, advance on the moderate methods employed in Ireland to that point. The census-taking was an exercise in state power, conducted by employees of the state and bringing with it the threat of sanction for those who did not co-operate. Yet, the state, in the person of the enumerator, was heavily dependent upon the co-operation of its subjects, particularly the head of each family whose duty it was to accurately complete the census return. This provided individuals with considerable leeway to register a protest, a fact recognised by the suffragists. A census form was not a ballot paper, but a message could be delivered to government through it. As Margaret Cousins's husband, James, put it, the census presented 'a prime opportunity of throwing metaphorical spanners into official machinery'.[8]

As with suffrage militancy in general, a boycott of the census was not an idea indigenous to Ireland. The proposal emerged in Britain where census night was also fixed for 2 April. There the boycott campaign originated with an organisation known as the Women's Freedom League (WFL). Its leaders had broken from the WSPU in 1907 because of their dissatisfaction at the extent to which the Pankhursts domi- nated that organisation.[9] As early as June 1910 the possibility of a census boycott had been discussed at the executive of WFL and a campaign to encourage such a boycott officially began in the pages of their newspaper, *The Vote*, on 11 February 1911. In an article in that issue, Edith How Martyn outlined the basic logic of the boycott when she wrote, 'any Government which refuses to recognize women must be met by women's refusal to recognize the Government.'[10] The campaign was taken up by the WSPU, and its slogan became 'No Vote, No Census'.[11]

Apart from suffragists' general and growing disgruntlement at the failure to grant the vote, there were particular factors encouraging protest in April 1911. When the new parliament met in February the government had not included any provision for female suffrage – such as a revived Conciliation Bill – in the King's

---

speech which outlined their legislative programme. This angered suffragists. Further, the 1911 census form itself included a series of new questions focused on the fertility of women and these drew objections from some women. The head of family in a household that included a married woman (usually her husband) was required to record the number of years that woman had been married, how many children she had given birth to, and how many of these were 'still living'. These questions were prompted by the desire to accumulate data that might inform contemporary debates surrounding the assumed differences in fertility rates and infant mortality rates between classes, and the alleged affects that these differences were having upon the overall health of society. These debates had grown out of contested ideas about welfare, public health, and eugenics; ideas that were then current in Britain.[12] Some women regarded the new questions as an unjustified intrusion into private matters by the state, while others worried about the conclusions that might be drawn from the collected data: would it, for instance, be used to exclude women from certain jobs or professions? Jill Liddington and Elizabeth Crawford have argued that once debate about the census boycott began in England a clear divide emerged. On one side stood militant suffragists, including the leadership of the WFL, the WSPU and the Women's Tax Resistance League. These women justified the boycott on the grounds of advancing the cause of female liberty. On the other stood many moderate suffragists – including the leadership of the National Union of Women's Suffrage Societies – and non-suffragists who opposed the boycott. Although holding opposing positions on the vote for women, they agreed that women, despite their votelessness, had obligations to the state, one of which was to participate in the census as a scientific exercise conducted for the civic good.[13]

Irish suffragists were slow to moot publicly the possibility of a census boycott, but the *Freeman's Journal* of 15 March did note that it had been discussed at a meeting of the IWFL on the previous evening. On the 24 March, the WSPU newspaper, *Votes for Women*, reported that the IWFL and Belfast suffragists were to co-operate in encouraging a boycott.[14] Because it was only in the final days of March that Irish suffragists began to campaign for a boycott, the resultant public debate was truncated compared to that conducted in England. Nonetheless, such debate as did occur in Ireland reveals divisions that mirror those identified by Liddington and Crawford in their study of the English census boycott. At a meeting on 9 March, the committee of the moderate IWSLGA decided 'not to give any support to the movement for refusing to fill up the census as such action would vitiate the returns for the next ten years'.[15] On 30 March, the *Irish Times* and *Freeman's Journal* published a letter from a correspondent from Clontarf calling himself or herself 'Arjapim' who complained that 'Census evasion is an attempt to diminish the value of an undertaking of immense importance and social value' and asked 'will the Irish Women's Franchise

League explain how they are able to justify such a crime against society as Census evasion?'[16]

Arjapim's view was endorsed by the editor of the *Irish Times*,[17] but the letter also prompted several responses justifying the boycott, including one from Mary F. Earl, a leading member of the IWFL. She outlined the thinking that underpinned boycotters' actions:

> Women have not votes, and therefore, are unable to bring influence of this sort to bear. Hence they are forced to adopt a method less conventional than that used by men. The Census is a numbering of the people. We are considered part of the people by the Government when it wants to tax us or to count us. We are quite willing to be part of the people as regards the Census when we are allowed to be part of the people as regards the Parliamentary vote.

Earl continued:

> We quite recognize the importance of the Census, but we are sure that the statistics obtained by it will be used as a basis of legislation, on matters affecting women, by a House of Commons consisting of men only and elected by men only. As laws passed by such a body can hardly fail to be unjust to women, we consider we are quite justified in our refusal to supply information for statistics.[18]

Earl's response was evidently modelled on a letter that Emmeline Pankhurst wrote to the London *Times*, defending the proposed boycott following a critical editorial in that paper.[19]

In the days leading up to the census, the press and the authorities in Ireland were curious as to the methods that those Irish suffragists committed to resisting the census would adopt. The *Freeman's Journal* reported that in Dublin speculation as to the suffragists' approach had 'imported an element of mild excitement' into the census-taking. This speculation was sustained, the patronising reporter for the *Freeman* continued, because 'in refutation of the popular belief that a lady cannot keep a secret, they seem to have guarded their plans successfully.' When a policeman called upon a committee meeting of the IWFL on the day before the census and asked if they intended holding a meeting on the following evening, he was informed that they did not, but had instead 'requisitioned a number of aeroplanes and submarines' for the occasion.[20] When interviewed on the day of the census, Marguerite Palmer, honorary secretary of the IWFL, told the *Irish Times* that she 'could not divulge any of their plans, but their scheme was entirely different to that employed in England' where the evasion strategies planned included collective public protest. Instead, she said, Irish suffragists intended to be 'conspicuous by their absence'.[21]

CENSUS OF IRELAND, 1911.

Two Examples of the mode of filling up this Table are given on the other side.

FORM A.

No. on Form B. II

RETURN of the MEMBERS of this FAMILY and their VISITORS, BOARDERS, SERVANTS, &c., who slept or abode in this House on the night of SUNDAY, the 2nd of APRIL, 1911.

Number	NAME AND SURNAME		RELATION to Head of Family	RELIGIOUS PROFESSION	EDUCATION	AGE (last Birthday) and SEX		RANK, PROFESSION, OR OCCUPATION	PARTICULARS AS TO MARRIAGE				WHERE BORN	IRISH LANGUAGE	If Deaf and Dumb; Dumb only; Blind; Imbecile or Idiot; or Lunatic
	Christian Name	Surname				Ages of Males	Ages of Females		Whether "Married," "Widower," "Widow," or "Single."	Completed years the present Marriage has lasted.	Total Children born alive.	Children still living.			
1	2		3	4	5	6	7	8	9	10	11	12	13	14	15
1			Head	Roman Catholic	Read & Write	32		Carpenter and Joiner	Married	3	1	1	Co. Cavan		
3 4			Wife	Roman Catholic	Cannot Read		28		Married	3	1	1	Dublin City		
4			Son	Roman Catholic	Read & Write	1		Scholar					Dublin City		
5	Mary		Servant	Roman Catholic	Read & Write		23	General Servant Domestic	Single				Waterford		
6			Servant	Roman Catholic	Read & Write		21	General Servant Domestic	Single				Dublin City		
7															
8															
9															
10															
11															
12															
13															
14															
15															

I hereby certify, as required by the Act 10 Edw. VII, and 1 Geo. V, cap. 11., that the foregoing Return is correct, according to the best of my knowledge and belief.

_____ Signature of Enumerator.

I believe the foregoing to be a true Return.

_____ Signature of Head of Family.

II

On the morning of 3 April 1911, the *Irish Times* expressed the hope that an accurate census had been completed, but admitted 'we do not know how far this aim has been frustrated by the campaign of the militant women suffragists.'[22] It was never likely that the suffragists' influence upon the accuracy of the census process would be significant. Some 910,748 separate family returns were made during the 1911 census and 2,198,171 females were enumerated,[23] while the numbers of active suffragists were few. In 1912, for example, the membership of the IWFL, by then the largest suffragist organisation in the country, stood at around 1,000[24] and the sum of these who were active members was a good deal lower. Despite the digitisation of the census records, the precise response of Irish suffragists remains unclear. It is possible, however, to begin to assess their actions on census night. As revealed by the census returns, these actions seem to fall into five broad categories. Firstly, there were those suffragists who did not use the census to assert their suffragist identity. Either these women filled in the form or the head of their family filled in the detail for them. On the other hand, there were women who responded to the campaign and took the opportunity to express their suffragist identity. The actions of these women fall into at least four categories. Those who sought to avoid the recording of their details in the census fall into two groups that might be labelled evaders and refusers. Two further groups emerge: these women, while not participating in evasion of the census, availed of the census form to register their views. They might be called protestors and identifiers.

Among those suffragists who do not appear to have made any effort to avoid enumeration or to register a protest were prominent members of moderate suffrage groups. Mary Hayden, a well-known history lecturer at University College Dublin, had chaired the IWSLGA committee meeting that decided against supporting the census boycott, and she completed her form.[25] Other regular attendees at IWSLGA committee meetings also appear in the census, including Nanno Keatinge and Beatrice Townshend. In Keatinge's case the form was completed by her husband, but Townshend assumed primary responsibility for completing the form as 'head of family'.[26] Census returns are also extant for prominent, yet moderate, northern suffragists such as Dora Mellone and L. A. Walkington[27] (both from Co. Down) who would be involved later that year in establishing an umbrella suffrage organisation called the Irish Women's Suffrage Federation.[28]

1911 also saw the establishment of the Munster Women's Franchise League (MWFL). Cliona Murphy has characterised it as 'a vague talking shop for writers and society women'[29] and so it is not a surprise to find census returns for its Cork-based founders, Susanne (Susan) Day and the literary cousins Edith Somerville and Violet Martin.[30] The Connacht Women's Franchise League, based in Galway city, would not be established until 1913.[31] In 1911, four future leading lights of that organisation Mary Donovan, Mary Fleetwood Berry, Florence Moon and Edith Young can be found among the census returns.[32] However, the feminist tendencies of these moderate suffragists are sometimes hinted at in their census returns. Somerville proudly proclaimed herself 'Author, Artist, Dairy Farmer'. An inclination to record their educational achievements is also noticeable in suffragists' returns. The return of Mabel Dodds, a Limerick-based member of the IWSLGA, records that she had a BA.[33] Those of Hayden and Donovan, both of whom would become professors of history, state that they held MAs. Suffragists were not alone, of course, in recording their university qualifications. Olive Purser, the first female student awarded a Trinity College Dublin College Scholarship,[34] was enumerated as 'BA, University Teacher' by her proud father, but he also noted that Olive's brother, John, held an MSc and was 'Assistant to Professor of Engineering'.[35] Nonetheless, female graduates were then few in number, had a keen sense of a shared identity (expressed in the establishment of the Irish Association of Women Graduates and Candidate Graduates (IAWGCG) in 1902), and were prominently involved in suffragism. Hayden was the first vice-president of the IAWGCG which campaigned for equity for women within third-level education.[36] It is surely significant that she filled in her household's census form as 'head of family' rather than her older brother, John, who she described as a 'barrister (not in practice)'.[37]

It is somewhat more surprising to find census returns for known associates, even leading members, of the IWFL, given that organisation's advocacy of the boycott. Among those to feature in census returns for Dublin is Katharina (Kathë) Oldham, the first president of the organisation.[38] Jane Gibson and Helen Morony, Limerick-based adherents of the IWFL in 1911, can also be found.[39] In the cases of Oldham and Morony this can almost certainly be explained by a discomfort with militancy despite their association with the IWFL. Margaret Ward has suggested that Oldham was selected as the first figurehead of the IWFL precisely because she was respectable and somewhat conservative. She, and her husband Professor Charles Hubert Oldham, continued to attend IWSLGA meetings during this period.[40] As for Morony, she would abandon the IWFL for the more moderate MWFL in December 1912 as militancy became a reality in Ireland.[41]

The same cannot be said of Kathleen Emerson and Lucy (Mabel) Purser. They would go to prison for militant acts carried out under the IWFL banner in 1912 and 1913.[42] Yet census returns are available for both.[43] This may indicate that these women had not radicalised by April 1911 or that they disagreed in principle with the census boycott. In the cases of Emerson – a recently widowed 26-year-old who had returned to live with her parents – and Purser it is also possible that they were enumerated against their will by their father and husband respectively. In his work on nineteenth-century censuses, Edward Higgs has illustrated the extent to which men dominated the census-taking process. Men framed the questions, acted as enumerators, processed the information and, perhaps most importantly in this context, men were expected to act as head of family and fill out the form.[44] This gave a male head of family a good deal of control over the capacity of his suffragist relatives to protest using the census. In one English case, Liddington and Crawford have been able to prove definitively that a suffragist was enumerated against her will by her husband.[45] Evidence for this – whether it be diaries, letters or a clear statement on the census form – is for obvious reasons difficult to find.

Suffragists with militant records were also enumerated by female heads of family. It is impossible to be certain whether Violet Jameson, who would be a regular speaker on IWFL platforms from the second half of 1911,[46] and Georgina Manning, who would be fined in 1913 for defacing a bust of John Redmond on display at the Royal Hibernian Academy,[47] were willingly or reluctantly enumerated by their mother and sister respectively.[48] In all these cases it is possible that the suffragists acquiesced in their enumeration because they did not want to expose their relatives to legal sanction. A head of family who did not complete the form was liable to prosecution and a £5 fine. Like Emerson and Purser, the artist Maud Lloyd would later go to jail for her militant activity. Unlike Emerson and Purser, as the sole occupant of 122.4 St Stephen's Green, it is certain that she was not constrained by another family member in her capacity to protest using the form. Nonetheless, she completed it.[49] It should be noted that, despite her imprisonment, Lloyd was a comparatively cautious militant, refusing to participate in or support hunger strike.[50]

The clash of loyalties, or contest for precedence, that a commitment to both female suffrage and Irish nationalism involved for some women is a central theme in the historiography of first-wave Irish feminism.[51] A shadow of this dilemma can be discerned in the census return of Rosamond Jacob. Jacob, a Waterford Quaker, was sympathetic to militant suffragism and advanced nationalism. In the estimation of her biographer Leeann Lane, when nationalism and suffragism came into conflict Jacob prioritised nationalism, although 'this was an uneasy choice for her.'[52] Her census return confirms this assessment as she, and her brother, made a point of filling out the form in Irish, using it to assert their cultural nationalism, while she made no mark to register her resentment at not having the vote.[53] Similarly, Mary MacSwiney, a founder member of the MWFL, made her return in Irish, as Máire Nic Suibhne. She too did not register a suffragist protest, although interestingly she returned the form as head of family rather than either of her younger brothers, Terence and Seán.[54]

The primary method employed to find the census returns of these women was straightforward. I compiled as comprehensive a list as possible of suffragists known to be active in Ireland during the period (along with relevant biographical detail) using the extant secondary literature, subscription lists, committee minutes, contemporary correspondence, and newspaper reports. This information was then used to search the digitised census records. This search of the census did reveal notable absences, indicating that a boycott took place and that a group that might be labelled 'evaders' did act on census night. There is no return, for instance, for a Marguerite or Margaret Palmer, matching the known biographical detail of the honorary secretary of the IWFL. It seems a reasonable assumption that Palmer successfully evaded the census (given that she was interviewed that day promising that suffragists would be 'conspicuous by their absence'). Similarly, it is very likely that suffragists, perhaps numbering in the dozens and including women such as Margaret Connery and Eva Wilkins, are absent from the record due to the boycott. All such absences cannot, however, be accounted for definitively. In the days after census night, when the enumerators began collecting the forms, the *Freeman's Journal* reported that they had been 'not unnaturally suspicious' when informed that the lady of the house was absent on the night of 2 April. The *Freeman* also acknowledged at least one case where such suspicions were aroused by a perfectly innocent absence.[55]

Nonetheless, using the extant digitised returns, it was possible to identify with certainty a number of women who attempted to evade the census. Among these were the co-founders of the IWFL, Cousins and Sheehy Skeffington. They adopted a strategy used by some English boycotters, collecting in groups at houses which, for various reasons, were not due to be enumerated. This increased the suffragists' chances of not being counted, while their heads of family could truthfully omit their details from the household form.[56] In later years, Hanna Sheehy Skeffington claimed that she spent census night at a cottage in Wicklow made available to her and some other boycotters by Countess Markievicz.[57] In 1950, James Cousins recalled that Margaret and Lizzie Duffy, their domestic servant, left to stay at a nearby house that had been vacant for some time and was therefore 'not on the enumeration list'. He remembered that he was suffering from scarlatina fever and so was left at home, in his bed, with the form, a pen, an envelope, and some disinfectant. He stated:

> When the official hour came, I wrote on the declaration form a note to the effect that I could not give a true enumeration of my household as its 'female' members were absent in protest against being officially classed with children, criminals, lunatics and such like. I added that I had filled the paper while laid up in scarlatina, but had duly disinfected it and the envelope.[58]

His actions appear to have acquired colour with time and telling. The census return for the Cousins' household at 35 Strand Road, near Sandymount in Dublin, reveals no explanatory note or health report while, despite his claims to the contrary, James Cousins provided Lizzie Duffy's details. It is also evident that the enumerator, Patrick O'Connell, sought to foil the protest by amending the form. Firstly, he crossed out Lizzie Duffy's details, then he attempted to record some basic details for Margaret Cousins – the sparse entry is largely inaccurate as he named her Gertrude and recorded her age as 38 (she was 32) – and below these he re-recorded Lizzie Duffy's details. He noted at the bottom of the form that 'Mrs Cousins who is a suffragette enumerated from enquiries made.'[59]

Like James Cousins, Francis Sheehy Skeffington did not enter his wife's details on the form at their home, 11 Grosvenor Place, near Rathmines. Again, the enumerator, James Crozier, attempted to mitigate the boycott by recording Sheehy Skeffington's details, but he was even less effective than Patrick O'Connell. Almost all of the information was incorrect. Crozier entered Sheehy Skeffington's given name as Emily (she was Hanna or Johanna), he recorded her age as 28 (she was 33), he accurately noted that she was married but stated that she had been married for three years (the Sheehy Skeffingtons had married in 1903), he was correct in recording that they had had one child and that this child was alive, before concluding that Emily (Hanna) was born in Dublin city (she was born in Kanturk, Co. Cork).[60]

The enumerators had extensive powers to make enquiries about those who did not comply with their obligations under the census.[61] That the enumerators in Ireland, unlike those in Britain, were drawn from the ranks of the local police enhanced their abilities to acquire information. The deployment of the police in this manner is typical of a process that Lowe and Malcolm have characterised as the 'domestication' of the Royal Irish Constabulary.[62] This does not appear to have brought uniformity to their response to evaders however, as different enumerators collected information on these women with different degrees of enthusiasm and success. While Crozier attempted (albeit poorly) to make a full return for Sheehy Skeffington, Hugh Roddy was satisfied with a good deal less in the case of Flaurence Ball, an IWFL member. She attempted to boycott by absenting herself from her residence at 17.3 Lower Sherrard Street, Dublin. In response, Roddy recorded Ball's name and an age, 40, before noting 'Left address and cannot be traced. Further particulars unknown.'[63] Lilly Gait's effort to evade the census was thwarted, but her census return raises a series of questions about the attitudes and agency of suffragists, heads of family, and enumerators. Gait was a boarder at the home of Emma Halpin at 3.1 Cliff Terrace, Kingstown, and Halpin recorded Gait's details before noting that she was 'absent'. It seems likely that Halpin was unwilling to assist Gait's boycott, but was willing to indicate Gait's intentions and actions. This may have been the result of an agreed compromise between Halpin and Gait or may have been done against Gait's wishes. Then, interestingly, someone drew a line through Gait's details as if to strike them from the record. It is possible that this was an act by Halpin or Gait, but it seems just as likely that it was that of the enumerator, Richard Grant, who may have believed that in doing so he was ensuring an accurate census return:[64] Gait was absent, therefore her return should be struck out.

In addition to those who evaded the census there were those women who 'refused' to fill in a form or part of a form. These women were heads of family and as such they were often forced to have a conversation with the returning enumerator during which they explicitly refused co-operation, although in some cases the task fell to a servant. One of these heads of family was Mary F. Earl. Michael Barry, the enumerator, recorded on the form for 39 Raglan Road, Ballsbridge, that it had been 'Filled as a result of enquiries made by the enumerator. Mrs Earl having refused to give any information.'[65] This is further confirmed by the fact that the space provided for the signature of the head of family is blank. It seems likely that the information was elicited from the household servant, Mary Dunne, because she was the only member of the household for whom Barry recorded a religious affiliation. This was certainly the case at 15 Highfield Road, Rathgar. In that instance the enumerator recorded 'This paper filled on information received from the servant (Julia Flynn) as the head of the family (Marie Hilles) is a "Suffragette" and refused information.'[66] It may have been the absence of a servant that so markedly hampered the capacity of one enumerator, James Marrinan, to complete a census return for 54.2 Willowbank Street, Belfast, when the female residents informed him that they were '"militant" suffragettes and refused to give information.' Although Marrinan managed to collect some accurate information on Mabel Small, a well-known northern-based suffragette who lived at that address, he was less successful in ascertaining the details for her colleague and housemate. Her surname, it seems, was Morris, although Marrinan failed to discover her first name. She could, he believed, read and write, was '(about) 43', and was born in England.[67]

Dr Mary Strangman of 17 Parnell Street, Waterford city, was another head of family who refused to provide her own details. Strangman would become a member of Waterford Corporation in early 1912; while in suffragist circles she associated with the MWFL.[68] It is clear that Strangman had a conversation with the enumerator, Maurice Kelleher, when he called to collect the form on 13 April because he noted that 'Head of family is a suffragette and states she did not sleep in the house on 2nd April but in Enumerator's opinion she did and probably was not enumerated elsewhere that night.' As a consequence, he recorded her details on the form.[69]

Clara Moser, who lived in Sandymount, Dublin, also refused to give her details. In addition, when, on 8 April, she returned her form she had written 'no vote no census' across it.[70] The census returns reveal a good many women who were not willing (or able) to join Moser in her boycott, but who, like her, desired to deliver a message of dissent through the form. These women might be described as 'protestors'. In some instances they were joined or facilitated by a male head of family in making their point. Adeline Tickell was a regular on suffragist platforms at this time, but rather than boycott she chose to protest using the form.[71] The last column on the census form provided a space where the head of family was expected to note those in the household who were either 'Deaf and Dumb; Dumb only; Blind; Imbecile or Idiot; or Lunatic' by writing 'the respective infirmities opposite the name of the afflicted person.' And it is in this column that Adeline Tickell was enumerated as 'voteless'.[72] This (or variants thereof) was the most common type of suffragist protest in the 1911 census of Ireland. Ellen Jane Bell and her cousin Maud Joynt, a suffragist activist, lived at 21 Annesley Park, Dublin. They were among those to describe themselves as 'unenfranchised'. Ellen Gregg Osborne of 23 Sandhurst Drive, Belfast was similarly described by her landlord, John James Smith, a 'Socialist (Unitarian)', who wrote in the infirmity column opposite his own name, 'none only bad tempered'.[73] The McClelland women, Elizabeth, Jane and Margaret, of 2 Woosley Street, Belfast, preferred 'Dis-enfranchised'.[74] Elizabeth Swanton and her daughter, Mary Beatrice Swanton, were originally from Cork, but lived at 10 Park Drive, Dublin. Under profession on the census form, Mary Beatrice noted that she was a vendor of *Votes for Women*, the newspaper of the WSPU, while she and her mother recorded that they were 'Voteless Alas, classed with Imbeciles having no vote'.[75] Kathleen Shannon, a former secretary of the IWFL who lived at Lower Lesson Street, wrote that she was 'Not naturally but legally classified with imbecile on account of sex'.[76]

Tom Kettle, journalist, academic and former Irish Party MP, and his wife, Mary Sheehy Kettle, sister of Hanna Sheehy Skeffington, also used their form to make a point. On their wedding day in 1909, Mary had 'worn a "Votes for Women" badge pinned to her white gown and another mounted in her floral wreath'.[77] She regularly appeared on suffragist platforms during this period. In the immediate aftermath of the census, on 6 April, she told a meeting at Kingstown, attended by Emmeline Pankhurst, that 'they had never got anything in Ireland from a hostile Government except by militant methods.'[78] A breach would open between Tom Kettle and the IWFL in 1912 when he argued that 'Home Rule comes first and everything else second', but he was an early associate member of the organisation and he would remain a believer in female suffrage.[79] Yet, at first glance, the Kettles' census form appears to have been filled out without fuss. A closer examination, however, reveals a modest if telling alteration. Tom Kettle signed the form, but either he, or his wife, amended this section from the official 'Signature of the Head of Family' to 'Signature of one of the Heads of the Family'.[80]

Those to fall into the fifth category of response described here are women who used the 'Rank, Profession or Occupation' column or the 'Religion' column to identify themselves as suffragists. For example, the religion of Helen Lawler and her sister, Louisa, of 15 Sherrard Street, Dublin, was initially recorded as 'suffragette', although this was crossed out and replaced by 'R Catholic', presumably by the enumerator.[81] Edith Colwill, of 21 Simmonscourt Road, Donnybrook, indicated that she was a 'suffragette', using the occupation column.[82] Blanche Emma Bennett of Skegoniel Avenue, Belfast, was more specific describing her occupation as 'Sec of Irish Women's Suffrage Sty'.[83] Sometimes individuals both protested in the infirmity column and insisted on their suffragist identity in other columns. Susan Manning and Elizabeth Duggan at Dartmouth Square, Dublin, described themselves as 'legally unfit to vote', leaving the enumerator in no doubt as to their reasons for doing so by giving their religion as 'militant suffragette'.[84] Finally, on Hollybank Avenue, Townshend and Bart did not boycott, instead they too declared themselves 'Unenfranchised' in the infirmity column while describing their occupation as 'suffragist'.[85]

III

Margaret Ward, a biographer of Hanna Sheehy Skeffington and perhaps the foremost historian of the IWFL, has suggested that evading or resisting the 1911 census was a matter upon which militant and non-militant suffragists agreed.[86] In this she is echoing some writing on the census boycott in Britain, although more recent historiography has tended to emphasise the link between the boycott and militancy of different varieties.[87] In the case of Ireland, Ward's claim seems to ignore the IWSLGA's official rejection of the proposed boycott and it is contradicted by the evidence offered here of widespread completion of the census by moderate suffragists and their heads of family. As Liddington and Crawford rightly point out, however, the census returns offer 'individuality rather than uniformity'.[88] Suffragists associated with moderate organisations such as Marie Hilles – who attended the IWSLGA committee meeting that rejected the boycott – and Mary Strangman participated fully in the boycott, while Adeline Tickell, who was also at that IWSLGA meeting, made a protest on the form.[89] On the other hand, some women declared themselves 'militants' on the census form even as they filled it, while other associates of 'militant' organisations did not use the census to register the suffrage agenda at all.

Ireland's suffragist organisations, whether moderate or militant, were not rigidly disciplined groups. Adherents drifted between groups and did not always view membership of groups as mutually exclusive. Such movement was encouraged by the fact that the policies and positions of the organisations – particularly the newly formed militant organisations – were mutable, adapting to the unstable political environment. In some cases adherence to a particular group may have been an accident of geography rather than an indication of philosophical compatibility. Strangman, for instance, would probably have joined a branch of the IWFL if this option had been available to her in Waterford. All of this is reflected in the variety of responses to the census. Neither does participation in the census boycott (or failure to do so) seem to be a strong predictor of an individual's future militant activity: the overlap between census boycotters and those suffragists jailed in Ireland between 1912 and 1914 is not particularly striking. Sheehy Skeffington, Cousins, and Mabel Small attempted to boycott the census and all would hunger strike in prison, but, as noted earlier, there are future hunger strikers who do not appear to have attempted any census protest.

The limited number of activists involved in these groups is also reflected in the response in Ireland. In London, the WFL and the WSPU planned very public resistance. They organised a series of collective public protests on census night, facilitating suffragists' absence from any residence where they might be counted. The Pankhursts attended a concert at WSPU Hall, followed by a protest march at Trafalgar Square organised by the WFL and attended by around 1,000 women, succeeded by further entertainments laid on at the Scala Theatre, before concluding the night by going to a WSPU event at Aldwych Skating Rink between 3.00 a.m. and 8.00 a.m.[90] The IWFL or IWSS did not organise similar public demonstrations, most likely because they would not have been able to rally large numbers in either Dublin or Belfast. Even if moderates and militants had been united in their attitude to the census it is unlikely that a sizeable protest could have been mustered while neither Dublin nor Belfast offered the range of public spaces that London suffragists had available to them, especially at night. Such a protest would inevitably have drawn considerable criticism from those who were then still discomfited by the sight of women independently organising themselves (whether collectively or as individuals) to occupy the public space.[91] Indeed, the organisers of the boycott almost certainly hoped that, by avoiding this, a less demonstrative approach would facilitate the participation of moderates in census evasion. A suffragette correspondent to the *Freeman's Journal*, on 1 April, wrote that 'several of our friends have recently congratulated us on the constitutional and eminently ladylike nature of Census resistance. In fact it is on that very account being very widely adopted in Ireland.'[92]

At the time, the lack of public demonstrations raised an obvious question, one which Arjapim noted in his/her letter to the newspapers. Arjapim had argued that silent evasion of the census was a pointlessly narrow form of protest as it 'cannot be a very successful method of advertisement, since, though militant, it is quiet, unostentatious, and incapable of proper estimation of its effects'.[93] The publication of Arjapim's own letter undermined this argument somewhat, as did the press coverage that the boycott received, although Arjapim was correct to this extent: it is extremely difficult, even now, to assess the extent of the boycott because it is very difficult to measure and analyse an absence. It seems quite clear, however, that the number of suffragists who attempted to evade enumeration in Ireland was very small indeed and the number that succeeded was even smaller. Hanna Sheehy Skeffington admitted in her memoir that 'our numbers abstaining did not greatly throw out the census figures.'[94]

At best we can speculate, with varying degrees of certainty, about the names and numbers of those who succeeded in evading the census. In most cases these protests remain lost to us: the consequence of a successful boycott is absence from the record. On the other hand, this analysis of the digitised census records has revealed 31 separate household returns in which a woman's or several women's suffragism was recorded because an enumerator noted an attempt to evade the census or a refusal to supply information, or because a suffragist declared her beliefs using the form.[95] In total this involved 47 individual women. The supportive networks created by Irish suffragists may have been small and may have lacked discipline, but these returns demonstrate that a woman who expressed a suffragist identity using the census was likely to have had access to, and to have engaged with, such networks. Perhaps the most significant indication of this is the concentration of protestors in the cities of Belfast and Dublin where the militant and, indeed, non-militant suffrage organisations were strongest. 27 of the 31 households identified were in Dublin or Belfast. Of four provincial protestors, two – Mary Strangman and Elizabeth A. McCracken[96] – were active in suffragist circles despite their comparative isolation in Waterford and Bangor.

It is surely no accident that protestors Flaurence Ball, and Helen and Louisa Lawler lived two doors from each other on Dublin's Sherrard Street, although, as northsiders, all three lived slightly at a remove from Rathmines, Rathgar and Pembroke, the centres of suffragist census protest in the city. Ellen Gregg Osborne and Sarah Hegarty Stewart[97] belonged to the small but growing network of female undergraduates at Queen's University Belfast. The suffragists among these undergraduates had become markedly more active in early 1911. In January, Margaret Cousins had addressed them on her prison experiences in England and, in February, the University's Literary and Scientific Society had debated female suffrage.[98] In organisations, educational institutions and neighbourhoods women supported each other to protest, but more than that they did so in households. It is striking that a woman was head of the family in 21 of the 31 households that registered a recorded suffragist protest, while 15 of these households were exclusively female. These included households such as those of Small and Morris in Belfast and Townshend and Bart in Dublin where it seems likely that these women chose to live with each other precisely because of their shared female suffragist views. It is noteworthy that no suffragist protestor resided in a household where her father was head of family. This very likely militated against younger women registering suffragist sentiments on the form, although those in the age bracket 20–29 years-of-age still constituted the largest cohort (32 per cent) of identified protestors.

Husbands seem to have been somewhat more sympathetic than fathers as eight identified women were assisted or facilitated in protest by a spouse who was head or joint-head of the family. In total 13 (27.6 per cent) of the 47 identified protestors were married while 28 (59.6 per cent) were single and three (6.4 per cent) were widowed. These figures may give a somewhat distorted impression because it seems likely that a married boycotter who had her husband's support had a better chance of escaping enumeration without any questions from, or comments by, the enumerator and is therefore more likely to have left no trace at all on the census record.

As addresses in Rathmines, Rathgar, Ranelagh, and Donnybrook suggest, the census protestors in Dublin were predominantly middle-class (even upper-middle-class) women. This was, for the most part, true of census protestors in Belfast and elsewhere in Ireland. The census returns reveal that all but one of the women registering a protest resided in first- or second-class housing stock; the exception was Bridget Nugent of Aghogan, Co. Tyrone.[99] It might be argued that the primary methodology employed here – to search the census for known suffragists, women whose actions have been publicly documented – would tend toward creating a middle-class bias in the results. However, it should be noted that a secondary methodology emerged which was free of this bias. It is possible to search the digitised census returns of every woman whose enumeration included an entry in the 'infirmity column' that did not conform to the standard, expected, answers suggested on the form; deaf, dumb, deaf and dumb, blind, idiot, lunatic or imbecile. There were 4,048 such women and each entry was checked for returns such as 'voteless' or 'unenfranchised'. The protestors revealed in this way shared the class origins of those revealed using the primary method, that of seeking out known suffragists. Liddington and Crawford, commenting on similar findings in England, make the reasonable point that the danger of receiving a £5 fine was a greater disincentive to protest for poorer women.[100] However, the fact that the suffragist movement in Ireland was at that time willing to settle for some form of limited female suffrage based on a property qualification, such as that offered by the Conciliation Bill, hardly encouraged working-class women to participate.[101]

That the Irish female suffrage movement was, for the most part, class bound is reflected in the attitudes toward female servants suggested in the census returns of these middle-class households. Despite his revisionist account of 1950, James Cousins enumerated his female servant, Lizzie Duffy. Similarly, Francis Sheehy Skeffington provided full details for his household's domestic servants Philomena Morrissey and Mary Butler. In contrast, all four women, including two servants, residing at the Lindsay household at 1 Marlborough Park, Belfast, were described as 'unenfranchised'.[102] Mary Walshe (who was domestic servant to Emily and Josephine Webb at 12 Brighton Square, Dublin) was also, with her employers, recorded as 'unenfranchised'.[103] In the Webbs' case this may reflect a democratic ethos informed by their Quaker background. Interestingly, although Mary Strangman refused to give her own details, she provided those of her servant, Julia Gibbons. She did protest, however, that Julia was 'unenfranchised' using the infirmity column. It is impossible to be certain whether the servants who provided details of their 'refusing' female employers to enumerators did so with the explicit or tacit consent of those employers. So too it is impossible to know the extent to which female servants in suffragist households had a voice in the manner of their enumeration. It seems likely that often they had none.

The Webbs' Quakerism raises the question of the religious affiliations of census protestors. Two further Quakers, Margaret Bulla and Catherine Jane Quayle, were among the Belfast-based protestors,[104] so that members of the Society of Friends constitute a very high percentage (8.5 per cent) of census protestors identified here when compared to their presence in the general population. Quakers, including Anna and Thomas Haslam, had consistently taken a leading role in suffrage movements in Ireland and elsewhere, influenced by their sect's emphasis on equality.[105] Ward has characterised IWFL activists as 'a mixed lot of Quakers, Unitarians, Church of Ireland, Methodists and Roman Catholics as well as non-believers'.[106] The profile of Dublin-based census protestors seems to confirm this. Of the 29 identified, eight described themselves as Catholics, eight as Church of Ireland, two as Methodist, two as Quaker, two refused to give information, a religious affiliation was not recorded in one case, one woman described herself as having 'no church', and five described their religion as 'suffragette' or 'militant suffragette'. This suggests that although these activists were a 'mixed lot', Catholics were significantly under-represented among suffragist activists. In Dublin, Catholics constituted 83 per cent of the city's population in 1911, but only 28 per cent of identified census protestors. Among the 14 identified census protestors in Belfast and environs there was not a single Catholic, although Catholics constituted 24 per cent of that city's population. Presbyterians were over-represented, on the other hand, contributing just under half of the identified census protestors while 34 per cent of the city's population was Presbyterian.[107]

Sheehy Skeffington's subsequent admission that the protest was unlikely to have influenced greatly the accuracy of the census was also the confident view of the officials at the time.[108] The number of activists was small and the actions of the enumerators in collecting some information on some would-be-boycotters mitigated the impact further. In Britain, where evasion was more widespread, the President of the Local Government Board claimed in parliament that the number of successful evaders was 'altogether negligible'.[109] It was in government's interest, of course, to minimise the effectiveness of the boycott and this informed their decision not to prosecute those heads of family who had failed to record the details of suffragist protestors.[110] This was sensible: although the numbers involved were small, the suffragist census campaign had already drawn a good deal of attention to their cause and the publicity attendant upon a series of court cases, fines, and perhaps even imprisonments would have benefited the suffragists more than the authorities.

When a subject or a citizen in a modern state is faced with an official form, especially a census form, she is imposed upon but she has opportunity to express her identity. The suffragist protestors of 1911 knew this. Some refused to recognise the legitimacy of any duty enforced by a state that refused to recognise them as full citizens. It is an irony that the identities of many successful boycotters are almost certainly now lost to us because they stridently asserted their suffragist identity through boycott. Others were certainly denied the opportunity to express their suffragist identity by their heads of family, while some women willingly submerged their suffragist identity, instead choosing to prioritise other aspects of their personalities; that of the dutiful citizen or Irish nationalist for instance. Perhaps most interestingly, a good many sought to balance their identity as suffragists with other identities: responsible citizen, considerate wife, obedient daughter, or moderate individual. Inventively, these women combined enumeration with protest.[111] As a consequence they emerge as complex individuals even through a medium as apparently limited in its potential to express personality as a census return. Similarly, the Irish suffragist movement as revealed by the census protest is an absorbing phenomenon, at once confined in its geographic and class base, yet fascinatingly complex, fluid, and various.

2

SPORT AND WAR

The 1915 All-Ireland hurling championship[1]

PAUL ROUSE AND ROSS O'CARROLL

Grant me, Oh Lord, a hurler's skill,
With strength of arm and speed of limb.[2]

On Sunday 24 October 1915 the All-Ireland hurling final was played between Leix[3] and Cork at Croke Park, Dublin, in front of a crowd which was estimated to have reached 12,000. On a day when the rain fell in torrents, Leix stunned the favourites Cork – one of the great traditional powers of hurling – and claimed victory by a margin of seven points. Accordingly, Leix won the All-Ireland championship for the first and only time in their history. Their success was rooted in a training regime backed by extraordinary financing, despite the fact that the Gaelic Athletic Association (GAA) was avowed in its rhetorical adherence to amateurism. The nature of the occasion of the All-Ireland hurling final of 1915 underlined the extent to which the GAA had adopted so many of the characteristics of the sporting revolution which had occurred in Britain in the second half of the nineteenth century. While the game played was a peculiarly Irish one, the occasion owed much to the new sporting rituals of Britain. This chapter places the evolution of the GAA in the context of the wider sporting revolution which occurred across the United Kingdom and beyond in the Victorian era.

The chapter also assesses the relationship between politics and sport in Ireland by reviewing the activities of GAA members at local and at national level before 1915. These activities related to the construction of an agenda around the promotion of cultural nationalism and – later – to engagement with war, whether in Ireland as part of a nationalist rebellion, or in Europe as part of the British army. At the time of the 1915 hurling championship a cadre of republicans was active at various levels of the Association, recruiting men and preparing for revolution in Ireland. This was no straightforward matter: the relationship between the members of the GAA and putative Irish revolutionaries was a complex one. So, too, was the relationship between the GAA and the British army. The scale of recruitment to the British army from the ranks of the GAA lends eloquent testimony, as will be seen, to the danger inherent in making broad assumptions about the politics of the membership of the Association.

I

The origins of the GAA

In the second half of the nineteenth century the social and cultural life of towns all across Ireland was transformed by the establishment of clubs to cater for men and women who wished to play sport. The phenomenon of establishing sports clubs had spread to Ireland from Britain, which was the crucible of the sporting revolution. Industrialisation, urbanisation, technological advancement, shifting social norms and unprecedented population growth radically altered the lifestyles of large sections of the British population in the nineteenth century. Patterns of play were moulded to fit this new society in a process which saw the informal, traditional recreations of previous generations recast as modern sport.[4] Some clubs catered for long-established sports such as cricket and golf; others catered for newly codified versions of old games, such as rugby and soccer; and still more catered for newly invented sports such as badminton and lawn tennis. These clubs were usually associated with a centralised governing body which regulated the manner in which a particular sport should be played, as the Football Association did for soccer after 1863 and the Rugby Football Union did for rugby after 1871. In Ireland, this process was emphasised by the foundation of the Irish Football Union in 1874 to legislate for rugby and the foundation of the Irish Football Association in 1880 to legislate for soccer.[5]

The sporting revolution was bound up with ideas of politics and of national identity. Sport came to play a significant role in developing the idea of the nation. This phenomenon was beautifully distilled in Eric Hobsbawm's phrase in respect of international soccer, where he wrote that 'the imagined community of millions seems more real as a team of eleven named people.'[6] Wrapped around all of this was the philosophy of the public school system which was vital to the codification of sport in the Victorian era. It was in these schools that an ideology was forged which entwined ideas of sport with those of education and religion. Sport became an essential part of a new curriculum, through which students were supposed to be inculcated with values of manliness, strength, loyalty, discipline and leadership.[7]

In Ireland, sports such as rugby and soccer were identified with the symbols of the British Empire. They courted the patronage of the key figures of British rule in Ireland, flew the Union flag at their events, and invited bands of the

British army to play the music of the Empire.[8] The establishment of the GAA was, in part, a reaction against this apparent 'Britishness' of sport in Ireland. Leading this reaction was Michael Cusack. Until 1882 Michael Cusack had actually been an avid enthusiast for cricket and rugby, and for the new sporting ideology. He wrote in July 1882: 'You may be certain that the boy who can play cricket well, will not, in after years, lose his head and get flurried in the face of danger.'[9] In respect of rugby, for the 1879–80 season he founded the Cusack's Academy Football Club and affiliated it to the Irish Rugby Football Union. Cusack was club secretary and trainer, as well as playing in the forwards, and described himself as a 'sterling lover of the game'.[10]

In founding the GAA on 1 November 1884, Cusack turned from 'British' sports and promoted the ideas of a Gaelic sporting 'revival' with messianic zeal.[11] Led by Cusack, the GAA ensured that sport – and ideas around sport – was another element in the evolving discourse on Irish nationhood. This discourse centred not just on political independence and on land ownership, but also on the promotion of domestic industry, the revival of the Irish language, and the reclamation of a distinctive Irish historical narrative. The fact that the key decade in the construction of the modern Irish sporting world was the 1880s sharpened the relationship between politics and sport in Ireland. This was, after all, a decade of profound social and political upheaval. The GAA received patronage from Archbishop Thomas Croke (the leading nationalist cleric in the Irish Catholic Church), Michael Davitt (the leader of the Land League) and Charles Stewart Parnell (the leader of the Irish Parliamentary Party). Soon this trinity was joined by the veteran republican revolutionary John O'Leary. Capitalising on the patronage of these men, the GAA presented itself as nationalist and patriotic. Further, it painted its opponents as pro-British and elitist. As Cusack so neatly put it in his newspaper column, Irishmen could now 'choose between Irish and foreign laws' when they went to play sport.[12]

II

The GAA, cultural nationalism and the Volunteer movement

By the time that Leix and Cork met in the 1915 All-Ireland hurling final, the championships run by the GAA in both hurling and in Gaelic football were a significant presence on the Irish sporting calendar. The GAA had first run an All-Ireland hurling championship in 1887. The decision to establish the championships was influenced by several factors. Firstly, inter-club contests were wildly popular and began to draw huge crowds. Clubs started to travel across the country to play against each other and these matches generated intense interest as the newspapers began to speculate which teams might be considered the best in the country. Secondly, although the number of clubs was growing, many were slow to affiliate to the Association, leaving it short of money. Establishing a central championship held the prospect of enticing GAA clubs to process their affiliations, just as the establishment of the Football Association Cup had done so much in the 1870s to promote the development of the Football Association in England. The championships were open to all affiliated clubs who would first compete in county-based competitions, to be run by local county committees. The winners of each county championship would then proceed to represent that county in the All-Ireland championships. These two basic ideas – county championships between local clubs and national competition between competing counties – provided the framework for the GAA's long-term development. From the very first All-Ireland championships in 1887 a trend developed whereby the champion clubs of each county selected a number of players from other clubs to assist them in inter-county matches. Over time, more and more players were brought in to supplement the county champions. By 1915, the idea of a county being represented by the best players from any club within its boundaries, rather than merely the champion club, was firmly established. It was a development which added greatly to the popular appeal of hurling.[13]

The rise in the popular appeal of hurling was also rooted in improvements in the standards of play. During the 1890s and the early 1900s rule changes were introduced which opened out the play. Hurling retained a devotion to physical combat but became more accommodating of the idea of skilful play. This, in turn, drew larger crowds to matches. By 1915, Croke Park in Dublin was the established venue for the All-Ireland finals. This was something which had only recently been confirmed. More than half of the first 20 years of finals were played outside Dublin. Some matches were held on private grounds; the 1901 and 1904 All-Ireland hurling finals were staged in a field at Maurice Davin's farm at Carrick-on-Suir, Co. Tipperary. As the GAA grew in the early years of the twentieth century, it sought to develop its own grounds and this led, eventually, to the purchase of Croke Park. This relatively small piece of land at Jones Road on the north side of Dublin had been used for horse racing, athletics and soccer in the late nineteenth century. The GAA used the grounds intermittently in the 1890s, but following their purchase in 1907 by the journalist and GAA man Frank Dineen, they became synonymous with Gaelic games. Dineen renovated both the sporting and spectating facilities at Jones Road, until the grounds were purchased by the GAA in December 1913 as its national headquarters and renamed 'Croke Memorial Park'.[14] This move had become all the more important because the 1911 All-Ireland hurling final had not been played due to a dispute over the venue for the match.[15]

The growth of hurling and Gaelic football as major spectator sports by 1915 was confirmed by the development of Croke Park. As W. F. Mandle has noted, 'by 1912 crowds of between 12,000 and 20,000 were commonplace at finals.' Such crowds were also witnessed at other sporting events in Ireland.[16] This emergence of a culture of attending events on a regular basis and in vast numbers transformed sport in the late nineteenth and early twentieth centuries. The single most striking consequential development was the building and enclosure of grounds for sport. Indeed, commercialised spectator sport for the mass market became one of the economic success stories of late-Victorian Britain. The influx of money placed pressures on different sports in different ways; it almost always brought into focus the idea of men (and a few women) being paid to play. The numbers of professionals grew across a whole range of sports as clubs tried to buy in success, or tried simply to compete. Indeed, by 1910, there were in England 6,800 registered professional soccer players, 400 professional jockeys, and 200 first-class professional cricketers.

Paradoxically, this development of professionalism in organised sport was complemented by the development of amateurism. Amateurism, in its essence, was apparently constructed around the simple principle that sport should be played for love, not money. Wrapped around this basic idea were associated notions relating to codes of conduct, not least that of 'fair play' whereby one would not simply play by the rules of the game but also demonstrate the spirit intended by those rules. This was an imagined world of integrity and manliness, where one might compete but equally one should always retain control, elegance and calm.[17]

The values of amateurism did not usually survive engagement with competitive sport. This was the case because, as the novelist Wilkie Collins wrote, far from teaching a man virtuous behaviour, sport taught him how 'to take every advantage of another man that his superior strength and superior cunning can suggest'.[18] The greater problem was that, at its core, amateurism in British sport was usually elitism dressed up as morality. For all that there were those who truly believed in the idea of amateur sport, there were many more who used it as a cloak to cover their elitism. Perhaps the most extreme example of social distinction disguised as amateurism came when stewards from the Henley Regatta founded the Amateur Rowing Association in 1882. In setting out its membership rules, it banned from the Association anyone who had ever competed for a material prize; anyone who had competed against a professional; and anyone who had ever taught, pursued or assisted in any form of sport to earn a livelihood. More than that, though, it also banned anyone who 'had ever been employed in or about boats, or in any manual labour for money or wages'; anyone who 'had been by trade, or employment, for wages, a mechanic, artisan or labourer, or engaged in any menial duty'; and anyone who 'was a member of a boat or a rowing club containing anyone liable to disqualification under the above clauses'.[19]

Sport in Ireland also divided along the lines of amateurism and professionalism. While soccer allowed for professionals to play the game, rugby did not. And neither did the GAA.[20] Nonetheless, by 1915 the various aspects of the modernisation of the game of hurling, and the parallel modernisation of the GAA, had brought dramatic change to how players prepared for games. Training regimes stressed the importance of physical fitness, skill-based drills and practice games. When Clare won the 1914 All-Ireland hurling championship, they were reputed to have prepared better than any team in history. This revolution in preparation was rooted in past failure. In July 1914, the Clare County Board issued an appeal for funds to help its team be 'properly trained and equipped', because 'we now find ourselves occupying a very insignificant position.'[21] The ambition was to ape what successful counties 'like Kilkenny, Kerry and others had done'.[22]

As a means of fundraising, Clare Chairman J. Shearin suggested organising some concerts throughout the county: 'Then they could get the players to Ennis to train.'[23] The Clare training fund – like that of training funds in many counties – was well-subscribed, with the GAA clubs, the general public and businesses all contributing.[24] As Clare progressed to the 1914 All-Ireland hurling final, they headed for a week's training in Lahinch and in Lisdoonvarna before all their championship matches, with Clare County Council, a local National Insurance inspector and a local doctor, Dr McDonagh, all giving use of their cars to convey the team.[25] Throughout the week before the 1914 All-Ireland final they stayed in the Temperance Hotel in Lisdoonvarna,[26] and among the exercises they undertook were running, walking, hurling, and gymnastics, as well as receiving massages.[27]

Each man was up at 7.00 a.m. for a five-mile walk and was usually in bed by 10.30 p.m. to rest and recuperate.[28] The training was overseen by the trainer for the team, Jim Ó Hehir[29] (father of the renowned Gaelic games commentator Mícheál Ó Hehir); he instructed that no drinking or smoking should take place, for even 'smoking of any kind is almost as harmful as drinking'.[30] There were strong rumours, however, that some members of the team had occasionally indulged in 'certain spa water brewed on the banks of the Laney'.[31] There were other distractions, too, as a letter writer to the *Clare Champion* wrote:

> Our boys being so good looking, and of course such heroes in the eyes of the fair sex, attract quite a number of fair ladies to the vicinity of their training quarters every evening and as a result we have some 'tripping in the light fantastic toe' which is all very well in its own way, taken in moderation … but it should not come off every night and on no account be prolonged after ten.[32]

Collective training was looked upon in disgust by some. Kerry's Dick Fitzgerald, the great star of Gaelic games in that era, lamented the increased emphasis towards professionalism, arguing that players were being 'unfairly forced to go into special training'.[33] The *Clare Champion* reported that some people in Clare were unhappy with the approach being taken by their players and were 'linking this as professionalism and are reluctant to donate'.[34] Most usually, the attitude was that adopted by a letter writer to the *Clare Champion*: 'If we want to win we have to go through with it.'[35] And win they did: Clare hammered Leix in the 1914 All-Ireland hurling final by a 5–1 (16 points) to 1–0 (three points) scoreline.[36] It was their first time to win the All-Ireland championship and, although Leix had been soundly beaten in 1914, they were soon to make amends.

III

How Leix won the 1915 All-Ireland championship[37]

Before Leix lost the 1914 All-Ireland final to Clare, an anonymous letter had been sent to the secretary of the Leix County Committee in October 1914 which implored the players to 'leave off work and train. If ye do not, ye will be not only beaten, but disgraced.'[38] As it was, the Leix team had actually trained together for the 1914 final every day for three weeks at the county grounds in Maryborough, using money raised by the county committee. The annual convention of the Leix County Committee had agreed that 'a fund be established to defray the expenses of training the Senior inter-county teams' and that that fund would be administered by a specially elected committee.[39] A circular was issued by the Training Fund Sub-Committee:

The preparation of the team for the Leinster Championship was carried out at the personal expense of the members of the team. This has involved a serious drain on the means of the men, who, in many cases, had to provide substitutes to fill their places of employment during frequent special practices. It would be too much to expect them to bear the expenses of the extra special course of training which it will be necessary for them to undergo for the playing of the All-Ireland Final. The team is mainly composed of working men to whom the loss of a day's wages is a serious matter, and they have, as stated, already sacrificed a considerable sum in this way.[40]

Contributions were received from GAA clubs across Queen's Co., from the Tullamore club in neighbouring King's Co., from local businesses and from people from Queen's Co. who were living across Ireland, particularly in Dublin.[41] To raise money, the committee had printed collecting cards where people could write in their subscriptions; receipt cards were printed to those who subscribed.[42] Some who were solicited for money wrote back in apology that they could not raise more. M. Collier wrote from 22 Ard Righ Road, Arbour Hill, Dublin that he had thought he would 'do better, but things are so upset with the war it's hard to get money'. Others were unable to raise any money. The GAA club in Monadrehid, Queen's Co. wrote that they could raise nothing because they 'had to pay one of our players 10s. a week last month that got hurt'.[43] The generosity of other donors was obviously rooted in self-interest, including a donation from the management of Wynn's Hotel on Lower Abbey Street in Dublin. Wynn's was already established as a venue for GAA players and supporters. It was in Wynn's that the Leix players ate breakfast and dinner on the day of big matches in Dublin.[44] Others still saw this as an opportunity to make money. John J. Higgins, the secretary of the Leix County Committee, received a letter from James F. O'Crowley, Wellington Square, Cork, offering to supply decorations in the Leix colours. With his letter O'Crowley enclosed samples of his decorations and suggested decorations bearing the legend 'Up Queens County'.[45]

The amount of money required was made clear in a letter from the captain of the team, Bob O'Keefe, a schoolteacher based in Borris-in-Ossory.[46] In a letter to Higgins, O'Keefe stressed the need to pay for substitute workers for members of the hurling team who would miss work. O'Keefe wrote: 'We will have to pay a man to take Jim Hyland's place also. He is a coach-builder. He is working at home but they are a very large family and they could not very well afford to have Jim away so long.' O'Keefe mentioned the costs of covering the expenses of the players, and understood that 'this will involve a big sum of money and it will go near the £80 that I had in my head all along. I would like, if at all possible to have every man free of any loss whatever.'[47] Replacing E. P. McEvoy, a farmer's son, cost 10s. per week for three weeks for a substitute worker and 1s. 3d. per day for 16 days to cover the cost of his train fare from Abbeyleix to Maryborough.[48] The money raised by the training fund covered not just the cost of providing those employers with substitutes for the hurlers, but also the cost of train fares and meals for the players. Leix was fortunate to be a crossing point for trains and, indeed, several of the hurlers were employed on the railways. Others worked as bakers, brewers and caretakers, in addition to a strong farming contingent.[49]

There were many other ancillary expenses. A dozen sliotars (hurling balls) were bought from Quigley's of Barrow Street in Dublin. They were 'made of the best Irish hide' and cost a total of 30s.[50] Another dozen sliotars were bought from James Lalor from Three Castles in Kilkenny, while his brother, Martin Lalor, was asked to make hurleys for the players, at a cost of 3s. 6d. apiece. Getting the sliotars from Lalor proved no straightforward task. He made six and sent them up to Maryborough. He then sent up two more, and then two more again, apologising for the delay. A rather bizarre letter was received from Lalor's wife in the midst of the transactions. She wrote to Higgins on 29 October 1914 and asked that her husband not be paid until she sent word for this to happen. A month later, on 30 November, Mrs Lalor wrote again to say that it was now fine to pay her husband and asked that Higgins 'not mention when sending that I caused the delay as he didn't know anything about it'.[51]

All of the efforts of Leix in 1914 had ended in dismal defeat, but 1915 offered a new opportunity. The Leix County Committee had attempted to keep Bob O'Keefe from the Ballycotton club as captain of the team for 1915, but Ballygeeghan had won the Leix championship and insisted on appointing a captain from their club. This was an important moment. The captain had the deciding say on who should constitute the team. Within the GAA, picking a county team was a delicate balance between avoiding alienating the members of your own club and picking the best players from the other clubs in the county. Indeed, it was a consistent challenge across the GAA to get the best players from all the clubs to represent the county. This was partly because of the tensions which emerged between clubs who competed against each other in their own local championship.[52] In Leix there was a new and intense rivalry between Ballygeeghan and Kilcotton.[53] There were also problems between other clubs. After one club match, O'Keefe had written that 'when we have cleared up [doctors'] fees for the battle with Clonaslee we may go bankrupt.'[54] Ballygeeghan nominated their best player, John Finlay, to captain Leix in 1915. Finlay (possibly under advice or pressure from the county committee) determined on picking the best hurlers in the county and the eventual team that represented Leix contained just six Ballygeeghan players.[55]

Finlay was also progressive in his approach to training. He believed that the team's preparations for the 1914 final had actually been hindered by the fact that they had trained too hard and that 'some of the players on the team were not able to stand the training they went through.'[56] Early in 1915 he wrote to his players advising that they do their utmost to win the Leix championship and then the All-Ireland: 'This we can do by acquiring the staying powers and speed necessary for a player to do his best for the whole of an hour's hard play.' He advised that players initially go on long, slow runs, reaching a distance of three miles. They should then start to build sprints of up to 50 yards into these runs.[57]

Leix duly beat Kilkenny and then Dublin to retain the Leinster championship by the end of August 1915.[58] It was then that preparations to win the All-Ireland final were properly put in train. Money was raised through renewed appeals to supporters and was now used to fund a refined training regime, with elaborate drills for the players to follow during practice. Copies survive of practice drills for catching, dribbling, striking, sideline pucks, free pucks and fighting for possession. In the drill which worked on fighting for possession, it was proposed to send a ball a short distance ahead of two players who would then fight for it 'somewhat like two dogs for a hare'.[59] In the two weeks before the final, the Leix players came together to train three times a week, for two hours on each occasion. To do this, some had to secure permission from their employers to leave work at 2.00 p.m. in order to be in Maryborough to train before the light faded.[60]

A significant input into training was made by Fr J. J. Kearney, chairman of the Leix County Committee and president of the Maryborough Hurling Club. In the weeks before the final he wrote to the players stressing the importance of speed and intensity: 'There will be no time for fancy play or raising the ball in an All-Ireland final. Men should practice striking ground balls when running at top speed.'[61] Kearney – in tandem with other members of the county committee – believed that the team needed outside expertise if it was to win an All-Ireland.[62] He wrote to Jim Doyle from Michael Street in Waterford and asked him to take charge of the team in the weeks before the 1915 final. Doyle was unavailable but offered the advice that Leix should be careful not to over-train before the final and suggested that they ask the great Kilkenny hurler Dick 'Drug' Walsh to take charge. Walsh knew all about winning championships. He had recently retired, having won seven All-Ireland medals, three of them as captain.

Walsh was approached and duly agreed. He did some work with the team, including bringing Kilkenny hurlers in sidecars to Maryborough to hurl practice matches on three successive Sundays.[63] Illness then prevented Walsh from attending training for several days, though he was in Croke Park for match day.[64] By then, the players had been given a type-written document: 'Notes for players previous to match'. This re-iterated all the work that had been done in training, stressed the importance of moving the ball quickly, of playing unselfishly and concluded: 'The team possessing the greater SPEED AND DASH will win.'[65]

Cork players, too, trained assiduously for the final. As well as training collectively, many players trained to their own regime. One of the stars of the Cork team in 1915 was Larry Flaherty who had won an All-Ireland as long before as 1903. Flaherty had learned his hurling ('as many') when playing the game as a boy using a sycamore branch and a can. As an adult, he developed a training regime which saw him train on a hill behind his house in Douglas, commencing at 5.30 a.m. He followed a regime of jumps, as well as tying a 6 lb. weight to his hurley, before working on his swing. (Flaherty lived into his 90s and later commented on watching hurling on television in the 1970s: 'To be honest, I don't like watching fellows doing things which I sometimes feel I could still do better myself.'[66]) Cork had already won six All-Irelands and their passage to the 1915 final had seen them defeat Tipperary, Limerick and defending champions Clare to win the Munster championship.[67] Many members of the Leix team travelled to watch Cork beat Clare in the Munster championship, 'each man to observe the style of his opponent'; Bob O'Keefe said that the match 'was not classic hurling ... [because] Cork were superior everywhere and their forward line is the best ever I saw working.'[68]

Cork entered the final as strong favourites with the press. In sections of the national press there was comprehensive coverage of the game. There were then several weekly newspapers in Ireland dedicated to the coverage of sport. One of those papers was *Sport*, whose GAA correspondent was Frank Dineen. Dineen's preview of the game included pen-pictures of the players. In compiling the preview, Dineen had travelled to Maryborough where he had interviewed the Leix captain, John Finlay. As Dineen later recalled, Finlay appeared to have already adopted the pose which was to become so associated with GAA teams: 'Speaking to Mr. John Finlay, I was made to think that they had not the slightest expectation of defeating Cork ... John Finlay, across a table, was a quiet, unassuming, sociable country gentleman, who talked of everything but hurling.'[69] Even if Dineen could winkle little from Finlay, the evidence which sat before him was enough to convince him of his team's worth. He wrote:

> The Leix team of this year are as fine a body of young men as could be found in any county in Ireland. The majority of them are over 6 feet in height, and all of them are handsome-looking athletes of power and strength and speed. They know how to hurl, they know how the Cork team will hurl, and they will play to the last minute.[70]

The memory of this Leix team as being big men has survived in local lore to this day.[71]

Both teams travelled to Dublin the night before the final. The Leix hurlers stayed in a hotel on Gardiner Street in Dublin. John J. Higgins had organised a team of four men to look after all the needs of the players in Dublin before and after the match.[72] These men included the brothers Joseph and William McDonald who said in a letter to Higgins: 'Anything that you want us to do, remember don't think bad of asking us.'[73] Their care of the players most likely included masseur work and the provision of oils and embrocation.[74] The four men were paid £2 each for their work. The night before the match, they waited in the corridors to restrain any man wishing to avail of a night in the city. This was done at the suggestion of Bob O'Keefe who noted that the 'caretakers' employed 'must be very strict on Saturday night. There is no use depending on any of the players.'[75] As it was, no player was thought to have successfully escaped. On the morning of the match, the Leix players togged out in their hotel rooms and, wearing black-and-amber horizontally striped jerseys, walked down Fitzgibbon Street, then down Jones Road, and into Croke Park.[76] Dineen had met their opponents and remembered 'a smile of confidence in every Cork face I saw on Saturday night'.[77]

Special trains were run from Cork and Queen's Co., and also from the hurling heartlands of Tipperary, Limerick, Galway, Offaly, Kilkenny and Waterford. In all, the Great Southern and Western Railway put on 17 special trains which were filled to capacity. Admission to the ground was 3s. for sideline seats, 2s. for the balcony, 1s. for the enclosure and 6d. to stand on the bank around the pitch.[78] In the end, around 12,000 people paid gate receipts totalling £362 on the day.[79] Amongst them was the former world heavyweight boxing champion Jack Johnston who was visiting from America to perform in a revue. It is claimed in local lore in Laois that Johnston 'appeared to be a supporter of Leix too'.[80] The crowd would most likely have been greater but for the wetness of the day. All morning it had threatened rain and that rain duly arrived before the game started. Leix were better prepared for the rain than Cork and appeared on the field wearing their overcoats. The *Irish Independent* was later to comment that the appearance of the Leix men was 'somewhat unconvincing because they all wore mackintoshes', but it was a decision rooted in commonsense.[81] On top of that, the Leix team had brought resin to put on their hurleys to improve the grip; Cork had not done this.[82] Journalists, though, were even more poorly prepared. They sat at a table on the sideline taking notes, but such was the rain that they were forced to resort to slinging 'sheets of water off our writing pads as frequently and as plentifully as if we were bailing water from a leaking boat'. When they tried to put up an umbrella, they were immediately brought to change their mind by the unsighted crowd standing behind them who made the journalists 'a target for their harmless missiles'.[83]

The referee, William Walsh (who, the press would later write, 'controlled the game in a masterful way, giving satisfaction to all'), called in the two captains and spun the hurley.[84] The Cork captain, Con Sheehan, had correctly chosen on which side the hurley would fall and directed that his team would defend the city end of the pitch (later known as the Canal End and then as the Davin Stand). Walsh threw in the ball to start the match at 2.54 p.m. and Cork started as if they were sure to justify their position as favourites and scored three early goals. Leix settled midway through the half, however, and scored two goals of their own, as well as two points, and trailed by just one point at the interval. The match was won in the early minutes of the second half. As the rain worsened to a downpour, Leix scored three quick goals and, despite a late rally by Cork, when the final whistle was blown the score stood at Leix 6–2 (20 points), Cork 4–1 (13 points).[85] In a somewhat wistful summary, Frank Dineen noted that he was growing old with the GAA and had now seen many All-Ireland finals, but that he was 'lost in admiration at one of the most magnificent battles that had ever been played in the final ... Every stroke of the hurley was like an electric shock, while the ball shot here and there and everywhere with lightning-like speed.'[86]

There were huge celebrations on the field after the match, with players and officials congratulated on their success. The team travelled home by train and are reported to have followed the passion for singing which GAA teams traditionally displayed on train journeys. The Leix men sang their local song 'Lovely Laois' and the Kilkenny standard 'The Rose of Mooncoin'.[87] Bonfires blazed across Queen's Co. Congratulatory letters arrived from many parts, not least from Sir Algernon Coote, Lord Lieutenant of Queen's Co., who wrote from the House of Commons: 'Will you convey my hearty congratulations to the Leix team, upon winning the hurling championship?'[88] A telegraph also arrived from Westminster from the nationalist MP for Queen's Co., Patrick A. Meehan.[89] There was praise for Bob O'Keefe from Frank Dineen: 'His hair has turned grey at the game for he has been over twenty years behind the camán [hurley] ... He has had a long and successful career as a hurler, and no one who ever knew him will grudge him his All-Ireland gold medal.'[90] O'Keefe had missed much hurling earlier in the year, not least because one of his daughters had suffered successively from pneumonia, measles and scarlet fever, but could now exult in that medal.[91] There was gratitude, too, for the work which administrators had done to achieve victory. O'Keefe was later involved in ensuring that a special commemorative watch worth £25 was struck and presented to Fr J. J. Kearney in recognition of his work in promoting the GAA in the county through the establishment of schools' leagues and proper structures for adult games.[92] O'Keefe also wrote to John J. Higgins to say: 'I am sure you can hardly take life seriously this week after Sunday's great win' and that he hoped that Higgins now felt 'fully rewarded for all your work [and] worry [and] trouble over inter-county hurling matches for the past two seasons'. He wrote that he looked forward to seeing the reports of the match in the press.[93]

O'Keefe was not to be disappointed. After the game, there was extensive coverage in the national and local press.[94] Lengthy match reports were accompanied by photographs of the teams, the referee and the play.[95] The report in the *Gaelic Athlete* claimed that 'the amount of vigour which Leix put into their work out-weighed the superior skill of their opponents ... it was though a hurling ball was thrown up between two teams, one side armed with stout ash camáns and the other side with frail tennis racquets. Leix were certainly not the side equipped with tennis racquets.'[96] The great exception was the *Irish Times*. The entirety of its coverage read: 'Hurling: All-Ireland Championship: Leix 6 goals 2 points; Cork 4 goals 1 point.' Against that, there was extensive sports coverage in the paper, including horse racing, golf, rugby, soccer, golf and billiards.[97] The *Irish Times* was not, however, entirely averse to covering hurling. In the week before the final it had recorded the details of an abandoned hurling match at the Markets Field in Limerick, where two teams had fought from start to premature finish, while one player was taken unconscious from the field and six more had to be brought to hospital to be treated for head wounds.[98] The antipathy towards hurling displayed by the *Irish Times* was, of course, related to the position of the GAA within the wider political and cultural life of Ireland.

IV

The GAA, cultural nationalism and the Volunteer movement

Despite a rule dating back to 1895 which declared the GAA to be a 'non-political and unsectarian organisation', there was no denying the nationalist aspect of the Association.[99] In the early years of the twentieth century, a new generation of officials emerged who were zealous in their belief in the transformative power of the GAA and saw the Association as primarily engaged in a project of national liberation. In their minds, the GAA would sit beside the Gaelic League in an attempt to define a particular Irish identity. The GAA, said a motion passed unanimously at the 1901 annual congress of the Association, was engaged in a 'struggle to crush English pastimes' and a 'patriotic effort to make young men more thoroughly and essentially Irish and self-respecting'.[100] Barriers were erected between the 'native games' of the GAA and 'foreign games' such as rugby and cricket. Between 1901 and 1905 the GAA at national level introduced a set of rules which ultimately decreed that anyone who played, promoted or attended 'foreign games' (the listed 'foreign games' were cricket, hockey, rugby and soccer) could not participate in the GAA. Later, it was added that anyone who was a member of the police forces or the British army was prohibited from membership of the GAA. Further, no GAA club was allowed to organise any entertainment at which 'foreign dances' were permitted, and any GAA member who attended dances run by either the British army or the police, or by 'foreign games' clubs, was liable to a suspension of two years. The problem for those who wished the GAA to be more than a mere sporting organisation was that there were many members whose involvement was rooted in a love of sport and who conceived of the GAA only in terms of sporting engagement. The pragmatism involved in running a broad-based organisation ensured that the ambition of drawing a line between Irish-Ireland and West-Britain was no straightforward task. Implementation of the 'Ban' rules was contentious. After all, there were almost annual attempts to have those rules weakened or removed.[101]

In certain clubs and in certain counties, the promotion of the GAA as a nationalist organisation was more heavily pursued than in others. One such county was Wexford. There, men such as Seán Etchingham (who was a columnist on GAA matters on the *Enniscorthy Echo*), Seán O'Kennedy (the outstanding Ross Geraldines footballer), and the Enniscorthy men Pádraig Kehoe and Frank Boggan, attempted to push the GAA in Wexford towards a more radical nationalist position. They promoted not just Gaelic games but also language revival through the Gaelic League and temperance through the County Wexford Temperance Council.[102] The failure of the GAA to match their cultural ambitions often drove Kehoe and Etchingham, in particular, into a state of high dudgeon. When a member of the Enniscorthy-based Volunteer GAA club, Robert Hanlon, looked for re-admission to the GAA having attended a dance run by a rugby club, the case was made by a member of his club that Hanlon understood he was doing nothing wrong:

> Mr Kehoe: What! Attended a Rugby dance and he understood he was doing nothing wrong?
> Mr Etchingham: What class of a dance is this? Is it like the Tango?
> Mr McGrath: A little above that.
> Mr Etchingham: He must come here and express his regret and make an apology.
> Mr Kehoe: What is the Association coming to? Here we have a man breaking the rules, and afterwards seeking to be re-admitted.[103]

It was one thing, of course, to promote an 'Irish-Ireland'; it was altogether another to fight for an independent Ireland. When the years after 1912 brought the renewed militarisation of Irish politics, this time with mass involvement and the threat of civil war, the GAA became involved in the Irish Volunteers from its beginning. The first public meeting of the Volunteers in November 1913 was addressed by the secretary of the GAA, Luke O'Toole, and evidence of close ties was readily apparent: for example the annual convention of the GAA in 1914 was addressed by a member of the Volunteer Executive; the newspaper of the Volunteers, *The National Volunteer*, carried a weekly GAA column; and GAA President James Nowlan urged Association members to join the Volunteers and 'learn to shoot straight'.[104] The founding of the Volunteers immediately impacted on the activities of the GAA at local level. In Leix, Bob O'Keefe wrote: 'Our lads are dying on the game lately. Between wet weather [and the] Volunteers, the hurling is going to the wall.'[105] 'Dalcassian', a *Gaelic Athlete* columnist, wrote in November 1914 that in Munster 'the game of hurling is now being neglected as all the wielders of the camán are engaged in the more serious work of drilling and learning the use of the rifle.'[106] In 1915, the *Clonmel Chronicle* wrote that applications had been received from the Cashel and Annacarty clubs for the postponement of their matches 'as they would be required at home on that date owing to important meetings connected with the National Volunteers and the holding of the county convention'.[107]

However, while many GAA members may have sympathised with the Volunteer movement, there were those who voiced their opposition to any formal link. A letter to the *Clare Champion* read: 'Allow no politics in, our Association is in existence alone to foster Irish pastimes.'[108] GAA officials in Limerick refused applications by the Volunteers for pitches for drilling purposes, as it would be 'wiser to keep clear as an athletics body of the Volunteer controversy.'[109] Indeed, within a month of the Volunteers being founded the GAA had decided against any formal link, against officially advising members to join, and against allowing the use of Croke Park for drilling purposes as it would cut up the pitch.[110] And there is also widespread evidence that the activities of the GAA actually impeded those of the Volunteers. The *Limerick Leader* reported in April 1914 that 'the usual drill of the Limerick Corps of the Irish Volunteers will not take place on Sunday next owing to the fact that the 1st Round of the Thomond Feis Shield Hurling Tournament will be played that day.'[111] Emphasising the need to avoid overstating the relationship between the GAA and the Volunteer movement, William Murphy has written: 'There were countless ordinary members of the GAA, who chose the hurley rather than the rifle.'[112] Indeed, prominent Volunteer J. J. O'Connell later remarked: 'When a match conflicted with a parade or a field day, too often the parade or field day was put into the background ... It was a fact that the Volunteers did not receive from the GAA the help they expected – nay to which later on they might fairly be considered entitled.'[113]

V

The GAA and the Great War[114]

The outbreak of the Great War in the summer of 1914 had a dramatic impact on Ireland and, of course, on its sports. F. H. Browning, president of the Irish Rugby Football Union, urged the young professional men of Dublin rugby clubs 'to do their bit' and join the war effort.[115] Shortly after, the Irish Rugby Union Corps was established along the lines of similar sporting battalions in Britain.[116] The *Sunday Independent* wrote that 'the attitude of the various rugby unions and their clubs is splendid ... The Irish players have branded themselves together to fight for their country.'[117] It was also decided that rugby matches would essentially be suspended for the duration of the war.[118]

Other sports such as soccer, horse racing and athletics also suffered severe disruption.[119] And, naturally, the GAA was not immune to the impact of the war; many of its games, including many high-profile matches, were postponed as trains[120] and GAA grounds[121] were commandeered by the British army. Nonetheless, some within the GAA saw in the war the opportunity to profit from the disruption to its rivals. In an editorial in April 1915, the *Gaelic Athlete* wrote that 'now that even the slightest shadow of West British competition which remained has made off with its tail between its legs, valuable propagandist work can be done in the sports promoting line ... Then, when the war is over, we will have an even bigger and better GAA to hand down as a heritage to posterity.'[122] And, despite the obstacles to be overcome, it seemed that the GAA was by 1915 'in every way a flourishing and more widespread institution than ever before'.[123]

For men such as Seán Etchingham in Wexford, the Great War represented an opportunity of a different kind. At a Wexford GAA meeting in November 1914, his suggestion that the GAA clubs of the county should establish rifle clubs was met with general agreement. There was, however, a concern expressed that the weather might then be unsuited to such activities. Etchingham was apoplectic: 'Do you want special weather for war? It is not a question of weather. It is a question of time, and you may be required to have knowledge on this point at any moment. If you wait till the summer the opportunity – the like of which you have not had for a century – may pass; an opportunity that may not occur again.'[124] When it was pointed out that the establishment of the rifle clubs was a subject for discussion at the forthcoming national convention of the GAA and that Wexford should await the decision of that body on a Kerry resolution to establish rifle clubs, Etchingham commented: 'Sure it's rifles I want, not resolutions. If resolutions could do any good, this country would have been free long ago.' Etchingham put before the meeting elaborate drills which the clubs would follow in their rifle training. As it turned out, the Kerry motion on rifle clubs was never put before the GAA's national convention and the idea of GAA rifle clubs was lost.[125] Nonetheless, in Enniscorthy, sections of the GAA continued to plan for nationalist rebellion. GAA rooms on Mary Street in the town were used for meetings of the Irish Republican Brotherhood, and football matches were used to mobilise the Irish Volunteers.[126] Ultimately, in Easter 1916, Enniscorthy was the only town in Ireland outside Dublin to experience revolution on a large scale, and Etchingham was in the vanguard, with other GAA members also taking up arms.

By then, though, many GAA members had already followed a different path and had joined the British army to fight in the Great War. Etchingham decried the notion that any GAA man should go and fight in the war, but many did.[127] Later, GAA historians usually ignored the fact that men from the Association had joined the British army, or simply denied that it had happened. The anonymous author of *Sixty Glorious Years: The Authentic Story of the GAA* (1946) claimed that 'efforts were, indeed, made to recruit GAA men for the British Army, an especial appeal being made to the hurlers and footballers of Munster, but there was no response.'[128] This was untrue and there should be no surprise that many GAA men joined the British army. After all, the leader of nationalist Ireland, John Redmond, had urged the Volunteer movement to enlist. Many GAA men who were members of the Volunteers responded to Redmond's call. That is not to say that all those who enlisted identified with the Empire. As well as responding to Redmond's call, many more joined because of economic circumstances, because of the sense of adventure which attended the war in its early stages and, most assuredly, for a whole host of other reasons. In general, the extent to which GAA members went to fight for the British army is impossible to quantify, although reports in local and national newspapers across the island help to give some indication of the numbers that saw action.

From Cork came reports that Florence Buckley, who lost his life through the torpedoing of the SS *Iniscarra* by a German submarine, was a well-known and popular hurler who played at centre-forward on the first team of the Redmonds club.[129] Rifleman Harry Burgess was also killed in France. He had previously captained the Cork junior team.[130] In Clare a local newspaper commented that 'the Gaels of the banner county will be glad to hear that Sergeant George Fitzpatrick, Connaught Rangers, who was seriously injured in the Dardanelles is now recovered, and it is the famous "Muff"'s fervent desire that the war may soon be over in order that he may once again don the Green and Gold.'[131] The report also mentioned that other prominent players from Clare were serving with the 16th Division and 'it is their foremost wish that the team would be kept going till they return.'[132] One of those players was John Fox from Newmarket-on-Fergus, who reportedly had had a magnificent game in the 1914 All-Ireland final against Leix.[133] His enlistment was seen as a minor propaganda coup for the British.[134]

From Limerick came the story of the bravery of Major Lawrence Roche, a former Limerick GAA county chairman and Munster Council member, who 'led the royal Munster fusiliers in the capture of Guillemont, a feat unequalled for bravery in the whole history of the War'.[135] From Tipperary there were similar echoes in the tale of Corporal John Cunningham, VC, Leinster Regiment, who was well known in Thurles where he was a leading member of the local GAA club. The report on his death described his award of the Victoria Cross as being 'for most conspicuous bravery and devotion to duty ... where although wounded he succeeded in almost alone in reaching his objective ... there is little doubt that the superb courage of this NCO cleared up a most critical situation.'[136]

The numbers who enlisted obviously varied from county to county, but were sometimes enough to truly inhibit clubs. The 'Belfast notes' of the *Gaelic Athlete* wrote that 'the European crisis has been responsible for many of our most prominent teams "going weak"', with the St Peter's club having been particularly hit, having lost 'no less than nine of their best players'.[137] Seán Kierse cites a report in the *Clare Champion* in January 1916 which stated that, 'unhappily the ranks of the Killaloe GAA have been sadly depleted owing to the war.'[138] Tom O'Donoghue also claims that enlistment into the army of local young men was a contributory factor in the depletion of the ranks available to John O'Leary's and New Tipperary GAA clubs.[139] Across the midlands, newspapers carried reports of GAA matches alongside news of recruitment and recruitment campaigns. In the week after it covered the 1915 All-Ireland hurling final, the *Leinster Leader* carried a full-page advertisement calling on the men of the midlands to join their peers at the front and replenish the Irish regiments stationed in France and elsewhere.[140]

Attitudes of GAA officials to members of the Association joining the British army were complex. The rhetoric of most officials was trenchantly against recruitment to the British army. In July 1915, for example, the honorary secretary of the Galway County Board, Stephen Jordan, was charged under the Defence of the Realm Act with having made statements which were considered prejudicial to recruiting.[141] In Wexford, members of the GAA led by Wexford County Board member Seán O'Kennedy called for some organised form of resistance amongst members in the county towards the call to join the war effort.[142] Against that, however, there were others within the upper ranks of the GAA who took an opposing view. There were reports of funds for wounded soldiers being raised from an athletic sports meeting held at Glasson, 'under the auspices of the Gaelic Athletic Association'.[143]

There was pressure, too, on the GAA to reverse its policy of banning from membership members of the British army. The *National Volunteer* reported, in an attack on the Association's policy of excluding men who were members of the British army and navy, that a large contingent of men who were members of the Association had joined the colours.[144] In addition, in April 1915, discussions took place in the House of Commons on the GAA's policy of exclusion and a question was put to the Under-Secretary of State for War, by P. J. Meehan, an Irish Parliamentary Party MP who represented Queen's County, on whether he was aware that the 'majority of Reserve Men and recruits who have joined in Ireland have been members of the Association'.[145] In many respects, the attitudes across the GAA towards the enlistment of its members in the British army can be seen in a motion put by the Leix County Committee to the annual congress of the GAA in 1915. This motion sought to permit volunteering for the British army during the Great War. The Leix County Committee argued that, with the increasing growth in the National Volunteers, it was due time that some move should be made to have deleted from the rules that portion prohibiting ex-army men from competing in the Association.[146] The motion was eventually withdrawn under pressure from other members within the GAA. The *Gaelic Athlete* expressed its annoyance that such a motion should be put forward in the first place: 'There are many Gaels who will totally disagree with it.'[147] More than that, the paper claimed the motion would have only entailed 'playing into the hands of parties who have never been distinguished by an inordinate display of affection for the GAA'.[148]

What is clear from all of this is that the relationship between the GAA and the Great War was not a clear-cut one. While many top officials continually saw the Association in terms of its commitment to nationalist ideals and were not at all enamoured by any involvement with the British war effort, it appears that many playing members, and even some high-ranking officials, failed to share in this sentiment. For all the nationalist rhetoric of the GAA, the simple fact is that many GAA members fought and died for the British Empire in the fields of Flanders and in the trenches of the Somme. A week after Leix won the 1915 All-Ireland hurling final, Wexford defeated Kerry to win the football final. They managed this without the services of one of their best players, James Rossiter. He had enlisted in the British army and had died of his wounds in France ten days before the final was played.[149]

VI

Conclusion

There are infinite complexities in the relationship between sport and politics, and sport and national identity. Ascribing motivations to men and women playing certain sports at certain times and under certain flags is no straightforward matter. The reasons why any person in any given place should play any given sport are complex and sometimes even contradictory. Those reasons are influenced by politics and personality and geography and history and tradition and friendship and religion and coincidence. For all that the GAA was usually profoundly nationalist in its rhetoric, the reality of the political engagement of its members was complicated. In 1916, about 350 of the estimated 1,500 rebels who rose on Easter Week were members of the GAA. This left very many more members of the GAA who did not rise. Ernie O'Malley later recalled that 'there were others who belonged to the Gaelic League or who played Gaelic football and hurling ... very contemptuous of rugby and golf, and soccer. They spoke of the English with inherited contempt, attended public meetings in the streets, approved of physical force in talk, but made no attempt to join the Volunteers.'[150] Indeed, while this has yet to be conclusively proven, it seems certain that more GAA members were wearing the uniform of the British army in the trenches of France than were fighting for an Irish Republic in 1916.

Marrying its twin commitments of fostering sporting development and encompassing its wider political function proved an enduring challenge for the

GAA. By 1915, this challenge had largely been resolved in favour of sport. For the great majority of members, games were the primary focus of their engagement with the GAA. Indeed, looking at the manner in which Leix pursued victory in the All-Ireland championship in 1915, it is apparent that, to the hurlers, politics may have mattered, but not as much as hurling. The primacy of sporting ambition was what drove the development of the GAA, not its commitment to nationalism, rhetorical or otherwise.

Roger Casement
24 June, 1915.

3

MICHAEL KEOGH

Recruiting sergeant for Casement's Irish Brigade

BRIAN MAYE

Descendants keep letters, diaries, memoirs and other documents faithfully because they know that in those pages lies a link with a time fast passing from memory into history.

The descendants of Michael Keogh are no exception as regards the practice of faithful document keepers. He led an exciting, adventurous and indeed at times dangerous life, about which he wrote in some detail and at various times. At the heart of that life was his devotion to Roger Casement, whom he first met in New York in 1911, and with whom he worked closely in Germany during the years 1914 to 1916 as part of Casement's project to recruit an Irish brigade from Irish soldiers who had joined the British army to fight in the First World War, and who subsequently found themselves prisoners of war in German camps. Casement's intention was to return to Ireland with this brigade to fight for Irish freedom.

Michael Keogh wrote a detailed account of those years in Germany with Roger Casement. It had always been his intention to publish that account in full in book form – an aim he did not get around to fulfilling during the course of a busy life, although he did publish many articles and give many lectures about his experiences with Casement's Irish Brigade.[1] Kevin Keogh kept many of the articles his father wrote. Another son, Joseph, now deceased, kept others. But they were deprived for more than 40 years of the longest and most detailed account their father wrote. Kevin recalls seeing his father working on that account at various times over the years. Sometimes Keogh senior would be working late into the night, drafting and redrafting, and would resume the process early the following morning. One of his daughters-in-law, Mary, says that he never went anywhere without these manuscripts, which he carried with him in a kind of briefcase.

When Michael Keogh was suffering his last illness in 1964, he was taken to James Connolly Memorial Hospital in Blanchardstown, Co. Dublin. It seems that he took the papers that contained the main account of his time in Germany with him into the hospital. His son Kevin concluded this to be the case because he remembers visiting the hospital one day and finding his father very distressed and calling out for his papers. When Kevin asked him where they had been, he replied that he had had them under his pillow and that they were no longer there. Kevin then called a nurse who had been attending to his father and asked her if she knew anything about the papers he was talking about. In the course of their conversation, she reported that Keogh senior had had a visitor the previous night – a priest whom none of the hospital staff knew by appearance or name. He was not a hospital chaplain or local parish curate but he had called to the hospital and had asked to see Mr Keogh. For the hospital staff, there was nothing unusual about priests visiting patients.

The Keogh family had no idea who the particular priest might be and they never found out who he was but they associate the missing papers with him. They could see how distressed the disappearance of his papers had left their father and they believe that his loss of these precious documents may have hastened his death, because he died around two days after they went missing.

Just over 40 years later, in 2005, Kevin Keogh's son, also called Kevin, was doing some research into his family's history with a view to compiling a family tree. He decided to do a search on the internet and he entered the name of one of his grandfathers, Captain Michael Keogh. To his amazement he discovered that the University College Dublin Archives (UCDA) had papers belonging to his grandfather who had worked for Roger Casement in Germany during the First World War.[2]

From the UCDA site, the Keogh family learned that their father's papers had been found among the Maurice (Moss) Twomey papers, which were deposited in the archive in 1984 by a Fr Maurice Twomey. The Keogh family could not say if their father knew Moss Twomey, who had been active in the IRA for many years and who ran a newsagent's and tobacconist's shop on O'Connell Street in Dublin from the 1940s onwards. He died in 1978. The Keogh family also did not know what, if any, was the relationship between the two Maurice Twomeys. The archivist in UCDA could see that the Michael Keogh papers had no direct or close connection with the Twomey papers and as a result archived them separately.[3]

Who was the mysterious priest? Why had Michael Keogh's papers disappeared? How did they come to end up among the papers of Moss Twomey? The Keogh family were glad to have the main segment of their late father's papers back but would like answers to those questions.

I

Roger Casement made a profound impression on Michael Keogh, an impression that did not diminish in any way with the passing of the years – the very opposite, in fact. Many years after Casement's death, Keogh's wife told her daughter-in-law that she had lived all her married life with 'the ghost of Roger Casement'.[4] But Keogh was in no way exceptional in this regard. One of Casement's biographers has remarked that so many who met him were immediately captivated by his charisma.[5]

One who met him for the first time in Germany during the First World War was Robert Monteith. Monteith had fought in the British army during the Boer War in South Africa from 1899 to 1902. When the Irish Volunteers were formed in 1913, his military background led to him instructing and drilling members of the new force. He was then sent by the Irish Republican Brotherhood (IRB) to assist in the training of the recruits to Casement's Irish Brigade at Limburg and Zossen prisoner-of-war camps in Germany. After many adventures and with extreme difficulty, he made his way to Germany via the United States in the latter months of 1915.

'To meet Casement was to institute a life memory,' he later recorded. This was how he recalled that first meeting:

> Feeling, as I did, that I was with one of the outstanding figures in the titanic conflict of arms and brains, it was the proudest moment of my life. Here was a man who had made, and was still making history; the man who had walked through savage Africa armed only with a walking stick, whose written word had shaken the throne of Leopold II of Belgium, a man who had saved millions of lives in the Congo and Putumayo.[6]

At times, Monteith wrote with deep emotion about Casement, of which the following is a good example:

> I have known no eyes more beautiful than Casement's. In his case they were truly the windows of his soul: blazing when he spoke of man's inhumanity to man, soft and wistful when pleading the cause so dear to his heart, mournful when telling the story of Ireland's centuries-old martyrdom. They were eyes that seemed to search the heart and read one's very soul ... A man is indeed fortunate who can say that he has clasped Casement's hand and received his kindly smile of welcome.[7]

Another who met Casement in Germany for the first time, and who left a record of how much he esteemed him, was Dr Charles Curry. This Irish-American academic was a mathematician and physicist and a professor at Munich University. He had a summer residence in the countryside near Munich on the shores of Lake Ammersee and invited Casement to spend time there whenever he wished. Later, writing to Casement's sister Nina, he referred to her as 'the sister of the man I worshipped and adored'.[8]

So it can be observed that men as diverse as the adventurous, soldierly Monteith and the quieter, academic Curry both found themselves spellbound by the charismatic Casement and remained devoted to his memory for the rest of their lives. Little wonder, then, that Michael Keogh's experience should have been so similar.

II

Keogh's background and life, up to the time that he became so closely involved with the brigade project in Germany, would certainly have predisposed him to see eye to eye with Roger Casement. In the first chapter of the story that is unfolded in his papers, Keogh writes about the importance of heredity: 'Consciously or unconsciously, heredity plays a powerful part in our destinies and lives. If its urge is latent in one generation, it returns with cumulative force in another. Circumstances may curb it, but no power can ever eradicate it.'[9]

Keogh's father, Laurence, came from Coolgreany, Co. Wexford, a county which saw much action and many struggles on behalf of Irish freedom from British rule, especially during the 1798 rebellion. His grandfather, Michael, had fought for the rights of tenant farmers during the late 1870s and 1880s, in the period known as the Land War, and his great-grandfather had been out in 1798.[10] Michael himself was born in Tullow, Co. Carlow, in 1891. He attended national school there and, at the age of 14, entered the seminary school of St Patrick's monastery on a county council scholarship. He stayed there for two years until, in 1907, he went to visit his aunt in New York; he was to remain in the US for the next five to six years.

He had joined the Gaelic League branch in Tullow and also joined a branch of the same organisation in New York. In that city, he also became a member of Clan na Gael, the American wing of the Fenian organisation. 'In these Irish-Ireland ranks, my mind was aroused to the more serious and wider aspects of Irish nationalism, and to a clearer perception of the influence which England never ceased to exert the wide world over in pursuit of international domination,' he later wrote.[11]

A military tradition also existed in Michael Keogh's background. His great-uncle was Colonel Myles Keogh who joined the Papal Zouave army in 1857 when he was just 16.[12] Four years later he went to the United States where the American Civil War was raging. With previous military experience, and showing natural leadership qualities, he was immediately elected captain of the volunteer company of Irish-Americans in the New York Irish Brigade. This brigade took part in almost every major campaign during the Civil War.

By the end of the war, Myles Keogh had risen to the rank of colonel – a temporary wartime rank – and he decided to make his career in the army. He joined the 7th Cavalry, then being formed at Fort Leavenworth, Kansas, with the rank of lieutenant. The regiment had Lieutenant-Colonel George Armstrong Custer as its second-in-command. Keogh was soon promoted to captain and became Custer's favourite subordinate officer. Keogh was to die by Custer's side at the Battle of Little Bighorn in Montana on 25 June 1876.[13]

In a newspaper article, which he wrote in 1952, and in which he referred to his illustrious predecessor, Myles Keogh's grandnephew Michael told about his own first military experiences in the United States. He recorded that his grand-uncle's horse, Comanche, survived the battle of Little Bighorn and that he himself sat on the horse's embalmed remains 34 years after the battle, at Fort Riley in Texas when he was doing a mounted infantry course in the American army. Michael Keogh had emigrated to America at the invitation of his uncle, Jack Tynan, who he described as 'a leading Fenian'. He enrolled in the American army four years later, joining the 69th Irish Volunteer Regiment of the National Guard. Of this he wrote: 'I was taking up again the fighting tradition of my family. For here I was, an eager Irish emigrant of 21, tossing aside my engineer's job in New York to go battling with Mexican guerrillas in Texas and New Mexico.'[14]

He explained that Mexico had been in revolt since the attempt to impose the Habsburg Archduke Maximilian on the country as emperor and that Mexican raiding parties were threatening the US border.[15] 'We rode out of Fort Riley for the Texas border after three months of tough training: riding 50 miles a day, making camp in the open, shooting with cavalry carbine and Colt revolver from both sides of the saddle at full gallop, tracking and, most important of all, learning how not to disclose one's presence while operating in strange country,'[16] he wrote. He held the rank of lieutenant in what he described as one of the dirtiest wars he had ever fought.

> I was 10 months on the frontier when we rode into an ambush and one of Pancho Villa's men knocked some of the family military tradition out of me. I was shot out of the saddle by a bullet in the abdomen. I rode out of Texas in an ambulance wagon, first to Fort Riley and then to Fort Siocum Hospital in New York. And three months later I relinquished my command and went back to my engineering job. The US government was forced in the end to send down regular troops and build blockhouses along the frontier to keep out the Mexicans.[17]

He was just a year home from what he called his 'first war' when he met Roger Casement, who was in America to meet President William Howard Taft and to press his appeal for an international commission to the Putumayo to expose the treatment of the indigenous people who were working as slave labour in the extraction of rubber for a British-based company. Keogh was introduced to Casement at a Gaelic League concert in New York: 'I shook hands with Casement for the first time on that occasion. It was a meeting that was to change my life and to lead me to many strange adventures.'[18]

III

Michael Keogh's narrative of his life from the time he met Casement in New York in 1911 until his return to Ireland in 1922, just as civil war threatened to explode, is what constitutes the main body of his recovered papers. The central part of that narrative is concerned with the years 1914 to 1916 in Germany and the travails of Casement's brigade project.

Keogh returned to Ireland in 1913 and enlisted in the British army. He did this, he said, 'in the same spirit and [with] the same aim that had inspired earlier soldier-Fenians'.[19] He was shipped to France in August 1914 with the Royal Irish Regiment and fought in the Battle of Mons. He was captured and sent to Sennelager POW camp. There, in November 1914, an English-speaking German officer made a sympathetic speech aimed at recruiting Irishmen into a brigade. Conditions were eased for Irish POWs and, in December, 1,500 Irish prisoners, including Keogh, were moved to a camp in Limburg. There were already 300 other Irish POWs in Limburg. Casement had paid a visit to the camp and had addressed the prisoners and distributed some leaflets – but to little avail.

Months of low-key recruiting followed. Keogh, who was one of the first to join the brigade, played a leading role in this process. In April 1915, Casement arranged for Keogh and two other men to meet Joseph Plunkett in Berlin. Plunkett had arrived from Dublin to step up the recruitment drive for the brigade. By the time Plunkett himself arrived at Limburg, in May 1915, fewer than 20 men had joined. He spent three weeks in Limburg recruiting and by the time he left, almost 60 men had enlisted in the brigade. However, the main reason the IRB had sent him to Germany was to secure a promise of a German arms shipment to coincide with a rising in Ireland.

Most of the brigade recruits were moved to Zossen prisoner-of-war camp in June. The conditions in Zossen were better; although the recruits were still prisoners of war, the move was to facilitate their training and bring them more under brigade discipline. In October, Robert Monteith arrived from Dublin to take charge of training the brigade. He visited Limburg to try to win more recruits and from there on 2 November he wrote to Casement suggesting that Keogh be sent back from Zossen to Limburg to help with the recruiting:

> Regarding Keogh, I am rather in doubt in this matter; I have learned that there are other attractions in Limburg for the Sergeant Major beside recruiting, but he might be able to help things along ... Up to the present, we have little to show for our work. I have interviewed seventy men, about ten of whom I intend to see again. The first twenty-five were inclined to be a bit rusty and insolent ... The men I saw today were of a far better frame of mind ... I think we stand to get eight or ten of them.[20]

However, it does not seem that many, if any, more men joined the brigade.

Gradually, Casement came to believe his mission to Germany had failed and became anxious to return to Ireland to prevent any possible rising breaking out. He believed it would be a hopeless endeavour without large-scale military support, in the form of men, equipment and arms, from the Germans. The Germans would have preferred to send the men of the Irish Brigade back to Ireland with Casement but he would not hear of it. He believed he was returning to face his own possible death but he refused to condemn the men to the same fate.[21]

Worth addressing here is the question of why Irish prisoners of war in Germany chose to join or not to join Casement's Irish Brigade. Michael Keogh never had any doubt that Roger Casement was absolutely right to go to Germany to seek aid there for Irish freedom and also that he was right to try to recruit an Irish brigade from Irishmen who had joined the British army and subsequently found themselves prisoners of war in Germany. In his narrative, Keogh points to Wolfe Tone's going to France in the 1790s to try to get the French to send military aid to free Ireland as Casement's historical precedent for going to Germany in 1914. He also makes mention of the numerous Irish Brigades who served against Britain in wars from the eighteenth century onwards, especially the brigade led by John MacBride that fought on the side of the Boers in the Boer War in southern Africa from 1899 to 1902.[22]

Robert Monteith, who had made his way to Germany via the United States in 1915 – with extreme difficulty and at considerable risk to his life – in order to join Casement's brigade was quite clear in his own mind about the purpose of the brigade and the motivation of the men who joined it: 'The men who joined the brigade in Germany never received one penny from the German government. They were asked by Casement, and through him by Ireland, to fight in and for Ireland only against Ireland's sole enemy – England. They were not asked to fight their own countrymen.'[23]

The historian Andreas Roth has proved unusual among commentators on the brigade in that he concerns himself with why men joined rather than why they did not join. He points out that the vast majority of those who joined had not been connected with the Home Rule movement before the war, never mind with more radical nationalist groupings such as the IRB. Roth puts forward the valid argument that it is difficult to say why exactly most of them joined because of 'the scant first-hand sources' available on which one could build some conclusions.[24]

Some who were repatriated after the war said they joined solely to see if they could get better conditions as prisoners of war. But there were a few who gave as their motivation for joining that they did so because they wanted to fight for Ireland. Most of them were probably too young (the average age of brigade members was 24) to have wives and children, so they would probably not have been worried about reprisals being taken against their families by the authorities back home in Ireland, Roth contends.[25] However, and Roth does not allude to this, it probably was the case that many would have enlisted in the British army in the first place for economic reasons, and their parents would have received financial support from the authorities while their sons were prisoners of war in Germany. If it became known that they had joined the brigade – the equivalent of desertion – that financial aid would have been discontinued.

Roth speculates that it may well have been the case that those without prior nationalist backgrounds joined 'in order to escape the dullness of prison camp routine'.[26] Nor did the prospect of going back to their former civilian lives promise much for them because only a third of them had some kind of professional quali-fication, he argues. Roth agrees with Monteith that no one joined the brigade as a result of sympathy with Germany. The Germans made no attempt to persuade Irish prisoners to join their army. Articles II and III of the German-Irish Agreement, signed by Casement and German Chancellor Theobald von Bethmann-Hollweg on 28 December 1914, stated that the brigade was an autono-mous unit and not part of the German army.[27] Roth concludes that one of the reasons for the failure of the brigade project was because of a lack of mutual German-Irish understanding, and he quoted one brigade member as follows: 'I needn't tell you the Germans knew damn all about us.'[28]

But *was* the brigade project a failure and, if so, to what extent? There is no doubt that all who have written about it consider it an abject failure and they give various reasons why it failed. One Casement biographer, Geoffrey Dudgeon, argues that the first Irishmen the Germans captured were mostly regular soldiers who were not going to be easily coaxed away from their comrades, unless they did not get on with them. The war in 1914 was still a popular cause among most combatants, Dudgeon contends, and Belgium, the perceived reason why the British went to war in the first place, was regarded by many Irish soldiers as a small Catholic nation invaded by Protestant Germans, who could be cruel in their treatment of British prisoners, especially as regards food and medical treatment.[29]

The German historian Reinhard Doerries has written the most detailed study of Casement's time in Germany. He believes that both Casement and the German General Staff organised attempted recruitment to the Irish Brigade extremely badly. The custom with Irish secret societies, he says, was to approach people individually but in this case it was decided to call prisoners together and explain to them in public about the brigade. Doerries thinks it natural that most men were unwilling to step forward and show their nationalism before all. Others, he speculates, were probably concerned about the financial security of their families at home. Looking back, he finds it hard to understand why the German General Staff officers responsible for Irish affairs let Casement address all the prisoners, including those loyal to Britain, who must have regarded Casement as a traitor.

Doerries refers to the men who eventually joined the brigade (he gives their numbers at between 55 and 60) as consisting of adventurers and republicans and others who appeared indifferent, which explains why the first two types but not the third joined up. He goes on to remark that Casement was not the type of man to organise successfully a military unit like the brigade or to instil the necessary morale and camaraderie in the men. On the other hand, he says, it should also be recalled that life for Irish prisoners of war in German camps was such that most would not have had any good reason to wish to co-operate with the Germans. Treated poorly since capture, even after they were sent inside Germany, many continued to complain of bad clothing and too little food. And neither the German military officers nor the civilian Foreign Office personnel detailed to deal with the Irish prisoners daily succeeded in forging a closer relationship with the prisoners of war.[30]

Michael Keogh's explanations for the limited numbers of men who joined the brigade agree and disagree with some of the foregoing analysis and add new perspectives as well. His narrative bears out Doerries's point that it was very difficult for men to step forward and show their nationalism in front of their comrades. Indeed, he suggested that intense intimidation was practised by pro-British and 'West British' elements among the men to prevent recruits coming forward to join the brigade. However, he would strongly disagree with Doerries's comment about Roger Casement not being the sort of man to organise such a unit or to instil the discipline and camaraderie required in the men. As far as Keogh was concerned, no fault whatsoever can be attributed to Casement. Yes, the Germans were incompetent and did not know how to deal with Irishmen; the IRB in Dublin and Clan na Gael in the United States – both of whom had a vested interest in the brigade project – also bungled and were ineffectual at times in their organisation and communication; but Casement held up his end of the bargain and did everything that was humanly possible to make a success of the brigade, Michael Keogh believed.

The sorting out of potential brigade recruits was done so badly that English-born prisoners were allowed to infiltrate the prison camp that was supposed to be for Irish prisoners only, Keogh pointed out. He also told of pro-British ladies' societies being set up in Ireland when news got out that Limburg prisoner-of-war camp had been set aside especially for Irish prisoners, with a view to persuading them to join a brigade. These ladies' societies sent large numbers of parcels to the prisoners at Limburg, parcels containing food, clothing, tobacco and even money. So, asked Keogh, why would men want to involve themselves in a risky project like the brigade when they were doing so well from this deluge of parcels from Ireland which were making their lives so much more comfortable than most of the prisoners in other German camps?

The existence of such societies is confirmed by the following anecdote that Monteith told in his book:

An amusing incident happened about New Year. A bag of mail came in. One man received two letters. They were both from the same person, Lady _____, Co. Kildare, Ireland. One was dated a week later than the other. The first informed the man that Lady _____ was pleased to adopt him as a 'war child' or 'war son' or 'war' something or other. By doing so, the writer pledged herself to send him a parcel monthly, papers at intervals, etc. The second letter informed him that her 'ladyship' had learned that he had followed that awful traitor, Sir Roger Casement, and was now in the Irish Brigade, and therefore she, more in sorrow than in anger, struck him off her exalted list of 'war orphans' or 'war babies' or what not. Quite a little tragedy in its way.[31]

In the final analysis, what might be worth commenting on is the fact that as many as up to 60 men joined Casement's Irish Brigade despite all the obstacles militating against their doing so. Some indeed were no doubt adventurers; from his ultimate fate, Timothy Quinlisk was perhaps the best example of this particular type. During the War of Independence, he attempted to betray Michael Collins to the British authorities and was shot dead in Cork city by the IRA in February 1920.[32] Others were certainly committed republicans or, at least, strong nationalists. Michael Keogh would count himself among these and so was Robert Monteith. According to Keogh's list of the names of brigade members, 14 of them afterwards served in the IRA during the Irish War of Independence, and two of them were killed in action.[33]

Why the other 40 or so men enlisted to follow Casement we shall probably never know. But, to the end of his life, Michael Keogh never expressed the least regret or doubt about his decision to follow a man he came to regard as the noblest being he had ever met or could ever hope to meet. It must say something about the quality of Roger Casement's character that he was capable of inspiring such devotion from men such as Michael Keogh and Robert Monteith.

IV

Following Casement's departure, the fate of the men of the brigade left behind in Germany seems to have been one of desultory neglect. In July 1916, they were moved to a camp in Danzig where, according to Keogh, he battled with the Germans to retain some status for the men above ordinary prisoners of war. They were sent out to work in farms and businesses in the surrounding area.

Keogh's narrative recounts that he joined the German army in the latter stages of the Great War (by which time he had married a German woman, Anna-Marie Seuffert) and that he fought on the Western Front in the spring offensive that began in March 1918. He gives an interesting account of two chance encounters with Lance-Corporal Adolf Hitler in the second of which he says he may even have saved Hitler's life. After the war, he was caught up in the chaos that engulfed the defeated Germany. He was in Munich, near his wife's home area, and claims to have fought against the Munich Soviet Republic early in 1919.

Berlin.

8 April 1515.

Private

Dear Captain Boehm

With reference to our talk yesterday afternoon the position to my mind is this.

I am not disposed to go on with the "idea of the Irish Brigade unless more serious efforts at co-operation are displayed by those who would derive the chief benefit — both moral and material — from the step I should be responsible for.

Once the Brigade is formed, even if numerically only a handful of men, and the Agreement on which it rests published, it is Germany and the German Cause and not Ireland or the Irish Cause will derive practically all the benefit.

He left Germany in December 1919, following his discharge from the German army, and returned to Ireland. For the next two years, he was involved in various capacities in the War of Independence. At least one of those capacities, as can be seen from his own story, entailed gun-running to the IRA from Germany.[34]

Kevin Keogh's mother, Anna-Marie Seuffert, told him some details of what life was like for her and her children during the Black and Tan era in Irish history. She said that the authorities had put a price on her husband's head. In later years, Kevin recalls seeing the poster with his father's photo and the reward offered for information leading to his capture – a poster that his father kept for many years. He was constantly on the move during the 1919–21 period and his wife had frequently to pack up house and move the children in her endeavours to be with him.

Initially Seuffert lived with Michael Keogh's parents in their house in Tullow, Co. Carlow. Any time it was raided by the Black and Tans she was subjected to extra abuse because she was German, she said. On occasions they threatened to kill her baby by throwing him out the window if she would not give them information about her husband's whereabouts. What made it extra difficult for her in her initial years in Ireland was that she spoke very little English, although her son believes it was probably just as well that she did not understand a lot of what the Black and Tans were saying to her.[35]

What of Michael Keogh's life after 1922? There is little or no evidence in his papers. According to information supplied by the Keogh family, and an abstract of his army service supplied by the Military Archives, Dublin, he joined the Irish army with another former member of the Irish Brigade on 10 April 1922.[36] He enlisted at Marlborough Hall, Dublin. He was assigned to the Army Corps of Engineers, 21st Infantry Battalion and was subsequently stationed in the Curragh Camp, Co. Kildare for a period; afterwards he was Foreman of Works in the Corps of Engineers at Collins Barracks, Dublin. Finally he was in the married quarters in Arbour Hill Barracks. While in Collins Barracks he was given permission to carry a loaded side arm by Command Intelligence Officer Comdt Shanahan and Intelligence Officer Captain Condon after it was discovered that an attempt on his life was being premeditated by three ex-prisoners of war who had been in Germany at the same time he was. He must have incurred the enmity of these men while there.

There is an official document among his papers which gives the dates and places of birth of his six children. Rosaleen, the third child, was born in the Curragh Camp on 6 December 1922, which shows that he was stationed at the Curragh nine months after joining the army. The fifth child, Kevin, was born in Arbour Hill in November 1925, some eight months after Michael Keogh is officially recorded as discharging himself from the army on 21 March.[37] He had asked for an extension of contract to bring him to December 1925 but was offered and took a 'free discharge' before this date. It seems likely that he held onto married quarters until the expiration of his original contract. Michael Keogh entered the civil service as a clerical officer in the Registry of Deeds in February 1928. He resigned in November 1929.[38] It seems that he left the country in a hurry because his resignation letter was written and posted in Nuremberg, Germany.[39] His sixth and last child, Anna Marie, was born in Nuremberg in 1930.[40]

So by 1930 he had gone back to his wife's homeland to live and work. There he worked as an engineer on the U-Bahn or underground railway system in Berlin. The family lived at 35 Jüdenstrasse in the city. The Olympic Games were held in Berlin in the first half of August 1936 and he worked as an interpreter at the games because of his fluency in both English and German (he was also fluent in Irish).

We learn from his own narrative that he left Germany and returned to Ireland in September 1936, where he spent the rest of his life. His son Kevin says that he returned to Ireland because Éamon de Valera wrote to him inviting him to do so, in view of his service to the national cause. Kevin, who was 10 or 11 by 1936, remembers his father's excitement as he came in the door of their Berlin home and showed them the letter, told them they were going back to Ireland and that he had been promised a house and a job.

They duly returned to Ireland and booked into a hotel in Dublin. Eight months later they were still in the hotel with no sign of either job or house. It was expensive keeping a wife and six children in a hotel for that length of time and Michael Keogh's savings became depleted as a result. The family moved to small rented accommodation around the city for some time until he managed to get a job contract, involving pipe laying, in Portlaoise, Castletown and Mountrath in Co. Laois.

When that particular contract was finished, he was idle for some six or seven months until he secured another contract in Scariff, Co. Clare. This was a much longer posting, lasting four years, and involved work on a large reservoir there. During the years of the Second World War, Michael Keogh was involved in the running of the Pigeon House power-generating station in Ringsend, Dublin. His fluency in German was a great advantage to him because many of the engineers who had run the station were German. They had been recalled to Germany by Hitler during the war and the plans and blueprints concerning the functioning of the station were in German (the machinery was all German). In fact, his son thinks it would probably be no exaggeration to claim that it was largely thanks to his father that the plant was kept going during the war. Following the war, he worked for some years in the Irish Sugar Beet factory in Carlow.

Now in his late 50s, his health was somewhat precarious because of an enlarged heart and he retired from regular employment. He occupied his time by writing articles and giving lectures about his adventurous young manhood. But there can be no doubt that he and his family had led somewhat of a peripatetic and uncertain existence from the time they had returned from Germany in 1936.

So, why the letter from de Valera that brought him back to Ireland in 1936, what promises, if any, were made, and why was the result so disappointing? Kevin Keogh has no explanation but speculates that it may have had something to do with his father's personality. He was a strongly independent person who would not toe any party line but preferred to express his untrammelled opinion on the issues of the day without fear of, or favour to, anyone. He had not taken sides in the Civil War and would not take any political side when he came back to Ireland in the mid-1930s. The country was a much polarised place politically at the time and it must have been difficult to maintain a neutral and independent line. Kevin Keogh wonders whether he was asked to run for political office for de Valera's Fianna Fáil and refused. But this is no more than speculation and, like other areas of his life, will have to remain something of a mystery in the absence of written evidence.[41]

V

Finally worth pondering is what sort of a man was Michael Keogh? Robert Monteith's account of his time in Germany gives us some insight into Keogh's character. Monteith arrived in Germany in late October 1915 and remained until early April the following year. He described Keogh as 'a quiet dispositioned man, of plump and short physique, prone to follow the line of least resistance, but possessed of the knack of getting things done'. Monteith said that Keogh spoke German well and continued: 'I attributed this to the fact that when out of bar-racks [he was] usually accompanied by a charming human dictionary, who made the study of the language a labour of love.'[42] The other member of Casement's Irish Brigade who had an account of his experiences in Germany published was Anthony Quinlisk.[43] Although he referred to Michael Keogh, he did not comment on his character.

So what insights into Keogh do we get from his own narrative? One character-istic of the man revealed is that he possessed a sardonic humour. An example has already been seen above from his account of his first military adventures along the US–Mexican frontier in 1910–11. His great-uncle, as already mentioned, was Captain Myles Keogh of the 7th Cavalry who perished at the Battle of Little Bighorn and Michael Keogh referred to himself as following in this family military tradition. However, as he wrote: 'I was ten months on the frontier when one of Pancho Villa's men knocked some of the family military tradition out of me. I was shot out of the saddle by a bullet in the abdomen.'[44] Another example is when he commented that he could have escaped to America when war was declared in 1914 but instead decided to take the chance of being shipped to France with his British army regiment because he had 'sufficient intuition' to make his way from there to Germany. 'Admittedly, it was not a trail over which one might carry an insurance policy for life,'[45] he remarked wryly and with some understatement. Again, when he was put in charge of the camp medical room at an early stage in the prisoner-of-war camp at Limburg, he said that he was in charge of 'the sick, the lame and the lazy'.[46]

While in Germany, Roger Casement kept a 'Diary for John Devoy' for a few days in late September 1915.[47] In it he considered his general treatment by the Germans as dreadful: 'Again and again I got rebuffs – and so rudely administered that I got quite despondent.' He still found the German 'civil element' a tolerable breed but the military men he considered hostile and stupid. He felt the Germans had shown a poor understanding of how to deal with Irishmen; they could not be brought to understand that Irishmen needed work and discipline but also freedom, humour, affection and a light rein.[48]

Early on in his narrative, Michael Keogh referred to Casement's difficulties with the Germans, not so much with the diplomats but with what Keogh called 'the military heads of baronial jackboot officialdom'. While trying to recruit men to the Irish Brigade in Limburg in the early stages, he felt he got little help from camp officials. He said they were 'all old reserve officers and preferred a quiet life. Isolated solitude was more in their line of soldiering.' But, unlike Casement, he was not about to get despondent as a result of their rebuffs. Nor was he about to let them enjoy a quiet life: 'I promised them a hot time and kept that promise.'[49]

It has been pointed out above that Robert Monteith considered Keogh a man of quiet disposition who was prone to take the line of least resistance. It was true that he took the sensible course of not causing unnecessary problems but he did not take things lying down either. He was not afraid of a fight when he considered that one had to be fought. An example would be when he was accused of desertion of his unit when he left Danzig in the spring of 1918 to join and fight with the 16th Bavarian Infantry Regiment of the German army. Although he could have stayed in Bavaria, he decided to go back to Danzig and to take on his accusers on their own ground. It was a tactic that would and did make his victory over them all the sweeter.

In his narrative, Michael Keogh does not gloss over or glamorise the horrors of warfare. This may be seen from his descriptions of his experiences at the first Battle of Mons in the very early stages of the Great War. There he referred to the German 'artillery belching death at short range'. The British forces found themselves facing overwhelming odds during the battle:

Scarcely had half an hour elapsed before word was passed down the extended firing line: 'Every man for himself! Save yourselves as you can!' We were in a veritable death-trap, and officers and men simply acted on their own instincts of defence.

I well remember one young Gael of immense stature, well over six feet, become suddenly bereft of all reason. He stripped off his jacket, rolled up his sleeves and, armed with drawn sword in one hand and a revolver in the other, dashed forward on his own, shouting and firing at random. It was a typical and tragic incident.[50]

Having become a prisoner of war, Keogh then joined Casement's Irish Brigade and finally moved on to enlisting in the German army. He said he took part in the major offensive launched by the Germans on the Western Front in the spring of 1918. When writing about his experience of the latter, he referred to modern warfare having become a 'hell on earth' and he also alluded to 'the sickening horror' of the process of machine-gunning huge numbers to death and of 'mowing down a retreating enemy like locusts before a hurricane on the African veldt'.[51]

The piece of prose just quoted is a good example of Michael Keogh's skill as a writer. He was capable of evoking a broad range of registers in his writing. In the following passage, he describes the terrain through which he passed as he was being transferred by train with other prisoners of war from Sennelager camp in north-west Germany to Limburg camp in the south west. It can be seen from the passage how he enlivens factual description with well-chosen adjectives, nouns and verbs that convey awe, enthusiasm and admiration but also a sense of homeliness.

> The journey from Sennelager, Westphalia, is a most instructive one to all lovers of the art of landscape scenery. One traverses great stretches of the fertile plains of Westphalia, inhaling the agreeable perfumes of the extensive pine forests which bear witness to the enormous forestry resources of the empire that came into being in 1870 under the German prince of politics, Count Bismarck. We gradually arrive in a valley of industry. The Rhine-Ruhr province was a veritable network of war-and-peace commerce, the sight of Krupps at Essen a marvel for the average visitor from the Green Isle.
>
> It was fast approaching the dusk of the evening as our transport train slowly chugged its way onwards through this roadway of modern enterprise. On each side of the permanent way, massive factory structures seemed to rise up, casting a ruddy glow upon the sky from the electric-lighted buildings which formed a vast beehive of mechanical energy and power. The hour of exchange in work between the day and night shifts told an impressive tale in itself. Great masses of tradesmen and munitions workers – men and women – thronged on each railway station platform awaiting the local passenger trains which conveyed them to a well-earned repast and the more pleasant surroundings of home and family, with a peaceful repose assisting to relieve the strain of a weary and dangerous toil among the grinding mechanisms which sent forth their deadly missiles of modern war.[52]

In the following example, Keogh displays one of the most necessary skills of the good prose writer: the ability to vary sentence type and style to maintain the reader's interest. Mixed in with this varying of sentence structure is a range of stylistic devices such as alliteration, assonance and metaphor.

> But in her insensate endeavour to extirpate the Gael, England has succeeded only in fortifying his spirit. In seeking victims, she has given us martyrs. The essence she thought to destroy flourished more richly in the frame her rapacity had emaciated. The soul, as ever, flourished even when the flesh succumbed, and its divine mission is yet to be accomplished. In homely phrase, the hero-tale was told around the fireside, while the spirit of patriot-heroism went forth as an element against which gun and gold alike have been impotent.[53]

Further examples of his skill as a writer may be found in his moving account of the death of one of the brigade members, Private Patrick O'Holohan, on the eve of St Patrick's Day, 1916 in Zossen prisoner-of-war camp, to which members of the brigade had been transferred from Limburg: 'St Patrick's Day 1916 brought sorrow to the brigade: Volunteer Patrick O'Holohan was carried to his grave on the shoulders of his Irish and German comrades. He had been in poor health for some time, having never recovered from the effects of the rigorous campaign of the first three months of the war.' On the day before Private O'Holohan died, Michael Keogh sat at his bedside: 'I asked him if he had any particular message, and I can never forget his reply. "My dear and kind-hearted Irish mother is in heaven," he said, "and there I hope to join her soon. One sister is in Ireland, another married in the United States. Let them know some day, if you have the opportunity, that I died a true Irishman."'[54]

The following day, Keogh returned to his bedside vigil beside the dying man, 'then, as the Angelus bell tolled in the village of Zossen, heralding the eve of Ireland's national festival, he peacefully closed his eyes in death ... Just as the sun prepared to sink somewhere west of the Green Isle on St Patrick's Day, Volunteer Paddy O'Holohan was borne to his final resting place with full military honours.' Roger Casement paid for the erection of a granite headstone over the grave and he also paid the cemetery committee to have the grave looked after for a period of 20 years. 'Patrick O'Holohan's grave and memorial make a centre of pilgrimage for Irish exiles in Berlin each recurring St Patrick's Day,' concluded Keogh's account of this sad occasion.

4

A SOURING OF FRIENDSHIPS?

Internal divisions in the leadership of the Irish Parliamentary Party in the aftermath of the Easter Rising [1]

CONOR MULVAGH

From its reunification in 1900,[2] the Irish Parliamentary Party saw the gradual and organic emergence of a body of just four MPs as the core ultimately responsible for the planning, direction and articulation of policy. Michael Wheatley has referred to the four-way alliance of John Redmond, John Dillon, T. P. O'Connor and Joseph Devlin as the 'inner leadership' of the party.[3] Redmond, as chairman, was the titular leader of the party. However, Redmond was not a chief in the way Charles Stewart Parnell had been in the 1880s. Since his elevation, Redmond's role had been to balance and manage the strong personalities within the party ranks. William O'Brien and Tim Healy, two other powerful figures within the party during the first decade of the twentieth century, were eventually ousted in the early years of the reunited party. John Dillon – formerly a leader of the anti-Parnellites during the divided 1890s – thus consolidated his already strong position.[4] As champions of the Parnellite and anti-Parnellite parties respectively, Redmond and Dillon's unlikely alliance became the fulcrum of the unified party. During the Home Rule crisis (1912–14), the leadership presented a united front, experiencing the high-point of its popularity and success in September 1914 when Home Rule eventually reached the Statute Book as the Government of Ireland Act, 1914. The accompaniment of an amending act, suspending its operation for the duration of the war in Europe and until a suitable accommodation could be found for the grievances of Ulster unionists, did not diminish this achievement. Confident of a speedy and glorious victory against the Central Powers and believing that nationalist participation in this struggle would unite orange and green in the trenches, Redmond cast his lot in with that of the imperial war effort. Although it caused a minority of hardliners to break away from the movement, the vast majority of the Irish Volunteers, established at the end of 1913, enthusiastically endorsed Redmond's appeal for them to go 'wherever the firing line extends in defence of right, of freedom and religion'.[5] It should be noted, however, that one contemporary document from a well-informed source puts the number of National Volunteers who actually joined the British army at just 25,000 up to February 1917. Given that there were approximately 158,000 members of Redmond's National Volunteers when the movement was formed after the Volunteer split in the autumn of 1914, this means that only slightly more than 15 per cent of Redmond's volunteers ultimately made good upon his call to arms.[6]

Redmond's pro-war policy had been announced without consulting either Dillon or Devlin and against the advice of O'Connor.[7] By taking this course of action, Redmond broke with precedents established over a period of 14 years in how he dealt with his most senior colleagues. Nevertheless, by acting unilaterally he did not precipitate an immediate crisis in the leadership; indeed, given the wave of popular approval for his stance on the war effort in both Britain and Ireland, Redmond's colleagues buried their misgivings and rallied behind their chairman despite private concerns about the advisability of his pro-war stance. Dillon in particular was not enthusiastic about the Irish party's co-operation with recruitment or its more general participation in the war effort.[8] Holding his tongue in the short term, Dillon wrote to O'Connor in March 1915 admitting that he differed greatly from the chairman on his deepening commitment to recruitment.[9] While such private misgivings did not cause a public split within the leadership, the ideological gap between Redmond and Dillon was intensifying by this point. What will be explored here is how geographical separation during the war, and unresolved differences over political tactics, would eventually push relationships within the leadership to breaking point. The turmoil of Easter 1916 and its aftermath would provide the catalyst for this reaction.

Among the leadership, John Dillon would undergo the most profound political metamorphosis following the 1916 Rising. Having witnessed events at first hand in Dublin, his whole outlook changed and hardened against the British government and the military establishment that had imposed a draconian martial law on Ireland and was responsible for the executions that began to turn Irish public opinion against the Irish party and towards Sinn Féin. While relations among the leadership of the Irish party remained outwardly cordial, and the bitter rivalries of the 1890s were not revisited, the party quickly found its leadership split down the middle as to the future of party policy. By 1917, disillusioned with conciliation, Dillon would refuse to take any part in the Irish Convention which had been summoned by the new prime minister, David Lloyd George, as a means of letting the Irish solve their own problems while the government got on with winning the war.[10] This signalled a clear shift away from the policies of Redmondism and made unambiguous and public the split over policy that existed at the head of the party.

That the 1916 Rising had a profound effect upon the internal stability of the Irish party leadership has been well documented.[11] That Dillon underwent a transformation in 1916 is not in question. What needs to be further explored is why this occurred and to trace the short and long term causes of the divisions within the leadership. It will be argued here that two factors, one long term and one more immediate, played a part in creating this divergence of opinion and ideology within the leadership. Firstly, the physical separation of participants has not been sufficiently explored in accounting for the short term causes of the rift. F. S. L. Lyons has noted the stark difference between Dillon and Devlin on the one hand – both keeping a watchful eye on the changing pace of events in Ireland – and Redmond and O'Connor – increasingly consumed with Westminster politics – on the other.[12] In these years, Redmond and O'Connor became increasingly divorced from the realities of political life in Ireland. This fostered something of a Dublin-London divide within the leadership.[13] Also worth exploring are the precedents for Dillon's unwillingness to negotiate in 1917. Here it will be argued that his decision not to partake in the Irish Convention stemmed, in part, from a long-standing unwillingness to participate in conciliationist tactics. In 1903 Dillon had zealously rejected William O'Brien's doctrine of 'conference plus business': a policy of negotiating with moderate landlords as a means of settling the land question.[14] Redmond, on the other hand, had participated directly as a representative of tenant interests alongside O'Brien in the Mansion House Conference which sat from December 1902 to January 1903.[15] Redmond gradually distanced himself from O'Brien's doctrine in the aftermath of the conference and O'Brien himself was hounded out of the party by November 1903 in a campaign led by Dillon.[16] Significantly, after 1903, the question of preserving conciliation as a desirable tactic within the party's arsenal remained largely unaddressed.

When attention turned to settling the Ulster question from 1913 onwards, an increasing degree of concession and conciliation was required of the Irish party leaders in attempts to secure the passage of a Home Rule Bill that was anathema to unionists on both sides of the Irish Sea. While Redmond and O'Connor viewed concessions to Ulster as pragmatic necessities for the salvation of Home Rule, both Dillon and Devlin were far more reluctant to yield. However, the entire leadership had conceded to some form of temporary exclusion for Ulster by the spring of 1914.[17] In July, delegates from all factions met at the Buckingham Palace Conference, which had been convened under the auspices of the king, and worked to find a last-ditch solution to the Ulster crisis before the outbreak of the First World War. There, Redmond and Dillon, as the nationalist delegates, showed their willingness to consider various permutations for the carving up of Ulster for an indeterminate time-period.[18] By so doing, they implicitly confirmed what had been already agreed with the British government: that an as yet undetermined section of Ulster would have to be excluded from the provisions of the Home Rule Bill for an undefined, but strictly time-limited, period. Thus, displays of good faith, both to the unionists on Ulster and to the British government in terms of support for army recruitment, represented a strongly conciliationist trend within the Irish party leadership at the beginning of the First World War. On the one hand, Devlin, who as a native and parliamentary representative of West Belfast and had made the greatest sacrifices of all by conceding to the temporary exclusion of Ulster, actively participated in recruiting and appeared as a loyal disciple of Redmondism. On the other hand, it has already been noted that Dillon's scepticism over Redmond's policies had been voiced as early as March 1915. Thus, by this point, the ingredients of a crisis were assembled.

The Rising and its aftermath would cause the problems within the leadership to boil over and the policy of conciliation would be stretched to breaking point by the failed negotiations, chaired by Lloyd George, which followed the Rising. From that point on, the leadership would remain nominally intact despite the ever widening gap between Redmond and Dillon. However, by refusing to participate in the Irish Convention, Dillon stood firm in his refusal to endure conciliation and negotiation as viable tactics for securing Home Rule and the survival of the party. By the end of 1917, Devlin shifted firmly into the Dillon camp, diverging from Redmond over the level of conciliation deemed acceptable by the chairman. Thus, months before Redmond's death ended a chapter in the history of leadership in the Irish Parliamentary Party, the four leaders of the organisation were split down the middle on policy. O'Connor had essentially been removed from any policy formation role in the leadership by the summer of 1917 after he was sent on an extended fundraising trip to America. However, both Dillon and Devlin, still on cordial terms with Redmond, had completely abandoned conciliation to the level that Redmond still advocated. By re-examining this complex episode in the final stages of the constitutional nationalist movement, it is hoped that new explanations for the emergence of this last ideological crisis in the Irish party leadership can be put forward.

I

The Easter Rising and the leadership of the Irish party: A tale of two cities

The role played by the London-Dublin divide in the comprehension gap between Redmond and Dillon prior to the Easter Rising is evidenced by a letter written by Dillon on the eve of the rebellion. Following days of intrigue and tension in Ireland, on Sunday 23 April, Dillon wrote to Redmond explaining that 'Dublin is full of most extraordinary rumours. And I have no doubt on my mind that the Clan men[19] – are planning some devilish business – what it is I cannot make out.

It may not come off – But you must not be surprised if something very unpleasant and mischievous happens this week.'[20]

Given the series of events that immediately preceded the outbreak of hostilities on Monday 24 April, written evidence that Dillon knew something was afoot in Dublin by Easter Sunday is hardly groundbreaking. What is significant about this letter is that it represents the last in a series of warnings received by Redmond prior to the Rising.[21] Dillon does not deserve much credit for sensing that something was afoot on the eve of the insurrection when Dublin was alive with rumblings but, at the very least, it shows he was not aloof from the reality of politics in Ireland in the way Redmond had become by this stage. At any rate, this last warning would come too late. By the time Dillon's letter reached Redmond in London, the Rising was already underway. Redmond would pay dearly for his inaction in the face of persistent warnings and indicators of danger. The implications for the party, its leadership, and the course of Irish politics generally would rapidly prove irreversible.

On Easter Monday 1916 the leadership of the Irish party was scattered across Britain and Ireland. Redmond and O'Connor were in London while Devlin was in his home constituency of West Belfast. Of the four, only Dillon was on the scene in Dublin when the insurrection that would catalyse the metamorphosis of Irish politics began. While the correspondence between three members of the Irish party leadership during and immediately after the Rising has been discussed at length by their respective biographers, Devlin's activities at this time remain the most intriguing. A flurry of correspondence went between Dillon and Redmond by the most extraordinary channels at this time: through the Irish Office's coded wire and in person via messengers and even soldiers.[22] These measures became necessary due to the crippling of communications that followed the seizure of the General Post Office and the imposition of martial law, compounded by the general sense of chaos that prevailed in Dublin into early May. While letters rushed between the rest of the leadership, Devlin, stuck in Belfast, appears to have been completely incommunicado for at least eight full days beginning on Easter Monday 1916.[23] A. C. Hepburn notes that he spoke at soldiers' families' fundraisers in the Falls and Smithfield wards on 25 April, and claims that Devlin was seemingly unaware of events in Dublin at that point.[24] While it seems unlikely that Devlin could have been wholly ignorant of events in Dublin, the reality was that – regardless of when he heard about the Rising – Devlin's closest colleagues were entirely unable to get in contact with him for the entire week of the hostilities. Given the reported state of Dublin, and with messages not reaching him, it is most likely that Devlin took a decision of his own volition to stay put and await clarification.

Devlin's importance within the leadership by this stage can be gauged by the fact that his colleagues were extremely anxious to obtain his views about the situation before determining the official party stance for public and governmental consumption.[25] Dillon's wish was that, when Devlin finally made it to Dublin and they had had an opportunity to talk, Dillon would remain there as the only member of the inner leadership to have been in situ during the fighting, and Devlin would then proceed to London as Dillon's emissary, to link up with O'Connor and Redmond and brief them fully on the situation. Presumably the three would then engage in talks with the government.[26] Whereas Dillon was anxious to get hold of Devlin as a means of safely transporting his own views to London, Redmond was keen to have Devlin's views in their own right, exclaiming to Dillon that he was 'very unhappy at being unable to get into communication with Devlin, and I think you should, by hook or by crook, get him to come to Dublin, so that you could let me know your joint views.'[27] Although Dillon had been on the ground throughout the fighting and Devlin had been stranded in Belfast, Redmond was nonetheless insistent on having Devlin's views as much as Dillon's before proceeding.

While A. C. Hepburn mistakenly records that Devlin made it to Dublin on 5 May, a letter from a greatly relieved Dillon confirms that he arrived on 2 May and was in Dillon's home on North Great George's Street by 4.30 p.m. that evening.[28] Having been reunited with his lost colleague, Dillon proceeded as planned, holding Devlin until the following morning and then sending him on to London, fully briefed. Dillon's insistence on remaining in Dublin at this point would have significant implications. Much like de Valera's decision not to attend the Treaty negotiations in 1921, the absence of a key player at such a pivotal juncture seriously impacted upon the negotiating power of the representatives of nationalist Ireland at Westminster. Dillon's decision to remain in Dublin must, therefore, be scrutinised further.

As the only member of the leadership to have experienced the Rising at first hand, Dillon had witnessed the realities of the fighting and its consequences. His house had seen both soldiers and the relatives of captured rebels crossing its threshold and he had been in close contact with government authorities in Ireland throughout the crisis.[29] In light of this, surely Dillon would have been in the strongest position to represent the party and the nation in London directly after the Rising? While a variety of reasons could be offered for why Dillon elected to stay in Dublin, the strongest, and the one which Dillon most frequently proffered himself, was that he could not bring himself to leave his children at such a time of danger.[30]

Left a widower with six children in 1907, it should not be forgotten that Dillon had family responsibilities far greater than any of his colleagues in the leadership. Redmond had become a widower in 1889 but, in Denis Gwynn's words, his second marriage ten years later brought him 'much domestic happiness and unfailing devotion'.[31] Such formulaic descriptions of marital bliss may seem unimportant but Redmond's ability to travel and work without having to worry about the welfare of his children gave him much more political and personal mobility than Dillon. Devlin was a lifelong bachelor with none of the domestic ties of his older colleagues. O'Connor enjoyed a similar level of freedom, albeit through a very different arrangement. By 1916 he was separated, childless and had been living with a Mrs Crawford – a Greek woman who had previously been married to a Scotsman – in a London flat for several years.[32] However, Dillon's attentiveness to his family and home life impacted on his ability to partake in political work at a key juncture, profoundly impacting the shape of the party's early responses to the Rising at Westminster.

II

Defending enemies: Redmond, the Rising, and Westminster

Without Dillon's counsel before having to explain his party's position to the House of Commons, Redmond decided to focus on the plight of prisoners who had been transported to camps in Britain after the insurrection and the need for urgent debate on the situation in Ireland. Both O'Connor and – when he eventually arrived – Devlin remained silent in the chamber, although they played key roles in negotiating with the government behind the scenes at this critical time. On 10 May, Dillon returned to Westminster, making his first appearance in the House in over two months. Prior to this, it had fallen to an out-of-touch Redmond to give the party's first official response at Westminster to the Rising and its aftermath. In Redmond's first contribution to these debates, wishing to prevent the insurrection from being used 'as a weapon against any party', he informed the House that 'the overwhelming majority of the people in Ireland ... [shared] the feeling of detestation and horror with which we [the Irish Parliamentary Party] have regarded these proceedings.'[33]

This was arguably a faithful representation of the mood on the ground at this time; the massive swing in public opinion, sparked by the executions rather than the Rising itself, would take time to gain momentum. Nonetheless, Redmond's statement has been labelled a 'sweeping generalisation' by Lyons who observes that, owing to the rapidity with which events were now changing in Ireland, Redmond's first statement after the Rising quickly became redundant and was superseded by events.[34]

When one compares Redmond's first post-Rising contribution at Westminster with that of Dillon, one can already begin to see the widening ideological gap between the two. On 10 May, Dillon re-entered the House with a renewed irreverence for parliament which had arguably not been seen since he had been suspended for comments he made about the Boer War in 1902.[35] Dillon immediately honed in on the continuing executions, seeking public assurances from Prime Minister Asquith that no more 'military executions by secret military tribunals' would be carried out and clarification that none had taken place since the last confirmed reports two days previously.[36] Furthermore, Dillon sought answers to a number of questions about matters which were then the subject of rumour in Dublin. This was at a time when Redmond was still coming to grips with the reality of events in Dublin from his seclusion in London.[37] Although a long list, it is worth quoting in full, as it emphasises the importance of geographical separation as a contributing factor to the growing comprehension gap among the leadership. It shows just how important Dillon's experiences in Dublin were in giving him a unique understanding of the situation in Ireland. Representing the real and pressing concerns of Dublin's citizenry, he asked Asquith:

(1) Whether any prisoners have been shot without trial or have been shot after trial without any public announcement of their names, and, if so, how many;

(2) Whether there is any, and, if any, what authority with power to check or control the military officers now ruling Ireland; whether the Lord Lieutenant or any officials of the Irish Government have any authority over them; and how long it is proposed to maintain this military dictatorship;

(3) On what ground the whole of Ireland has been placed under martial law, and why searches of houses and wholesale arrests are being carried out in districts where there was no disturbance and in which the population remained peaceful and loyal;

(4) Whether he can state the circumstances under which Mr. Sheehy-Skeffington was shot at Portobello Barracks;

(5) Whether he can explain why Sir Roger Casement has been brought to London, and is apparently to have a public trial before a civil tribunal, whilst comparatively obscure men whom he has been largely responsible for seducing into rebellion have been sentenced and executed in Ireland by secret military tribunal; and

(6) Whether the censorship is preventing the publication of expressions of opinion from the United States of America and other neutral countries on the policy of the military executions in Dublin?[38]

All at once, Dillon had identified the most pressing and central issues emerging in the aftermath of the rebellion in a way no other Member of Parliament was capable of articulating. It is true that Redmond had been working to put a halt to the executions, both in private and in parliament. However, his pleas to Asquith lacked the sincerity and conviction of Dillon's and Redmond proved more malleable on this subject than his colleague ever would. In a memorandum of an interview with Asquith on 3 May, Redmond recorded that he had 'urged the PM to prevent executions. He said some few were necessary, but they would be very few. I protested.'[39] The following day, a seemingly assuaged Redmond wrote to Dillon, informing his colleague that 'Asquith solemnly assured me that no one had been shot except the three men named yesterday ... He intends that there shall be practically no more executions, although he did not pledge himself that there might not be one or two more in Ireland.'[40] Lyons has shown that Dillon did not hold the guarantees of Asquith in the same high regard as Redmond, and that he smarted at the broken assurances given to the chairman that no more executions would take place when he found out that four more rebels, and only one of them a signatory of the Easter Proclamation, had been executed on 8 May.[41]

While Dillon issued strong public denunciations of the executions, Denis Gwynn shows that Redmond may not have been entirely in sympathy with the plight of all rebels, openly accepting that harsh justice should be meted out on certain high-profile individuals. In his first press statement after the Rising, Redmond described the insurrection as a 'wicked move' by an 'insane movement' that had committed 'treason to the cause of Home Rule'.[42] With words like these, it is questionable to what extent Redmond did in fact wish for clemency to be extended to the ringleaders of an insurrection that was as much an attack on him and his party as it was on British rule in Ireland.[43] Further inference can be drawn from Redmond's utterance in the House on 3 May – when he knew that the first of the executions had already been carried out – that the insurrection had been 'dealt with with firmness, which was not only right, but it was the duty of the Government to so deal with it'.[44] He proceeded: 'I do beg the Government ... not to show undue hardship or severity to the great masses of those who are implicated, on whose shoulders there lies a guilt far different from that which lies upon the instigators and promoters of the outbreak.'[45]

While this could have been interpreted as an appeal to his audience for clemency, it had a clear inference that the punishment of the ringleaders was justified. Redmond only wished for the rank and file to be spared harsh treatment and, at this early date, he showed no concern whatsoever for their superiors. The first three rebels had been executed that very morning.[46] At this point, Redmond failed to comprehend the transformative effect which the executions were having on opinion in Ireland. Later that day he wrote to Dillon, apparently satisfied with the situation regarding executions, stating that

> Asquith tells me that he gave orders to the War Office to go slowly, and said he was shocked when he read the news of the three men being shot. I begged him to promise me that no one else would be executed. He said he could not give an absolute promise to that effect but that except in some very special cases that was his desire and intention.[47]

Those before the firing squads had been no friends of the Irish party and, despite his public denunciations of the executions, Dillon shared Redmond's contempt for the ringleaders then in Kilmainham Gaol. In early May, he admitted to Redmond that he was 'not concerned personally to save [James] Connolly or [Thomas] Kent', a fact he had openly stated to the Lord Lieutenant.[48] Dillon had harboured a 'detestation of the socialism of Connolly' since the Dublin Lockout of 1913, and he viewed Kent as indefensible and a 'cold blooded murderer' as he had been implicated in the shooting of an RIC head constable in Cork.[49] However, despite his personal attitudes towards some of the ringleaders, and in direct contrast to Redmond's ambivalence, Dillon saw the absolute political necessity of stopping the executions due to their continuing effect on public opinion in Ireland. Before coming to London, while the executions were still ongoing, Dillon had told Redmond that 'the feeling amongst the working classes in the City is becoming extremely bitter – over the continuation of these executions – and ... this feeling is strong even amongst those who had no sympathy whatever with the Sinn Feiners – or with the rising.'[50]

Thus, what had been apparent to Dillon from the outset thanks to his experiences in Dublin would only become clear to Redmond with time. As the executions dragged on and the tide of public opinion moved towards sympathy for Sinn Féin, Redmond would be left behind. While Dillon could not ride this wave, he could certainly follow the shifting tide and understand its causes and its potential ramifications for the constitutional movement.

Mindful of the changing public mood, Dillon precariously stuck his neck out in parliament on the subject, showing just how far he stood from Redmond in his sympathies. In a move that provoked outrage, especially from Conservative and Unionist members, Dillon defended the rebels' actions, telling those assembled in the most outspoken terms:

> I declare most solemnly, and I am not ashamed to say it in the House of Commons, that I am proud of these men. They were foolish; they were misled ... I say I am proud of their courage, and, if you were not so dense and so stupid, as some of you English people are, you could have had these men fighting for you, and they are men worth having.[51]

The difference in the public stances of Redmond and Dillon on the Rising could thus not be more evident. As already stressed, an outward cordiality was still maintained between the two but, with such a profound divergence in their reactions to the Rising, a watershed had been reached. Furthermore, Dillon's reference to the bravery of the rebels, along with the failure of the British to recruit them to the war effort, could be viewed as a slight on Redmond, given that he was so intrinsically linked to the Irish recruitment campaign.

This was not the first instance of discord between Redmond and Dillon. The latter had disagreed on the party's participation in the war effort in 1915. In a letter to O'Connor in March of that year, Dillon admitted how he had 'never felt enthusiastic about this British recruiting campaign' and vented at length about his differences with Redmond on the issue.[52] Underlining their disagreement, in a particularly revealing passage of this letter, Dillon exclaimed how 'for a long time I have had a strong feeling that Old Parsons[53] was an Ass – and a rather Orange Ass – but the Chairman would hear nothing against him.'[54] Unlike the estrangement of 1915, this time there was little evidence of palpable bitterness on either side. However, the stark difference between the recruiting issue and the fallout from the Rising was that Dillon now set a new political course for himself. By 20 May 1916, Dillon confessed to O'Connor that he differed 'profoundly' from Redmond on the way forward.[55] While there would be frequent instances of co-operation in the two short years Redmond had left, a Rubicon had been crossed, and the professional relationship between the two most powerful members of the Irish party had been fundamentally altered.

III

Picking up the pieces: The Lloyd George negotiations and the limits of concession

The Rising provided a renewed impetus within government to solve the Irish question once and for all. As much as the geographical separation of its members had exacerbated the ideological divide in the Irish party leadership during and after the Easter Rising, the negotiations that would follow in its wake exposed a much more serious and more deeply rooted issue at the centre of the party. Dillon's political metamorphosis in 1916 might better be described as an ideological reversion. In his biography of Dillon, Lyons has noted how his subject had been cast into a deep dilemma in reacting to the growth of Sinn Féin both before, and particularly after, the rebellion. On the one hand, Dillon was 'absolutely opposed to everything Sinn Féin stood for'.[56] However, Lyons qualifies this, explaining how 'the memory of his [Dillon's] own passionate youth rose up to prevent him from joining the chorus of execration which was the usual reaction of less complicated constitutionalists to their rivals.'[57] Here it will be argued that a different facet of Dillon's more radical past was reawakened in 1916: his distaste for conciliation.

On 20 December 1902, a land conference between landlords and tenants had been convened in Dublin's Mansion House. The negotiations eventually led to the passage of George Wyndham's 1903 Land Act. In the minds of Dillon and other hardliners, including Michael Davitt, the provisions of the bill were overly generous to landlords. Following its enactment, Dillon became heavily involved in a campaign against William O'Brien and his new model of 'conference, conciliation, consent' as a means of solving not just the land but also the national question.[58] Dillon's position eventually won out and the party adopted the policy that 'half measures' would not be accepted in settling the demand for

Home Rule.[59] However, in 1913 and 1914 there had been a growing acceptance within the Irish party that some form of concession would have to be extended to Ulster as the Home Rule crisis intensified. While outside of constitutional channels the formation of rival unionist and nationalist volunteer forces signalled a hardening of attitudes on both sides of the sectarian divide, within the Irish party there was a gradual and, in some cases, grudging acceptance that certain concessions would have to be made on Ulster. Within the leadership, the conviction that conciliation would be necessary for the safe passage of Home Rule was exemplified by O'Connor. However, Redmond, Dillon and, eventually, Devlin all fell into line, acknowledging that at least some form of temporary exclusion or concessions for a portion of the north-east would have to be conceded. Crucially, any such compromise would have to be balanced with outward displays of defiance in order to save face.

The high-point of this two-pronged strategy came at the Buckingham Palace Conference at the end of July 1914.[60] The conference eventually became bogged down over the issue of where to draw the line of what nationalists steadfastly maintained could only be the temporary partition of Ulster. However, the fact that Redmond and Dillon, as the nationalist delegates, participated in conceptualising this boundary gave unequivocal recognition to the principle of partition as a necessary compromise for the passage of Home Rule. An exasperated Asquith, who had earnestly tried to work through the intransigence confronting him at the conference, observed that 'nothing could have been more amicable in tone, or more desperately fruitless in result.'[61] When the conference broke on a stalemate, Redmond and Edward Carson, leader of the Ulster Unionists, were even seen to publically share 'a good shake hands for the sake of the old days together on the circuit'.[62]

In the spirit of pre-war statesmanship and under the eyes of the monarch, this was a high point in conciliation. Dillon had dutifully accompanied Redmond throughout, even partaking in what he instinctively would have viewed as fraternisation with the enemy after the conference.[63] The level to which Dillon was a willing participant in this type of brokerage is debatable. However, that he was convinced of the necessity of concessions to Ulster is undeniable.[64] The degree to which the Lloyd George-led negotiations in the summer of 1916 precipitated a reversion on Dillon's part to the anti-conciliatory spirit he had displayed in 1903 will now be explored.

Returning to the aftermath of the Rising, Asquith and his colleagues saw the need to remove the uncertainty surrounding the Irish question. The Dublin insurrection had shown that the policy of postponing Home Rule for the duration of the war was no longer workable. With this in mind, Lloyd George was charged with reopening negotiations with nationalist and unionist representatives beginning in May 1916. The starting point for the new settlement would be where both parties had left off at Buckingham Palace.[65] However, unlike the previous conference, these were not face-to-face discussions between nationalist and unionist representatives. Rather, the Lloyd George negotiations were conducted as what would today be called 'proximity talks'. Unlike the formulaic deadlock that had been speedily arrived at in 1914, this was to be a functional attempt at settling the grievances of nationalists and unionists quickly, efficiently and permanently, thereby allowing the government to get on with the war.

As the closest of the Irish party MPs to Lloyd George, O'Connor played a significant role in these renewed negations. Denis Gwynn has noted that the other members of the leadership remained suspicious of Lloyd George, twice shy since they had been bitten in their dealings with him over the 1909 budget. Back then, verbal assurances given by the then Chancellor of the Exchequer had not been upheld.[66] O'Connor, on the other hand, believed that he had a strong relationship with Lloyd George, and he saw this closeness as his conduit to influence within the cabinet.[67] However, his biographer, L. W. Brady, believes that O'Connor's perceived level of influence over the future prime minister was overestimated and of more theoretical than practical value by this point.[68] In real terms, the implication of O'Connor's links with Lloyd George, when coupled with their shared personal enthusiasm for a settlement, was that the negotiations of 1916 lasted longer than otherwise would have been the case.[69] As much as O'Connor acted as an important intermediary for the Irish party on matters in London, he also kept Lloyd George informed on the sentiments of his nationalist colleagues regarding proposals for settlement of the Irish question.[70] Indeed, Lyons suggests that O'Connor was at this stage 'hypnotised' by the personality of Lloyd George.[71]

By mid-May 1916, O'Connor and Devlin had held preliminary meetings with Lloyd George and others close to him in London to discuss the terms of a settlement. In one of the most significant of these early meetings, Lord Northcliffe, as a friend of Lloyd George's and an Irishman by birth, met with Devlin.[72] In the course of their discussions, concentrating on the Ulster question, Devlin told Northcliffe that he felt an immediate settlement for Ireland was of paramount importance following the Rising.[73] For this to have come from Devlin, as the only nationalist leader representing Ulster, it was a clear signal to Lloyd George that there was some fertile ground for a settlement in the nationalist camp. However, a letter from O'Connor to Dillon three days later gives a little more insight into Devlin's personal misgivings on the subject. Here, O'Connor told Dillon that he had 'been with Joe almost night and day ... he is a man of somewhat uncertain moods, as you know, and now and then he relapses into regrets that he ever consented to help us with regard to Ulster two years ago; and things of that kind, which to me are sheer madness.'[74]

Relations between Devlin and the rest of his colleagues were at their most problematic in these years. For Devlin, negotiating for Home Rule with Ulster already off the table was a far more painful prospect than he would betray to any member of the British establishment, but now he was revealing the depth of his crisis of conscience to one of his closest colleagues. Returning to the practicalities of Devlin's uncertainty and pessimism, O'Connor went on to explain that he was confident that, despite these private misgivings, Devlin could yet again be encouraged to toe the line, arguing that 'this, however, is not his ordinary mood, and I think I am justified in regarding him as in entire agreement with … Redmond and myself.'[75]

Much more so than Devlin, Redmond and O'Connor were anxious for a settlement. Indeed, they appeared desperate to reach one and they did not hold the Irish party's bargaining position in nearly as high regard as Devlin, and especially Dillon, did at that point. Highlighting the internal differences over the perceived strength of the nationalist position, R. F. Foster notes that, in softening his opposition to Carson's preference for the partition of six rather than four Ulster counties, Redmond displayed a 'desperate need to achieve any settlement going'.[76] Thus, the geographical separation between the leadership resurfaced: the London men – Redmond and O'Connor – were again out of touch with the situation in Ireland and more influenced by the pressures of individuals directly and indirectly linked to the government in London.[77]

Lloyd George eventually proposed a scheme which would see the immediate enactment of Home Rule for 26 counties only, and the continued attendance of Irish MPs at Westminster for the duration of the war. Once the European conflict had ended, an Imperial Conference would be held to forge a final settlement for Ulster.[78] In what Eamon Phoenix has dubbed 'pre-meditated duplicity', Lloyd George gave written assurances to Carson that the border would be a permanent feature while he simultaneously allowed Redmond to believe that partition would be of a strictly temporary nature.[79]

As his colleagues fully realised, without Devlin – as MP for West Belfast – on board, it would have been impossible to sell any deal that included temporary partition in the north-east. O'Connor worked hard to counter Devlin's instinctive aversion to such a deal, and he appears to have been very anxious to get Devlin on side while they were in London together with Redmond working on the early stages of the settlement. O'Connor reported back to Dillon in Dublin that he had 'been a little anxious about Joe's position, especially as he varied it from time to time. But he has now definitely made up his mind that there must be some sacrifices about Ulster.'[80]

Capitalising on Devlin's acceptance, Dillon and Redmond accompanied him to Belfast where, on 23 June 1916, they entered into the herculean task of winning the approval of a convention of Ulster nationalists for Lloyd George's proposals.[81] Devlin's influence on the assembled delegates was profound. Following a 45-minute speech from Devlin in support of a policy on which he himself still harboured doubts, the convention expressed its support for Lloyd George's proposals: 475 delegates in favour and 265 against.[82] Bearing in mind that Devlin was bartering his native province and his own constituency for the general survival of Home Rule, this can be viewed as conciliation at a level none of his colleagues could ever be asked to replicate. Despite the magnitude of the sacrifice asked of Devlin, he would defend conciliation as a tactic for some time to come. As the Lloyd George settlement unravelled, it was Dillon rather than Devlin who would emerge as the most vociferous opponent of further dialogue.

Although he was not opposed to the idea of the negotiations, throughout the 1916 deliberations Dillon was deeply self-aware about his inherently combative nature and his heightened personal feelings concerning the state of Ireland. Consequently, while he did not oppose the Lloyd George negotiations, he realised that the prospects of arriving at a workable settlement would be greater in his absence. In this frame of mind, on 20 May 1916, Dillon told O'Connor: 'It is I am convinced much better for me <u>not</u> to be in London – at the time of the first Conference between Redmond and Asquith – as I am almost certain I should feel compelled to dissent and object – it is far better to leave the field clear to those who believe that a workable arrangement is possible.'[83]

Such scepticism on the prospects of a deal and such candid mistrust in the intentions of the government from a figure as central as Dillon show more clearly than anything the scale of the ideological gap that now separated him from Redmond and O'Connor. Furthermore, the role of the Rising in this souring of relations is clear. A week after this communication, having been convinced to participate in the London deliberations through the joint efforts of O'Connor and Redmond, Dillon re-emphasised his conviction that he would be a negative influence on any chance of settlement, reflectively observing to O'Connor that his mood at the time was due to the 'horrible nervous strain I have undergone for the last month – and especially for the last ten days ... it would have been better for me to keep out of these conferences and negotiations. The truth is that I am in a frame of mind wholly unfitted for conference or negations.'[84]

In reality, Dillon's frame of mind stemmed from more than just stress: it reflected a deeper disillusionment and exasperation over the contemporary political situation. In this way, Dillon's choice not to attend the Irish Convention can be seen as a crucial turning point in the leadership of the party. In finally agreeing to enter into talks with Lloyd George in 1916, Dillon had given concilia-tion one last shot. The breakdown of the Lloyd George initiative convinced him of the integrity of his position. From the moment these negotiations broke up, it was clear that Dillon would have nothing to do with future talks, regardless of what format they would take. This was a central element to the regression towards Dillon's instinctively anti-conciliationist stance. Dillon's self-conscious unwillingness to negotiate and his natural tendency to be a hardliner rather than a compromiser took prominence in his new political position. Following the failure of the Lloyd George negotiations, again confiding the true nature of his position to O'Connor, Dillon exclaimed that he had gone 'to the utmost limit, and I shall not be party to *any* further concessions'.[85] Yet again, the Rising was the catalyst for the hardening of Dillon's stance. In terms of cohesion within the party leadership, Dillon had experienced the changing mood in Ireland in a way Redmond and O'Connor still could not begin to recognise. Even though the absentee O'Connor had come to Dublin and witnessed at first hand the altered mood of the Irish public in the aftermath of the Rising, the fact remained that only Dillon had fully understood its severity and its full destabilising potential.[86]

In the end, the party's hard-won success in selling the Lloyd George scheme to Ulster came to nothing through the cloaked duplicity upon which the entire settlement had been based. Bending to the influence of unionist sentiments in cabinet, Lloyd George was forced to agree to a revision of the scheme that would formally make partition permanent and also see the immediate removal of Irish MPs from Westminster. When a bill containing these terms was introduced on 25 July 1916, Redmond had no option but to reject such a fundamental betrayal of the terms he had initially agreed with Lloyd George.[87] On foot of this betrayal, a dejected Devlin issued a vitriolic attack on the government, expressing a wish that the whole scheme would collapse.[88] Significantly, Redmond appears to have been influenced by Asquith, who wrote him a strictly personal note following the failure of the Lloyd George negotiations urging him 'to keep the "negotiating" spirit alive'.[89] The impact of this letter on Redmond's own thinking is hard to gauge: in a sense Asquith was preaching to the converted.

At this point, the government gave up on direct intervention and Lloyd George – who became prime minister in December – decided to leave it to Ireland to sort out its own problems as he set his sights on winning the war in Europe. What was important in terms of the leadership is that, as Redmond turned his mind to future settlement, he increasingly saw himself as the custodian of conciliation within the party. The lines of demarcation between Dillon and the chairman were thus re-emphasised. Disillusioned at the failure of the Lloyd George settlement, Devlin would soon face a difficult choice as to his stance on the future of party policy. With Redmond determined to give negotiation another chance and Dillon steadfastly in opposition, Devlin in effect held the casting vote. Initially he would side with Redmond, accompanying him to the Irish Convention. However, even there the limits of compromise would be pushed. By the end of 1917 Redmond would be alone in believing that negotiation could solve the Irish question and, just as in 1903, the party rapidly moved away from the tactic of conciliation.

IV

The Irish Convention: A divided leadership in the public eye

The failure of Lloyd George's 1916 negotiations resulted in a temporary stagnation of the Irish question. However, by May 1917, Lloyd George, as prime minister, was committed to the idea of leaving resolution of the question in the hands of a representative body of Irishmen.[90] Despite the abstention of Sinn Féin, the most powerful emerging force in Irish nationalism, the Irish Convention, which met at Trinity College Dublin between 25 July 1917 and 5 April 1918, brought together an otherwise broad section of representatives and Redmond was able to assert that 'for the first time ... Ireland has been asked ... to settle these problems for herself.'[91] Among the Irish party, none was more committed to or enthusiastic about the prospect of a convention than the Irish party chairman. Taking the 'negotiating spirit' entrusted to him by Asquith, Redmond now cast his lot in with that of the Convention with a zeal comparable to that which he had displayed in getting behind the war effort in 1914. Just as his association with the war had a negative impact upon Redmond's career and popularity, the Irish Convention would further damage Redmond's image. The wholeheartedness with which Redmond committed himself to certain initiatives can be seen as a positive trait in his personality. However, his inability to choose the right causes represents a major flaw.

Having made his views on conciliation apparent after the failure of the 1916 negotiations, Dillon's attitude towards the Convention was deeply hostile from the outset. Although he gave significant consideration to, and commented on, the various permutations for the composition of the Convention that were circulating in May 1917, he was adamant that he himself would not participate.[92] Far from representing a last instance of co-operation in settlement, Dillon's involvement in determining the shape of the proposed assembly stemmed from an anxiety that the government was out to 'pack the Convention'.[93]

In analysing his decision not to include himself in that body, one could point to past instances where Dillon – aware that he was frequently more a hindrance than a help – had taken a step back in the interest of consensus. However, on this occasion, it seems that Dillon seriously doubted if a settlement could be reached and that he was only prepared to observe its collapse at a remove. Only a few days after the Convention held its first meeting, Dillon told O'Connor not to be 'too enthusiastic about [the] Convention, or put all your money on its success'.[94] By this point, O'Connor was in America, fundraising for the financially beleaguered *Freeman's Journal*, the de facto official newspaper of the party.[95] O'Connor's mission to America would eventually extend into the summer of 1918 and thus he was effectively removed from the decision-making process of the party from the opening of the Irish Convention onwards. With Redmond and Devlin at the Convention as delegates, Dillon initially took up a position of lonely isolation on the margins of the leadership. However, deliberations at Trinity College quickly stagnated. By the end of 1917 it was Redmond who found himself out of favour. In November a 'memorandum on fiscal autonomy', circulated by the southern unionist Earl of Midleton, had proposed a compromise whereby all purely Irish services would be entrusted to a parliament in Ireland while control over 'imperial services', including customs, would be retained at Westminster.[96] This was more than had been promised under the 1914 Government of Ireland Act and, when the Convention broke for Christmas, Redmond saw in it a workable scheme upon which the whole Convention could agree.[97] In the new year, Redmond brought the issue to a head by moving an amendment asking the Convention to agree to Midleton's scheme provided it was accepted by the government and given prompt legislative effect.[98] His desire to push Midleton's modest settlement lost him the support of his two most senior colleagues at the Convention; Devlin and Patrick O'Donnell – the Bishop of Raphoe and a longstanding Irish party supporter – who publically split from Redmond at this point. On 15 January, the morning on which his amendment was supposed to go before the Convention, Redmond informed the assembly that, although he was still confident of passing the amendment, having just learned of the opposition of Devlin, O'Donnell, and others, he would not now put it to a vote, as 'such a division could not carry out the objects I have in view.'[99] Without any hope of unity within the ranks of constitutional nationalism, any vain hope Redmond still harboured of a united, Home Rule Ireland evaporated.

Stephen Gwynn, the MP for Galway city who would go on to write the first major defence of Redmond's legacy, perhaps best summed up the situation at the top of the Irish party as it faced into the year of its electoral destruction.[100] Although personally supportive of his chairman's position, Gwynn wrote frankly to Redmond outlining how both Devlin and O'Donnell were being led in their views by Dillon and his anti-conciliationist policies. He continued: 'I fear, as too often happens, Dillon and not you will shape the line. Dillon has more tenacity and more persistence and by these qualities he has again and again ... prevailed against your larger and wiser judgement.'[101]

Whatever the relative merit of their positions, it was Dillon's that won out. Having dwelt in the political wilderness as the party officially pinned its hopes on success at the Convention, Dillon's hardline approach was vindicated as prospects for an acceptable settlement faded. Conciliation was a failed policy. For the Redmondites, 'the convention's failure was added to the Parliamentary Party's collection of lost opportunities.'[102] For Dillon, however, nationalism was moving on at a rapid pace, and he was desperately struggling to fight the rising tide of Sinn Féin. Shortly before his death, Redmond conceded to Dillon that he was 'probably out of sympathy with the general view of the Party as to policy'.[103] Combined with the deteriorating state of his health, and mindful that an impending surgery – which would in fact take his life – would leave him *'hors de combat* for a very considerable time', Redmond relinquished the chairmanship, leaving it to Dillon and Devlin to decide the future course of the party between them.[104] Redmond's premature death on 6 March 1918 only formalised a fait accompli. Having lost the support of the majority of his party and his ability to speak for the nationalists of Ireland, Redmond, unlike Dillon, had failed to appreciate fully the sea change that had occurred in 1916. As Michael Wheatley has observed, Redmondism had traditionally been a 'minority taste' which had arguably reached its apogee by 1914.[105] By 1916, the Rising had precipitated, or at least contributed to, a reversion towards a more radical brand of nationalism for many both inside the party and throughout the constitutional movement generally.

V

Conclusion

In conclusion, by revisiting a well-documented period in the history of the Irish question, new light has been shed on some important factors influencing the internal dynamics of the Irish party leadership. It has been shown how the geographical separation between Redmond and O'Connor on one hand and Dillon and Devlin on the other played a role in widening the ideological split within the leadership, particularly as the Easter Rising converted previously reconcilable differences between Redmond and Dillon into an outright policy rift.

More importantly, it has been argued that the longstanding divergence between Redmond and Dillon over the tactic of conciliation stood as a deep and unresolved issue at the centre of the party which had roots going back almost as far as the reunification of the party itself. Whereas Redmond had gone along with William O'Brien in negotiating with the moderates of the landlord interest in the winter of 1902–3, Dillon had been to the fore in attacking O'Brien and forcing him into the margins of political life. Early in the Home Rule crisis, a firm anti-exclusion stance had been adopted. However, Redmond and O'Connor's willingness to appease and cater for Ulster as a means to safeguard settlement created a new enthusiasm for compromise within the wider Irish party. In the short term, Dillon acceded to this. As a parliamentarian, he would follow the will of the majority. The important distinction was that the will of the party majority and the wider nationalist public were not necessarily one and the same. Dillon was the first in the party to perceive their separation.

The Rising, and more particularly the disastrous Lloyd George negotiations that followed it, would entirely alter Dillon's attitude to conciliation. If the history of the Irish Parliamentary Party can be viewed as a series of splits and reunifications from 1890 to 1918, then the period under consideration here witnessed one of the most profound ideological splits among its policy-making core since the schism of 1890. While the rift of 1916 did not force the break-up of the movement as it had done during the Parnell crisis, it played a decisive role in the already declining fortunes of the party. By the opening of the Irish Convention, Dillon publicised his dissent through his abstention. No more than the absence of Sinn Féin, Dillon's refusal to attend the convention damaged the ability of the nationalist delegates there to claim to represent a broad section of public opinion. When Devlin eventually crossed over to the Dillon camp – albeit with a reluctance either to offend or abandon his chairman – the fate of Redmond, as well as that of the Convention, was all but sealed.[106]

Patrick H. Pearse

A Sketch of his Life

By "COILIN"

PRICE **3d.**

DUBLIN :
PRINTED BY CURTIS, 12 TEMPLE LANE.

5

PAINTING PICTURES AND TELLING TALES

The scholarly and popular portrayal of Patrick Pearse, 1916–27

SHAUNA GILLIGAN

There is properly no history only biography
RALPH WALDO EMERSON *Essays: History*

Two of the most recognisable images of Patrick Pearse show him in profile: a close up of his face and the photograph of him surrendering at the GPO in April 1916.[1] What is generally understood and known about Pearse is also one-dimensional and based on his involvement in the 1916 Rising and subsequent execution. This chapter examines the scholarly and popular portrayal of Patrick Pearse from the 1916 Rising through to the formation of Fianna Fáil in 1926 and the June 1927 general election. Through a chronological analysis of biographies of Pearse, historical publications, popular theatrical productions and political party election propaganda, we shall see how representations of Pearse were used to explore notions and portray images of Irish identity.

This chapter will consider the idea that in the formation of a new state, the death of an iconic figure as influential as that of Patrick Pearse 'helped to bring about a new reality [and] was the thing that made the Pearse myth so compelling and also what made it so threatening to those who wanted to stabilise that new reality'.[2] The process of beatification of the executed leaders of the 1916 Rising came 'as a result of individuals in the Irish nation trying to make sense of these events using the already present and popular building blocks of national myths, memories and symbols'.[3] While the selection of works analysed within this chapter is broad, it is not within its scope to examine every text written about Pearse; however, it is hoped that a clear picture will be painted of how Pearse was portrayed through publications in Ireland during these years.

The historiography of this period illustrates that the *meaning* of 'history' has a direct connection not only with the development of the writing of history, but also with the *type* of history being written. The texts examined in this chapter show how 'social environment impregnates the author of any historical work in advance and sets him within a framework predetermining him in what he creates.'[4] The pictures painted and tales told from 1916 to 1927 were often based on the idea that Patrick Pearse embodied the Easter Rising. His life's work – including his achievements in the field of education – was viewed from the endpoint of his execution. Through an examination of the use of Pearse as an historical figurehead, this chapter demonstrates that rather than any popular notion of Pearse, it was the scholarly portrayal and the *intellectualisation* of him during these years that laid the foundations for the more familiar emotionalised portraiture, which has since prevailed.

While Ireland was engaged in two bitter wars – the War of Independence and the Civil War – people were also searching for a stable sense of national identity. Many of the early writings both on Pearse and on the 1916 Rising were hagiographical in tone which suggests an immediate link between the telling of stories and the writing of historical fact. The biographies published during this time painted a picture of a storyteller, dreamer and prophet who, at the same time, 'was never a legend, was a man'.[5] Seán MacGiollarnáth went so far as to declare that 'to understand Pearse is to understand in great measure how the insurrection came to happen.'[6] The language used in the titles of the early biographies reflect how Pearse was viewed as a complex but essentially human character caught up in the rush of events of the time. Between 1916 and 1922 numerous biographies appeared. In 1917 MacGiollarnáth's *Patrick H. Pearse: A Sketch of His Life* (under the pseudonym 'Coilin') was published, followed by the influential *The Man Called Pearse* by Desmond Ryan. Ryan, a friend and former secretary of Pearse's went on to edit much of Pearse's work and in 1932 published a translation from French of Louis Le Roux's biography *The Life of Patrick Pearse*. In 1920 James Hayes published *Patrick Pearse: Storyteller* and the writer M. J. Hannan published a booklet in the United States. Hannan claimed of Pearse that 'the novelist will find the most fertile field for his pen ... the soldier will find in him the most disinterested patriotism ... the statesmen may well learn from him what goes to make for real democracy and true contentment ... the countrymen will see in him Irish thought, culture and nationality developed to their highest.'[7]

After 1922 many more biographies were to follow. Ryan, MacGiollarnáth and later Le Roux presented Pearse as the natural leader of the people.[8] Through these publications, the Irish public was shown an image of Pearse both as a born leader and peaceful Gael. Desmond Ryan declared 'he was always a moderate and always a revolutionary.'[9] Louis Le Roux believed that:

> Two men lived in Patrick Pearse and both influenced his life and his work. One was the warrior, drawn towards an enterprise full of dangers, the type of Gaelic hero to be found on every page of the history of Ireland's wars ... the other ... was a man very

difficult to characterise because that man of his own free will renounced all desire to lead his own life.[10]

Pearse then, as we have observed, was all things to all men. To understand his mind was to comprehend the whole of Irish history.[11] Pearse's involvement in the Rising was portrayed not as a desire to see the red wine of the battlefields, but as the only option left to him at the time. He was:

A Nationalist in the fullest sense long before he came into association with the 'extreme', or Republican, group, and he joined that group because he believed that it was the only one that would offer any protest in action against English Rule ... The granting of a decent measure of Home Rule would undoubtedly have prevented that decision, but in the political circumstances of Easter, 1916, the most natural thing on earth for a man of Pearse's temperament and tendencies was to revolt.[12]

These early accounts used Pearse's fiction as a lens through which to view his political career, unlike later scholarly accounts which focused on the political and the personal, including his sexuality in the 1977 biography of Pearse by historian Ruth Dudley Edwards. Furthermore, these early publications were generally presented as objective and as complete accounts of Pearse's life, despite the numerous reprints of his literary, educational and political writings (for example, the 1922 publication of *The Collected Works of Padraic H. Pearse: Political Writings and Speeches*), which clearly showed that his achievements were not solely fictional or political in nature.

The image of Pearse in James Hayes's *Patrick Pearse: Storyteller* was constructed out of an examination of Pearse's short stories. Hayes analysed Pearse's method of writing in Irish and English as well as his subject matter. He maintained Pearse had 'the characteristic the people of Rossnageeragh found in "Brigid of the Songs"[13] – the characteristics of sweetness and loneliness ... that sweet, sad loneliness that the righteous feel in the valley of tears.'[14] Hayes attempted to merge the personal with the political through his readings of Pearse's fiction. Similarly, both Louis Le Roux and Desmond Ryan felt that Pearse's play *The Singer*[15] was the most autobiographical of his writings. This point has been reiterated repeatedly by historians and other scholars, many failing to see that the original point made by Ryan and continued by Le Roux was exaggerated through reinforcement.[16] Like all writers, a fraction of self goes into the fiction, but not the whole self. Le Roux painted the picture of Pearse the prophet: 'In *The Singer* Pearse sums up and exteriorizes himself ... and foretells the event with such force that the event ... comes into being soon afterwards exactly as Pearse had foreseen ... in a word *The Singer* is the key to the mystery of Pearse ... it explains Pearse, it explains the Irish.'[17] To assume that one play 'explains' Pearse is reductive of his career and character but to believe that a play explains 'the Irish' is ludicrous. Ryan's earlier interpretation of *The Singer*, however, is far more applicable, although by no means the final say on the play. He claimed that 'Pearse's *The Singer* recaptures the clash of thought and policy in the divided leadership of the time.'[18] Ryan resisted passing judgment on Pearse because 'we are too near him in time and too much under the spell of his personality, his genius, his deeds.'[19] This perhaps explains how some writers felt able to portray Pearse by way of a fictionalised version of him.

1918 and 1919 saw two plays – Maurice Dalton's *Sable and Gold* and Daniel Corkery's *The Labour Leader* – offer a partially disguised portrayal of Patrick Pearse. One of the main characters in *Sable and Gold*, Gregory, gets his sense of nationalism from the tales his mother tells him – just as Pearse did from his great-aunt Margaret. Unlike Pearse, though, Gregory secretly escapes a violent death. Corkery's *The Labour Leader* was staged in the Abbey Theatre in October 1919. Set in Cork, it tells the story of the conflict between a strike committee whose members are unwilling to break the law and a charismatic leader who preaches that violence is the way to shock people into action. It would seem that the leader, Davna, who cites both the Bible and Cúchulainn,[20] is a thinly disguised *version* of Pearse.[21] The dramatic narrative of his role in history that Pearse himself had portrayed through political speeches and writings (both educational and fictional) had become, after his death, a fractured narrative of *self*.

Even through this brief examination of a small sample of the written and performed words invoking Pearse, we are presented with fractured visions (or versions) of him, none of which show the full picture of Pearse. Other publications of the time, not devoted to Pearse himself, still feature him strongly – particularly in relation to his writing and, of course, the Rising. Unlike later accounts (such as that of William L. Thompson in 1967[22]), these early accounts of his writings did not have a bad word to say about his politics. Cathaoir Ó Braonáin in *Poets of the Insurrection* believed that Pearse's 'personal virtue, his intense religion, his unquestioning faith are qualities perpetually found in the pupils of the Christian Brothers.'[23] Stephen MacKenna in his *Memories of the Dead* dedicated more space to him than any other personality and claimed that Pearse 'hoped no less than to see Ireland teeming with Cúchulainns; he conceived education as the art or act of giving Cúchulainns to the country; his ideal Irishman, who he thought might be a living reality in our day, was a Cúchulainn baptised.'[24]

MacKenna found the idea of Pearse as President of the Republic strange: 'A poet, a philosopher, a mystic, one would say, not a leader of the people in the hard tussle of politics ... yet he did lead and the people followed. They hung on his slow, melodious words, dreamed his dream and very largely did his will.'[25] Other narratives of this era declared Pearse to be 'not only a born teacher, but a poet and idealist, a practical patriot, a loyal comrade, and one of the most lovable of men'.[26] Again, it is Pearse 'the man' rather than Pearse's deeds which are highlighted. Francis P. Jones, however, emphasised the importance of Pearse's contribution to education in stating that 'apart entirely from its national significance, St Enda's was a most important contribution to the science of pedagogy.'[27]

In 1916, what was of concern to the national newspapers was how Ireland could be *perceived* as a result of the actions of Easter Week rather than the Rising itself. The *Irish Independent*, owned by William Martin Murphy (the industrialist who had been in the vanguard of the employers' clampdown on union activities which led to the 1913 Lockout), declared 'no terms of denunciation that pen could indicate would be too strong to apply to those responsible for the insane and criminal rising of last week ... they were out, not to free Ireland but to help Germany.'[28] The *Irish Times* took a broader outlook, expressing concern for the effect on future generations:

> In the verdict of history, weakness today would be even more criminal than the indifference of the last few months. Sedition must be rooted out of Ireland once and for all. The rapine and bloodshed of the past week must be finished with a severity, which will make any repetition of them impossible for generations to come.[29]

The attitude of the general public to the 1916 Rising moved from one of indifference to that of anger, so that prisoners' recollections of the period contained statements like 'if it weren't for the fact that we were so strongly guarded by British troops, we would have been torn asunder by the soldiers' wives in the area.'[30] Press commentators, whether overtly hostile or somewhat sympathetic, based their comments on emotion. The *Irish Times* and the *Irish Independent*, for example, both gave brief accounts of the lives of the leaders while the *Irish Catholic* described Pearse as 'a crazy and insolvent schoolmaster'.[31] The public's attitude and international opinion changed, however, as the executions began and gathered momentum. George Bernard Shaw epitomised the moral outrage felt in Ireland and in America by the Irish-Americans at the prolonged executions. In a letter to the editor of the *Daily News* he wrote:

> The men who were shot in cold blood after their capture and surrender were prisoners of war and it was therefore entirely incorrect to slaughter them ... the shot Irishmen will now take their places beside Emmet and the Manchester Martyrs in Ireland and beside the heroes of Poland and Serbia and Belgium in Europe; and nothing in heaven or earth can prevent it.[32]

The image of Pearse the patriot was also formed because of how the 1916 Rising was portrayed. Immediately after the Rising a range of handbills were printed circulating Pearse's last letter, some of his poems and his oration for O'Donovan Rossa.[33] Clearly answering demand, pictures of the executed leaders of the Rising were also produced with Pearse among them.[34] Privately, some writers condemned the Rising in wholly moralistic terms, for example, Edith Somerville (best known for the Somerville and Ross novels), dismissed the rebels as 'tom fools' and 'half-educated cads and upstarts'[35] while W. B. Yeats wrote to Lady Gregory informing her that he was 'trying to write a poem about the men executed – "A terrible beauty has been born again" … I had no idea that any public event could so deeply move me.'[36]

In her book *The Irish Rebellion of 1916 or the Unbroken Tradition*, published in New York in 1918, Nora Connolly, daughter of James Connolly (who was tied to a chair when executed because of the severity of the wounds he sustained in the Rising) explained the very personal anguish around the executions: 'We heard of the executions of Tom Clarke, and of Padraic Pearse, and of Thomas MacDonagh. Every time we heard the newsboys call out, "Two more executions", or "One more execution" we dreaded to look in the paper for fear we might read my father's name.'[37] Horace Plunkett stated in a letter to an American friend that 'the military executions will be a black chapter in Irish history … the disproportion between the punishment and the crime was given the worst possible appearance by minimising the gravity of the rebellion in order to save the faces of the civil government.'[38]

James Stephens's *The Insurrection in Dublin* published in 1916 provided a first-hand narrative of and reaction to the events of Easter Week. For Stephens, the *feeling* was anti-Volunteer but the *opinion* of the significance of the events was one of indifference: 'The feeling I tapped was definitely anti-volunteer, but the number of people who would speak were few … I received the impression that numbers of them did not care a rap what way it went; and that others … were merely machines or registering the sensations of the time.'[39] The choice of Pearse as President of the Republic was unexpected. Stephens

> would have said that Pearse was less magnetic than any of the others. Yet it was to him and around him they clung … I think that Pearse became the leader because his temperament was more profoundly emotional than any of the others. He was emotional not in a flighty, but in a serious way and one felt more that he suffered than he enjoyed.[40]

This representation of Pearse as being more emotional than the rest of the leaders was to be used in later elections by politicians such as Éamon de Valera. It was the *emotionalisation* of Pearse's politics and death that placed him in the tradition of martyrs alongside Emmet and Tone, rather than any *intellectual analysis* of his ideas.

Simultaneously with Stephens's narrative, W. B. Wells and Nicholas Marlowe published *A History of the Irish Rebellion of 1916*.[41] Wells and Marlow analysed the part religion played in the Rising and declared that 'it is a fact of first-rate significance that all the men of the revolution of 1916, Connolly and Casement included, died Catholics,' while on the other hand, the rebels 'did not hesitate to seize a convent'.[42] Failing to source their assertions, they claimed Pearse 'was a man of brooding imagination, with a strong introspective tendency; and it seems that the idea that the Irish cause demanded a blood sacrifice haunted him in later years ... It is generally believed that the famous Republican Proclamation of Easter Monday was the composition of his pen.'[43] The Proclamation of the Republic was issued by Pearse on 24 April 1916 to 'the People of Ireland' on behalf of 'the Provisional Government of the Irish Republic' and proclaimed 'the Irish Republic as a Sovereign Independent State'. The Proclamation stressed the equality of all men and women, the continuity of the tradition of armed resistance and the important role of the Irish Republican Brotherhood and declared the 'right of the people of Ireland to the ownership of Ireland ... to be sovereign and indefeasible.' Wells and Marlowe paint a particular picture of Pearse as bowing to an inevitable call to bloodshed and tie this in to the words of the Proclamation. While many of the ideals contained in it are certainly those of Pearse and the language used typical of Pearse's orations, the Proclamation also bore the signatures of Thomas J. Clarke, Seán MacDiarmada, Thomas MacDonagh, Eamonn Ceannt, James Connolly and Joseph Plunkett.[44] Their 'history' of the Rising ends 'like the skeptical German philosopher, with a question mark. Would the influence of the Rebellion produce ... a secure and lasting Irish settlement? "Or else"?'[45] Stephens ended *The Insurrection in Dublin* equally dramatically, declaring 'from this day the great adventure opens for Ireland. The Volunteers are dead and the call is now for volunteers.'[46] Wells and Marlow clearly echoed themes of the day in connecting religion, freedom and blood sacrifice. One must not forget that at the time in which these texts were written Europe was engulfed in the First World War.

For Pearse's biographers and those writing on the Rising directly after 1916 it was the leaders' occupations combined with their execution, which made them all the more worthy of the martyr label. Irish-American publications at this time, such as F. A. Mackenzie's *The Irish Rebellion: What Happened and Why* declared Pearse was 'a man of letters, of delicate and fine sensibilities, a barrister, an Irish scholar, and above all profoundly religious' while Padraic and Mary Colum declared he 'could have been a great lawyer, a great writer, or a great scholar'.[47] Francis P. Jones stated that Pearse 'was a man who personified in himself the noblest traditions of the country he loved and for which he sacrificed his life'.[48] In *Poems of the Revolutionary Brotherhood,* we are told that Pearse 'was first of all a Christian man ... [He] was a man of supreme value Ireland ... he was a mystic, and for him a cause would become a call ... He was the very type of the implacable idealist.'[49] Referring to the much-told tale of Willie and Patrick Pearse as children vowing to 'strike a blow for Ireland's liberty or to die in the attempt to free her', the anonymous author of a pamphlet issued in 1917 declared that 'the Rebellion of 1916 abounded in romance of every kind, but I know of none more dramatic than that with which the brothers Pearse were associated ... the brothers were inseparable all through life and were not separated even in death. In writing of one the story of both is told.'[50] The 'man in the street' came to view Pearse *as* the 1916 Rebellion during this time because of the emotional portrayal of Pearse in the context of the Rising. Pearse was beginning to symbolise Ireland and all that it meant to be Irish for the public, so that by 1966 Hedley McCay was able to say:

> Of all the worthy leaders of the 1916 Rebellion Patrick Pearse has become the accepted symbol and reflection of the freedom movement and why this should be so remains rather difficult to understand. For the snob type diehard Republican the name of Tom Clarke is more meaningful with its long Fenian and IRB connections. For the rabid Socialist and trade-unionist James Connolly is the name to be exalted, to the man in the street since the Twenties Padraic Pearse and his name alone has come to mean the 1916 Rebellion.[51]

Just as the disgust expressed by the public as those involved in the Rising were led through the streets of Dublin on the day of surrender and the subsequent horror at the executions of the leaders was a moral, emotional reaction, so too was the use of Pearse by religious and political parties a specific moral and emotional use. There was a marked difference between the use of Pearse by de Valera and anti-Treaty Sinn Féin (and later Fianna Fáil) and by W. T. Cosgrave and pro-Treaty Sinn Féin/Cumann na nGaedheal (and later Fine Gael). Although both parties used Pearse in order to gain support, their method of doing so differed in relation to how emotion was evoked. Interestingly, even though Pearse was called upon almost twice as often by opposition than by government parties from 1922 to 2008,[52] the use of him for political gain, it may be argued, still remains of significant note.

While the 'relationship between the Parnell myth and its political context was cemented during the first years after Parnell's death',[53] the Pearse myth and its political context was not cemented until de Valera was established in power, through his use of historical figures for his own purposes.[54] However, as Joost Augusteijn, in his biography of Pearse, points out, 'the uncritical admiration that characterized the writings on Patrick can also be detected in the way politicians referred to him in Dáil Éireann from 1919 well into the 1970s.'[55] The Pearse myth – that of martyr imitating both Christ and Cúchulainn, writer of prophetic, self-confessional literature, eager to engage in the Rising to see bloodshed

– stemmed as much from the picture painted in biographies we have discussed and from a public adoration of Pearse's *image* (demonstrated by the huge turn-out at his mother's funeral in 1932) as from de Valera's self-conscious formation of his *own iconic status*. In the 1917 East Clare by-election de Valera used the same rhetoric, and to the same effect, as Pearse did in 'Peace and the Gael'[56] with the same aim: to gain popular support. De Valera referred to the 'government' of 1916 when he stated: 'To that government when in a visible shape I offered my allegiance and to its spirit I owe all my allegiance still ... we want Ireland a sovereign state, not a province in slavery. Nothing less will satisfy our national aspirations. Nothing less is worthy of our past or of the later glorious centuries of struggle and martyrdom.'[57]

While the representation of Pearse in scholarly works after the Rising was evidently plentiful, governmental use of and referral to Pearse *as icon* was scarce until the late 1920s. The use of Pearse during this time centered around the formation of notions of both nationhood and Irishness. It was during the Treaty debates where notions of Irishness were most obviously muted.[58] Of course, the revered symbol of the perfect Irish mother, Pearse's mother Margaret Pearse, opposed the Treaty in his name: 'Anyone else who invoked his name during the bitter arguments about the negotiations with Britain lacked the authority of the pre-eminent mother of 1916.'[59] To gain votes and to use the 'unleashed tide of emotional nationalism' the emotions of the electorate had to be played on.[60] A pro-Treaty pamphlet headlined 'Arguments against the Treaty' played on the emotionalisation of recent fighting and had no words, just a picture of a can of petrol and a gun.[61] In contrast, a pro-Treaty leaflet encouraged support by intellectually justifying the Treaty, using Pearse's own words:

> Means to an End!
> The anti-Treatyites are fond of voting *the dead who died for Ireland!*
> And invariably they vote them *against* the Treaty! If Collins, Mulcahy etc., had died they would be voting 'Anti' also!
> Listen to Padraig Pearse himself '... Home Rule to US would have been a means to an end. Repeal to Davis would have been a means to an end.' (*The Spiritual Nation* P. H. Pearse)
> Vote for the Treaty![62]

Here Pearse's words formed the voice of reason, as if he were speaking from the grave. Readers were asked to 'listen to Padraig Pearse himself' and then vote for the Treaty because it was a means to an end. The quote from *The Spiritual Nation* is, as with many quotations from Pearse, used for a purpose other than what it was intended to achieve. Comparing Davis and Repeal to Home Rule and the Volunteers was Pearse's attempt to consider Davis 'chiefly as one of the

Separatist voices'.[63] Anti-Treaty Sinn Féin also used Pearse in their pamphlets advertising that the 'liberty of the person [is] inviolable' and that 'the greatest soldier of this generation – Patrick Pearse – has testified to these truths in word and in deed,'[64] indicating that the acceptance of the Treaty would violate all personal freedom.

After the Civil War, Cosgrave's government was regarded (by its political enemies) as standing for the Treaty of 1921 and the establishment of a separate entity, Northern Ireland. The challenge, as Lionel Pilkington points out, 'was that of engendering a form of Irish identity that would be transparent, centralized and constitutional'. This period was one of 'reining in revolutionary expectations and reconciling the population to constitutional government'.[65] One of the attempts at reconciling recent rebellion with current constitutional government was the plan by Cosgrave's cabinet, only weeks after the establishment of the Free State, to hand over the ruins of the General Post Office in Dublin to the Catholic Church for conversion into a cathedral. The plan was abandoned on legal advice. As Michael Laffan puts it: 'What a shrine that would have been, uniting triumphalist Catholicism and nationalist rebellion!'[66] That Pearse, as a figurehead, was used by Cosgrave's government illustrates Mansergh's claim that 'Pearse is an absolutely central figure in creating an Irish national democracy, not a marginal one.'[67]

From 1924 onwards there was an annual, state-sponsored religious service at the Arbour Hill cemetery in Dublin where the executed 1916 rebels had been buried. Given the political divisions in the country by then, the figure of Pearse – particularly in relation to his use of religious symbolism – fitted well with the alignment of the Catholic Church with commemorations of the Rising. In the first formal military commemoration of the Rising under the Cumann na nGaedheal government in 1924, Michael Mallin's widow was the only relative of the executed leaders to accept the invitation to attend.[68] With the 1925 Boundary Agreement, which accepted the border with Northern Ireland as permanent and workable, it was becoming increasingly difficult for Cosgrave to align himself with images or symbols which had once represented the nation. Cumann na nGaedheal TD Osmond Esmond asked Cosgrave in the Dáil if he was 'aware that this is the only state in Europe that has not a legalised national flag? Does the President expect that the people of other states can pay proper respect to the Irish Free State if it fails to legalise its flag? … The President said that the second part of the question was not admitted and the first part did not arise.'[69] In 1926 Cosgrave implemented the official renaming of Great Brunswick Street as Pearse Street (it having been informally named Pearse Street in 1920), and declared the Irish national anthem to be 'The Soldier's Song'. His concern for the image of Cumann na nGaedheal as a *national* party was also evident in his speech at the fourth annual convention of Cumann na nGaedheal:

Those false prophets who tell you that the country is 'going to the dogs' are not to be credited. The country, on the contrary has improved very considerably since 1922 ... Everyone with an axe to grind is out against the government. Every disruptive and antinational agency in the country is busy. We need a strong and live organisation to combat their misrepresentations ... The Cumann na nGaedheal organisation provides a platform sufficiently broad to embrace all the best elements in the country.[70]

The image of Cumann na nGaedheal centered on the idea of the peacekeeping party, the party that would encompass all *good* elements of the country. Indeed, Ernest Blythe would later describe Cosgrave as being more than anything a 'practical man'.[71] In other words, Cosgrave was the leader whose task it was to *ground* Ireland. And in this practical grounding, rather than a *nationalistic* party (like Sinn Féin), Cumann na nGaedheal appeared as a *national* party. Not unlike portrayals of Pearse being all things to all men, Cosgrave declared that Cumann na nGaedheal

has a great advantage over rival political organisations in that it represents no isolated interest, no faction group; it embraces every interest and every walk of life; the secret of its cohesion being a sincere desire for the country's progress and prosperity and an appreciation of the fundamental basis of organised society, namely, that considerations of the common good must override the claims of any particular section.[72]

In 1926, Sinn Féin's *An Phoblacht* carried the headline '1916–1926 Make it a great Commemoration' and contained various accounts of the Rising and its personalities. 'Pearse,' Frank Gallagher explained, 'the singer, the poet, the gentle schoolmaster, had become the warrior because the nation looked as much for the fiery sword as for the angel who bore it.'[73] Pearse, not only an angel bearing the fiery sword of freedom, was also 'the last great secular champion of the Gaelic tradition. On that tradition he had made his soul believe that the soul of Ireland was for Irish Independence.'[74] It is clear, then, that Sinn Féin had made its claim on Pearse. If Sinn Féin's purpose was to attain full Irish independence, Cumann na nGaedheal's purpose was to retain what they had by keeping peace and 'asserting and upholding the will of the people' so that they would find 'the turn in the long road which leads upward and onward'.[75]

A rather different narrative of Irishness and Pearse was played out in the Abbey Theatre (the national theatre which the government subsidised annually by £850). In Seán O'Casey's *The Plough and the Stars*, where the characters are ordinary people of Dublin, bent on survival, the words of Pearse are spoken by a shadow and heard over squabbles in the pub.[76] While in Act II Lieutenant Langon declares that 'Ireland is greater than a mother' and Clitheroe that 'Ireland is greater than a wife,' the Figure in the Window, a silhouette of Pearse, proclaims that 'bloodshed is a cleansing and sanctifying thing.' The silhouette then declares, from Pearse's O'Donovan Rossa graveside speech with an added exclamation mark, 'the fools, the fools, the fools – they have left us our Fenian dead, and while Ireland holds these graves, Ireland unfree shall never be at peace!' Meanwhile the prostitute Rosie and Fluther leave the pub laughing, arm in arm.[77] What O'Casey does, of course, is to remind the audience how political rhetoric is no match for human emotion. When Captain Brennan of the Volunteers suggests that Nora's grief at Jack's death will be replaced by joy when she hears she 'had a hero for a husband', Bessie simply replies 'if only you seen her you'd know to th' differ.'[78] With the behaviour of O'Casey's characters, similar to the portrayal of Pearse's personality as shown in previously discussed popular narratives, there are constant contradictions. They support a bid for freedom on the one hand and on the other, do not. What O'Casey does is bring 'reality, and not an idealised notion of it, before the public's gaze'.[79]

The full-scale riot which occurred after the fourth staging of *The Plough and the Stars* in 1926 occurred partly because of the perceived attack on the men in the Rising, partly in protest in opposition to the animated appearance of a prostitute and, indeed, partly because of the *portrayal* of life in inner-city Dublin. Reality in the new Ireland was a far cry from the picture of freedom that Pearse had painted. The ideal and ideas Pearse had once stood for had become, by 1926, a representation of the myth of Pearse: caricatures of ideals and he himself, a caricature of a rebel. It was not a coincidence that on this night, Thursday 11 February, the audience comprised of people with such deep connections to the Rising as Margaret Pearse, Kathleen Clarke, Hanna Sheehy Skeffington, Maud Gonne and members of Cumann na mBan, among others. While the riot echoed the public's reaction to J. M. Synge's *The Playboy of the Western World*, the protest, however, was more than a protest of portrayal. It was, as Chris Morash points out, 'an effective means of embarrassing the Cosgrave government (and Ernest Blythe in particular), in that it cast them as the subsidisers of a scandalous attack on the sacred traditions of republicanism'.[80]

Sheehy Skeffington summed up the high emotions in a letter to the *Irish Independent*: 'In no country save in Ireland could a State-subsidised theatre presume on popular patience to the extent of making a mockery and a byword of a revolutionary movement on which the present structure claims to stand.'[81] In fact, what both the writing of *The Plough and the Stars* and the subsequent reaction to its performance showed was how much a part of the national psyche the events of 1916 and Pearse as *figurehead* had become within ten years.[82] It would not be until many years later that a view devoid of myth could be taken whereby the revolution could be examined as 'an outgrowth of national self-discovery' and that 'as much as anything, they fought for each other, their brothers, cousins, neighbours, workmates, and friends.'[83] Indeed, O'Casey himself would later regret this portrayal of Pearse and describe him in his autobiography as 'a thoughtful, literature-loving educator and idealist'.[84]

The use of Pearse in the years preceding and during the June 1927 general election illustrates how he was used for specific *party* politics, as opposed to individual purposes. The dual significance of the Rising in Irish politics is reflected by the dual use of Pearse during these years. On the one hand, the Rising is seen as a mythical legacy to be proud of (a view upheld by Sinn Féin, de Valera and Fianna Fáil) and on the other hand, it is connected with revolutionaries (a view upheld by Cosgrave, Cumann na nGaedheal and later Fine Gael). It is clear, then, that while 'Pearse's martyrdom and apotheosis placed him firmly in the company of those who had spurred him to action … For many who came after him, Pearse would become the most insistent ghost of them all, whose reproach would in turn have to appeased.'[85] Whereas in the Treaty debates, pro-Treaty TDs were able to directly cite Pearse to support their policies, by 1927 the focus had shifted. Cumann na nGaedheal defended the party position by attacking that of the opposition – Fianna Fáil. In election advertisements, the government party declared:

> Who are the war makers? Fianna Fáil – the party whose leader caused the Civil War of 1922 over what has since become an 'empty formula' now claims that it is the party of 'National Peace'. It proposes to establish this 'perfect peace' by … having 'another round' with England … Fianna Fáil wants to make pieces of the country … Give your vote to Cumann na nGaedheal and keep the peace you have.[86]

Again, cleverly using phonetics, Cumann na nGaedheal put its campaign in the form of a poem, of which part is quoted:

> From Donegal to Bag-anBun
> Fianna Fáil is on the run.
> Like old tin can to donkey's tail,
> Hangs broken oath to Fianna Fail
> … But the Cosgrave bunch will never fail
> Vote for them and Cumann na nGaedheal.[87]

With the consolidation of partition by 1927, and given that those in 1916 had died for a *united* Ireland, support for or allegiance to Pearse and the Rising did not sit comfortably with the image Cumann na nGaedheal wished to portray. Thus, the 'aims and purposes of the Cumann na nGaedheal Organisation are an ordered society, hard work … upright economic public service … a national revival of Irish culture, the maintenance of peace.'[88] De Valera, however, was very much in a position to use Pearse and the Rising in a direct attempt to gain support for Fianna Fáil. He declared there was a place in Fianna Fáil 'for all who believe with Padraig Pearse in one Irish nation and that free'[89] and that the constitution of the Republican Party (Fianna Fáil) embodied the declarations of the 1916 Proclamation.[90]

While Cosgrave upheld the image of the morally upright, ordered party, 'portraying himself as the guardian of law, order and stability against de Valera, a wild and reckless adventurer',[91] the Christian Brothers upheld the moral goodness of Ireland by upholding those very elements of disorder, the martyrs of 1916. The use and ownership of Pearse had shifted, then, from those in (and with) political power to the holders of moral and religious authority. It was to shift again when de Valera gained power in 1932, but what is evident here is that coupled with the use of Pearse by Sinn Féin in the 1926 commemorations of the Rising and the references to him by religious organisations such as the Christian Brothers, the 'ownership' of Pearse had moved from Cosgrave. Like Ryan and Le Roux, the Christian Brothers of *Our Boys* saw Pearse's fiction as solely autobiographical. Like politicans, *Our Boys* only incorporated Pearse into its ideology because of what he could be made to *represent.* In other words, the representation of Patrick Pearse by politicians and religious orders at this time was a *selective* representation chosen solely to uphold the values of the representer. Pearse was not upheld because of his many careers but because he could be easily moulded into a specific age.

What Pearse seemed to represent, then, could no longer be used to appeal to all men in political terms as it had done in the years after the Rising. Now his image represented something rather dangerous to the extent that Seamus Clandillon, director of broadcasting at 2RN, the first radio broadcasting station in the Free State, refused to broadcast an item on a speech by Pearse in 1926 because it 'might not be suitable, as we have a very mixed audience indeed. We have to be very careful about broadcasting anything of a political character.'[92] Cosgrave chose to concentrate on the practicalities of his government and party during elections, rejecting the ideological heritage that the tradition of martyrs seemed to leave him as the leader of the first legitimate Irish government – a tradition to which the public in general were *emotionally* sympathetic after the executions. For the Irish public what the leader in power *symbolised* was more important than how he articulated his political theories. It was to de Valera's benefit, as the Fianna Fáil party was founded, that the Cosgrave government by 1926 chose to uphold an image of a morally upright and practical party rather than the image of any one historical figure.

The seeds of the party political use of Pearse were sown in the period examined in this chapter (1916–27). The initial intellectualisation of Pearse illustrated by his usage in pro-Treaty and anti-Treaty propaganda alongside the many scholarly accounts in this period laid the foundations for an emotionalisation of the Pearse image that was to prevail in the de Valera era and beyond. It is clear that

Pearse has been assessed personally and politically predominantly in relation to his involvement in the 1916 Rising and subsequent execution. His life's work has been judged by his last action; his early career in the Gaelic League and time as editor of *An Claidheamh Soluis* have been, in the main, ignored.[93] While throughout the twentieth century various parties and groups invoked the names and ideas of those involved in the 1916 Rising for different reasons, this chapter has shown how Pearse has been invoked not for his politics or ideas but for what he could be *shown* to represent.

A political prisoner in Koestler's *Darkness at Noon*, referring to the Communist Party during the 'purges', stated 'the Party is the embodiment of the revolutionary idea in history ... history makes no mistakes.'[94] Similarly, it could be said that Irish political parties are the embodiment of the idea of *tradition* in history illustrated by the way the present is often (and was often) interpreted in terms of a unifying past. In twenty-first-century Ireland, Pearse is now 'a marker of what once was, not what might be'.[95] In essence, what he marks now is a direct result of what he was shown to represent in these years after 1916, or as Ruth Dudley Edwards so aptly phrased it in the title of her biography of Pearse: *The Triumph of Failure*.[96] What remains is O'Casey's Figure in the Window. Speaking as the 'Voice of the Man'[97] Pearse, a mere shadow of a former self, is looking, searching for the future and finding only fragments of the past. The other histories of 1916, as James Moran states, 'remain largely untold, as each subsequent generation uses the ideas of the 1920s and 1930s in order to inspire new versions of the insurrection that suit their current ideological needs.'[98] That this has happened is due, in part, to what has been described in this chapter: the formation of the myth of Pearse through painting pictures and telling tales.

6

PHYSICAL FORCE WITHIN THE BOUNDS OF POLITICAL CONSTRAINTS

GHQ's role in the War of Independence[1]

KATIE LINGARD

Between its formation in January 1913 and the spring of 1918, the Irish Volunteer Force was noticeably bereft of formal military leadership at the highest echelon. In the wake of the 1916 Easter Rising's evident military failure, the Volunteers[2] explored the obvious need for guidance from a dedicated military leadership body, resulting in the creation of a General Headquarters (GHQ) Staff in March 1918. This chapter discusses the establishment of GHQ and how it developed and implemented a policy of discriminate violence. GHQ not only ordered but also restrained Volunteer actions in order to promote the image of the force – both nationally and internationally – as a legitimate army, with a defensive mandate to protect the people and the civil authority. Throughout 1919, GHQ's strategy was largely political, not military.

While local initiative is a necessarily dominant feature in guerrilla warfare, central control ensures that local operations do not exceed public tolerance of the use of force and of the likely repercussions of violent actions. In order to maintain public support, appearing to operate under the auspices of a legitimate political body is equally important. In a conventional setting, the military wing is responsible for defending the freedom of government and people. In a guerrilla context, where the political wing is under constant threat of arrest, the mainte-nance of political legitimacy becomes all the more pressing. During the War of Independence, GHQ was responsible for ensuring that political restraints, designed to maintain public support, were upheld. This meant, firstly, that GHQ adopted a strategy of ordering discriminate use of force in order to provoke the British forces to respond with indiscriminate violence, which would in turn garner public support for the Volunteers. Secondly, GHQ had to ensure that the legitimacy found in the form of Sinn Féin, and later the Dáil, was maintained by safeguarding members from arrest. Ultimately, GHQ employed military strategy for political ends, not only ordering but also controlling the use of violence.

The Rising's aftermath saw rebels become martyrs, interned innocents educated by separatists, and a dramatic shift in public opinion. In blaming the Rising on Sinn Féin, a small, independent political party with no involvement (although some sympathy with the rebels' cause), the British government made the party the rallying point for future separatist initiatives. Beyond capitalising on the wave of public support, however, Sinn Féin had to offer a viable alternative to the ailing Irish Parliamentary Party, whose approach was purely constitutional. Having brought Ireland to the brink of civil war, the Ulster crisis and its aftermath had clearly demonstrated the limits of constitutional politics. On the other hand, previous armed rebellions – such as Robert Emmet's rebellion in 1803 or the Fenian uprising of 1867 – indicated that use of force alone had no hope of success against a militarily superior enemy. Rather, Sinn Féin and the Volunteers sought to combine the two traditions, thus providing legitimacy for military actions and protection for members of the Dáil. Margery Forester summarises the rationale: 'To harass the British out of Ireland by force of arms would be useless if it left an administrative vacuum behind. There must be a second line of men armed with pens and sound economic policies waiting when the British were gone. In the elected representatives of Sinn Féin this civil rearguard would find its leaders.'[3]

The practical co-operation of Sinn Féin and the Volunteers was symbolised in the election of Éamon de Valera, the sole surviving commandant of the 1916 Rising, as president of both bodies in 1917. Neither body could effectively operate in the long term without the other, and their co-operation played to the strengths of both the constitutional and physical force approaches: 'A combination was forged in 1917 which made possible the mobilisation of the nation's maximum strength, and based the claim for national independence firmly on the consent and approval of the great majority of the population.'[4]

The close relationship between the Dáil and the Volunteers alleviated many potential tensions between political and military endeavours, but this was largely enabled by Michael Collins's presence as a liaison. Collins was not only Minister for Finance in the underground Sinn Féin government established in 1919, but also president of the Supreme Council of the IRB and Director of Intelligence for the Volunteers. He was 'the ministerial presence in the army and the army's link to the government'.[5] This meant that policy could be decided and implemented with minimum disruption, and the Dáil's suppression (it was declared illegal in September 1919) did not adversely affect the Volunteers' functionality. The close relationship between Collins and Richard Mulcahy, the Volunteers' Chief of Staff and the Dáil Minister for Defence from January to April 1919 (and Assistant Minister for Defence thereafter), 'obviated the need for stricter control of the army by the Dáil ministry or a more attentive minister for defence'.[6] Collins's effectiveness as a liaison also countered the potential problems of an autonomous military. As Mulcahy's biographer, Maryann Valiulis concludes, 'Collins's dual roles covered over much of the ambiguity surrounding the relationship between the IRA and the Cabinet. For the rank and file of the IRA, Collins's high-ranking positions in both the government and the army obscured the subordination of the military to the civilian government.'[7]

While ideally suited to guerrilla warfare, combining the physical force tradition with politics had one substantial flaw – it was an informal arrangement and the Volunteers retained a large measure of autonomy; as Valiulis notes, the government–army relationship was 'built on cordiality rather than obedience'.[8] But given the Dáil's suppression eight months after its first meeting, and the continued escalation of the conflict, this autonomy was essential for effective operations: 'In the absence of an effective Dáil and full-time functioning cabinet, [the Volunteers] decided policy, made decisions and directed the revolutionary struggle.'[9]

To some, the military's dominance in crafting political strategy was evidence that the Volunteers saw the gun as the primary agent of change in Ireland. Writer and civil servant P. S. O'Hegarty, who was active as a propagandist for Sinn Féin, argued that 'the greatest achievement of any Irish generation was brought about by a military terrorism in which civilian government existed merely as a machine for registering military decrees and under which every argument, save the gun, was eliminated.'[10] He further claimed this was not an unconscious attitude or an unfortunate side effect; the Volunteers deliberately manipulated the Dáil for its own ends: 'The political machine became a tool in the hands of the military side of the movement so that in the end the whole thing was moulded by men who were capable of regarding the government seriously only in so far as it could be manipulated or forced to do what the military mind wanted.'[11] What O'Hegarty did not take into account was the possibility that the Volunteers had strived for a functioning civil–military relationship but the Dáil seemed indifferent to their efforts; the military was dominant because the government ignored its responsibilities, only taking formal responsibility for Volunteer actions in the spring of 1921, near the end of the War of Independence. Allowing the Volunteers to be politicised would later contribute both to the outbreak of the Civil War and to a crisis over control of the Free State army in 1924. However, during the War of Independence, it actually aided GHQ to implement policy with minimum disruption.

After the Easter Rising, the Volunteers' progress in reorganisation was initially slow, lacking purpose and direction. While the pace increased with the release of internees between the end of 1916 and the general amnesty of summer 1917, the Volunteers' reorganisation did not become focused until their involvement with marshalling Thomas Ashe's funeral in October 1917. After his success at Ashbourne, Co. Meath, during the Rising, Ashe had been identified as a serious threat to the British government and his capture 'was looked upon by the Castle authorities as a serious blow to Sinn Féin'.[12] Determined to be granted political status at Mountjoy, Ashe began the tradition of hunger-striking, which later became synonymous with republican campaigns in Ireland. Equally determined to withhold political status, the British government denied the prisoners' claims and instituted a policy of forcible feeding to counter the hunger-strike. 'But rough and inexpert handling caused the unfortunate Ashe to drown on the life-giving fluid.'[13] The horrific circumstances of his death at the hands of his captors triggered an unprecedented response nationwide in a remarkable show of strength and solidarity. The repercussions of his arrest, death, and funeral would galvanise the entire republican movement.

The funeral's aftermath united the Volunteers with three lasting ramifications. Firstly, it led to the immediate formation of the Dublin Brigade, with Mulcahy as commanding officer, from battalions that had previously lacked leadership and direction. Secondly, Collins's prominence at the graveside increased his profile and influence, enabling him to take on a key role in the Volunteer leadership. Finally, as a result of these crucial factors, the GHQ Staff was born. As Mulcahy concluded, 'the loss of Ashe at this important stage in our national affairs was a grievous and tragic blow but his death and funeral provided an important opportunity for the public assembly of the volunteers and for the subsequent formation of a national volunteer executive.'[14]

Deliberately scheduled to take advantage of the cover offered by the Sinn Féin Ard Fheis that took place at the same time, the Volunteer Convention of October 1917 sought to establish central control by bringing together 'all volunteer influences into a more coherent and disciplined organisation'.[15] The Volunteer National Executive was formed as a result of the Convention and it in turn elected a Resident Executive as the military equivalent of Sinn Féin's new Standing Committee. Primarily comprised of Dublin officers, 'this smaller group was responsible for the day-to-day activities and organisation of the volunteers.'[16] Cathal Brugha was elected Chairman of the Resident Executive, but held the position as a civil authority[17] – military status was never assigned to the chairmanship.[18] Mulcahy explained that specific military duties were then delegated to certain individuals: 'Much urgent work was required to be done to routine and standardise many aspects of the military work of the Volunteers and following discussion on these matters, it was decided that there were certain branches of this work which required to be looked after by having a Director specially to take charge of each.'[19]

Mulcahy became Director of Training, (D/Training); Collins D/Organisation; Rory O'Connor D/Engineering; Michael Staines D/Supplies (the position later became Quartermaster General); and Diarmuid Lynch D/Communications.[20] Between the Convention and GHQ's establishment, the Volunteers' priority was to conduct training, inculcate discipline, and procure equipment for future operations, with the goal of moulding an effective fighting force. Mulcahy maintained that the Resident Executive was a fundamental element in shaping the Volunteers and sustaining their momentum: 'The work of the Resident Executive brought increasing life and cohesion into the Volunteer movement.'[21]

GHQ was established on the eve of the conscription crisis in April 1918 when, facing mounting pressure on the Western Front, the British government introduced the Military Service Bill which was intended to extend conscription, which had existed in Britain since January 1916, to Ireland. Its implementation was postponed after a united opposition from Irish church and political leaders, but Mulcahy insisted that the threat of conscription confirmed the necessity for GHQ, rather than having created it.[22] While some Irish politicians viewed conscription as a declaration of war, the Volunteers were still expected to react in self-defence, rather than organising any offensive opposition. Mulcahy recalled the instructions given to the Volunteers:

> Volunteers were required to take all possible precaution to avoid arrest, and even to avoid creating occasions that invited disorder and the danger of the use of force. If arrested they had orders to be defiant of authority and non-cooperative on detention. If, while in possession of arms their arrest was attempted, the arms should be used in an effort to prevent their loss and to evade being taken into custody.[23]

The conscription threat 'made it clear that there was a realistic necessity for having a General Headquarters Staff, for having an organisation of the Volunteers, and it came as a timely confirmation of our lines of development'.[24] Florrie O'Donoghue, of the Volunteers' Cork No. 1 Brigade, observed that supervision of the Volunteers was 'most essential if their exuberant enthusiasm was to be disciplined, controlled and directed into effective, combined action. It was time

to lay down guidelines for their internal problems of organisation, training and arms, and for their relation to the political wing of the movement in which many of them were deeply involved.'[25] The ease of GHQ's establishment was a tribute to the Resident Executive's valuable work, which had ensured the military leadership was set up 'along practical and functional lines'.[26] GHQ thus took over the responsibility of military organisation.

The establishment of GHQ defined a new era for the Irish Volunteers. Within the space of six months, the Volunteers had evolved from a loose organisation to one with clear structures and plans to instil training and discipline throughout the country. However the Volunteers' focus would stay largely defensive until the Dáil's suppression in September 1919. The movement had originally been formed to defend the passage of Home Rule and its status as a defensive force was reinforced when its members occupied buildings as defensive positions during the 1916 Rising. Even after the Volunteers' reorganisation and training in 1917 and 1918, their response to the conscription crisis, despite its perceived gravity, was still to use physical force only in self-defence.

As Dáil Éireann held its inaugural meeting on 21 January 1919, two members of the Royal Irish Constabulary (RIC) were shot dead by Volunteers at Soloheadbeg, Co. Tipperary. Although most historians recognise that Soloheadbeg was not stage-managed to punctuate the Dáil's political statements, the accidental timing is still frequently perceived as a convenient starting point for the War of Independence.[27] Yet the Volunteers were deliberately kept on a defensive footing until the Dáil was suppressed nine months later, and even then organised military offensives were not sanctioned until the following January, nearly a year after Soloheadbeg.

In early 1919 Mulcahy still saw the Volunteers as a defensive force; while he believed that conflict was inevitable, he did not yet envisage initiating a military offensive. Always conscious of the need for public support, he expected the Volunteers to only use physical force in self-defence or as a means to protect the people, so the public would view them as the victims of aggression, rather than the perpetrators. He believed that blood should only be spilt where absolutely necessary, and repeatedly cautioned Volunteer leaders around the country 'to take every possible precaution against taking life and against losing life'.[28] This policy was difficult to implement as local leaders initiated attacks on the RIC and grew impatient in the face of increasingly repressive British measures. Nonetheless, Mulcahy maintained that the most effective course of action for maintaining support from both the Irish public and the international community was to 'move slowly and educate the people'.[29]

In addition to the escalating conflict, there were a number of political events that 'weakened the position of those who wished to avoid violence'.[30] As part of its campaign for international recognition, the Dáil appointed a delegation to attend the Paris Peace Conference following the First World War in the hope that those countries that had championed the right of small nations to 'government by consent of the governed' would grant them a hearing. Their request was denied, however, on the grounds that Ireland was an internal problem for the United Kingdom. This rejection propelled the Volunteers further away from their defensive footing. Valiulis concludes that 'the failure of the Paris peace conference to acknowledge and support Ireland's claim for independence pushed Irish leaders to a more militant position.'[31]

The political situation deteriorated further when Sinn Féin was proscribed, together with the Gaelic League and the Volunteers in July 1919, 'severely weaken[ing] the political sector of the nationalist movement and strengthen[ing] the military faction'.[32] However, the Dáil's continued existence gave the Volunteers legitimacy and was crucial in presenting the 'government by consent of the governed' argument to the international community. As Mulcahy noted, 'it would not have been reasonable or useful to encourage an attitude of aggression as long as the Dáil was there for propaganda purposes.'[33]

GHQ was responsible for developing a military strategy that would authorise discriminate strikes on the enemy without alienating the public. As the Volunteers' military policy evolved from its defensive roots to a carefully planned offensive, GHQ had to manage the tension between local initiative and central control by not allowing the 'spirit of resistance [to] die down',[34] while preventing seemingly unprovoked aggression that would alienate support. Thus it was crucial that GHQ develop a cohesive military policy within the context of political constraints.

GHQ's vital role in forming the Volunteers' military policy is often overlooked, in part due to the frequent accusations of impotence made against it by prominent county brigades. Why was there friction between the county Volunteers and GHQ? Was GHQ out of touch with the counties and making decisions about the entire country based solely on the situation in Dublin? The Tipperary Volunteers certainly thought so. The Soloheadbeg attack reflected a growing impatience among the Volunteers; further frustration was apparent when GHQ condemned the ambush and rejected Tipperary's plan for further action.[35] The British government established a Special Military Area in South Tipperary as a visible attempt to support the police in the aftermath of Soloheadbeg. Instead of quelling further rebellion, the government's punishment of the entire community triggered a militant response from the activists they were trying to target.

Séamus Robinson, a prominent member of the Tipperary Volunteers who had authorised and participated in the Soloheadbeg attack, drafted a proclamation ordering all members of the British military and police to leave South Tipperary, under penalty of death. He requested permission from GHQ to issue the proclamation, and was stunned when his request was denied. Robinson met with his brigade, and expressed his disappointment at GHQ's refusal: 'I wished GHQ were here for one week even, and they'd probably change their minds.'[36] Equally disappointed and puzzled, Robinson's better-known subordinate Dan Breen later recalled that 'we could not understand their reluctance, seeing that ours was the only logical position.'[37] The Tipperary Volunteers had assessed their local situation and employed their own initiative to address the issues. Most local initiative operations that followed received retrospective authorisation, and yet GHQ was quick to condemn Tipperary's early actions.[38]

To a local Volunteer, GHQ's position was certainly not logical. The Tipperary Volunteers argued that physical force was the only reasonable policy in the face of British aggression, and believed that GHQ did not understand the situation outside Dublin. What these Volunteers lacked, however, was an appreciation of the wider context. GHQ was not opposed to offensive action, and would soon demonstrate its willingness to order the taking of life where it was deemed necessary and proportionate. GHQ's refusal to sanction Robinson's proclamation was based on a perception of how the escalation of conflict in Tipperary might affect the rest of the country, and not just the local area. GHQ objected to the Tipperary Volunteers' timing rather than their plans, fearing that even if these plans were initially successful in Tipperary, local initiative employed outside the bounds of political constraints and public support could be counterproductive for the entire country. Thus 1919 can be seen as a year of preparation, of county brigades eager for action but denied permission. The evolution of the Volunteers' strategy might have been gradual and action restrained, but 1919 was crucial both for their development and for ensuring that military offensives would not alienate the public.

The primary aim of guerrilla warfare is to win public support through the clever employment of physical force to exploit the enemy's weaknesses, forcing them to choose between capitulation and replying with indiscriminate force, thus loosening the enemy's control over the public. Mulcahy saw the importance of 'persuading the Irish people that they were being forced into fighting a justified defensive war against foreign aggression'.[39] So, rather than attacking the British military directly, GHQ would order discriminate violence to 'undermine civil authority to an extent where Britain was forced to rely on the crudest expression of that power, namely coercion'.[40] This strategy was designed to wear down British will and morale. As Robert Taber accurately summarises, 'the object of the guerrilla is not to win battles, but to avoid defeat, not to end the war but to prolong it, until political victory, more important than any battlefield victory, has been won.'[41] Ultimately, for GHQ, it was hoped that such a strategy would create a political situation where the Crown forces could not control the country without resorting to indiscriminate violence, which in turn would bring international condemnation.

Despite the failure to achieve admission to the Paris Peace Conference, international pressure was one of GHQ's strongest weapons in the War of Independence. Britain's wartime and post-war defence of a small nation's right to self-determination and 'government by the consent of the governed' presented an opportunity to level accusations of British hypocrisy before the international community: 'As long as [Britain] was fighting as the champion of small nations' independence, Irish Nationalists had a trump card, which they lost no opportunity to play.'[42] International support for using violence to suppress a nation was highly unlikely when that nation had made the same claim to independence as other small nations Britain gladly defended. So, rather than devising a military strategy with the end goal of conventional victory, GHQ resolved to place Britain in the untenable position of a perpetual state of war, which it could not justify suppressing without international condemnation.[43]

Although it cannot be argued that the Volunteers had unequivocal support from the masses, the change in public opinion owing to continued aggression from the Crown forces presented them with a welcome window of opportunity. M. L. R. Smith concludes that 'Britain's inability to restore civil control implied the lack of popular legitimacy in Ireland for British rule ... correspondingly, the republican cause enjoyed greater support ... As a result of both of these implications Britain would face a long, drawn out conflict.'[44] As Joost Augusteijn further explains:

> This violence seriously damaged the image of the Crown Forces as upholders of the law. Although officially condemned by the government, it was, and was felt to be, supported by higher military and police officers ... Members of the Crown Forces became less able to distinguish civilians with good intentions from Volunteers. As a result they started to regard the whole population as hostile. In the worst affected areas this turned most civilians against them.[45]

Increasingly, the Dáil could portray itself as 'government by consent of the governed' and the Volunteers were better employed in protecting this position than in undertaking actions that might undermine the long-term strategy. Thus, 'a combination was forged in 1917 which made possible the mobilisation of the nation's maximum strength, and based the claim for national independence firmly on the consent and approval of the great majority of the population.'[46] This consent was essential as dominance achieved through force could only ever be temporary. 'The reason', S. E. Finer explains in his assessment of the military's role in politics, 'is simply that the claim to rule by virtue of superior force invites challenge; indeed it is itself a tacit challenge, to any contender who thinks he is strong enough to chance his arm.'[47] Maintaining popular support for Sinn Féin was a way to ensure that any independence achieved would not just be temporary.

Public support also depended largely on the legitimacy of the Volunteers, and as the Dáil's continued existence provided that legitimacy, its safety was of paramount concern to GHQ. Mulcahy argued that 'it was the prime task of the army to protect the lives of the Government personnel and to establish and secure the arena of the Government's work and authority.'[48] Furthermore, maintaining possession of Dublin was crucial for the maintenance of the Dáil's authority. As the county brigades resented Dublin's priority and dominance in the conflict, a defensive Mulcahy sought to explain on several occasions why holding Dublin was critical to victory of any description: 'This is the first Irish War in which Dublin has been in National hands. This is a factor that may by itself prove decisive if turned to full account, for it places at our disposal all the resources of the capital city … All these factors taken together make Dublin by far the most important Military Area in Ireland.'[49]

He elaborated further elsewhere: 'Therefore, the grip of our forces on Dublin must be maintained and strengthened at all costs … It cannot be too clearly stated that no number nor any magnitude of victories in any distant provincial areas have any value if Dublin is lost in a Military sense.'[50] In order to maintain control of Dublin, described in a recent history of the city during the War of Independence as 'the cockpit of the Irish revolution',[51] GHQ needed to ensure both the Dáil and the Volunteer leaders remained safe from capture.

In Dublin, the detectives of the Dublin Metropolitan Police's (DMP) G-Division, with their growing arsenal of information on both Sinn Féin and the Volunteers, presented the greatest threat to the leadership. Collins suggested a pre-emptive strike against the G-men to avoid further mass arrests, and with such a clear and present threat Mulcahy agreed to Collins's proposed solution. Mulcahy later claimed they had destroyed 'a very dangerous and cleverly planned spy organisation whose purpose was to destroy the directing corps of the Volunteers'.[52] He shared Collins's assessment of the G-men as legitimate and proportionate targets because selective shootings would have a substantial effect on enemy morale and efficiency without necessitating collateral damage.[53] To act on his intelligence information, Collins established his 'Squad', a hand-picked unit of gunmen, to carry out targeted assassinations. Starting in July 1919, the squad first eliminated the threat from the G-Division, and then began to deal with British intelligence agents, most notably in the killing of 12 men and the wounding of several more on Bloody Sunday, 21 November 1920.[54]

In his 2002 introduction to recently published reports on British intelligence in this period, Peter Hart argues that the G-men were well known, and easy to identify. Thus, Collins's first victories (prior to 1920) were not against the expertise of British intelligence, but over his own countrymen who made no effort to disguise their identity or activities.[55] Furthermore, ordering the execution of someone who was blatantly following you hardly demonstrates proficiency in analysing intelligence. So while Collins's reputation grew more fearsome for effectively paralysing the G-Division, Hart contends that in reality Collins had preyed on easy targets.

Hart's argument does raise a valid point, and if Collins's goal was to achieve a military victory (albeit unconventional), or to prove the effectiveness of his intelligence, the current high estimation of his network should be revised. However, Collins had long realised that military victory was unrealistic and sought a political solution from the outset; targeting the G-Division was a military means to a political end.[56] Certainly, intelligence gathering needed to start from scratch because each G-man took his knowledge to the grave, but this was merely a beneficial side effect and not a desired end-state.

In contrast to Hart's appraisal, a closer analysis of Collins's strategy and modus operandi highlights three elements which suggest his envisaged end-state was political. Firstly, Collins always warned the detectives to desist from their activities or continue at their peril, in many cases several times. These warnings sent more than a ripple of fear through the division; it dented what little morale they had under already strenuous working conditions, and thrust them from the status of policemen to enemy spies. Naturally, this feeling was compounded when Collins carried out his threats against those who disregarded the warning and continued to threaten his operations. It should also be noted that Collins did not view these warnings as a polite formality; he never ordered the killing of any detective who chose to desist.[57]

Secondly, on a political level, Collins's warnings were aimed at the British government. Its refusal to order the G-men to desist and withdraw would result in the killings as threatened; thus it would be the politicians who would be depicted as responsible for these deaths. While the loss of individual G-men would not affect an enemy with enough manpower to replace them and time to rebuild their knowledge, the political ramifications were too damaging to be ignored. Further, the government would either be compelled to reply in kind, at great risk of international condemnation, or do nothing and allow the Volunteers a tangible victory Britain could ill afford.

Finally, Collins 'anticipated that once the detectives were neutralised or eliminated, the British would inevitably react blindly and in the process hit innocent Irish people and thereby drive the great mass of the people into the arms of the republicans'.[58] Thus the key to Collins's campaign lay with Britain's response. Michael Foy succinctly summarises Collins's strategy as 'a masterly combination of defence and aggression. On the one hand, by assassinating G-men he protected the Volunteers from enemy pressure and infiltration; on the other, he goaded the British authorities and police into retaliation and overreaction, encouraging nationalist Ireland to unite behind Sinn Féin.'[59] These arguments counter Hart's appraisal, not by disproving his valid claim, but rather by underlining that Collins's desired end-state was always political, not military. He combined military and political strategies with lethal effect.

In the shorter term, pre-emptive strikes against G-Division meant that the British government's eventual suppression of the Dáil in September 1919 was counterproductive. According to Mulcahy, 'it will be seen that the initiative against the detectives was only begun barely in time ... [and it] may be regarded as the ... central activity which stimulated the volunteer military activity ... and saved the parliament as an institution.'[60] Undertaken without the intelligence necessary to easily identify the ring-leaders before they went underground, the suppression had little practical impact. At the same time, it provoked public indignation at such treatment of democratically elected representatives. Had suppression resulted in the Dáil's inability to function, continued military operations without that vital legitimacy would have risked alienating the public, both in Ireland and internationally. By protecting the deputies from arrest, GHQ could turn the suppression of the Dáil into a propaganda victory and thus gain public support for a more active military offensive across the country. As described by Mulcahy, 'it was not continued violence that "ultimately let loose the guns of the Volunteers". What turned passive resistance and defensive tactics into an offensive, was the suppression of the Dáil as the national assembly in September 1919.'[61] This suppression was pivotal in the development of GHQ's military strategy and would come to mark a watershed that divided defensive from offensive action.

Clearly GHQ was closely involved with military operations in Dublin, but the county brigades, frustrated by the inherent challenges of insurgency communication, accused GHQ of not understanding the situation outside Dublin and of hampering local initiative. By nature, insurgency requires a higher degree of flexibility in both command and communications, as orders must convey the commander's intent while allowing units to improvise appropriate tactics for each unique situation encountered. The frequent immediacy of insurgency engagements can hinder direct and detailed consultation with superiors, thus forcing brigade commanders to use initiative and report their operations after the fact. So while GHQ's strategy and intent was conveyed to rural units, direct involvement was dependent on the logistics of timing and communication. After his success in West Cork, Tom Barry was invited to visit GHQ in Dublin, and his opinion of GHQ changed upon closer acquaintance:

> It became fashionable after the Truce with the British for inefficient units to throw
> the onus for their lack of action on the shoulders of G.H.Q. The truth demands that this

should be faced up squarely. Never throughout 1920 and 1921 did G.H.Q. repudiate or reprimand any Unit for its aggressiveness or its activities. On the contrary, Headquarters encouraged and urged the Army to fight and to keep on fighting.[62]

Aware of the limitations that communications and timing imposed, GHQ largely encouraged local initiative, but within set guidelines. It provided discipline, training, and encouraged ethical boundaries, all within the context of a national political framework which local units did not always appreciate or understand. For GHQ, it was all about timing and public support; it was essential to show the public that they were fighting a justified war against foreign aggression

7

VIOLENCE AGAINST WOMEN DURING THE IRISH WAR OF INDEPENDENCE, 1919–21

MARIE COLEMAN

I

The historiography of women in the Irish revolution

The role of women in the Irish revolution was largely ignored or marginalised by historians until recently. This was in part due to the absence of archival material relating to Cumann na mBan, the women's auxiliary of the Irish Volunteers (later the Irish Republican Army (IRA)). However, the release of the Bureau of Military History (BMH) archive in 2003, which contains approximately 150 statements by women who were involved in various aspects of the revolution, has resulted in a much greater focus on the role played by women; this has been most noticeable in recent books on the 1916 Rising.[1] This situation will improve over the coming years with the phased release of the Military Service Pensions Collection.[2]

During the 1930s some women published first-hand accounts of their involvement in the revolution, including Eithne Coyle's history of Cumann na mBan, which was serialised in the Sinn Féin newspaper *An Phoblacht* in 1933, and the Sinn Féin president Margaret Buckley's *Jangle of Keys* (1938) which focused on her imprisonment by the Free State during the Civil War. Some memoirs written by women, including Kathleen Clarke and Josephine O'Donoghue, were not published until decades later.[3] The *Fighting Stories* series, a compilation of veterans' accounts from counties Dublin, Cork, Limerick and Kerry (with the telling subtitle of *Told by the Men Who Made It*), relegated the role of women to one or two small chapters usually at the end of the books.[4] There are also a number of biographies of female revolutionaries, but they tend to focus on the most prominent women in the movement, what Gerda Lerner has termed 'women worthies',[5] such as Maud Gonne, Hanna Sheehy Skeffington and Constance Markievicz.[6]

Memoirs written by men often emphasised the domestic role undertaken by women and even deliberately ignored their role in crucial actions. The best example of this is the varying accounts of Michael Brennan's escape from the town of Bandon provided in his own version, *The War in Clare*, and that of Kathleen Keyes McDonnell (née Healy) in *There Is a Bridge at Bandon*.[7] Brennan was sheltered by the republican Healys for two weeks while trying to avoid detection in a unionist stronghold with a heavy police presence. Brennan mentions the assistance that he received from the Healys in general but McDonnell refers in particular to the role of her sister, Peg Healy, a Cumann na mBan courier, in driving him out of the town. Brennan makes no specific reference to the role of Peg Healy. It has been argued that the side-lining of women in this way might have been a conscious effort to reinforce gender roles, avoiding women appearing as a threat to the dominant role of men in the revolution, or a reaction against the strong republican line adopted by Cumann na mBan during the Civil War.[8]

Prior to the release of the Bureau of Military History, the best treatments of the role of women in the revolution were: Margaret Ward's general study of women and Irish nationalism, *Unmanageable Revolutionaries*, first published in 1983; Aideen Sheehan's essay in a collection produced by the Trinity History Workshop in 1990; the relevant sections of Roger Sawyer's general survey of women in Irish history; and Sinéad McCoole's treatment of female nationalist activism that drew heavily upon and highlighted the richness of the Kilmainham Gaol archives for studying the experience of women during the Civil War.[9] My own work on Cumann na mBan in Co. Longford benefited from access to draft applications for military service pensions, enabling me to paint a picture of the activities of Cumann na mBan at a regional level in the fields of intelligence-gathering, acquisition and transportation of arms and ammunition, and the care of Volunteers on the run during the War of Independence.[10] Since the release of the BMH there has been a noticeable increase in the volume and quality of such literature, as witnessed by the survey works of Cal McCarthy and Ann Matthews, and the diversification of biographical studies to include figures such as the medical doctors Kathleen Lynn and Brigid Lyons Thornton.[11] The political and propaganda activities of active women republicans have also been brought to the fore by recent studies.[12]

There still remains considerable scope for research on this aspect of the Irish revolution. The Military Service Pensions Collection will hopefully provide a fuller picture of what a wider range and greater number of female activists did during these formative years. Irish historical biography is underdeveloped both in general and with regard to women in this period in particular. Mary MacSwiney, Albina Broderick and Margaret Skinnider are a few whose activities deserve closer scrutiny. Yet, such an approach must go beyond merely putting women into the picture. In setting out an agenda for the future direction of research on the Irish revolution in 2003 Peter Hart identified under-studied areas that have not been adequately tackled in the intervening period; pointing out that 'there has been little critical consideration of ... factors such as ethnicity and gender,' he warned that 'the gender of the revolutionary movement cannot be fully analysed by just adding women to the narrative or by compiling female activist biographies, valuable though these are.'[13]

The aims of this chapter are to explore the female experience of violence during the War of Independence by categorising the forms of violence experienced by women from various sectors of the community and also to adopt a broader gender-based interpretation in seeking to explain the actions, or lack of them in some cases, of the males who were the principal perpetrators of such violence.

II
The nature of violence towards women during the War of Independence

1. KILLING

The violence experienced by women in Ireland during the years 1919 to 1921 can be categorised as physical, psychological, gendered and sexual. Fatally violent attacks by either the republican or Crown forces were quite rare. There were very few deliberate killings of women. The most notable were those of the loyalist Mary Lindsay in Cork and the intellectually-disabled poitín-maker, Kate (or Kitty) Carroll in Monaghan.

The former was executed by the IRA in January 1921 for giving information to the Crown forces about the Volunteers who were planning an ambush near Dripsey. There was knowledge of the planned ambush in the local community and Mrs Lindsay gave the information to her friend, General Strickland, in Ballincollig. The IRA disregarded a warning from a local priest that the army was aware of its plans, resulting in an attack by the army on the would-be ambushers, the deaths of two IRA members, and the capture of five who were subsequently court-martialled and executed, along with a haul of weaponry and documentation.[14]

Carroll had fallen foul of both the Royal Irish Constabulary (RIC) and the republican police for her illegal activities and paid the price for informing on her competitors to the RIC. When her communication was intercepted she was treated in the way that had become customary for the IRA to deal with spies by 1921 – she was shot dead on 16 April and a note warning spies and informers that they would meet a similar fate was left on her body. While she did give information to the police, it was about rival poitín distillers, not IRA men. Therefore, the motivation of the Monaghan IRA in this regard is worthy of closer scrutiny, and the conclusion of Fearghal McGarry that 'the charge of spying appears to have been a convenient rationale for the execution of an obvious antisocial security risk' is compelling.[15]

Both of these killings have usually been examined by historians from a sectarian rather than a gender perspective, although Terence Dooley notes that Carroll was dispatched in contravention of the following IRA General Order issued in November 1920 that spared women convicted of spying the ultimate punishment:[16]

> Where there is evidence that a woman is a spy or is doing petty spy work, the Brigade Commandant whose area is involved will get up a Court of Inquiry to examine the evidence against her. If the Court finds her guilty of the charge, she shall then be advised accordingly and, except in the case of an Irishwoman, be ordered to leave the country within seven days. It shall be intimated to her that only consideration of her sex prevents the infliction of the statutory punishment of death. A formal public statement of the fact of the conviction shall be issued by Poster or Leaflet form or both ... Ordinarily it is not proposed to deport Irish women, it being hoped that the bringing of publicity on the action of such will neutralise them. In dangerous and persistent cases of this kind, however, full particulars should be placed before GHQ and instructions sought.[17]

This deliberate rejection of a General Order has led historians to question whether there was a sectarian motive to Carroll's killing.[18] However, this interpretation appears to have been based on the mistaken assumption that she was a Protestant, whereas she and her immediate family were all listed as Roman Catholics in the 1911 census.[19] What the Carroll affair does highlight is the lack of uniformity in IRA General Headquarters (GHQ)'s control of local units. Lindsay's killing was also a breach of the IRA's General Order, and as she was a Protestant, the evidence produced by Peter Hart on sectarianism in Cork brings this issue to the fore as a possible motive for the IRA's action in this episode. According to Hart, 36 per cent of civilians deliberately shot by the IRA in Cork between 1920 and 1922 were Protestants, equating to 'five times the percentage of Protestants in the civilian population'. Similarly, attacks on property were disproportionately aimed at Protestants; only 15 per cent of houses 'burned by guerrillas in Cork ... belonged to Catholics'.[20]

Other IRA units in Cork did adhere to GHQ's direction on the execution of suspected female spies; Seán Healy recounted how his unit received orders 'to deal with a woman informer', who had 'openly boasted that she would get all the IRA men whom she knew hanged or shot by her English masters'. The local IRA considered the shooting of women to be 'abhorrent' and decided to take her prisoner while she was on her way to Sunday religious services. However, having been in receipt of previous warnings from the IRA, she appears to have realised the danger and disappeared before any action was taken.[21]

Some elements within the IRA appear to have been willing to shoot women whose actions were seen as a threat to their security. In Killonan, Co. Limerick, a maid, formerly a workhouse inmate, who was employed by a Mrs McCormack, whose husband and son were in the Limerick IRA, was rumoured to be 'a pal of the Tans' and acting under an assumed name. Michael Collins (of the Limerick IRA) was warned by the master of the Tralee workhouse that 'if we did not have the girl executed ... some members of the local company there [in Tralee] would come to Killonan and shoot her.' She avoided this fate through the intervention of the sympathetic Mrs McCormack, who 'facilitated her escape by opening a back window'.[22]

In many cases where women died during the War of Independence, it was as a result of non-targeted or random acts of violence. Such incidental fatal attacks on women included the deaths in Galway of the pregnant Ellen Quinn in a drive-by shooting by police on 1 November 1920, and Lily Blake, the wife of a police District Inspector whose vehicle was ambushed by the IRA in May 1921.[23] Jennie Boyle was the only female casualty of the indiscriminate shooting of civilians by Black and Tans in Croke Park on 21 November 1920.[24] Women were often the direct or indirect targets of reprisal attacks by both sides, which will be described below, but none of these appear to have been fatal; in his research on the Black and Tans and Auxiliaries, David Leeson did not find that 'a single woman was ever murdered in a reprisal'.[25]

2. NON-SEXUAL PHYSICAL ASSAULTS

There is ample evidence attesting to assaults on women by the Black and Tans and Auxiliaries. Frequently this took the form of cutting off their hair. In September 1920 five members of Cumann na mBan in Galway were subjected to this unofficial punishment in reprisal for a similar attack carried out by the IRA on a woman who had given evidence to a military court. This incident indicates that the IRA was equally liable to commit such attacks and there are many instances of women who were friendly with the police or who worked for them being treated similarly.[26]

This type of assault is a good example of what Elisabeth Jean Wood has termed 'gender violence', as distinct from sexual violence: 'gender violence ... includes violence that occurs because of the victim's gender without the kinds of sexual contact included in sexual violence,' whereas '*Sexual violence* is a broader category that includes rape, coerced undressing, and non-penetrating sexual assault such as sexual mutilation.'[27] The use of such a form of violence by the IRA against Irish women also conforms to Elizabeth Heineman's idea of 'insider violence', deployed as a method of disciplining women, including those who were, or were expected to be, on the same side as the perpetrators.[28]

In addition to such examples of 'insider violence', the majority of violence against women perpetrated by the IRA was what the British Labour Party's commission of inquiry labelled 'victimisation of policemen's wives and barrack servants'. This included eviction from and destruction of their homes; verbal and written threats; enforced resignation from employment in police barracks; ostracisation; and exile. One example of a serious physical assault on a female by the IRA, cited by the Labour commission, was that of a woman who was held down and had three pig rings put into her buttocks with pincers, for supplying milk to the police.[29]

Black and Tans and Auxiliaries also earned a reputation for rough treatment of and threats against women, much of it related to the circumstances surrounding raids on their homes in the search for male relatives suspected of involvement in republican activities; Kate O'Callaghan, wife of the Sinn Féin mayor of Limerick, Michael O'Callaghan, and later one of the six Sinn Féin women TDs in the second Dáil who voted against the Anglo-Irish Treaty, provided a heartfelt account of the impact of these raids of women:

> A search means carpets pulled up, presses, wardrobes, cupboards and beds pulled out and ransacked, writing desks rifled, private letters read aloud and commented on, jeering questions put to an unarmed man, the humiliation of the women of the house standing for hours in their night clothes and hastily-donned dressing gowns ... The women searched the wardrobes, linen press, cupboards, drawers, beds, etc., etc., very carefully. Even the heels of my boots and the shoes and the hems of my gowns were examined. The manner of the senior woman searcher was insolent in the extreme. At last she searched me personally. This seems a small matter, but the circumstances – the time, 11 o'clock [p.m.], the place, my own house, the insolent manner – were such as to cause me great humiliation. This woman, I could see, had learned her methods and her manners in London dealing with a class of English crime very different from my offences under the Restoration of Order in Ireland Act.[30]

There are some instances of the Black and Tans showing sensitivity in the treatment of women during raids. When Michael Kilroy's wife was forced out of her house in May 1921, while carrying a baby, 'a Tan, with an English accent, followed her with a rug and said, "Take this. We have babies ourselves".'[31] Kilroy, who was one of the most active republicans in the west of Ireland, and remained so during the Civil War, certainly had no cause to include such a story merely to reflect well upon the Tans.

Women also had to endure being present during physical assaults, including fatal ones, against their close male relatives. The wife of Cork Lord Mayor Tomás MacCurtain suffered a miscarriage soon after witnessing her husband's killing in 1920. The wives of successive Sinn Féin mayors of Limerick, Michael O'Callaghan and George Clancy, were also eyewitnesses to the shooting of their husbands in their own homes the following year; both men were shot dead in their homes on the night of 7 March 1921, most probably by members of the Black and Tans or Auxiliaries.[32] Nor did the IRA spare women in this regard.

Richard and Abraham Pearson were shot and fatally wounded by the IRA at Coolacrease in Co. Offaly on 30 June 1921 while their mother and sisters were nearby.[33] At least one of the intelligence agents shot on Bloody Sunday, William Frederick Newberry, was killed in the presence of a woman, probably his wife.[34]

3. SEXUAL ASSAULTS

The stereotypical depiction of the Black and Tans portrays them as a bunch of rogue, lawless, lower-class criminals: 'According to legend, the Black and Tans were ex-convicts and psychopaths, hardened by prison and crazed by war.'[35] Similar depictions in BMH statements are also accompanied by claims that women were not safe in their presence; the Limerick Volunteer James Maloney characterised them as being drawn 'mainly from the dregs of English cities and jails ... They robbed, looted or burned after any particular foray by the IRA. Prisoners were shot "trying to escape". IRA men's sisters and other girls had to go "on the run" fearing rape.'[36] An IRA commandant in Fingal, North Dublin, whose unit intercepted Black and Tans' correspondence described the letters which they wrote home to their wives as 'horrible and filled with sex and sensuality which clearly indicated the type of men they were and the lives they led'.[37] and 'the Archbishop of Dublin was counselled to keep the nuns of his archdiocese confined to their convents with such desperate men about.'[38]

Definitive evidence of actual sexual assaults on women is more difficult to find. For the purposes of this analysis, Wood's definition of sexual violence as 'a broader category [than gender violence] that includes rape, coerced undressing, and non-penetrating sexual assault such as sexual mutilation', will be used.[39] The British Labour commission explained that it was 'difficult to obtain direct evidence of incidents affecting females, for the women of Ireland are reticent on such subjects', but clearly suspected a sexual assault, and perhaps even a rape, had taken place in a case where 'a young woman who was sleeping alone in premises which were raided by the crown forces was compelled to get out of bed and her nightdress was ripped open from top to bottom.'[40]

Probably the clearest case of a sexual assault, so serious that its consequence was fatal, was that of Kate Maher, from Dundrum, Co. Tipperary. On 21 December 1920, Maher, a 45-year-old unmarried mother of one daughter, died as a result of a 'fracture of the base of the skull accelerated by haemorrhage from [a] wound in the vagina', both of which injuries 'were probably caused by some blunt instrument'. At the court of inquiry into her death it was reported that on the night before her death Maher, who was described by the local police as 'a woman of dissolute habits', was seen leaving a local public house in an intoxicated state in the company of a number of soldiers from the Lincolnshire Regiment. When she was discovered 'lying unconscious bleeding from her eye and from her womb' in a yard at the back of local dwellings and pubs, one of the soldiers,

Private Thomas Bennett, was lying close by, also in an inebriated state. Bennett was eventually cleared by court-martial, largely because the RIC witnesses were either unable or unwilling to link him to the crime and no other witnesses or evidence were forthcoming.[41]

The army's leadership was dissatisfied with both the incident and its handling by local commanders. While no one appears ever to have been convicted of involvement, the court of inquiry considered the responsible 'person or persons unknown' to be guilty of manslaughter, and General Sir Nevil Macready, the General Officer Commanding the army in Ireland, was in no doubt 'that the death of this woman was caused through ill treatment at the hands of soldiers' and considered 'the affair ... most discreditable to the Military and to the 1st B[at] t[alion] Lincolnshire Regiment'.[42] There is no evidence of a political motive to the crime, and the army authorities viewed it in the context of a breakdown of leadership and discipline:

> The Officer in Command, Lieut M. N. Ormond ... accidentally shot himself on the 18th [Dec]. Had he been there, this sort of conduct would never have occurred. It was impossible to send out at once another Officer as we had no subaltern at the moment available. The Sergt who was left in charge, Sergt Williamson, is one of my best NCOs, but unfortunately on the evening of the occurrence he was sick, and this was apparently taken advantage of by some of the men.[43]

Other specific allegations of rape and serious sexual assault committed by Crown forces during the War of Independence are to be found in the *Irish Bulletin*, the principal organ of Irish republican government propaganda. The edition of 14 April 1921 focused on 'Outrages on Irishwomen' and carried two reports by a Mrs Healy and a Nellie O'Mahony who claimed respectively to have been raped and sexually assaulted by members of the Crown forces. As Louise Ryan notes, these instances are unusual in that the women consented to being named. In addition to detailing their stories they gave accounts of how little regard the British authorities paid to their complaints and spoke of the climate of fear in which they lived. The *Bulletin* carried similar reports in subsequent issues – the last issue before the Truce (which ended the War of Independence on 11 July 1921) was headlined 'The War on Women and Children' – but was less specific, stating that women were unwilling or afraid to pursue complaints against their aggressors.[44] The principal difficulty with this source is the propaganda nature of the *Irish Bulletin*; the veracity of these reports is difficult to judge and cannot be relied upon too heavily in the absence of more concrete evidence.

The other sources available to date to historians of the revolution tend towards the impression that serious sexual violence, and rape in particular, were rare in Ireland during the War of Independence. Erskine Childers's propaganda pamphlet *Military Rule in Ireland*, dedicated a chapter to the effect of the war on women, but this dealt largely with the psychological impact of raids and did not refer to sexual violence.[45] The weight of the evidence presented before the American Commission on Conditions in Ireland in 1920 indicated that there was very little sexual crime.[46] Daniel Crowley, a young RIC police constable who had resigned in June 1920, told the commission that while he had witnessed Black and Tans harassing and searching young women, 'there was no rape.' In their evidence to the commission, British labour suffragists Annot Erskine Robinson and Ellen Wilkinson of the Women's International League for Peace and Freedom[47] 'made a special point to ask about ... impropriety against women' but 'did not hear of one single instance about that', though this was disputed by Hanna Sheehy Skeffington. The lord mayor of Cork, Donal O'Callaghan, presented an affidavit from Ellie Lane, a servant in Ballincollig, who was the victim of what was alleged to have been an attempted sexual assault when Crown forces raided her employer's home:

> The big fellow took the screen off my face and kissed me in spite of all endeavors to prevent him. He tried to force me to go back to the bed, and to do so caught me by the throat with his two hands, but I resisted all his efforts successfully ... The two then left, and about five minutes afterwards, the big fellow came back again to my room.
>
> He made me sit on the bed. I asked him what did he want me to do. Was it to assault me? He said no, but that I should get back to bed before he would leave. I refused. He then exposed his naked person to me, and tried to seduce me by telling me he had plenty of money.

This was the only such case of which O'Callaghan was aware, though he had heard rumours about similar attacks. Nevertheless, he was of the opinion that 'that class of assaults [sic] is not very general in connection with raids.'[48]

A simple search of the online BMH for the word 'rape' returns ten hits, four of which are transcription errors.[49] Of the other six, one is a reference by a Connaught Ranger mutineer to the depiction in India of Irish rebels, another is James Maloney's generalisation about the perceived conduct of the Black and Tans cited above, and a third is the use of the term 'rape' by John McCoy to describe the abandonment of republicanism in Northern Ireland in 1922. The remaining three relate to actual allegations of rape. In Cork, Seamus Fitzgerald of the Cork No. 1 Brigade, based in Cobh, reported an instance of rape and one of attempted rape in his brigade area: 'I regret to say I had two such cases. One, an already middle-aged pregnant woman was raped in Blackpool by the Black and Tans, and in the same locality another middle-aged woman successfully resisted a similar attempt.'[50] The second reference relates to a letter received by George

Berkeley, an Irish nationalist based in Britain, from a correspondent in Ireland who informed him that 'a woman was raped, and when she made complaint (to the authorities) her house was burnt as a reprisal.'[51]

In the final instance, Frank Henderson of the Dublin Brigade described a case of alleged rape that came before a republican court. Before issuing their decision the judges sought clerical advice. Unfortunately, Henderson's description of the case is extremely vague:

> All parties concerned having agreed to abide by the decision of the Court, the judges examined the accused and the other parties who had been summoned to give evidence. The Court took a certain view in regard to the case, but as it was thought it would be well to obtain expert advice on the moral side of the question it was agreed to defer announcing a decision pending consultation with a clerical authority. The prisoner in question was set at liberty on his undertaking not to leave the city and the judges … called on a priest of a certain Order and asked his opinion on the moral issue involved. The priest in turn consulted a colleague who was expert in matters of the kind who agreed with the view taken by the Court. The decision of the Court was then made known to the parties concerned in the case.[52]

This does not appear to have been a conflict-related incident, and is in many ways most instructive for what it tells us about the operation of the republican courts.

The paucity of definitive or reliable evidence on the extent of sexual violence during the War of Independence is reflected in the historiography. Writing in 1995, Sarah Benton could find no evidence for the use of rape as a weapon of war: 'This does not mean that no soldier ever raped an Irish woman during either the war against the British or the Civil War. But for rape to be a *weapon* of war it must have mass intimidatory effect and thus must be publicized.'[53] Similarly, in a more recent study of the Black and Tans and Auxiliaries, David Leeson found 'surprisingly few reports of sexual assaults on Irish women by members of the security forces' and concluded that rape 'was not very common'.[54]

A sense that rape and sexual assault was more widespread emerges from the work of Ann Matthews and Louise Ryan,[55] but as Gemma Clark has shown 'Ryan's supposedly "convincing evidence" of widespread attacks and sexual violence on women and girls during 1919–21 is actually based on only a handful of examples.'[56] Much of Matthews's contention that there was a 'war on women' in which rape and sexual assault were prevalent is based on a pamphlet produced by Hanna Sheehy Skeffington probably in late 1920 or early 1921 entitled 'Statement of atrocities on women in Ireland'. Yet, this four-page account, which relates principally to the type of physical and psychological violence referred to above, contains only one reference to an alleged actual rape: 'the rape of a girl in the presence of her father reported in Galway near Gort but not yet investigated fully.'[57] Contemporary sources indicate that the fear and threat of rape and sexual assault were more prevalent than actual assaults, but the atmosphere and intimidation created by such a perception should not be mistaken for evidence of actual assaults.

The discussion so far has focused largely on the southern Irish counties and the actions of the IRA, Black and Tans and Auxiliaries. A third paramilitary police force operating in Ireland during the War of Independence was the locally-recruited Ulster Special Constabulary. Tim Wilson's comparative study of ethnic conflict in Ulster and Upper Silesia between 1918 and 1922, suggests that rape and sexual assault were not weapons deployed by this controversial force either: 'Rape, torture, mutilation of the dead, denial of proper burial and massacre were all far more common practices in Upper Silesia than in Ulster.'[58] Where examples exist, they date from 1922. This was a much more disturbed period in the conflict in Ulster that followed the creation of Northern Ireland and the upsurge in sectarian attacks by both sides in the context of the IRA's failed northern offensive of early 1922 that aimed to destabilise the new northern government.

The best-known examples of such assaults were in Co. Derry where a Catholic girl 'managed to get away' from B-Specials[59] who 'attempted to outrage her' during a raid on her family home, and the alleged attempted rape of the wife of a prominent republican, James McGuill, in South Armagh, that formed the backdrop to the controversial killing of six Protestant civilians by the IRA at Altnaveigh and Lisdrumliska, in Co. Armagh, on 17 June 1922.[60] Both incidents – the assault of Mrs McGuill and the killings by the IRA – took place during a period of escalating hostility between the two communities in this contested border area over the preceding few years.[61] It is noteworthy that both of these incidents of attempted rape took place in the context of raids by the security forces on the homes of suspected republicans or sympathisers. This adds weight to the sense that rape and aggravated sexual assault were opportunistic rather than used as weapons of war.[62]

There was a flurry of discussion of incidents of rape and sexual assault in Ireland in both the British press and Parliament in June 1922. In the House of Lords, Sir Edward Carson[63] raised two cases of women who had been 'outraged', and a number of newspapers in Britain and Northern Ireland carried reports of alleged assaults against women, primarily in Ulster.[64] In most of these cases it is difficult to identify the perpetrators. In one case in Tipperary it is possible that the attackers were National Army soldiers as they claimed to be raiding a house to prevent guns from falling into the hands of the anti-Treaty IRA. In another case, also in Tipperary, the Protestant maid servants were assaulted but not the Catholics, indicating that the attackers had local knowledge of the religion of the domestic servants.[65]

wot in Cdl N·IC 102

Statement of Atrocities on Women in Ireland, Made and Signed by Mrs. Hannah Sheehy-Skeffington

I have been asked to furnish details for your convention on atrocities and terrorism of women in Ireland. It is impossible at present to send sworn statements but I send pamphlet on Cork which emobdies some and deals incidentally with terrorism of women. For the rest my material is drawn from Irish or British press (of latter Daily News, Manchester Guardian, and Herald notably) from investigation by members of Irish Women's Franchise League, from Irish Bureau for propaganda or from my own personal experiences or observations at first hand. I can only take **typical** cases in this brief statement and group these under various headings.

1. **Terrorism of Wives, Widows, Mothers and Sisters** of prominent Sinn Feiners, many of whom are "on the run." For last three months over 79,000 raids of private houses, usually at curfew hours (often between 1 and 4 a. m.) of armed and often drunken soldiery or police. When the man on the run is not found his wife, sister, etc., frequently threatened, separated for hours from her terrified children and sometimes compelled to stand in the street under the rain barefooted in her nightdress while her house is being sacked and dismantled or even burned. Recently blood-hounds accompanied these searches and added to their terror. Among such cases I mention the frequent raids upon Mrs. Maurice Collins, Parnell street, Dublin (see Erskine Childers' pamphlet "Military Rule in Ireland") Mrs. Kent, widow of Eamonn Kent shot in 1916, Mrs. Pearse (house at St. Enda's destroyed as "reprisal") Mrs. Cathal Brugha, wife of speaker of Dail Eireann (Irish Parliament). (To her house blood-hounds brought), Mrs. Wyse-Power, member of S. F. executive, etc.

2. **Wanton Terrorism of Young Mothers.**—Two pregnant women Mrs. Quinn, Gort, County Galway, Mrs. Ryan, Tipperary, shot dead. First shot by lorry of Black and Tans (auxiliary police) and left to bleed to death. Mr. Lloyd George described the murder in the House of Commons as a "precautionary measure." Mrs. Ryan owned a shop in Tipperary and all the traders were ordered to close their premises during the funeral of some officers killed in outlying district as form of compulsory mourning and trade reprisal. After the funeral had passed Mrs. Ryan ventured to open her door to let out a friend and was instantly shot dead. She was within a few months of her confinement. Mrs. MacCurtain, Lady Mayoress of Cork, was also within two months of her confinement when police invaded her house and killed her husband who died in her arms. She was delivered shortly after of still-born babies, two boys. Instances of this kind could be multiplied (v. Evelyn Sharp on Terrorism of Women, Daily Herald, February 7). Medical doctors report terrible effects to have resulted from constant strain on young wives and mothers. Two women (friends of my own) have gone mad as result.

It must be noted that these events took place in the much changed political atmosphere that coincided with the outbreak of the Civil War and many seem to have been concentrated in the contested area of the new Northern Ireland. Nevertheless, Clark's recent research on the nature of violence in Munster during the Civil War, which includes a more detailed account of the cases referred to above, has concluded that rape and sexual assault were relatively rare during that conflict also: 'Neither the anti-Treaty IRA nor National Troops utilized the breakdown in law and order to carry out unfettered violence against women, children and the wounded, as did paramilitary groups in Central Europe after World War I. Rape never became a systematic tactic in Ireland.'[66]

A question asked in the House of Commons about one incident which took place in Tipperary also highlights the way in which such occurrences could be mistakenly attributed a political motivation because they took place at a time of heightened political tension. Winston Churchill, Secretary of State for the Colonies, was asked if he was 'aware that a number of Sinn Feiners recently entered the house of a Loyalist in Tipperary and, having locked up the owner of the premises and an aged relative in a room, proceeded one by one to outrage the wife of the owner'? In response, Churchill cast doubt on any political motive for the assault: the attackers were 'not necessarily Sinn Feiners' and 'so far as can be ascertained there is no political element in this crime.' He also highlighted the unusual nature of such attacks in Ireland – 'this crime ... is one, I am glad to say, of rare occurrence in Ireland' – indicating that rape and sexual assault in general, but specifically in the context of the contemporary political turmoil were not commonplace in early 1920s Ireland.[67]

III

Analysis: Possible reasons for the absence of sexual assault during the War of Independence

The available evidence indicates that while there were instances of rape and sexual assault committed by the Crown forces in Ireland during the War of Independence, sexual violence was not a prevalent form of violence during that conflict. Where such assaults occurred they were not systematic or used in any deliberate way as a strategy or weapon of war. It is difficult to find any allegations of such assaults having been perpetrated by the IRA. Such allegations as do exist date from 1922, appear to have been more prevalent in Ulster, and in some cases, were mistakenly identified as political, or might well have used the political upheaval of the time as a cover.

Recent modern conflicts have perhaps created an impression that sexual violence is common in nationalist conflicts, as seen in cases such as Bosnia, Bangladesh and Sierra Leone.[68] However, the work of scholars such as Elisabeth

Jean Wood show that there is in fact a much greater variation in both the extent and form of such violence, and 'in some conflicts [it] is remarkably limited, despite widespread violence against civilians.' Her research has found relatively low levels of sexual violence in Peru, Sri Lanka and El Salvador, while the most notable contemporary conflict in which sexual violence is not prevalent is the on-going dispute between Israel and Palestine.[69]

There is evidence for the prevalence of sexual assaults in conflicts which occurred elsewhere at the time of the Irish revolution, especially in the defeated powers of central Europe after the First World War. Robert Gerwarth has drawn attention to the extent of both sexual and non-sexual violence against women by paramilitary forces in these regions, which appears to have been linked to ideals of masculinity, the impact of the defeat, and a sense that modernism, feminism and communism were the roots of the losers' ills.[70] Similarly, in his comparative study of Ulster and Upper Silesia, Wilson highlighted the noticeable contrast between the prevalence of sexual violence in both areas.[71]

There is still considerable disagreement among scholars as to why sexual violence is more common in some conflicts that others; according to Wood, 'the literature on sexual violence during war has yet to provide an adequate explanation for its variation across wars and armed groups.'[72] The final section of this chapter will examine some of Wood's arguments about this variation in an effort to seek explanations for the paucity of sexual violence during the Irish War of Independence.[73]

The argument that war creates a greater opportunity for sexual violence by grouping young men together away from normal social controls seems to have some applicability to the case of Ireland as most of the instances of sexual violence that we have evidence for appear to have been opportunistic, rather than targeted, often occurring in the context of raids on houses by the Crown forces. By contrast, much of the gender violence, especially hair-cutting, committed by both sides was targeted, often being used as a reprisal by Crown forces and as a form of insider violence by the IRA to keep women in line.

There was limited contact between combatants and enemy women during the War of Independence. In April 1919 Dáil Éireann instituted a boycott of the RIC, advising against any social or commercial interaction with policemen or their families and this kept many women from nationalist or republican backgrounds away from the Crown forces. Loyalist women would have had very little contact with the IRA other than in cases where their houses were raided for arms or where they had deliberately crossed the republicans as in the case of Mary Lindsay. While some republican women were imprisoned, there were no large scale detention centres, along the lines of those used by the British in South Africa during the Boer War. Therefore, the limited social intercourse between the combatants and women from the opposing sides in the War of Independence is a possible reason for the rarity of sexual violence and the opportunistic nature of it where it did occur.

The case of Kate Maher was possibly the most serious sexual crime committed by any of the combatants during the War of Independence. The emphasis placed by the army on indiscipline as a factor in her death might lend some weight to the suggestion that 'variation in sexual violence is better addressed by variation in military discipline than training and socialization.' By contrast, the overall absence of sexual violence by both sides might indicate that there was a relatively high level of discipline among both the Crown forces and the IRA.

It is possible to argue that, far from being a lawless mob, the violence of the paramilitary police forces was somewhat orchestrated – a certain level of venting of frustration and retaliation was permitted but this was controlled and curtailed. Unofficial reprisals by the Crown forces in response to IRA attacks became increasingly common throughout 1920, to the extent that reprisals against property became official policy between December 1920 and June 1921 in order that they could be controlled better. This policy of official reprisals and the efforts of the police advisor, Sir Hugh Tudor, to curtail hair-cutting attacks, could be cited as evidence to reinforce this hypothesis that a certain degree of violence was permitted.[74]

IRA units were small, tightly-knit and embedded in their own communities, factors which might have reinforced an informal discipline that drew a line at certain forms of violence that were seen as unacceptable to that society. There are also indications that IRA GHQ exerted greater influence as the conflict progressed; the fact that the General Order against executing female spies was largely adhered to, except in the two notable cases of Kitty Carroll and Mary Lindsay, reinforces this view.

A stronger case can be made to ascribe the IRA's disinclination to resort to sexual violence to its dependence on the support of the community in which it operated, as, according to Wood, many scholars agree that 'if an armed group is dependent on civilians, leaders will probably attempt to restrain sexual violence.' The cultural, ethical and moral norms of that community can also be cited as restraining influences on guerrilla fighters. In explaining the absence of sexual violence in the El Salvador conflict of the 1980s, Wood argued that 'it is difficult to imagine the organization embracing liberation theology while violating one of Catholicism's central norms, the sanctity of womanhood.' Most of the research on the social make-up of the revolutionary IRA has shown its members to have been overwhelmingly practising and in many cases devout Roman Catholics, reflecting the society in which they lived and operated.[75] The edict against the killing of women spies was a product of this society's attitude to violence against women and it is legitimate to argue that similar attitudes explain the virtual non-existence of sexual assaults by the IRA against women during the War of Independence.

While domestic attitudes were important, presenting the Irish case for independence in a good light to foreign powers can also be considered as a restraining factor in regard to both combatant sides in the War of Independence. Parallel to the IRA's military campaign for independence, the first Dáil was pursing an ultimately unsuccessful effort to seek foreign (and in particular American) recognition of the legitimacy of the revolutionary republic, a strategy that would have been hampered by reports of callous treatment of women by its military wing. While the republic might never have been officially recognised, the Irish did gain a high profile and sympathetic hearing in many sectors of the USA, parts of the Commonwealth and influential institutions such as the Vatican.

The Dáil's propaganda outfit was among the most successful aspects of its foreign policy and exploited incidents of Crown force violence effectively to garner greater sympathy. In light of these two factors, the British authorities in Ireland would have been well aware of how much damage would be done to Britain's reputation internationally if stories of rape and sexual assault of Irish women began to emerge. The evidence given to the American Commission on Conditions in Ireland relating to attacks by the Crown forces in Ireland and the international publicity given to reprisals such as the burning of Balbriggan were examples of this.[76] The case of the Irish War of Independence therefore gives added weight to Wood's argument that 'dependence on international allies may also constrain sexual violence if those allies have normative concerns about such violence.'

The presence of a significant number of female combatants among their own numbers has been cited as a reason why some forces constrain their use of sexual violence. The prominence of women in the Israeli army and among the Tamil Tigers possibly form parts of the explanation for low levels of such violence in the conflicts in which these groups are engaged.[77] While the presence or otherwise of women does not explain why the Black and Tans, Auxiliaries, Ulster Special Constabulary or British army did not use sexual violence in a more widespread manner during the Irish War of Independence, it is a strong argument to employ in explaining why the IRA shied away from such a tactic. While republican women did not take part in actual combat, Cumann na mBan, the IRA's female auxiliary, worked closely with the IRA and many leading IRA men had sisters or girlfriends in Cumann na mBan. Women were also prominent in the political side of the republican campaign. The significant role played by republican women in the Irish independence campaign is therefore a possible explanation for why male republican fighters did not resort to one of the most objectionable forms of violence against women.

The extent to which 'military forces in democracies are more accountable for their practices to civilian authorities' is also seen as a factor affecting the extent, nature and form of sexual violence perpetrated by such armies. The first Dáil placed a strong emphasis on democratic accountability as highlighted in its constitution, which made the executive answerable to the legislature, although this was not always possible to live up to in the context of an underground government that rarely had an opportunity to consult with the legislature. Similarly, the Minister for Defence, Cathal Brugha, fought with some, though not complete, success by the end of the conflict to bring the IRA more closely under the control of the civilian government. Thus, a commitment to the ideals of democratic and constitutional government might be a plausible explanation for the IRA's general eschewal of sexual violence.

From the British viewpoint, the emphasis on democratic accountability and the avoidance of sexual violence allowed them to draw a clear contrast with their recent enemy, the autocratic Germany of the Kaiser, whose army had resorted to widespread rape and sexual assault in Belgium at the start of the First World War. Clive Emsley has shown that 'reports of rape and sexual assault by British and Imperial soldiers both at home and overseas [during the period of the First World War] are rare in both the military records and the press.' While this might have been the result of a conscious desire on the part of British soldiers to differentiate themselves from 'the German Army's "rape" of Belgium and of the assaults and violence perpetrated by the invaders in 1914', the desire to keep up appearances cannot be discounted: 'Such reports in the press would, however, have undermined the moral and ethical crusade against the Prussian militarists who had raped poor little Belgium. For the sake of a regiment's name, it is possible that some units concealed such offences, either by encouraging or pressurizing the victim not to complain or by punishing at company level.'[78]

In addition to seeking explanations for the absence of sexual violence in revolutionary Ireland, it is worth considering what might have been gained by either side from resorting to it? The IRA was fighting what it saw as a war of national liberation on its own soil, and resorted to violence against women primarily as a means of disciplining Irish women seen as consorting with the enemy. Therefore, it is arguable that the IRA did not resort to sexual violence or rape because it had nothing to gain from doing so; it was not a means that helped achieve any of its aims and its employment would have been counterproductive if anything.

Similarly, the aim of the Crown forces in Ireland during the War of Independence was to quell an uprising. The tactics employed by the Black and Tans and Auxiliaries, especially the burning of homes, businesses and towns, did a good job of terrorising civilians without having to resort to rape to achieve this end. The Crown forces favoured methods which terrorised the civilian population through attacks on property, rather than on persons, which is broadly similar to the 'everyday violence' in the subsequent Irish Civil War.[79]

Joanna Bourke has shown that one of the principal justifications of wartime rape is that 'male sexual needs must be met.'[80] This raises the question of whether or not rape or sexual violence could have served a purpose for the Crown forces in meeting such 'needs'. Historically there was a tradition of prostitutes providing their services in proximity to army camps, most notably in the Irish context the so-called 'wrens of the Curragh'.[81] For most of their sojourn in Ireland, the Black and Tans and Auxiliaries were confined to barracks, and had few opportunities for recreation as it was considered too dangerous to venture outside when not on patrol. One of their few recreational pursuits was alcohol, which when combined with boredom and a siege mentality, goes a long way to explaining many of their actions.[82]

This raises the question of how, or if, their sexual 'needs' were met, especially as it would appear that they were not met by the rape of the Irish female population. More research needs to be done, if there is evidence available, to ascertain whether prostitutes were procured for the Crown forces in Ireland at this time (as might have been the case with Kate Maher) or whether there were any sexual assaults committed within the confines of the barracks, raising the spectre of intra-male sexual violence that is not within the remit of this chapter, but has yet to be considered by historians of the conflict and would throw further light on the issue of gender during the Irish revolution.

IV

Conclusions

Violence towards women was certainly a feature of the War of Independence, yet the evidence available indicates that it was limited in nature and scope, especially by contemporary European standards. The targeted killing of females was very rare. Most of the violence carried out against women by both the Crown forces and the IRA can be categorised as physical, gendered and psychological. Sexual violence took place but was rare; rape was not employed by either side as a common weapon of war.

This chapter has suggested some possible reasons for this. Both sides lacked opportunity, were possibly restrained by a level of military discipline or were constrained by contemporary societal norms. Their political masters or partners were aware of the significance of international opinion, and they themselves placed importance on ideals of democratic accountability. In regard to the IRA, the specific circumstances of its guerrilla campaign, including its reliance on the support of its community and the significant role played by women in the independence campaign, might be further explanations for the absence of this form of violence.

This chapter does not purport to be the definitive word on women's experience of violence during the revolution. Further research, as more archives are released, might yet challenge some of its conclusions about the nature and extent of such violence. The subject of this chapter is also an area where the documentary evidence might not tell the whole story. In dealing with a sensitive issue such as rape, there needs to be an awareness that women, especially in the context of early twentieth-century Ireland, were reticent about reporting it. The absence of a clear judicial authority to which it could be reported might also have affected our sense of how prevalent it was. Furthermore, one of the most important potential sources of evidence, the files of the Irish Free State's personal injuries compensation commission, do not appear to be extant.[83]

The possibility that the IRA played down evidence of sexual attacks on Irish women by the Crown forces because to admit such attacks had taken place might have reflected poorly upon republicans' ability to defend their women must be considered. However, in light of the way in which republican propaganda exploited instances of reprisals, and taking into account the allegations of assaults on women that were carried in the *Irish Bulletin*, it is more likely that republicans sought to publicise such incidents in order to embarrass the British rather than suppress them to protect either their own reputation as defenders of their community or the sensibilities of the victims.[84]

The aim of this chapter is to ignite a debate on violence and gender in the Irish revolution. The focus on sexual violence seeks not only to broaden the discussion of the experience of women in the Irish War of Independence, but also to take up Peter Hart's challenge to look at the revolution through the broader lens of gender. Seeking to explain why men did not employ rape as a weapon of war in the War of Independence is an important way of writing gender into Irish revolutionary historiography.[85]

THEN AND NOW!

THE SAME "SPOTTERS" WHO — IN 1920 — WERE HUNTING DOWN REPUBLICANS FOR BRITISH PAY

ARE STILL AT WORK — IN 1922 — HUNTING DOWN REPUBLICANS FOR FREE STATE PAY

ARE YOU ON THEIR SIDE?

'SPIES AND INFORMERS BEWARE...'

ANNE DOLAN

One night in March 1921 Bridget Walpole did not come home. While the nieces she lived with went about their daily business, shopping and fetching and carrying in Tralee, a small boy found her lying in a ditch in John Murphy's field. Bridget Walpole had been shot in the back of the head, thrown into a ditch, and left for dead 400 yards from her own front door. When the police arrived they examined the pool of blood she was found lying in, they noted the bullet hole through the folds of the shawl she was wearing on her head, they picked up the blue pencil thrown on top of her body, and they transcribed the words that were on the piece of paper tied around her neck: 'Convicted spy, and all others beware. RIP.'[1] The court of inquiry which investigated Bridget Walpole's death assumed they had another case of a now familiar type. She seemed like the others who were taken from their homes, often in the middle of the night, often to be found in the mornings at the side of a road, or in the corner of a field, or in a shallow grave, often found with a crudely fashioned label, sometimes blindfolded, sometimes with their hands and feet bound, sometimes with Rosary beads clutched in a dying grasp. By June 1921 the clerk who filed the records of the courts of inquiry that had replaced traditional inquests under the Restoration of Order in Ireland Act, 1920 was simply writing 'usual spy notices on body', such was how 'usual' this kind of death had become.[2] But when District Inspector Thomas Reilly began to give his evidence at the court of inquiry into her death, it quickly became clear that Bridget Walpole's was not a 'usual' death. He mentioned a life assurance policy, he spoke of some 'friction' having 'recently arisen in the house between herself and the other inmates', he knew of no reason why the IRA would want to execute this woman in this way. He believed that the label had been placed round her neck 'to avert suspicion from the real culprit or culprits'.[3]

There were many things that might have aroused the District Inspector's suspicions – inconsistent evidence about dates and times, a niece not even stopping to look at the body before rushing back to Tralee for food for the funeral, the failure to notify the police for a whole day after the death. But there was one other reason. So much had been very correctly done – the bullet to the back of the head, the label around the neck, even the choice of a blue pencil, a colour reported to have been used in other cases. There was just something wrong with the words. 'Convicted spy, and all others beware' – that part was fine, 'usual', familiar. Ending the message with 'RIP', with 'Requiescat in pace', was not. The Irish Republican Army signed almost every label it left on the men and women it had 'convicted' of spying or informing with its own acronym. Even the labels supposedly left by Crown forces to incriminate, to imply IRA involvement, closely copied the words; the label was only a poor insinuation if it did not name the organisation to be blamed.[4] The label's function was, after all, to warn all those who read not to do what the dead had done, to behold the nature of revenge, the indignity of death on the roadside in the half nakedness of the night, to behold the threat, the menace, the very terror of the words themselves, the hidden hand behind the very letters I, R, A. The IRA did not implore that its victims rest in peace, and it certainly made no pious entreaties for the men and women it chose to kill in this way. For generations Irish nationalists had called down all manner of imprecations on the head of the 'spy' and the 'informer'; a restful eternal repose was rare among them.[5] So the RIP was simply a sentiment out of place.

Despite this mistake, no one seems to have been charged with the murder of Bridget Walpole; hers was just one violent death in the midst of so many other violent deaths, over 1,000 by this stage since the IRA's war for independence began in January 1919, just one of over 2,000 killed before its end, two and a half years later in July 1921.[6] The best place to hide a murder, if Agatha Christie is to be believed, is among a lot of other murders.[7] And so, someone may have got away with murder in Kerry in 1921.

Bridget Walpole's murder might say much of the hatreds and frustrations and jealousies District Inspector Reilly suspected of life in that house. But Bridget Walpole's death, the manner and the nature and the way of it, says something more. She might have been beaten or bludgeoned, smothered or stabbed, but these deaths could not be passed off so readily as the work of the IRA. To hide her murder among all the others, it had to look precisely like them. It had to follow the by now established pattern, appropriate the disappearance, the wounds, the label, the indignities. She had to be killed in a way that could only be recognised as an IRA execution. And so her death suggests that there was a pattern to follow, that by this point there were certain acts of violence that denoted certain things, a language of violence, almost, that was there to be read through the nature of wounds, just as it was there to be read on the crude label tied round Mrs Walpole's neck. In the act of imitation, in the attempt but perhaps more in the failure to deceive, Bridget Walpole's killers confirmed that the bodies of the dead have something to tell us about the nature of Ireland's revolutionary violence.

This chapter does not intend to prove or disprove, name or shame or declaim those who were or were not the 'spies' and 'informers' of Ireland's revolution. This kind of proving and disproving has been undertaken before; it will go on being part of the questions that need to be asked about sectarianism, about local grievances and suspicions and old animosities and how much they shaped the violence of this time.[8] It will no doubt go on, particularly as more and more evidence is picked over and revealed. The concern here is not with guilt or innocence, not with proving one death more terrible than another, not with raking over the proofs whether real or circumstantial, even invented or imagined. Suspicion comes more readily than trust; a name on a blacklist is more willingly written than erased; and procedures for dealing with suspected spies – rules and regulations, requisite proofs and approvals from a Brigade Commandant – are more likely overlooked as suspicion grows, as the threats seem to increase, as spies and informers can be seen in every staring face and treason heard in every whispered word, when the violence moves with a more desperate momentum towards its end.[9]

One Cumann na mBan organiser, Brighid O'Mullane, proves how easily this kind of suspicion came. New to Naas, she was quickly thought to be the 'woman spy' rumoured to be operating in Co. Kildare. When warned by an IRA man that she was in danger she insisted that she 'could explain everything at my court-martial' and volunteered to be held under arrest while proof was sought at Cumann na mBan headquarters in Dublin.[10] She was rather taken aback when the 'young man' who claimed to have 'been present at the meeting at which my death was decreed' admitted 'Oh! There is to be no courtmartial, nor will the fellows show themselves. They have decided to crouch behind the ditch near the bridge with only the rifle barrels protruding.'[11] She learned that instead of procedure, due process, she was just 'to get a volley from each side of the road which would riddle me with shot; and the label, "Spy", was already prepared to be attached to my body after death, while they made a getaway.'[12] She decided to heed the warning and fled from Kildare. While it is possible to say that fear invites these kinds of mistakes, that rules were broken, that here was the intention to shoot a woman even though General Headquarters (GHQ) prohibited the shooting of women spies, this example is just to suggest how easily the label 'spy' was to come by, how simple it was to meet this kind of end.[13] The competition of evidence, of 'right' and 'wrong', is not to be played out here. 'Guilty' or 'innocent' by whosoever's measure or morality, the bodies themselves have other things to say – what was the nature of a 'spy's' or an 'informer's' death, what did it say to those who found the body, to those who lived nearby, to those who read of it in the next day's news, who read in the deliberate choosing of one person and not another a different kind of death than the innocent caught in the crossfire, than the prisoner shot while trying to escape, than the unlucky taken in anger or reprisal or revenge? What did this kind of death ask of those who had to carry out the deed? What can be read in this particular kind of dead body – the labelled 'informer' or 'spy'?

The executed, or the punished, even the assassinated, only account for a limited number of the dead, yet somehow these particular dead seem to cast quite a long shadow over IRA violence during the War of Independence. This might be explained by the emphasis placed on the importance of the 'intelligence war', on the sense that the lessons of the past had been learned, that spies and informers were not to be allowed infiltrate the movement, that 'to paralyze the British machine it was necessary to strike at individuals. Without her spies England was helpless.'[14] For others 'spies' had to be spies to justify what had been done. This fits a narrative that casts Michael Collins as an uncomplicated winner of the intelligence contest. It is not so often noted that the labelled bodies continued to be found during the Civil War; that even a cursory look finds the body of John Powell discovered near Nenagh, Co. Tipperary in November 1922, with bullet wounds in his head and body, and with a label pinned to his clothes warning 'Spies and informers beware – IRA';[15] that it finds Ben McCarthy, a 16-year-old taken at 4.00 a.m. from his home at Ardagh, near Bantry, Co. Cork in March 1923, and left dead with the label 'Convicted spy. Shot as a reprisal for our comrades who were executed during the week', shot even though General Order no. 12, issued by the anti-Treaty IRA in November 1922, insisted that 'boys under 18' were not to be killed.[16] 'Spies and informers, beware. Your brother and sister will meet with the same fate if they are not careful' was the message found on John Melvin's body near Ballina, Co. Mayo in April 1923.[17] Indeed, a case in Kingstown District Court in October 1924 suggests a longer legacy still. Michael Dalton alleged two men had threatened and assaulted him. He testified that William Peggs and Francis Murray came to his home, ordered him outside, where he heard them say they were going to 'label him', that 'his body would be got in the Park', that 'he must be done in tonight'.[18] As late as September 1948 Margaret D'Arcy Daly wrote to James Everett, then Minister for Posts and Telegraphs in the first Inter-Party government, to complain about the appointment of a postman to her hometown, Cooraclare, Co. Clare. He was, she claimed, one of the men who had killed her brother Patrick in June 1921 and left him with the label of a spy.[19] The labelled 'spy' and 'informer' could cast an even greater shadow than has yet to be conceived.

Yet these particular dead dominated enough in 1920–1 to be imitated, to be copied by those trying to implicate the IRA, to be described as 'usual', to be the subject of parliamentary questions, to be the fascination of the *Morning Post* and several other English newspapers.[20] They added to, encouraged, the impression that terror was abroad, that murder in Ireland needed to be stamped out, 'grasped by the throat' as Lloyd George quite graphically put it.[21] And here it has to be borne in mind what this kind of death asked of those who killed. Even accepting the unpredictable nature of guerrilla warfare, the nature of the violence set these deaths apart. In this kind of death there is none of the anonymity of the chance encounter or the planned ambush, where combatants were maybe separated by a couple of hundred yards, where those firing back were burdened with no more detail than that they were soldiers or police, or just someone in a uniform, where perhaps across fields the dead or the dying may never have even been seen to fall. There was none of the distance between the sniper on a Belfast roof and the unseen face that just stopped moving on the street below; there was none of the uncertainty of a bomb thrown that had to wait for the next day's newspaper to be certain of the damage done. Rather this kind of execution was a violence that began in seeking and gathering and listening for information, in finding out where a person lived, in watching their movements, in knowing the times when they rose in the mornings and lay down at night, in looking into their wife's or their mother's or their children's faces while they took them away, in holding them still as they bound their wrists or put a blindfold across their eyes, in shooting them through their prayers or their pleas or their silence, in standing over them in the darkness and knowing how deliberately death had come. It was not war's traditional violence and it was not meant to be. It was to be understood as punishment, as intimidation. It was reserved for those who were to be killed as an example and thought of as spy. It was to frighten beyond its own reach, to shift all sense of what could be conceived as war, choosing kitchens and bedrooms, churches and graveyards and fields and turning them into uneven battlefields, where the enemy was alone and unarmed and even half dressed. It replaced an army of recruits and volunteers and conscripts and fought farmers and teachers and shoemakers and labourers one by one instead. It sent combatants in civilian clothes, it came in the night and took men and women, pensioners and teenagers, Protestants and Catholics, ex-soldiers and ex-IRA alike; it acted on the word of rumour and suspicion, it killed to punish and to pre-empt, and it made terror its own type of war.

Isolating this type of violence, the methods used in these deaths, suggests that there are patterns there to be read. There are similarities in the wounds, in the one or two or three shots to the head, in the numerous bullets fired into the chest and abdomen, in the repeated random firing at legs and arms and necks and groins, in the oftenness of frenzied firing when perhaps a tied and bound victim meant there was no apparent need. For a force that had such constant and complained-of difficulty in arming itself, where in some areas it sent men into ambushes with an allocation of no more than six bullets each, the ammunition it was prepared to expend on killing these 'convicted' one person at a time, is worthy of remark in itself.[22] But what is most common in these deaths is the one bullet or several bullets to the head and face. Depending on how far one wishes to read the wounds, this repetition can be interpreted as an attempt to obliterate the identity of the 'tried and executed' spy. To remove the trace of them, to make them foul in death to all who beheld them, to make mourners shiver at the sight of what might be done to them in turn, to cause a body to be waked in a closed coffin because it was too damaged for the grieving to look upon. It is clear from even a small sample that there did seem to be an anxiety or an intention to attack and disfigure the face and head. Hugh Duffy, an army pensioner and 'loyal citizen' from Monaghan, was shot in April 1921 in the chest, the shoulder and through the chin, but his head was also beaten with a blunt and heavy instrument even though the gun shots were quite enough to ensure that he was dead.[23] An unknown man, found in Mullingar, Co. Westmeath in July 1921, was similarly bludgeoned before the shot of a flat-nosed bullet to the head made sure that he remained unknown.[24] Martin Scanlon's skull was 'smashed' in front and behind; William Good the same.[25] William Elliott was shot in the face as well as through the chest, the groin, twice in the back, through the neck and also through the back of the head.[26] Kate Carroll and Michael Coen were shot in the face in addition to a long list of other wounds that would most certainly have caused their deaths.[27]

There are other intentions to be read in the wounds if so desired. Writings on the case of the Pearson family in Co. Offaly have chosen to regard the targeting of the genitalia as symbolic of the desire to cast out the Protestants from the land, seed, breed and generation.[28] Alternatively, all of this might be just trying a little too hard, looking for patterns in what was just panic or enthusiasm or inaccuracy or practicality from the killer's point of view. For every studied significance attributed there are a number of equally plausible and simple explanations. Bludgeoning the head was perhaps a way to stop the struggling, and the shouting, and the noise, and the running away. It might have been just a way to quieten the victim, to make it easier for those who had never shot or killed before to summon up the will to shoot. It might be just the mark of the man who maybe had no weapon of his own; who, wanting to be part of it, of the enthusiasm of it, of the boasting of it later, simply picked up the nearest and the deadliest thing to hand and took his part. The five, six, seven or eight bullet wounds might be an expression of hatred or untempered vengeance. They might also suggest that these men were poor shots, not sure where to shoot, firing again and again because they could not trust poor weapons and, for some, home made ammunition, because they had heard or read in the newspapers that one or two or three wounds had not been enough to kill.

This was quite a different demand to what might have begun as drilling to the tune of old fashioned army manuals, or joining because your pals had joined, or because in a quiet townland it seemed like something to do. When training amounted to maybe getting to watch someone else fire a weapon in anger possibly once before, there was scant preparation for this kind of work, not enough to prevent shaking hands or erratic shots or wounds in parts of the body that would never kill. For others it might well have been down to zeal and enthusiasm and just warming to the task; firing again and again because it might be the only engagement of their war, their one chance to have a war to retell. For others still there may have been power and fear and curiosity in death; the making of a reputation, the creation of a persona that changed the boy previously playing at war in the fields into a force to be feared and reckoned with instead. In turn, the excess of bullets may have made it seem like a proper firing squad, where each man fired, and one performed the coup de grâce, making it resemble the official, something sanctioned – as the label also said, an act of war authorised by a legitimate power, the sentence of a court-martial and not an act of murder by maybe masked men, fumbling and furtive, in a field in the dark. The wounds simply give themselves to too many explanations to hang anything too significant upon them; elaborate constructions or interpretations should only be suggestions instead.

Indeed, it is not the wounds themselves which make these bodies different, which alter the sense or the atmosphere of war. Recounting these wounds is no more or less terrible than recounting the wounds of say the Auxiliary cadets killed by the IRA at Kilmichael, or the men, women and children fired upon at a football match in Croke Park by Crown forces in November 1920. The blood and the sights and the senses are filled just the same. It is only in placing these bodies back into their fuller contexts, into the set of circumstances where it is clear that etiquettes of war have been breached and disregarded and undone, that one can begin to understand why this particular violence, these self-styled executions, had such a disproportionate effect. It explains why Ireland, with its comparatively low death toll, could cause such anxiety and concern, such discomfort in Westminster and Whitehall, why it could be considered such a bad example to the difficult and determined corners of the Empire, why it just simply would not do to have a war of 'savage tribes' conducted on the doorstep, a war of 'savages' that threatened to come far more disquietingly close to home than many of His Majesty's ministers may have realised.[29] These bodies reveal more than their wounds and it is perhaps for that reason that they remain a source of concern and, for some, a source of shame, why so much of the historiography has torn itself apart justifying the rightness or the wrongness of these particular deaths, why they can be read as the brutal cost of revolution or the impetus to rewrite a noble narrative as nothing more than a sordid, vicious squabble amongst ourselves.[30]

What this chapter has been trying to say in a particularly roundabout way, is that these deaths cannot be separated from the way they were and were meant to be read and interpreted, from the significance of an almost ritualised sequence of acts that set these deaths somehow apart. This killing cannot be isolated from the panic and the fear, from the foreboding of what was to come. To be understood as it was perhaps conceived, it needs to be set against the screams and the struggles of wives and elderly fathers and squealing children, it needs to be felt in the long drawn out hours waiting for the taken to come home, or to be heard in the shouts or cries or shots that confirmed they were gone, felt in the waiting hours or days for a body to be found, and hoping still that the body was not the father, husband or brother gone. It is to be seen then in the living after, in the consequences of that type of death, labelled as the wife or father or child of the 'spy' as sure as if the label on the body was tied around each of their own necks, isolated by a community that had no wish to be visited by the same fate.

Ranging across a sequence of inquests, through the evidence of eye-witnesses and doctors and police, certain repetitions begin to be revealed.[31] There are patterns of how this violence works; there are the disturbing associations of the strange and the familiar, building up to the moment of violence, and in themselves an integral part of how this violence terrifies, of how terror works. The sound of a knock echoing through a house in the middle of the night seems to be the place where most witnesses begin. It was a sound that tolled all sorts of dangers – raids for arms, demands for food or shelter, the coming of Crown forces in their many forms, the spectre of Black and Tans 'firing their rifles, and frightening our wives and daughters, murdering ...' in the middle of the night.[32] But there is a constant repetition of this sound in the recounting of these particular deaths. Mary Ann Cunningham remembered being woken at close to 3.00 a.m.:

> I saw two men who were masked pass my bedroom window and afterwards heard a knock at the door ... I went to the door, opened it and saw 4 masked men who told me not to get excited they only wanted to talk to my husband ... I was kept inside my house. I then heard three shots and then went out and found my husband lying on the ground about 20 yards from the door ... My husband died in my presence about 10 minutes later without speaking ... He had no enemies that I know of.[33]

That gap between seeing them and hoping the knock would not come, hoping her house would be passed over for another, is found again and again as mothers and sisters and wives repeatedly answered doors, maybe in the hope that their presence might make men hesitate or delay or change their minds. In many respects this opening the door, this letting them in when every instinct must have fought against it, makes little sense. Maybe there was too little time for makeshift barricades, too little time, too little space or opportunity to hide everyone inside; no point perhaps when it might be assumed or imagined that the house was surrounded, that the best hope was to obey, to do what was asked in the hope that the worst would be postponed until another night. Maybe it just suggests that there was no suspicion, no inclination as to what the knocking might bring.

The distress was the same regardless of which side came calling. Mary Cosgrove's husband, John, was taken and killed in the night, probably as a reprisal for two men killed by the IRA in Camlough, Co. Armagh in early June 1921.[34] She recounted the men's pity for her when she insisted that her husband could not go where they were taking him without his socks and boots; the reassurance of 'it's alright', of allowing him to 'bid me goodbye', a deception just as disquieting as the injuries Phillip Dunne's mother suffered as she struggled with the IRA to keep hold of her son.[35] These reassurances were more unsettling still when Mary Cosgrove was not allowed leave the house to follow her husband; it was only ever false hope that he might come back. Thomas Byrne's mother was told not to bother putting his scarf on because he had no need for it where he was going. She stated that the men who came asked her to point out her son's room, shot him on the spot and then asked had she any other sons.[36] She was put in the position, like many others, of having to give her son away. While most of the IRA are recorded in the courts of inquiry accounts as trying to keep the families away, stop them following, stop them from seeing and identifying who fired the shots, in some instances there was less concern: Kate Donovan watched the men who came, apparently to ask her husband about life insurance: 'I turned to call my husband and was pulled between the two men. I saw one of them put a pistol close to my husband's face and fire.'[37] Bridget Gilligan was held back at gunpoint and heard one man whistling as he walked away from the body of her husband left behind.[38]

Men with masks, men with blackened faces, men with goggles, with hats pulled down over their eyes, strangers with strange voices coming in the night, are the figures that populate this testimony. The trench coats that made them blend in with most other men during the day became a sinister kind of uniform at night. As the months of this kind of death went on, witnesses started to stop recognising faces, stop noticing details, stop, in some incidences, giving evidence at all. A court of inquiry commented on the witness Edward Elliott, that 'he probably knows more than he will tell, but considers that the same fate as that of his brother awaits him if he gives further evidence.'[39] His brother, William Elliott, had been found dead in a bog, his body telling he was kneeling, his clasped hands saying his prayers. The message of this death, as was intended, had not been wasted on Edward Elliott, even if the court of inquiry could not appreciate the point. Thomas Coen only went out to look for his brother at 6.00 a.m. admitting that 'I was frightened to' go out any time before.[40] The delay, not telling, not going out straight after the shot had been heard to find the body, resisting that temptation even though every impulse must have been stirred to run, to help, to bring home the dying or the dead, suggests how this kind of death worked, how it policed small communities, how it bred an instinct to look the other way, to shun the dead, to forsake any small kindness in case kindness was construed as complicity, in case kindness courted the same fate.

As these deaths continued and increased people were schooled quickly in its etiquettes and retreated further and further from the dead. Francis Caulfield claimed that the men who found his cousin Kate Carroll were afraid to carry her home, 'afraid of being shot if they moved the body'.[41] Indeed, the bodies seemed to become increasingly untouchable. Ellen Byrne stated that 'none of the neighbours came to condole because I suppose they are afraid of the Sinn Féiners. I had to get the police to help to put my son in his coffin.'[42] A Dr O'Driscoll in Timoleague, Co. Cork refused to come to see the body of John Good when he was shot in March 1921. He admitted bluntly that he was 'afraid to do so'.[43] The Royal College of Surgeons in Ireland confirmed that 'it is contrary to the traditions and instincts of the Profession to refuse aid to a seriously injured man on the grounds of personal fear', but but General Macready, the General Officer Commanding the British Army in Ireland, just accepted it as a natural consequence of what he referred to as 'the terror caused by gunmen' in Ireland.[44] Bridget Daly explained 'I went to my cousin's house, David Daly, and asked him to come with me to bring back my brother's body. He would not go. He said he was too much afraid.'[45] In this simple way Bridget Daly explained how this violence was intended to work, the atmosphere it created, and to an extent, why so relatively few had to be killed for the lesson to be learned.

This emphasis on time, or rather on how long it took the body to be found, was part of the other message of this kind of death. The repetition in newspaper reports of how long the body was left lying in a ditch or in a field or on the side of the road was part of the indignity to be taken from this death. Cast aside on the road, and 'the public road' at that, it drew out the humiliation of being left to die like the beasts in the field, a cast-out, brutish and unwanted thing.[46] Though most were found within hours, or at least found the next morning, some like John Sheehan, missing for 16 days, could only be identified by his prominent teeth and his ill-matched clothes.[47] The unknowns, the men missing so long that they could not be identified, were the anonymous witnesses to the indignity of this kind of death, to the time suffered without the relief of a Christian burial. The body also revealed other indignities. John Doran, who died without his trousers, and Thomas Walker, who died in his bare feet, were not even permitted to meet their maker fully clad; both ragged half-ready examples of men rushed to their deaths.[48] The blindfolds, hiding their eyes from their fate, but also saving their executioners from their stares, were, like the bonds on the wrists or ankles, further markers of a prisoner's death; men knew as they went to their death that whether the charge was true or not, these accoutrements of execution would always belie the facts. The same was true of the labels, the crudely written condemnations that tried to convey that an official process had been observed, that a verdict had been handed down, that this was the will of an

IRA court. 'Spies, Traitors, Informers associate with military, police and Black and Tans in Kanurk, You are all listed. Beware. IRA', was the quite elaborate message pinned to John Sheehan;[49] 'Spies and informers this is your fate. IRA', was the more direct warning left on John Wymes.[50] The label left on John Fitzgerald, spotted with his blood, shows that it was pinned to him before he was shot, that he went to his death knowing that he had been labelled in this way, knowing that this insult and indignity was to be added to the injury that his family would endure.[51] With the words written on the back of a flattened cigarette packet, the familiar was again called upon to do its macabre work.

These same accoutrements of execution – the blindfold, the bonds, the pinning or placing of the label, the shots fired at close range, the singed clothes, the beaten, bludgeoned, broken faces – suggest a physical closeness that can only begin to imply what this kind of death meant for those who killed. To bind hands or feet, to write a label, to bring a pin and pin the label on while all the time feeling the panic and the fear that throbbed beneath the coat or the shirt between their fingers; all the time close to the sights and the sounds, the sensations of execution, the sensation of dragging a woman out by the hair, of fighting off the scratching and the struggling, the sensation of tears and prayers and pleading, the sensation of silence, of resignation, the surprise of nothing said at all. There are remnants of these men's nervousness left behind: a first label written and left aside, ruined by a mistake or a slip of the hand, cast aside perhaps for a more impressive formulation of the words.[52] There are maybe more obvious remnants of callousness found in the explicit crafting of this kind of death, in learning its ways, in elaborating on its pattern, in knowing what to say, what to write on the label, where to leave the body so that it would most certainly be found. John Cathcart was killed in Youghal, Co. Cork, in March 1921: a piece of paper was left by his body inscribed with 'Convicted spy, spies and informers beware, IRA'. It was reported that 'a board bearing the inscription "Revenge" was put on a tree' in his garden after his death.[53] This was Youghal's own elaboration of the method, a further message, if one was needed, to all who passed by that house not to do as Mr Cathcart had done. Rumour of one of Roscommon's variations reached the *Manchester Guardian*: after John McGawley's body was labelled 'Convicted spy. Tried by IRA' and left by a trench in the road with another dead man, Martin Scanlon, McGawley's daughter was said to have been left hanging by her hair from the church railings in the town.[54] The *Manchester Guardian* was largely sympathetic to Ireland's case, but it openly reported these breaches of what it considered war.

There are signs, though, of an enthusiasm for this kind of death; it took on a greater urgency with time, a perhaps understandable and encouraged urgency, when GHQ prompted all IRA battalions to make lists, to report all loose talk, when it kept asking 'who do you suspect as enemy SPY AGENTS in your area?'[55]

The constant reminders to be vigilant possibly granted a licence to see spies at every turn. By the end of July 1921 the East Limerick Brigade was regretting the stop the Truce had put to its gallop – 'One spy was shot lately. A few others would have met [the] same fate were it not for truce.'[56] 'Spies are too numerous to mention' was simply the report from Carlow in October 1922.[57] In some places killing 'spies' was used as a type of discipline within the IRA: 'These actions had the effect of keeping "our own weak ones" right. We had South Monaghan safe.'[58] General Orders made rules about spies for the very reason that regulation was needed, and GHQ continued to insist on those orders being kept because they clearly continued to be broken and breached. Rules were one thing in the abstract, up in Dublin in GHQ; they were quite another in small places where every stranger was suspicious, where violence kept time with local fears and grievances regardless of the pace Headquarters tried to set. The Chief of Staff, Richard Mulcahy, wrote to Kilkenny in June 1921 that 'it is a very serious matter that a junior Officer should take upon himself the responsibility for executing two alleged spies.' He reminded Kilkenny that the 'Brigade Commandant's authority is necessary before a spy can be executed. There must be no slacking with regard to this Order.'[59] By July 1921 he had to ask the Adjutant General to send 'South Wexford a copy of the General Orders up to [no.] 16 or they will be shooting a Woman Spy on us; or something else'.[60] The case of the 16-year-old Ben McCarthy, cited above, is further proof that this enthusiasm continued to break the rules through the Civil War as well. And it was an enthusiasm that continued to be expressed in IRA pension applications in the decades beyond. Seán Mac Eoin's papers contain details of many of the IRA pension applications of men from his battalion and brigade area. 'Assisted in capture & execution of enemy spy', 'was at the execution of spies', 'I was at the arresting of a spy', 'I took part in the ex of (a spy) (the fellow with 9 lives)', 'Did you execute [a] spy? Yes' – suggests that it was cited as certain proof of service, that something notable had been done.[61]

Yet this simple, straight retelling for a pension application is quite at odds with what can be read in the additions and adaptations made to those patterns of death in 1920–1. The variations made imply a number of things, not least the fears and nervousness and the ways and means needed to bring a group of men to the point of committing this kind of act. Patterns of behaviour can be seen, some more or less complex. It is easy to note that a lot of these kinds of deaths took place in the middle of the night, and also that a lot of those nights seemed to be Fridays or Saturdays, weekend nights when it was maybe easier to assemble a larger group, when they had a bit more freedom to be out later, when they had maybe money or opportunity enough at the end of the week for the Dutch courage necessary to carry it through. These things can be read and misread at length. What is less often cited or said is what this kind of death left behind. John L. O'Sullivan recalled in later life the part he played in the death of two members of the Essex Regiment in Cork. Along with his brother he was told to dig them a grave. When the brothers went home for a pick and shovel their mother stopped them to say 'don't ever do anything you'll be sorry for.' He continued: 'I can remember the weight of this thing on our minds as we were walking down the road ... Finally, I said to my brother, "We'll have to get it postponed".' The punishment for delaying the execution 'was that my brother and myself were appointed to the firing squad ... The revulsion of taking a human life goes very deep in a person, if he's been reared in a family.'[62] O'Sullivan's views on the influence of family life aside, that revulsion has to be balanced with the details of these executed dead.

But there was a different kind of revulsion read in these deaths by many at the time. They were meant to terrify, otherwise the dead would simply have disappeared: no labels, no details, no bodies on 'the public road' begging for their story to be told and retold at length. The English journalist Wilfrid Ewart's first thought when he was questioned by a group of IRA men on the road from Kilcormac to Tullamore, Co. Offaly was of 'the number of people who had lately been found in bogs with brief notes attached to them'.[63] His fear was a learned one, bred of rumours and newspaper reports, of the sensational and the sensationalised. He had imbibed the language of a certain type of violence and understood precisely what a stranger to rural Ireland had cause to fear in 1920 and particularly in 1921.

The terror of this kind of death was also heightened by its frequency or by its repetition, but also when more than one body was found in this way. Brothers were killed together: the Skeltons in Wexford;[64] the Watters, possibly killed by the IRA, possibly by the Crown forces, in Dundalk;[65] John and then William Good, father and then son, in the same month in Cork;[66] Patrick Sheehan in Limerick together with the 17-year-old boy who worked with him delivering coal;[67] two men on the same night in Ballinalee, Co. Longford, one at 12.30 a.m., the other at 2.00 a.m.;[68] John Wymes and John Gilligan, left either side of a trench in a road near Loughglinn, Co. Roscommon;[69] the Waldron brothers killed together, near the same place, Loughglinn, just three months after Gilligan and Wymes.[70] Loughglinn and Ballinalee were small places for so much death in one or two nights, small enough places for the dead to be more than just names in some solemn newspaper report. They were small enough to know all the reasons why the dead had died.

The executed were killed for reasons real or imagined: for being too loyal, too friendly with the police, too keen to help, for feeding the RIC when they had been told to stop, for reporting a raid, for living above a room where Sinn Féin meetings were held and just possibly letting the police know, for being rumoured to be in the Auxiliaries, for being new to a town and asking too many questions and maybe trying to spy. In the case of the Watters brothers, the court of inquiry believed it was because 'they were assigned duties by the IRA which they failed to carry out'; for John Buckley the inquiry surmised that 'since his marriage which took place a few months ago he had not been attending night operations' with the Soloheadbeg IRA.[71] The IRA believed he had been killed by police in plain clothes.[72] Whether aged 17 or 71, whether staunch loyalist or wavering Irish republican, whether dissenting or just diverted by a new wife, this was the violence of punishment and bad example. It was the violence of quieter places, where houses were more isolated, where men and women could be taken in the night and the taking unlikely to be interrupted or disturbed, where it was easier to disappear without the observances of passers-by, where curfew could be evaded, where Crown forces were less likely to be driving by. By contrast, the suspected spy William Doran was shot in the foyer of the Wicklow Hotel in Dublin, but there was no time to take him and tie him up and label him; just enough time to shoot him and run back into the cover of the crowded streets outside.[73] Unlike Doran's death, this was possibly the violence of smaller places, shaped by towns and villages where strangers were noticed and suspected, where old rivalries and jealousies mixed with new politics bred dangerous suspicions. The Waldron brothers of Loughglinn were killed over a mixture of things, over land, over inheritance, over a dowry and, as the British military officer in the area suspected, because 'they lived in a district where practically every man is a Sinn Fein' and they were not.[74] They lived in a place where the whispered retelling of a death like theirs had more power to terrify because it could be whispered and everyone knew who was being whispered about. This was a violence that took root in counties that could not be stirred to fight in many other ways just as much as it thrived in the most violent county, Cork; it was found in places that had little or no IRA activity, but somehow seemed always to suspect a surfeit of 'spies' and boasted men ready and willing to get rid of them. It shocked because it could be so intimate and so local; it was resorted to because in smaller places the lesson was more quickly learned, with village certainties quicker to adapt, with curtains twitching swiftly closed when the knock came to a neighbour's door.

At the inquiry into William Charters's death the Reverend Henry Johnston of Ballinalee, Co. Longford 'asked for permission to address the Court'. 'He stated that the whole of the loyalists in that Area were living in a state of terror, as the Sinn Feiners did what they liked at night.' He asked for some more police; he was afraid because murder had 'been committed in the midst of his parish and it might be anyone's turn next'.[75] When the labelled body of Crosby Boyle was found on the 'public road' near Killusty, Co. Tipperary, 'much alarm prevailed' in the village, 'several people left their houses, while others removed their furniture.'[76] After Kate Carroll's death in Monaghan in April 1921, the House of Commons heard that 'the murder had caused a feeling of terror in the district.'[77] From the IRA's perspective this is precisely how Reverend Johnston, how the people of Killusty, how the MPs in the House of Commons were supposed to feel; this is what this violence, what this kind of death was supposed to do. It reinforced divisions, it isolated communities, it bred the fear of being taken from your bed by masked men in the night to be found dead in a ditch with the mark of a spy.

republican movement 30 gardiner place, dublin

LIAM MELLOWES

A GREAT FENIAN WHO SAW THE POOR AS THE FREEDOM FORCE OF THE NATION ; AS TONE DID.

SHOT BY FIRING SQUAD, MOUNTJOY JAIL,   DEC. 8. 1922

9

'HAVE WE BEEN PLAYING AT REPUBLICANISM?':
The Treaty, the Pact Election and the Civil War in Co. Galway[1]

ÚNA NEWELL

I

The Treaty

In January 1922, a visiting correspondent for the London *Times* wrote:

> I have talked with many inhabitants of Galway, and they all look to a revival of the industries of the city – jute mills, flour mills and other industries – which aforetime promised a reign of prosperity for the West of Ireland. The vision is bright with promise, and it is not surprising that most of the people of the county desire to see the establishment of peace and the opportunity for development.[2]

Yet the approval of the Anglo-Irish Treaty met with little of the boisterous enthusiasm which normally marked local political events.[3] The Republic seemed lost in the small print and among the people a pressing mood of relief rather than triumph greeted the endorsement of the Treaty by the Dáil. An editorial in the *Connacht Tribune* on 4 February 1922 asked 'where are the rejoicings and the jubilations of a liberty-loving and impulsive race which has regained its freedom after seven-and-a-half centuries of bondage? As far as can be judged, they are entirely absent.'[4] The *East Galway Democrat* noted 'an entire absence of anything like jubilation', but acknowledged that 'nobody would doubt that all were relieved that the great strain was over at last, and the issue decided formally.'[5]

In the Dáil, the seven Galway deputies voted four to three in favour of the Treaty settlement. Patrick Hogan, Padraig Ó Máille, George Nicholls and Joseph Whelehan voted in favour of its ratification. Liam Mellows, Frank Fahy and Brian Cusack voted against it. However, this division is somewhat deceptive. When the Treaty was first published Joseph Whelehan[6] acknowledged that he 'was rather more or less against it', but knowing that his actions would misrepresent

173

his local (North Galway) Sinn Féin executive, he felt 'bound to stand for the Treaty'.[7] Had he not done so, Galway would have returned a verdict of four to three against the agreement. Of the three anti-Treaty deputies, Mellows[8] dismissed it out of hand; Cusack,[9] like many of his republican colleagues, stressed the inviolability of his oath to the Republic; and Fahy[10] put it to his colleagues, 'is not the declaration of the Republic ... *a fait accompli*, or have we been playing at Republicanism?'[11]

It is of course, as J. J. Lee and more recently John M. Regan have argued, too simplistic to paint all pro-Treaty supporters as instinctive democrats and all anti-Treaty supporters as instinctive autocrats.[12] To cast the Treaty debate as a battle between the pragmatists and the idealists is equally unfair. We can certainly argue that Michael Collins was pragmatic in signing the Treaty, but it is difficult to argue that he was not also an idealist. There was a mix of moderates and radicals on both sides, and it was precisely because the split was not so clear-cut that it became so divisive. The Treaty was fought over many things. Broadly speaking – and even this may be an over-simplification – the debate was fought over the oath of allegiance (more accurately an oath of fidelity) to the Crown, the Republic, and essentially over power. It was not fought over class or partition. Cyclically, the same questions were rehearsed over and over on the floor of the Dáil. Was the Treaty an abandonment of the Republic, or did it contain the seeds of further development? Was there ever to be a 'living Irish nation', was Ireland always going to be 'the dead past or the prophetic future', to use Arthur Griffith's phrase, or indeed, had the Treatyites, as Éamon de Valera later maintained, abandoned their journey across the desert on catching their first glimpse of an oasis, when paradise may have been just over the horizon?[13] This notion that, if they stopped, the people might get comfortable and they might never regain their momentum was repeated °over and over in the speeches on both sides of the House. For Patrick Hogan[14] (pro-Treaty), the Treaty was not a final settlement – the words 'forever' and 'permanent', he maintained, 'are words that should not be used in connection with the Treaty'.[15] But Frank Fahy (anti-Treaty), while accepting that the stepping stone theory was comprehensible, feared that 'this road under other guides may also lead rapidly to the sacrifice of principles to the Imperial idea, to smug prosperity, and obese content.'[16] Writing in *An Saorstát* a few months later, Griffith attempted to counter such criticisms:

> Certain well-fed people have expressed a fear that if the body of Ireland be well nourished the soul of Ireland may get gross. Let them be reassured, the children of the Irish farmer, the children of the Irish artisan, the children of the Irish labourer will not love Ireland the less if they get butter and jam on their bread ... The Irish poor will not cease to be true to their love of Ireland when the Irish Free State has abolished pauperism and provided them with [the] means of [a] decent livelihood.[17]

The difficulty was that up until this point, the meaning of 'the Republic' had never really been specifically clarified. The time-honoured demand was for independence but it was clear that the Republic meant different things to different people.[18] Was it to be a Gaelic Republic, a Workers' Republic, an all-Ireland Republic, an externally-associated Republic? The definition was clouded in ambiguity. In 1918, the general election was fought on the basis of self-determination; in 1921 it was fought for the continuance of a republican government, but Irish statesmen had at no time shown an inclination to be meticulous about defining what the words the 'Irish Republic' actually meant. The form in which independence should clothe itself was secondary to its actual attainment. The Republic was as much a rallying-cry as it was something tangible. The Treaty forced a debate on what form Irish independence would now take and the cracks began to show openly. As Brian Cusack (anti-Treaty) made clear to the Dáil, 'we have visualised this Republic far more clearly than we ever visualised this Free State.'[19]

For the Galway anti-Treatyites, the war-weary western people had to be saved from themselves. By rejecting the Treaty, they argued, they were preserving the virtue of their constituents who were unwittingly abandoning the Republic. Material might must not vanquish moral right. Virtue must not be subjugated by fear. As Fahy explained: 'Had a vote been possible prior to the Rising of 1916, does any Deputy imagine that we would have received the sanction of 10 per cent of our people? Yet the people now admit that our action was justified ... should a demand inspired by terror be hearkened to as the real voice of the people?'[20] Endorsing Fahy's belief that 'the great majority of the people are in favour of acceptance, lest worse befall,'[21] Mellows claimed that:

> The people are being stampeded; in the people's mind there is only one alternative to this Treaty and that is terrible, immediate war. During the adjournment I paid a trip to the country and I found that the people who are in favour of the Treaty are not in favour of the Treaty on its merits, but are in favour of the Treaty because they fear what is to happen if it be rejected. That is not the will of the people, that is the fear of the people.[22]

In their view, and in the minds of some of their anti-Treaty colleagues, the majority of the Irish people were supporting the Treaty on tactical grounds, and not on principle.[23] But even Mellows in his emotional appeal that 'we would rather have this country poor and indigent, we would rather have the people of Ireland eking out a poor existence on the soil; as long as they possessed their souls, their minds, and their honour,'[24] seemed to have lost sight of the fact that many people in the west of Ireland were already poor and indigent, and looked upon the Treaty as a means of economic and social salvation.[25]

Protesting against a hostile press, Cusack complained that 'the daily papers in Ireland are full of "ratify the Treaty" resolutions – public bodies falling in one after another. We saw the same before, and one gets suspicious.'[26] Arguing on the same lines, Fahy declared that 'a venal Press that never stood for freedom and now with one voice advocates ratification has, by *suppressio veri* and *suggestio falsi*, prejudiced the issue and biased public opinion.'[27] Their protests were not unfounded. Terms such as 'disorder', 'chaos', 'ruin', 'war' abounded in the local press as its editors tried to impress on their readers what would ensue if the Treaty was rejected. The effusive *Tuam Herald* was particularly forthright in its attacks on the anti-Treatyites. Commenting on the necessity for people to accept the settlement, it declared, 'they cannot possibly do otherwise unless they are bereft of intelligence and that they have been drugged and thereby their common sense is abandoned.'[28]

The Treaty did not grant unfettered freedom for Ireland, and, if one recalls the famed remark of Seán Lemass in 1928 that Fianna Fáil was 'a slightly constitutional party', then perhaps it is fair to suggest that, for the pro-Treaty Galway deputies, the peace settlement presented 'a slightly independent Treaty'. In the Dáil, Galway's pro-Treaty deputies, and Patrick Hogan in particular, challenged the attitude adopted by their anti-Treaty colleagues over divine right and majority right. Public opinion could not be flouted. Reiterating Michael Collins's call for government by the consent of the governed, Hogan reminded those assembled that any deputy who voted in favour of the Treaty, knowing that his or her constituents were against it, was doing wrong. 'That may be a bitter thing', he conceded, 'but it is democracy'.[29] While acknowledging that the Treaty did not provide complete independence, local solicitor George Nicholls[30] (pro-Treaty) argued that it brought them very near to what they wanted. Responding to those who were expounding constitutional law in connection with the Treaty, he stated: 'One of my constituents was speaking to me, and he used these words to me: "We are bewildered and moidered with high faluting talk about constitutional law ... But we do feel certain of one thing; that is, if we once get the British forces out of Ireland, it will require more than constitutional law to get them back."'[31]

Adhering to public opinion, and echoing Collins's reluctance to commit the people to a renewed war without their consent, Padraig Ó Máille[32] (pro-Treaty), a celebrated member of the West Connemara flying column, announced:

> I support this Treaty because I feel in my heart and soul that the supporting of that Treaty is the best thing for Ireland. I support it on other grounds. I support it because I know that it is what the people of Galway who sent me here want. I live in Galway. I go among the people every day and I know their feelings on the question, and I would not be true to the people of Galway if I held opinions on this matter contrary to theirs, and if I were to stand up here and give a vote on such a vital issue as this which threatens the very lives of the people of Ireland and the people of Galway.[33]

Defending the Treaty in a later speech he argued that 'when a man got nine-tenths of a road, that man was a fool if he went back to the starting point, and began the journey again.'[34] Ó Máille's speeches in favour of the Treaty gained him the congratulations of the *Connacht Tribune*, which applauded his 'shrewd intuition, common-sense, and moral courage ... a tribute which we are particularly pleased to pay him inasmuch as we actively opposed his return at the 1918 election'.[35] For Joseph Whelehan (pro-Treaty), like Collins, and like Ó Máille, the situation and the decision which must follow was 'not a Republic *versus* Association with Great Britain', but whether 'this Treaty be approved or, shall we commit the country to war'.[36]

While the Articles of Agreement fell short of the people's expectations, public opinion in Galway, as in much of the country, expressed a desire for peace. Support for the Treaty was stronger among the citizenry than the small margin of victory (64 votes to 57) in the Dáil suggested. But it was difficult to gauge accurately. As one local reporter noted, 'into one ear is whispered an assurance that public opinion is solid for the Treaty, and into the other an assertion that it is Republican to the core.'[37] On 30 December 1921, Galway County Council passed a resolution stating that:

> Although the terms of the Peace treaty between England and Ireland do not satisfy the aspirations of the Irish people we are of the opinion that it is the best that our plenipotentiaries could have got under the circumstances. On that account, and on that account only, we on behalf of the people of Galway, approve of it, and we call upon our representatives in the Dáil to vote for its ratification.[38]

This was hardly a ringing endorsement of the Treaty, particularly coming from what was a particularly conservative body. Other political groups were more outspoken. In a letter to Brian Cusack, the Tuam town commissioners wrote: 'The people of Tuam, who were among your most ardent supporters in the 1918 election, are almost unanimously in favour of ratification. By opposing the Treaty you are acting in direct opposition to their wishes and the wishes of the men who worked so hard for your return.'[39]

The difference between the oath agreed to by the plenipotentiaries and that embodied in de Valera's proposed alternative to the Treaty – Document No. 2 – sparked little debate in the local pro-Treaty press. The *Tuam Herald*, rather flippantly, deemed it a matter 'more verbal than vital', and reiterated John Devoy's disparaging claim that de Valera's amendment would establish little more than a 'Royal Irish Republic'.[40] In similar fashion the *East Galway Democrat* cast it as a choice between Tweedledum and Tweedledee.[41] Described somewhat disparagingly in the Dáil as 'a quibble of words' by Arthur Griffith and 'a red herring' by Eoin MacNeill, de Valera's bold concept of external association – of an Ireland associated with but not part of the British Empire – was a formula undoubtedly ahead of its time.[42] Yet the differences between the proposals in Document No. 2 and those of the Articles of Agreement were portrayed as nothing but a 'shadow'. Deploring the manner in which his alternative was handled by the pressmen, de Valera accused them of being guilty of 'a violation of the canons of all reputable journalism'.[43]

The Sinn Féin organisation across the county was divided. At a meeting of the South Galway Comhairle Ceanntair at Loughrea on 2 February, members narrowly voted by 15 votes to 14 to support the republican policy at the Árd Fheis. In Galway city, the standing committee of the Thomas Ashe Sinn Féin Club carried an amendment, by 36 votes to 22, 'that we uphold the constitution of Sinn Féin as it stands at present pledged to the Republic'.[44] The North Galway Comhairle Ceanntair, on the other hand, was unanimous in its support of the Treaty and the East Galway Comhairle Ceanntair also voted in favour of ratification by 18 votes to eight. While many Sinn Féin clubs instructed their delegates to support the Treaty at the February Árd Fheis, not an insignificant number declared in favour of de Valera.[45]

Within the IRA, two of the three Western Divisions, contained within the county boundary, declared against the Treaty.[46] Yet the recurrent procurement and relinquishing of local barracks across the county by both factions of the army did little to clarify the situation. In one episode, Portumna Barracks, recently vacated by the RIC, changed hands three times in one week.[47] In Galway city, Renmore Barracks, previously the depot of the Connaught Rangers, was taken over by Commandant Thomas Duggan on behalf of the republican (anti-Treaty) forces, while the regular (pro-Treaty) forces, under Commanding Officer Austin Brennan, commandeered the Railway Hotel in Eyre Square. Commenting on her new 'tenants', Miss Clancy, the manager of the hotel, remarked: 'The lounge of the building has been turned into a guardroom. It is worth noting that the British who were recently in occupation took over the best rooms in the hotel, whilst the IRA have left the best rooms for the visitors, whom they have endeavoured to inconvenience as little as possible.'[48] The anti-Treaty IRA, as has been well documented in other accounts of the Civil War, held the dominant position in the country during the first months of 1922. In Galway, the fact that the republicans occupied both Renmore Barracks and Eglinton Barracks (former headquarters of the RIC in Galway city) illustrated the initial weakness of the Provisional Government's forces. And, among local pro-Treaty supporters, the influx of new recruits to the republican cause since the ratification of the Treaty, was a source of bitter resentment. At a St Patrick's Day rally in Galway city, George Nicholls declared: 'I can understand the attitude of the man who throughout thought this Treaty was bad and should not be accepted, but I cannot understand the attitude of the man who wrote to us to vote for the Treaty, and after we had won the evacuation turned round on the other side and said we were traitors.'[49] Criticising the actions of these new recruits, these new playboys of the western world (as the Treatyites perceived them to be), Commandant Reddington, a native of Galway city who had fought alongside Seán Mac Eoin in Longford during the Anglo-Irish War, stated how he witnessed in Galway

> men who funked the fight and did nothing to help them; never lift[ed] a revolver or rifle when the fight was there … Those would-be soldiers going around now looking for a Republic were insulting the men who did fight when the enemy was up against them … Men in Galway who never fired a shot for the murder of Fr Griffin were the men who would lead them now into the fight and let them down.[50]

However, there was to be no military standoff between the IRA rival units in Galway. Unlike the initial crisis which developed in Limerick city a degree of civilised co-operation existed between the pro- and anti-Treaty troops in Galway city. The wounding of Captain Seán Hurley (pro-Treaty IRA) outside the Railway Hotel on 3 April was an isolated incident. At a public meeting held in Eyre Square to condemn the shooting, Austin Brennan declared:

> We are not here for intimidation … we are not here for war, but I wish to warn the other side that we are not here to be made cock-shots of either. We will afford protection to the people of Galway, and it will be my desire to inconvenience them as little as possible. I will control my men and I will let the other side do the same, and I hope we will come together again.[51]

While reconciliation seemed increasingly unlikely, both sides wished to avoid military confrontation. Similarly in Limerick, despite Ernie O'Malley's plan to take over the Provisional Government positions in the city, and his warnings that the Provisional Government forces would gain an advantage if the republicans did not act decisively, the majority of the anti-Treaty leadership showed no desire for a military showdown.[52] The tension between rival forces in Galway, however, was less pronounced than in Limerick. In Galway, despite the shooting of Hurley, the *Connacht Tribune* reported that 'good feeling appears to prevail between both sections, who move about the city freely without arms.'[53] Speaking at Clifden on 8 April, Padraig Ó Máille TD (pro-Treaty) conveyed a similar sentiment: 'I knew that even though some of my friends of the flying column may differ from me they would not stand for anything in the nature of tyranny. Thank God that in this county, at least, we are able to keep our heads.'[54]

II
The June Pact Election

With the party and the army divided, the Collins–de Valera electoral pact of May 1922 was designed to salvage the fragile unity of Sinn Féin by denying a popular verdict on the Treaty. Under the provisions of the pact, a joint panel of Sinn Féin candidates, proportionate to their existing strength in the Dáil, would be offered to the voting public in the hope that electoral contests would be reduced to a minimum. After the election, a national coalition government representing the rival pro- and anti-Treaty factions of Sinn Féin would be formed. A crucial aspect of the agreement, however, was the clause which allowed other parties to run candidates against the Sinn Féin panel and, despite republican intimidation, many of them did so.

In Galway, in an election contest with eight candidates for seven seats, the question was not who would win, but who would be eliminated. The pact election result saw the ousting of the most prominent republican candidate, Liam Mellows, by the Labour nominee and General Secretary of the Irish National Teachers' Organisation (INTO), T. J. O'Connell. The republicans were the only ones to suffer a defeat in Galway, and had other pro-Treaty candidates entered the contest their position might have been more vulnerable.[55]

According to the published figures, Galway registered the lowest percentage turnout in all the contested constituencies, recording a figure of 44.81 per cent compared to the national average of 60.27 per cent.[56] With an estimated population of a little over 170,000, 47 per cent of the population of Galway was eligible to vote in the June pact election, yet less than half of the electorate recorded their vote (figure 1).[57] If only half of the population was eligible to vote and if only half of this half actually voted, could the government really claim such a decisive victory? Yet a general election was the only way, even in an admittedly imperfect manner, in which public opinion could be measured. The clause enabling other parties to contest the election was the ultimate contradiction, but the pact did

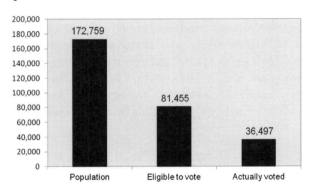

FIGURE 1. **Voting turnout for Co. Galway, June 1922**

affirm 'the primacy of the ballot box, at a time when this seemed very much in the balance'.[58] And this is precisely what Collins needed – a popular mandate for the Treaty and for peace. The pact enabled an election to take place. Without it, it seems likely that the anti-Treaty IRA would have attempted to forcibly prevent any election contest from taking place. Yet not even Collins could have expected it to have worked so well – every 'third party' vote cast in the election was translated as a vote in favour of the Treaty and these successes came at the expense of the anti-Treaty candidates, not candidates who supported the Treaty.

If, for the anti-Treatyites, the pact was designed to silence or at least 'muzzle' the electorate, it failed.[59] In Galway, the Treaty dominated the local election campaign. The central message, stressed by both sides, was that responsibility for acceptance or rejection of the proposed settlement rested with the people. George Nicholls (pro-Treaty), at a public meeting in Clifden, advised those gathered that if 'you do not want the Treaty and are prepared to face the consequences, and if you think that we did wrong, your absolute duty is to kick us out'.[60] The *Galway Observer* reported a speech made by Frank Fahy (anti-Treaty) at a republican meeting in Athenry on the same day:

> It was to secure a Republic he trained his men there in 1915. He and those with him in the rising of 1916 took seriously the declaration of the Republic. If the people wished by acceptance of the Treaty to turn down the Republic he was willing to give [his] place to somebody who would better express their changed opinions. It was entirely a question to be decided by the people.[61]

But 'if you turn me down', he later proclaimed at Loughrea, 'be honest and admit that it is not because you accept the Articles of Agreement, but because of the fear of war or of injuring your business.'[62]

Much to the frustration of the press, local issues almost entirely failed to impinge on the debate. On 8 April the editor of the *Connacht Tribune* declared: 'Unemployment is rife, everywhere, although the stern fact has been lost sight of in the political ferment. It is doubtful if any of those who talk politics so glibly realise the menacing groundswell of discontent that is heaving in their very midst.'[63] The pact was widely criticised by the local pro-Treaty press. Claiming that it was a negation of the first principle of democracy, the *Tuam Herald* insisted: 'It is not a real election for its effects will be practically a mere stereotyping of the present situation.'[64] William O'Malley declared the election to be 'a farce'.[65] Yet however-much inflated and frenzied the pronouncements of this former Irish Party MP for Connemara were, the election campaign in one of the largest constituencies in the country produced little enthusiasm among the voting public. After months of debate on the merits of the Treaty, the people, as the *East Galway Democrat* noted, were 'tired of talking'.[66]

The Labour Party's decision to offer a challenge to the Galway panel candidates was an important one. Labour, on the whole, was not very well organised in Galway, although the Town Tenants' League and local trade associations were occasionally visibly active. In May 1922, for instance, one month before the election, in a protest against the conditions of the tenants on the Clanricarde estate (East Galway) and the Urban District Council's inability to provide adequate housing in the city, the Galway branch of the Town Tenants' League, led by Stephen Cremen, pulled down the bronze statue of Lord Dunkellin which stood in Eyre Square, paraded it through the town, and unceremoniously hurled it into the sea at Nimo's Pier.[67] In selecting T. J. O'Connell the party chose a prominent figure to contest the June election and with the help of local trades councils and supporters of the INTO, a strong political union, it ran a short yet effective campaign. Perhaps the size of the constituency influenced the party's decision. As O'Connell pointed out at the opening of his campaign in Ballinasloe (East Galway), there were seven seats and Labour was looking for only one. O'Connell also recognised a growing spirit that was 'antagonistic to the ordinary people having a say in the affairs of the country'.[68] While some support for the party could be perceived as a reactionary vote against Sinn Féin, Labour also clearly identified a frustration among a populace tired of hearing about the nation and eagerly seeking an end to economic stagnation.

No independent candidates came forward. However, unlike the incidents which occurred in Sligo, Clare and Mayo and several other counties, there were fewer reports of disruptions at public meetings and intimidation preventing other candidates from contesting the election. The tempestuous meetings that characterised the election campaign in Sligo-East Mayo, the only other Connacht constituency where an election was held, were for the most part absent in Galway, where cordial fellowship seemed to abound between the two factions of

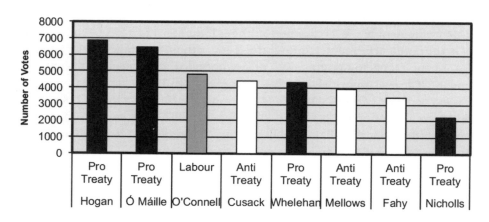

FIGURE 2. **First preference vote in Co. Galway, June 1922**

the IRA and the local body politic. In Sligo-East Mayo, the campaign was particularly bitter. Two pro-Treaty Sinn Féin candidates – John Hennigan and Seamus McGowan refused to withdraw from the contest, as the pact required them to do, and the republicans were especially hostile and aggressive in consequence.[69] Up until the last moment it seemed as though Co. Galway would fall into the habit of its nearest neighbours and not hold an election contest at all. The Galway branch of the Irish Farmers' Union, recognising that Patrick Hogan and Padraig Ó Máille (both pro-Treaty Sinn Féin) were themselves farmers and members of the organisation, took the decision not to nominate candidates for the coming election and agreed instead to give first and second preference votes to them.[70] It was hardly surprising then that, in a county where 75 per cent of the work force was involved in agriculture,[71] Hogan from East Galway, and Ó Máille from West Galway, topped the poll on the first count (figure 2). Overall pro-Treaty Sinn Féin won 54.5 per cent of the Galway vote compared to anti-Treaty Sinn Féin's 32.3 per cent and Labour's 13.2 per cent.

The local Urban and Rural District Councils' minute books are filled with entries relating to the severe distress prevalent in parts of Connemara and the housing, unemployment and agricultural crisis affecting the whole county. Labour's ability to side-step the Treaty debate and identify with these immediate social and economic concerns was certainly advantageous. The alleviation of the destitution in Connemara may well have been an overriding factor among a voting community that was merely striving to exist on patches of bog and rocks. O'Connell ascribed a certain level of political naivety to the Galway populace when he asked: 'What did the starving fisherman in the West of Ireland, the houseless workers, the men living in unsanitary slums care whether there was a governor-general here, or whether they signed Document No. 1 or Document No. 2?'[72] Yet he expressed a clear understanding of the compromising mind-set of a war-weary western people desperate to follow any course that might improve their social conditions. O'Connell did not crawl in in last place, but was elected on the first count receiving the third highest number of votes in the county (figure 2). The majority of the electorate, by recording the highest number of first preference votes for the two farming pro-Treaty Sinn Féin representatives and the Labour candidate, and by rejecting a principal member of the republican garrison in the Four Courts, made a clear statement in favour of peace, the Treaty and economic regeneration.[73] The local electorate decisively voted for pragmatism over radicalism.

In theory, the coalition panel presented a united front to the electorate, but the cracks and fissures within Sinn Féin were perceptible and palpable. The vibrant and resourceful campaign fought in 1918, in an election characterised by the swift organisation of the party, was on this occasion altogether absent. In June 1922, Sinn Féin, as a unit, won 86.8 per cent of the first preference votes cast in Galway. This figure is often quoted to indicate the strength of the party, but in an election

183

contest in which seven of the eight candidates were guaranteed to be returned, the result, relative to the provisions of the pact, was a disappointment (although the Treatyites were no doubt pleased to oust one of their most fervent opponents).

The government candidates retained each of their four seats. The successful election of the popular Galway city representative George Nicholls, who polled the lowest number of first preference votes, illustrated a clear loyalty in transfer votes on the part of the pro-Treaty supporters (figures 3 and 4). Nicholls was elevated to fifth place overhauling the anti-Treatyite Brian Cusack whom he had trailed by four places and 2,167 votes after the first count. With the republicans already losing one seat to Labour, the final seat was fought out by two of the republican camp's most divergent supporters – Frank Fahy, the moderate republican, and Liam Mellows, the uncompromising radical.

Fahy had urged restraint throughout the campaign. At an anti-Treaty meeting at Athenry, he declared that he 'would rather let the Free State win, without a contest, than to see a divided army and Irishmen who had fought side by side, turn their arms against one another in fratricidal strife.'[74] No doubt, as the *Connacht Tribune* suggested, his speeches in favour of the restoration of order and goodwill brought him an accession of voters from all classes.[75] Mellows, on the other hand, rarely left his position in the Four Courts to address the Galway electorate during the contest. Failure to address one's electorate in person, however, did not make inevitable a failure to secure election in Galway. In December 1918, both Cusack and Fahy had been elected for Sinn Féin while interned in Birmingham under the German Plot allegations.[76] On this occasion, however, the electorate may well have felt there was less excuse for a candidate's absence, especially one

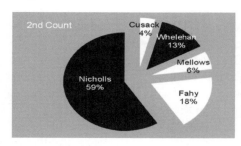

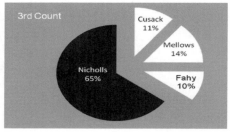

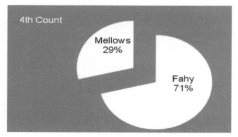

FIGURE 3. *above left*
Patrick Hogan (pro-Treaty) surplus (2,269)

FIGURE 4. *above*
Padraig Ó Máille (pro-Treaty) surplus (1,882)

FIGURE 5. *left*
T. J. O'Connell (Labour) surplus (258)

who was not a 'native' of Galway. Mellows had been returned unchallenged in 1918 and 1921. Perhaps he took the electorate somewhat for granted.

The closely run fight between these two republican figures reveals some interesting voting patterns. Fahy received the second highest number of transfers from Hogan's surplus, coming second to Nicholls and gaining 103 more votes than Joseph Whelehan, the other pro-Treaty candidate (figure 3). Hogan's large surplus was clearly a factor in Fahy's high tally, but he was also the beneficiary of a certain degree of localism with both Fahy and Hogan hailing from Loughrea in South Galway. Mellows secured the highest number of surplus votes among the anti-Treaty candidates on the third count (figure 4). However it was the distribution of O'Connell's surplus which was most revealing (figure 5). Electors who gave their first preference to Labour clearly paid little heed to the social policy of Mellows and showed no desire to pass on their lower preferences to the man who in 1916 had brought about a short-lived merger of land and revolution in East Galway.[77] Lower transfers, of course, do not mirror as strong a reflection of voting patterns, but they still produced a high margin of 70, 71 and 88 per cent in favour of Fahy over Mellows (figure 6). Fahy had trailed his fellow anti-Treatyite after each successive count, yet secured sufficient pro-Treaty and Labour transfers to beat Mellows to the final seat by a slim margin of 39 votes on the seventh count.

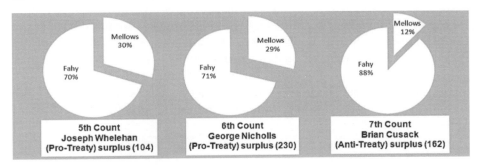

FIGURE 6. **Destination of Lower Transfers, Fahy versus Mellows**

The defeat of Mellows was unexpected. To lose such a commanding figure of the republican army and one of their most outspoken leaders was a disappointment to the anti-Treatyites. Of the three anti-Treaty candidates, Cusack's position seemed to be the weakest but he polled the highest number of first preference republican votes, narrowly failing to be elected on the first count. Cusack's high tally may well have been the result of republican supporters giving their first preferences to their weaker candidate, expecting both Mellows and Fahy to be elected on merit, thus securing each of their three seats.[78]

The national result was conclusive: 58 pro-Treaty Sinn Féin, 17 Labour Party, 7

Farmers' Party, 6 Independents and 4 Unionists, amounting to 92 candidates that could be expected to support the Treaty in the new Dáil, against 36 anti-Treaty Sinn Féin candidates.[79] However, as long as the Collins–de Valera pact could be regarded as still being in existence, the result could be interpreted (and was interpreted by the republicans) as a vote which returned a total of 94 pro- and anti-Treaty Sinn Féin candidates to form a coalition government as originally negotiated in the electoral agreement. The deterioration of the military situation, the attack on the Four Courts republican garrison on 28 June and the outbreak of heavy fighting in Dublin shelved any lingering likelihood of the continuation of Sinn Féin's dualist approach. In truth, any such possibility had been extinguished with Collins's alleged repudiation of the spirit of the pact days before the poll, the decision of non-panel candidates to contest the election, and the publication of the new Free State constitution on the morning of the poll in a form, insisted upon by the British government, that was wholly unworkable for the republicans.

III

The Civil War

The war in the west, as Michael Hopkinson has suggested, was an isolated campaign.[80] On 2 July 1922, republican forces in Galway, following the national pattern, abandoned attempts to hold fixed positions, destroyed their posts and evacuated the city. Four buildings – Renmore Barracks, the naval base at the Docks, Eglinton Street Police Barracks, and the Freemasons' Hall on Presentation Road – were set on fire. A fifth republican base at Dominick Street police station was spared. A notice posted by Thomas Fahy, O/C at Dominick Street, explained that the house was left intact because it was felt that a fire started in the building would endanger the entire street and the lives of non-combatants.[81]

Abandoned republican posts in the city were targeted by looters. After the evacuation of Renmore Barracks, the *Connacht Tribune* reported that 'every portable piece of property that remained after the evacuation was looted. Doors, tables, kitchen furniture, window-sashes, even permanent woodwork were torn down … and removed.' At the naval base, military tables were removed on donkeys and at the Freemasons' Hall, which had not been badly damaged by the fire, looters carried away doors, window-frames, furniture and floors. One man was in the process of removing the kitchen range when National troops arrived and put a stop to it.[82]

The withdrawal of the republican forces and the re-employment of guerrilla war tactics, however, meant that Galway city did not become a focal point of the military struggle. Unlike events in Dublin and in Limerick, for instance, there was no military showdown in Galway. Limerick city had considerable strategic importance. If controlled by the anti-Treaty IRA a link between Munster and the west could have been established, leaving Michael Brennan's command in Clare and Seán Mac Eoin's command in Athlone dangerously isolated. Conversely, if the city was held by the pro-Treaty IRA, republican units in Clare and the midlands would have been cut off from their colleagues in Munster.[83] Galway city, in a military sense, was not such a strategic pivot.

The Civil War, particularly the guerrilla phase of the war, did not spread across the whole county. Republican resistance was strongest in Connemara and in North Galway. Yet, raids on banks and post offices; the destruction of roads, bridges and railways; the interruptions to the postal service and telegraphic communications; the cancelling of market fairs; theft; the postponement of the Galway Races festival; and the damage to public and private property, greatly disrupted transport, trade and commerce both in the city and in the county. In Tuam, in North Galway, for example, the destruction of the Crumlin bridge near Ballyglunin, prevented a rail service running from Athenry to Tuam for three months. As the main road from Galway to Tuam was also impassable in places, people wishing to get to Tuam from Galway had to take a train to Athenry and then travel by road to Tuam. In July 1922 a journey of 22 miles became a journey of 46 miles.[84] In Galway city, in an effort to conserve food supply and prevent profiteering, the Urban District Council ordered that no trader was to charge more for any goods than the market price of 1 July and that all citizens were to be as sparing as possible in the use of foodstuffs and report any waste to the council.[85] In Oughterard, in West Galway, old age pensions, which had not been received since July, were eventually delivered when the first train to travel on the Clifden line, since the outbreak of the war, ran from Galway to Oughterard and Maam Cross on 17 October. From Roundstone in Connemara, Dr T. T. Collins, dispensary medical officer for the area, wrote to the Local Government Ministry in Dublin in July declaring:

> We are absolutely cut off here, no post or telegraph communication, no railway, and, worst of all, no petrol. I am seriously hindered in the execution of my professional duty by the want of petrol. As you are aware I have a very large district to attend to, and there is an exceptional amount of sickness just now ... This is due mostly to the extreme poverty prevailing, attended by the shortage of necessary foodstuffs ... I have appealed to the IRA (the Irregulars) in Clifden (who have seized the available supplies) but with no result.[86]

It has been suggested, particularly in regard to republican activity and support in Connemara, that the people were more active in this area because they were poor, their situation was more desperate and therefore they had less to lose – in short, that revolutions were more easily made when people were starving.[87] Revolutions, however, require energy and many would-be Volunteers were too poor or too weak to fight. Some could not afford to leave their land untended and take to the hills or go on the run. The economic cost to those they would leave behind would be, and often was, far too high (the consequences of such activities had already been seen in other parts of the county after the widespread arrests and imprisonments of local Galway 'sympathisers' in the aftermath of the Easter Rising in 1916).[88] For those who did fight, the localised nature of Volunteer enlistment, activity, and loyalty were important factors, as were the aspirations towards an Irish Republic and the anticipation of a radically altered way of life. For many others the desire for land and land redistribution was as fundamental as any patriotic aspiration.[89]

Nonetheless, the poverty in many of the western areas, coupled with a lack of food supplies and a shortage of arms, was an important factor in reducing the prospect of effective republican activity. Reporting on the conditions in East Connemara, Colm Ó Gaora of the 4th Western Division wrote to his divisional O/C in December 1922 stating that:

> Since the commencement of hostilities last June our ASUs [Active Service Units], numbering about 80 men, are in a pitiable and most desperate condition [and] in need of proper clothing and feeding, especially since the Winter months. As you will see by the geographical position of our area it is the poorest in Ireland, and the shops in our area which are small did not stock the stuff required by our men, and therefore the necessaries needed could not be commandeered.

The people 'who have stood with us are of the poorest type in Ireland', he continued, 'and I consider it a crime to trespass much longer on their hospitality'. Ó Gaora ended by stating that if a sum of at least £800 was not immediately provided the fighting spirit of his men would be broken.[90] The O/C of the West Connemara Brigade offered a similarly depressing account, writing that his men could not stand always being out in the cold and rain without overcoats and with wet feet.[91]

A report on the general state of the Western Command compiled on 14 March 1923 stated that the 2nd Western Division was weak of officers, arms, and ammunitions. The 4th Western Division was in a stronger position, but the round up before Christmas had a demoralising effect. Communications were 'very bad all round' and it was considered a very good result if a reply to a dispatch from the 4th Western Division HQ to Connemara reached the Division in less than seven days.[92] In October 1923, the 2nd Western Division requested that each man 'be given a complete suit of clothes as most of them are very badly off in that respect, only having received a breeches or jacket when the old one went to rags'.[93] Moss Twomey, reflecting on the position in the west after the civil war, noted that:

Before hostilities began a great proportion of the Brigade Officers deserted to the enemy. Even worse still others ... remained only to desert a short while after hostilities began. The result is that these areas never properly recovered from the effects of these desertions and consequent disorganisation.[94]

Participation in the Sinn Féin clubs was also unsatisfactory. A report submitted in December 1923 recorded that the clubs simply existed nominally, that meetings were poorly attended and that no business was transacted. The 'right type of man', it noted, 'does not control the Clubs' and 'several volunteers have walked out ... in disgust.' The report also criticised members of the committee who arrived at meetings with their accounts in a bundle of raggy papers, with no balance sheets, no appearance of satisfactory business, and concluded: 'no wonder people ask are we really serious.'[95]

Notwithstanding the earlier advent of new volunteers to the republican side, the local organisation was in a particularly poor condition. Yet, Galway was not playing at republicanism. Although a defeated and dejected military force by the spring of 1923, they retained a reservoir of political support in the west.[96] In the next election of August 1923, despite the flood of other party candidates and the fact that many prominent members were interned, on the run, dislocated or dead, the republicans not only retained but marginally increased their vote in Galway from 32.3 per cent to 33.5 per cent.[97] The huge support recorded for Barney Mellows, no doubt, in part, a demonstration of compassion for his executed older brother, nonetheless indicated an enduring sympathy for the republican cause. After the Civil War the local IRA continued to drill and organise and implemented orders and directives from General Headquarters.[98] However ineffective they might have been in the aftermath of a demoralising military defeat, republicanism was still a potentially potent force,[99] and the continued presence of this rumbling if not particularly radical republican bloc posed a challenge to the process of legitimising the new state.

10

'ALWAYS IN DANGER OF FINDING MYSELF WITH NOTHING AT ALL'

*The military service pensions and the battle
for material survival, 1925–55*

DIARMAID FERRITER

I

Tom Barry, an IRA activist from Cork, lived a long and eventful life. Following service in the British army, he became one of the best known and most admired of the flying column leaders during the IRA's War of Independence from 1919–21, as a result of the Kilmichael ambush of 28 November 1920, when he led an attack on a patrol of Auxiliaries, 16 of whom were killed. The ambush had a profound impact, resulting in the declaration of martial law for much of Munster the following month, official reprisals and wide scale internment. By the spring of 1921, his flying column, with 104 men, was the largest in Ireland. Barry survived the War of Independence and the Civil War, during which he fought on the republican side, and was instrumental in efforts to end that war. He remained on the run until 1924, the same year in which he became involved in the Cleeves Milk Company based in Limerick and Clonmel, and from 1927 until his retirement in 1965 he was general superintendent with the Cork Harbour Commissioners.[1] In 1949, his book *Guerrilla Days in Ireland* was published and became a bestseller.[2]

Barry has been described in the *Dictionary of Irish Biography* as 'often prickly and autocratic' but also generous and charismatic. Intelligent yet impatient, he was quick to take on lawyers and bank managers over matters relating to his IRA column's activities.[3] He also took on the Military Service Pensions Board over another perceived slight – its decision that his activities during the revolutionary period did not merit the award of the most senior rank and grade for the purposes of payment of a pension that, following a number of legislative initiatives in the 1920s and 1930s, was made available to veterans of the War of Independence and Civil War, who applied and fulfilled the required criteria. In December 1938 Barry submitted his form, which claimed IRA service from July 1919 to the end of September 1923:

I would like to point out that I have not included what I would term the lesser fights, shootings or actions. I have only dealt with the major activities ... I claim that I was continuously engaged without a break for the period mentioned. In justice to myself and the officers and men I commanded, I claim Rank A. Apart from the post of Liaison officer for the martial law area to which post I was appointed in the day preceding the Truce, by virtue of my rank as deputy divisional O/C prior to that date, I had under my absolute control all the fighting organisation of active service units in Cork, Kerry, Waterford and West Limerick. My post was <u>NOT</u> vice O/C but Deputy O/C. The late General [Liam] Lynch handed me over all the Active Service Units about three weeks after his own appointment. My rank and activities also during the Civil War period entitles me to rank A.[4]

Days later, Barry wrote another letter, suggesting 'it is possible that the Board would be facilitated by a more detailed statement in deciding the issue of my rank' and also to make the point that, at the outset of the Civil War 'the ranks on 1 July 1922 were indeed very vague for any of the GHQ officers.'[5] During his sworn statement before the Military Service Pensions' advisory committee, he was asked was there a difference between deputy divisional commander and vice divisional O/C? He replied: 'Certainly there was a difference ... Deputy Divisional O/C is one which ranks co-jointly with the O/C, whereas the Vice O/C is only a staff officer.' In reply to the question about a later period – 'You claim your rank at that period was Rank A?' – his reply was adamant: 'Certainly. I would accept no other rank.'[6] Barry's complaint was that it was unacceptable that he could be considered as having had any military rank in the IRA lower than Deputy O/C.

Grave disappointment was to follow for Barry. In January 1940, he received his Military Service Pension award of Rank B for just under six years of IRA service, which, he wrote, 'I reject ... on the grounds of both length of service and of rank.' He was livid that the Board had disallowed him full-time active service on certain key dates, including the periods October 1919 to July 1921 and July to September 1923: 'It is sufficient to state that my award was humiliating to a degree.' As was usual with Barry, such a concise assertion of his grievance was not sufficient; a few lines later in the letter he wrote: 'I do ask the Board now to understand that I am feeling ashamed and ridiculous at the award and that I am entitled at least to have this humiliation removed from me.' He insisted on his appeal being heard in person and maintained that he had many former IRA officers who were prepared to verbally testify on his behalf. Senior politicians, including Taoiseach Éamon de Valera and P. J. Ruttledge, Minister for Local Government and Public Health, had already written statements of evidence on his behalf.[7]

Bill Quirke, who was a member of the army executive and O/C of the 2nd Southern Command, and who had also been awarded Rank B, wrote the following month in relation to Barry: 'I always regarded him as my superior officer and if any man in Ireland is entitled to special consideration for special services, surely he is one man.'[8] De Valera intervened, suggesting to the Board that it should avail of its power to review individual cases and award Barry a pension based on Rank A service.[9] The honorary secretary of the Old IRA Men's Association of Cork County, F. Begley, gave evidence on Barry's behalf in April 1940 and followed this up with a letter suggesting:

> Re. Mr Barry's claim – As far as I can recollect he forfeited a pension from the British authorities by his actions in 1920. This should also be taken into consideration in his favour by your Board when deciding his case ... My experience on Wed. last in the presence of Board members has led me to believe that you are not a bad lot of chaps at all, though mind you I had not such kind feelings towards all of you previously. How-ever time will I presume prove whether the moderately good opinion I have formed will be justified by the treatment of claims awaiting assessment from this area.[10]

Tom Barry gave further evidence in May 1940 and in August 1940 he was granted the rank of Grade A for pension purposes on the basis of which an annual pension of £149. 7s. (roughly €9,500 in today's terms in relation to pur-chasing power) was payable.[11] His perseverance, self-righteousness, attention to detail, friends in powerful positions, and the adamant testimonials on his behalf had paid off.

The saga surrounding Barry's application for a pension and his vehement rejection of the Pensions Board's initial decision is a reminder of the longevity of battles over the legacy of the War of Independence in the state that was created at its end. Significantly, Barry's struggle in the late 1930s and early 1940s with the Pensions Board involved the issue of status rather than money. Given his profes-sional life and job security and the success of his memoir, he was presumably relatively well off materially. But for many others, the award of a pension could mean the difference between material survival and destitution. The list of those awarded military service pensions at the highest grade under the 1924 and 1934 Military Service Pensions Acts reads like a roll call of some of the best known gunmen and later politicians of that era – including Emmet Dalton, Piaras Béaslaí, Dan Breen, Oscar Traynor, Seán Moylan, Seán MacEntee and Frank Aiken. However, the bulk of the files in the Military Service Pensions Collection, which the Department of Defence began to release to researchers on a phased basis in 2014,[12] is filled with the experiences of those who were not household names, and includes many voices of desperation and urgent pleas for pensions due to the abject circumstances of a host of War of Independence and Civil War veterans. Undoubtedly, as with Barry, status was a preoccupation for many of them, but the monetary award could be of more immediate consequence.

The archive, with its wealth of information on military service, engagements, tactics and strategy will provide historians of the War of Independence and Civil War with abundant material to deepen an understanding of the nature and logistics of the wars, but it is also an archive that opens a window on social and economic history. Many were not as fortunate as Barry; some were the relatives of republican icons, but such a family connection was not always a guarantee of material comfort.

II

The Military Service Pensions Collection owes its origin to the decision of the Dáil in June 1923 to recognise and compensate wounded members, and the surviving dependents of deceased members, of various groups that had participated in the events of 1916 to 1923 and were deemed and proven to have had 'active service' during this time. From the 1920s to the 1950s, two streams of legislation, the Army Pensions Acts from 1923 to 1953 and the Military Service Pensions Acts of 1924, 1934 and 1949, were introduced to facilitate recognition of military service. The legislation generated an enormous administrative archive, including the pension applicants' files and supporting material (such as reports of military activities, the nature of military service and family circumstances, information on degrees of dependency, societal circumstances, and where applicable, medical reports); requests for investigations by the military authorities; reports from An Garda Síochána; and the issuing of recommendations. There was also considerable correspondence between the Army Pensions Branch and the Secretaries of the Departments of Finance and Defence and Old IRA Associations; reviews of individual cases; the details of payments of pensions, gratuities and awards; and individuals' proof of service, including references and testimonials.

To assist the Department of Defence (which had overall responsibility for the assessment of claims), specific bodies were set up to decide on the merit of each applicant's case; for example, a Board of Assessors under the Military Service Pensions Act of 1924 and Referee and Advisory Committees under the 1934 and 1949 Acts respectively; membership of these bodies included senior civil servants, former senior IRA officers and members of the judiciary.[13]

Under the provisions of the Army Pensions Act of 1923, individuals were entitled to apply for the payment of wound pensions to veterans of, and allowances and gratuities to the widows, children, dependents and partial dependents of deceased members of, 'Óglaigh na hÉireann, including the Army and the Irish Volunteers and the Citizen Army, 1916, who were killed in the course of duty while on active service between April and May 1916 and the beginning of the Civil War in April 1922'. Provision was also made for the supply of medical appliances and vocational training. In order to be successful, applicants had to prove they or their relative had been 'on active service', killed or wounded 'in the course of his duty', and not guilty of 'any serious negligence or misconduct'.[14] The Army Pensions Act of 1927 provided for the grant of disability pensions in respect of diseases incurred due to, and the grant of allowances to dependents of those who died as a result of diseases attributable to, service in the period ended September 1924. This 1927 Act also provided for the establishment of the Army Pensions Board which assisted the Department of Defence in compiling evidence to investigate claims under the act.

The Army Pensions Act of 1932 amended and extended the scope of the Acts of 1923 and 1927 to include members of Na Fianna Éireann, the republican youth organisation established in 1909; the Hibernian Rifles, established in 1912 as a military offshoot of the offshoot of the Ancient Order of Hibernians; and Cumann na mBan, the female auxiliary of the Irish Volunteers, established in 1914. In terms of the 1932 definition of military service, 'pre-Truce military service' referred to military service during any part of the period from 1 April 1916 to 11 July 1921, when a truce halting the War of Independence was agreed. 'Post-Truce military service' referred to military service during any part of the period beginning on 12 July 1921 and ending on 30 September 1923. In effect, this meant those who had pre-Truce service but took no further part in hostilities, and those who fought on the republican side in the Civil War, now came under the terms of the legislation. This new legislation was largely as a result of the change of government in 1932, when Fianna Fáil, political representatives of the losing republicans during the Civil War, won power for the first time and was determined that military service pensions would apply to republicans who had been excluded from the earlier legislation, framed by the pro-Treaty victors in the Civil War.

The Army Pensions Act of 1937 extended the time limit for applications in some cases covered by previous legislation and made special provision for the relatives of the signatories of the Proclamation of Easter Monday 1916. Provision was also made for the grant of special dependents' allowances to those whose means were less than £40 per annum and ex-gratia payments to certain persons wounded or injured during the period from 1 April 1916 to 30 September 1923, once again incorporating the full period of the Civil War to include republican combatants during that conflict.

Further acts in 1941 and 1943 extended the time limit for application for wound and disability pensions and widows' and dependents' allowances, and provided for a special additional allowance to those whose means did not equal or exceed a prescribed amount, who were incapable of self-support, and who had been awarded pensionable service under the pensions Acts of 1924 to 1934 in respect of service or a wound or disability during Easter Week 1916. Finally, Acts of 1946 and 1953 made further amendments to the previous acts, widening the range of eligibility and providing for allowances to each child of a signatory to the 1916 Proclamation.[15]

The Military Service Act of 1924 created a Board of Assessors chaired by District Justice Cyril J. Beatty and its membership included Eamonn Duggan, Parliamentary Secretary to the Executive Council, Minister for Fisheries Fionán Lynch and retired Lt Gen. Gearóid O' Sullivan, who acted as secretary. This Board approved payment of pensions to 3,855 applicants; almost 10,000 other applicants were refused.

The amount of pension payable varied according to the rank held by the applicant based on the rank structure of the National Forces/Defence Forces, with a sum of £5 applying per year of service and per grade, awarded up to a maximum of £25. Thus in the case of privates and non-commissioned officers, £5 applied, while £25 per year (roughly €1,750 per year today) applied in the case of officers of rank higher than major general. The number of years of continuous service counting towards pension was computed to arrive at a maximum of 14 years, as active service throughout Easter Week 1916 was counted as four years' service. The maximum pension thus awarded was £350.[16]

Applicants completed a six-page form setting out details of their service, specifying the periods, the commanding officer they served under and the details of three officers who could verify their service. These officers were subsequently contacted by the Board and required to complete verification forms. Applicants were then summoned to appear before the Board, with evidence taken under oath, and a one- or two-page summary of service, evidence and other relevant information was compiled. A successful applicant received a signed certificate of military service with their rank defined. Unsuccessful cases were informed: 'Act does not apply' as active service could not be established to the satisfaction of the Board. Each successful applicant also generated an associated administration or payments file with details of address, income and tax affairs.

The Military Service Pensions Act of 1934 was designed to amend and extend the 1924 Act and brought Cumann na mBan within the definition of the bodies already listed as constituting 'the forces', as with the Army Pensions Act of 1932. The new act also established a Referee who was given significant statutory powers and advised by a committee of four people, it being required that two of these four had held senior rank in the IRA prior to the Truce of July 1921.

Each applicant applying under the 1934 Act completed a 19-page form, divided into different parts specifying service at different stages. Individual files also contain copies of sworn evidence; in some cases the Referee questioned claimants at length. Between 1937 and 1945, the Referee and his committee also created 'brigade committees', composed of people who had previously held high rank in the IRA forces, in order to gather reports of brigade activity, membership of flying columns, details of organisation and operation, and structure and membership rolls for the groups that came under the legislation. Under the Military Service Pensions Act of 1924, 25 people were awarded pensions at the highest grade, while under the

1934 Act, 39 people were awarded pensions at the highest grade. The Military Service Pensions (Amendment) Act, 1949 provided for the review of cases previously refused under the 1924 and 1934 Acts, the restoration of pensions forfeited under clauses of those acts, and new applications from veterans.[17]

III

Those affected by the events of Easter Week 1916 and who were in drastic financial circumstances as a result of the Rising feature prominently in the correspondence generated by the pension scheme from the 1920s. However, it is clear that Civil War politics intruded in some of the decisions that were taken. In May 1925 Mary Malone from Drumcondra in Dublin wrote to the Minister for Defence on behalf of her sister Annie Malone, from the South Circular Road in Dublin, who had been 'badly wounded with a bullet that lodged in her hip' on Easter Monday outside the College of Surgeons in St Stephen's Green. The bullet was extracted more than a week later at Mercer's Hospital:

> Previous to her injuries she was training as a draperess, which occupation she is unable to follow owing to the injury to her hip, as she is absolutely unable to stand all day, as is required in drapery establishments as the injured hip to the present day gives her great pain, especially during the winter months ... After my sister was wounded a claim was lodged on her behalf, but owing to the fact that our brother Michael was 'killed in action' Easter Week, her claim was dismissed because we were 'rebels'. If our brother Michael had not taken part in the Rising, my sister would have got compensation for the injury to her hip. I feel sure that my sister's case has only to be brought to your notice, when you will have it satisfactorily dealt with. As our mother died on the 4th ult. my sister must now look out for herself. Were it not for the injury to her hip she would be independent earning her living as a draperess.[18]

Three weeks later a confidential letter to the department from the Office of the Director of Intelligence reported that 'this lady appears to be a sister-in-law of Dan Breen's. In that case, the whole family is tainted with irregularism.'[19] Breen had been a key figure in the establishment of the IRA's South Tipperary Brigade, and his fame had been established by the Soloheadbeg Ambush on 21 January 1919 at the outset of the War of Independence. He subsequently worked for Michael Collins in Dublin. During the War of Independence he had married Bríd Malone, another sister of the letter writer, and had often stayed with the Malone family while on the run. Breen had reluctantly opposed the Treaty and had led a republican column during the Civil War; in August 1923 he was elected a Republican TD for Tipperary.[20]

One of the interesting aspects of the report from the Director of Intelligence, Colonel M. Costello, was the assertion that the Malone family 'are supporters of the Irregulars in a similar sense to Dan Breen, probably for outward appearances and contrary to their better judgement.' It was claimed that Mary Malone's brother Brian sympathised with the republicans during the Civil War 'but was not known to have taken any active part himself. I believe the only case that could be made against the family is an effort to keep up the "family traditions" exemplified in "My Fight for Irish Freedom".' [21] It was also noted that two grants of £100 each had been paid to Michael Malone's family by the National Aid Association, established by republican sympathisers in the aftermath of the 1916 Rising to financially assist those affected by the death and imprisonment of republicans, in respect of his death. [22] The compensation claim was rejected.

Others in difficult circumstances in the aftermath of the Rising included Lily Connolly, the widow of James Connolly, a woman long used to penury. Writing on her behalf to Minister for Defence Richard Mulcahy in February 1924, William O'Brien of the Irish Transport and General Workers' Union pointed out that she was still waiting to hear about her application for a pension: 'She has found it rather difficult to make ends meet during recent years and at the moment is rather embarrassed for the want of some ready money. She has one daughter who is a medical student in her last year and it is hoped she will be qualified in the next six or eight months.' [23]

At the time of James's execution in the aftermath of the Rising, the National Aid Association had given Lily Connolly £1,500 and she also received £75 from the White Cross. Two days after the letter was written on her behalf, the Secretary of the Department of Defence wrote an irate note to an army finance officer, complaining of the 'utterly inexcusable' delay in getting the matter sorted:

> It should not take one day to get evidence that James Connolly was executed in 1916. It should not take one other day to verify that the applicant is his widow … those dealing with the matter of such pensions might have some appreciation that if a woman loses her husband and has a family that she has been through very difficult circumstances and is actually in very difficult circumstances at the present time. [24]

Nonetheless, an army sergeant interviewed her the following week and suggested that 'she appears to be in comfortable circumstances as she has one unmarried daughter practising medicine and a daughter a boarder at the Loreto convent in North Great George's Street.' [25] But as she was deemed to have been wholly dependent on James, she was awarded an annual pension of £90. By 1927, due to increases in allowances payable, she was entitled to a pension of £180 per annum, and her daughter was entitled to £40 per annum until she reached the age of 18. By the time Lily died in 1938, her pension was worth £500 per year [26] (the equivalent worth today would be about €39,000).

In July 1941, Nora Connolly O'Brien, a daughter of James who had been an active member of Cumann na mBan and principal organiser of its Belfast branch, and who was dispatched to Tyrone on Easter Monday 1916 to attempt to mobilise the northern Volunteers, wrote to one of her referees that, in relation to the pension she sought for her own service, she had not

> heard a word yet from the Pensions Board, so don't know what is going to happen in my case ... I am at my wits end. We are absolutely on the racks. This week will see the end of us unless I have something definite to count upon. Seamus [her husband] has had no luck in finding any kind of a job. I was hoping that the pension business could be hurried up and what I could get might tide us over this bad spell. There seems no prospect of anything here so we have written to England applying for jobs. I'm absolutely blue, despondent, down and out, hopeless and at the end of my tether.[27]

Kathleen Clarke, the widow of 1916 Proclamation signatory Tom Clarke, and a former Fianna Fáil senator who served as lord mayor of Dublin from 1940–1, wrote to one of the judges on Nora Connolly's behalf, pointing out that her husband 'is idle through no fault of his own and they have nothing. It is an awful position for James Connolly's daughter.'[28] There was relatively good news in October 1941 when she was awarded an E grade pension for just under six years of active service, amounting to £29. 7s. 6d. per year[29] (this would be worth roughly €1,900 today).

For other relatives of executed 1916 leaders, financial support from the state was vital in allowing them to qualify as professionals, even decades after the Rising; it helped that their names carried considerable political clout and that they had relatives and friends who lobbied politicians on their behalf, ensuring some did not experience the impoverishment that threatened others. In June 1930, the sister of Muriel MacDonagh, widow of Thomas MacDonagh, another signatory of the Proclamation who was executed after the 1916 Rising, wrote to Dr Thomas Hennessy TD (she was also lobbying Seán T. O'Kelly TD) to point out that Muriel and Thomas's two children, Barbara and Donagh, were supported and educated by an allowance of £80 per annum each and payment of school fees under the Military Pensions Act of 1923, but as Donagh was approaching the age of 18, both allowances would soon cease.

His aunt was pleading for the pension and allowances for education to be continued for Donagh MacDonagh's third level studies:

> His father, who was a lecturer in the National University, refused to my knowledge, at least 2 professorships in Universities abroad in order to remain in Ireland and play his part in the 1916 Rising, thereby leaving his family to the care of the nation. Thomas MacDonagh would certainly have given his son a university course. His Mother was drowned in 1917 and her two children have since been in the care of friends, as none

of their relatives are in a position to keep them. Had she lived, she would have been in receipt of the pension awarded to the widows of the 1916 leaders and this present application might not have been necessary.

She also pointed out that there was a sum of just under £3,000 invested for the children but that 'Donagh's share, if realised now, would produce only about £1,200. This sum would be sufficient to maintain him till qualified but would leave him with nothing to carry him over the first few years until he could be self-supporting.'[30]

These representations were successful, as in October 1936, Donagh himself, then living in Sandymount in Dublin, contacted the Department of Defence to inform it that with the payments made to him to date he had completed both his BA and BL degrees:

As you probably know the first few years at the Bar are at once hazardous and unremunerative; of those who have been called in the last few years I know only one or two who have made more than £20 or £30. I hope you will find it possible to extend my allowance for some period as otherwise I can see no possibility of practising – as it is we are living on capital. Further grants would need to be much less than in the past as now there are no educational or examination fees to be taken into consideration. I hope you will be able to do something; I am very grateful for your help in the past, without which I could never have qualified and I hope you will be able to help me further until I am able to actually earn money.[31]

At that stage his pension was £80 a year which, along with National Aid money, was, as he had earlier that year noted in a letter to Éamon de Valera, 'the whole of my income ... this leaves very little, if any, margin, so that I am always in danger of finding myself with nothing at all.'[32] He was then looking for an increase. Early the following year, in 1937, a priest acquaintance of his appealed to the Minister for Finance, Seán MacEntee, to reimburse MacDonagh for expenditure in connection with his final examinations: 'The purpose of the annual grants was to equip the two MacDonaghs for the battle of life and I put it to you that it is not fair on Donagh to saddle him as he starts in life with a debt of £116.18.0 ... surely if we wish an end we must also wish the means to that end.' MacDonagh was granted the extra funds through means of 'extra statutory grants'.[33]

As mentioned in the letter written by his aunt, Donagh MacDongah had had a difficult childhood; he was only three years old when his father was executed and his mother Muriel Gifford drowned in 1917 while MacDonagh was in hospital with tuberculosis. A talented writer, he was noted as being an exceptional student in University College Dublin and had spent his second undergraduate year at the Sorbonne in Paris. In 1934 his talent for poetry was revealed in a published collection. By the time he wrote the letters referred to above he was married and would soon have two children to support. He was later to describe himself as a 'briefless barrister'. He lost his wife when she drowned in the bath during an epileptic seizure and he subsequently married her sister. But his professional life improved, as he was appointed a district justice in Wexford, which provided him with a steady income until his death in 1968.[34] His was a life marked by both the privilege and burden of his father's legacy, but it is clear that the pensions he received were essential to his education and professional status; quite simply, as he recognised, he could not have succeeded without them.

IV

The Board of Assessors overseeing the Military Service Pensions Act of 1924 approved the payment of pensions to 3,855 applicants, but rejected the applications of 9,900 other applicants. Overall, by 1957, under the 1924 and 1934 Acts, 82,000 people applied for pensions and, of these, 15,700 were successful and 66,300 were rejected.[35] Even allowing for dubious or even dishonest claims, such a gulf between the numbers of applications and awards meant it was inevitable that there was a very large constituency of people who would have been, at the very least, disappointed at the decisions of the assessors.

Individual material circumstances did change and, for some, prompted a rethink about an application. In March 1944, James Hogan, the historian and political scientist, applied for a pension. Hogan had joined the 3rd Battalion of the Dublin Brigade of the Irish Volunteers in 1915; his promising academic career had been interrupted at University College Dublin by the outbreak of the War of Independence and he was a member of the East Clare flying column. He took a leading part in military engagements in Clare, Galway and East Limerick. He was successful in his application for the Chair of History in University College Cork in 1920 but did not take up the post until 1924; he subsequently became a very active member of the Irish Manuscripts Commission and was active in Fine Gael politics. He married in 1935 and had six children.[36] In his letter to the Pensions Board, Hogan noted that he had not applied for a military pension in 1924:

> I was at that time unmarried, and holding a professorship ... my circumstances were such that I did not think it necessary to look for any compensation for my services such as they were. But my position is very different now. I have been married for several years and have heavy domestic responsibilities. Moreover, my health has deteriorated in such a way as to impose upon me the duty of providing for the future of my family, and this disimprovement in my health I believe would not have arisen were it not for my participation in the national struggle. This then is why I have altered my old attitude and beg to submit to you my claim for a military service pension.[37]

The following month, the Secretary of the Department of Defence noted that the Minister for Defence, Oscar Traynor, 'does not consider as satisfactory the reasons put forward' by Hogan for the delay in his application but significantly, indicating that senior politicians could and did intervene to reverse refusals, Traynor wrote in May that 'in view of certain information conveyed to me verbally, I have now decided that Professor Hogan's application may be accepted.'[38] From September 1945 Hogan was awarded an annual pension of £120.[39]

Hogan's case was unusual in the length of time it took him to apply, but also because of the speed with which his case was processed. Some applicants had to endure years of waiting, frustration and tortuous correspondence, often with no positive outcome from their perspective. The tone of their letters conveys an anger with seemingly endless bureaucratic delay and, as many saw it, inertia. What was an added insult to some was their genuine dismay that their services and sacrifices were not officially recognised, sometimes because of the difficulty of verifying the exact level of service or number of military engagements. Poverty formed the backdrop to many of the cases being considered, which gave an added urgency to appeals.

In November 1937 Annie Maher from Friar Street in Cashel, Co. Tipperary, made an appeal 'on behalf of my daughter', noting that:

> My son always voted for the government and my son William did 3 weeks hunger strike in Hare Park camp and he has always given his services to the cause since 1916. He has not received any pension so far and is now out of work for the past 10 months and living on me, a widow on the side of the street, but so far as I can see it is the parties that are up against the government are getting all. My daughter who has worked for the cause since 1916 is employed in the Labour Exchange Cashel on a wage of 10/- per week to keep herself and her brother. It was Mr Lemass that gave her this job as she was in communication with him for some time … is not that a miserable wage for a girl to work for. Surely the people that suffered should get more consideration. My daughter also is in for a pension but was not called yet and is waiting nearly three years … if things don't improve I must send my son and daughter to England to seek for a better living.[40]

The file containing William Maher's application includes correspondence that ran for over 20 years. He gave sworn evidence before an interviewing officer in January 1942 in which he detailed his IRA service blocking roads and carrying despatches as well as transporting IRA men and taking part in one military engagement before the Truce in July 1921. He also had extensive Civil War service and was interned for 18 months, ultimately in Hare Park internment camp at the Curragh, Co. Kildare where he partook in a hunger strike for 19 days in March 1924. A note attached to the end of the transcript of his sworn evidence for the advisory committee reads: 'Good Civil War service. His one scrap before the Truce may pull him through.'[41]

But it did not pull him through. In April 1942 Maher was informed that he was 'not a person to whom the act applies' and was therefore not eligible for a pension.[42] Under the terms of the Military Service Pensions (Amendment) Act 1949, a Referee could reconsider applications. The next batch of correspondence concerning Maher commenced in October 1956 when William's brother John, who was town clerk of Cashel, wrote to explain that a letter had arrived requesting that William appear at the courthouse in Cashel to deal with a review of his case. John explained that his brother had in fact died in November 1955 and that the letter regarding the review of William's case had been sent to the wrong person. He pointed out that two IRA colleagues of his brother were available 'to vouch for my late brother's service'.[43] He was informed in November 1956 that his brother's application was still under consideration. In September the following year those reviewing the case noted that the 'applicant claims an exchange of fire which lasted 20 minutes with British military. This incident has not been verified by witnesses. The act doesn't apply.'[44]

Verification of that alleged 20 minutes of gunfire was the difference between the award of a pension and refusal. In June 1958 John Maher was again 'reluctantly compelled' to write to the office of the Referee. Not unreasonably, he suggested that 'surely after such a long time and especially in view of the fact that my brother is dead since November 1955, close on 2 ½ years ago, a decision as to whether he was or was not entitled to a service certificate and allowance should long since have been arrived at.' The following month he was informed that reconsideration had resulted in the same conclusion and decision as before: that William was not a person to whom the act applied.[45]

An emotionally charged John Maher wrote to the Secretary of the Department of Defence, maintaining he could not understand the decision, given his brother's obvious sacrifices during the revolutionary period: 'Incidentally, I may remark that I am not in receipt of either a certificate or allowance and though qualified for such, I have declined [to apply] for same.' John had been in prison in Maidstone prison in England. With regard to his brother, he added that:

Within the past week spring cleaning and painting was being carried out by my sister in the house where she and my brother resided, and in an old box put safely away was found some papers on which were written details of his activities since he joined the IRA in 1917 ... they show sufficient evidence to prove that he was certainly a person to whom the provisions of the act of 1934 apply.[46]

The reply he received informed him that the minister had no function in the matter, that the Referee's decision was 'final, conclusive and binding', and that there was no action that could be taken to further review the case.[47]

The archive of the Military Service Pensions Collection is littered with such disappointments and desperate pleas against what must have seemed like a cold, harsh bureaucracy. It was not just the Department of Defence that had a role in the pensions process; for obvious reasons relating to expenditure controls, the Department of Finance was also involved and could be calculating in seeking to minimise spending on the pensions. Such an approach was evident in the Department of Finance's reaction to a successful appeal by Denis Doran against the abatement of pension payable to him due to his employment as a district court clerk. Doran, from Enniscorthy, Co. Wexford, who had been a member of the Irish Volunteers, was active in 1916 and interned in Frongoch camp in Wales, had been employed as a district court clerk from October 1934 to May 1938. His pension had been abated for that period, as part or all of pensions could be suspended under the terms of a public service abatement for those in receipt of other remuneration from the state. But the pension was not awarded to him until 15 months after he had ceased that employment, at a time when he was not in receipt of any remuneration. He had been awarded a Grade E pension based on service of just over two years; his annual pension was £11. 17s. 11d.

In January 1942 Doran approached Richard Corish, the mayor of Wexford, informing him that he had not been in the employment of the government at the time the pension was granted and that he had sent four letters, from December 1939 to December 1940, to no avail:

> You will therefore see that another 12 months have now passed and still no word … surely it doesn't take 2 years to decide a simple legal matter? My whole argument is: The Pension was not awarded to me until I was 15 months out of the government's employment and consequently, I was not in receipt of salary or remuneration during the continuance of such pension. There could be no continuance until there was a beginning and I was not in their employment at the beginning of the pension.[48]

Doran's solicitor alleged that the reason for the department's stalling was an obvious desire to prevent the payment of money legitimately due to pensioners. The Attorney General agreed with this interpretation; he had 'no doubt' that a court would agree likewise, and the Department of Defence knew that

> there are a considerable number of cases which would be affected by whatever decision may eventually be reached in the present case … these are the cases of persons who on the commencing date of the pension (1st October 1924 or 1st October 1934, as the case may be) were in receipt of remuneration payable out of public moneys, but who were not granted military service pensions for some time after that date. Their pensions were abated with effect from the commencement date of pension. In view of the advice received in the present case it would appear that abatement of pension should not have been effected during the period from the commencing date of pension to the date when pension was actually granted, in each case.[49]

A civil servant from the Department of Finance recommended that Doran be repaid the pension amount previously abated but that this should not be seen as a precedent; he suggested that in general the policy of pension abatements should continue, with repayments only being approved where the pensioner challenged the practice in his own case and to ensure that, when repayment took place, it did so before legal action commenced. It was estimated that the approximate number of cases of this nature was a substantial 2,001.[50]

In October 1942 a clearly distraught but dignified Doran – and this dignity was characteristic of many of these letter writers who struggled not to become too emotional in the face of bureaucracy's stone wall – wrote to the Secretary of the Department of Defence: 'I am a married man with a wife and 3 children to keep and being unemployed, I am at a big loss in not receiving the pay order punctually.'[51]

Understandably, the Department of Finance was continuously vigilant about policing the cases of those whose pensions were liable to be abated or suspended, as arose in relation to Patrick Wade from Balla, Co. Mayo. In 1943, he was indebted to the Department of Agriculture for £59 under levies incurred under the Slaughter of Cattle and Sheep Acts; the amount due was to be recovered from the military service pension payable to him and the payment of his pension was suspended. In October 1946 he wrote a plaintive letter to the Department of Finance:

> My pension has been stopped for years for cattle levy due ... I have 11 children and my wife dead. I lost £620 in the fight for Irish freedom in Cork and Mayo. My shop was closed for a few years owing to this levy ... I am now starting the world over again with a big expense over my head and my 11 children and can't get a job for them.[52]

Forfeiture of a pension could also occur if a recipient was convicted of a criminal offence. In 1940 John Guiney, a small farmer in Meath who was in receipt of an annual pension of £50, was convicted, along with eight others, under the Offences Against the State Act, 1939, arising out of a milk strike in Dublin that year which had involved picketing and the destruction of fresh milk. Guiney was convicted of unlawful assembly and malicious damage and was bound over to keep the peace for 12 months. In this instance, however, 'the special criminal court considered ... that the loss of pension consequent on the conviction constituted an unduly severe punishment for the offence' and the pension payments were resumed.[53]

V

Financial penury was certainly a factor in prompting applications, but intertwined with that were issues of pride and status and the difficulty of verifying the historical record, particularly 30 years after the events. In this regard, the judgements handed down by the pension bureaucrats were short, sharp and potentially devastating. In October 1941, Katie Walsh from Clonmel, Co. Tipperary, wrote to the office of the Referee to appeal the refusal to award her a pension. She had been a member of the Touraneena branch of Cumann na mBan and she wrote: 'I claim that my services which entailed hardship, privation and danger from the time of my enrolment to the end of hostilities entitle me to a just consideration from the government of this country.'[54] She requested an opportunity to testify in person, which she did in July 1941. On the basis of this testimony, the interviewing officer informed the advisory committee:

> Applicant had fair activities. She seemed to be very vague about periods. Her principal activities would appear to have been catering for the men who came to her cottage, none of whom stopped overnight, owing to lack of accommodation. She may probably have done more work than she can recall and her case may be worth consideration. Hold for officers.

Three months later the verdict from the advisory committee was succinct and negative: 'No Change. On appeal, applicant gave evidence. There does not appear to be anything outstanding in her service.'[55]

Others who, like Tom Barry, were disappointed with the decision reached about their rank expressed their dismay but did not pursue an appeal, being well aware how long the process could take. As John Scollan from Drumcondra, Co. Dublin, on whose behalf leading politicians Seán T. O'Kelly of Fianna Fáil and Richard Mulcahy of Fine Gael testified, put it in May 1938: 'The question of rank is certainly disappointing. As I am now 62 years of age it would only delay matters considerably if I were to appeal. This I am not going to do.'[56] Scollan had been director of organisation, intelligence and munitions for the Hibernian Rifles and a member of the Executive Council of Sinn Féin and had, at various stages, been a prisoner in Frongoch and Wormwood Scrubs and Reading jails. Although he had made his sworn statement in October 1935, he had still heard nothing by November 1936. In May 1938, he had been informed that his pension would be £20 per annum.[57]

Many of the pension files also reveal the long-term effects of the loss of a significant earner within the family and the levels of dependency within individual families. In January 1933, Margaret Murphy, an invalided 68-year-old widow with an unmarried daughter, sought a pension. Her only son, John Murphy, had been executed in Beggars Bush Barracks in November 1922 at the age of 19: 'He was a promising boy and a great help to me in keeping my home and if by the will of God he had been spared to me he would now be able to replace his father in keeping a home for myself and my only daughter.'[58] The Secretary of the Army Pensions Board subsequently received a report of an investigation of her claim which involved a personal visit: Mrs Murphy was 'confined to her bed and barely able to move'. At the time of her son John's execution her husband had been a labourer in the Guinness brewery and her eldest daughter was married and living elsewhere; her 22-year-old daughter was earning 15s. a week in a draper's shop. According to the report, John

> appears to have been a very intelligent lad because at the age of 16 ½ years he secured a clerkship in the railway ... he was stationed in Tullow ... and had, his mother thinks, about £2.10s. a week. He used to send her on an average of 25 shillings a week ... about a month before his death he told his mother and sister that he had secured a job in Suffolk Street, but they have never been able definitely to say what it was ... the probability is that he was wholly engaged in IRA work.[59]

Margaret Murphy's situation in 1933, two years after the death of her husband, was bleak; she had an allowance of 16s. a week from her late husband's employer, Guinness; she was keeping her middle daughter's two children, aged seven and ten, although the children's father gave her 10s. a week for their upkeep. Of these two children she wrote, 'their mother it was who opened and first read the official notification of her brother's execution, and she never recovered from the shock.' The matriarch was paying 5s. a week in rent and her younger daughter 'is obliged to devote her services to the household duties'. It was decided that this applicant was 'obviously in necessitous circumstances' and that there had been a 'partial dependence' on the executed son in terms of the income of the house.[60]

Understandably, at a time of high unemployment, economic stagnation, and very limited prospects for the next generation, the issue of dependency permeates the Military Service Pensions Collection. In 1946, the 34-year-old daughter of an army pension recipient who had recently died asked the Department of Defence if her father's last cheque could be made payable to her

> as I am v. absolutely dependent for my support on my father's pension ... I should also like to point out that I am an invalid for over twelve years and I am not in receipt of any monies from any source whatsoever. I am unable to work, I get no relief or insurance benefits, and I have nothing left out of my death policy as any money received went to pay doctors for my father's illness and funeral expenses. My brother in law has asked me to live with him for the future.[61]

The sum was paid to her as requested; it amounted to 13s. 9d. For those seeking to survive or eke out a bare subsistence in the 1930s and 1940s, every penny generated by War of Independence service was precious.

11

FROM ROGUE REVOLUTIONARY TO ROGUE CIVIL SERVANT

The resurrection of Bulmer Hobson[1]

MARNIE HAY

Prior to the 1916 Easter Rising, Bulmer Hobson (1883–1969) was one of the leading propagandists and organisers within the advanced nationalist movement in Ireland.[2] As a Sinn Féin propagandist, he was second only to Arthur Griffith. He also co-founded the nationalist youth group Na Fianna Éireann with Constance Markievicz in 1909,[3] served on the Supreme Council of the Irish Republican Brotherhood (IRB) from 1912 to 1914, helped to establish the Irish Volunteers in 1913, and co-ordinated the landing of guns and ammunition at Howth in 1914. His open opposition to an insurrection with no hope of military success provoked his comrades in the IRB to kidnap him on Good Friday 1916 and hold him captive until the rebellion was underway. This, combined with his subsequent evasion of arrest, ensured that his disappearance from the nationalist scene lasted longer than that historic Easter weekend. To the general public it was as if he had been executed along with the rebel leaders, but without the posthumous benefit of their spin-doctors.[4]

Some of Hobson's former colleagues, misunderstanding his motives for not participating in the Rising, not only denounced him as a coward and a traitor, but subjected him to ostracism.[5] Despite this, Hobson managed to stage a quiet resurrection after the establishment of an independent Irish state as a civil servant and economic propagandist. In 1924 he secured permanent employment as Deputy Director of Stamping in the Office of the Revenue Commissioners. Frustrated, however, that successive Irish governments did not institute 'a bold national policy of reconstruction' to tackle poverty, unemployment and emigration,[6] he resuscitated his propagandist career by turning his pen to these issues in the 1930s.

Hobson, the product of a liberal Belfast Quaker family, believed that a strong economy in the Irish Free State would lead to the eventual reunification of Ireland.[7] His concern for Irish unity dated back to his teenage admiration for the combination of non-sectarianism and separatism espoused by Theobald Wolfe Tone and the United Irishmen, and his own early efforts in Belfast to bring Ulster Protestants into the nationalist movement through such propagandist organisations as the Protestant National Society, the Ulster Literary Theatre and the Dungannon Clubs.[8] As a civil servant, he had to publish some of his writings on economic issues anonymously or under a pseudonym. Despite these precautions, however, his criticism of the government's economic policies landed him in trouble at work, provoking the censure of Minister for Finance and fellow Belfast native Seán MacEntee. This chapter will not only uncover Hobson's little-known activities as an economic propagandist and their impact on his civil service career, but will also help to bring his life after 1916 out of the shadows.

In the period 1900–16 during his years as an advanced nationalist activist, Hobson's devotion to nationalist activities had impacted negatively on his ability to secure steady employment, particularly in the north. As a single man with no dependents this had not been overly problematic. His situation was to change when, while on the run in June 1916, he married Claire Gregan (1887–1958), a member of Sinn Féin and Cumann na mBan who had been his secretary at the Irish Volunteer office.[9] Consequently, when Hobson emerged from hiding after the June 1917 amnesty for individuals connected to the rebellion who had escaped arrest or were still serving time in prison, he had to find steady employment that would enable him to support a family in Dublin.

Prior to the 1916 Rising, Hobson had been a printer and journalist by trade.[10] He built on this experience from c.1918 to 1923 when he worked in book publishing as co-director of the Candle Press and Martin Lester Ltd in Dublin. By 1920 the Hobsons had set up home in the Mill House on Whitechurch Road in Rathfarnham.[11] Their children Declan Bulmer and Camilla Claire were born in 1921 and 1928 respectively.

In addition to their involvement in the advanced nationalist movement, Hobson and his wife, whom an *Irish Times* columnist described as 'strikingly handsome',[12] shared an interest in literature and theatre and helped to support the establishment of the Gate Theatre in the late 1920s.[13] The Hobsons were known for hosting gatherings at which 'the most diffident artists' were encouraged 'to express themselves'.[14] They also shared a concern for social issues. For instance, Claire Hobson gave evidence on behalf of Saor an Leanbh (the Irish Save the Children Fund) to the Committee on the Criminal Law Amendment Acts (1880–5) and Juvenile Prostitution (otherwise known as the Carrigan committee) (1930–1).[15]

Perhaps finding that book publishing did not provide a reliable enough income to support his young family, Hobson sought employment in the civil service of the new Irish Free State established in December 1922. He was initially hired in August 1923 as Temporary Technical Clerk in the Stationery Office at a salary of £250 per annum. He moved up to a permanent, pensionable position in

October 1924 after he successfully interviewed for the post of Deputy Director of Stamping in the Office of the Revenue Commissioners. The creation of this new position may have been a result of the Minister and Secretaries Act of 1924, which led to the increased formalisation of staffing of the civil service and of the titles of individual civil servants. The job initially came with a salary scale of £350–£500 per annum plus bonus.[16]

Ironically, Hobson was based in Dublin Castle, the former bastion of British authority in Ireland. He managed the printing section of the Stamping Department in the Office of the Revenue Commissioners, which was responsible for all of the government's 'secure' printing needs, such as postage stamps, pension books, licenses and various government forms.[17] By the late 1940s he had about 60 people working under his supervision.[18]

The Revenue fell under the remit of the Department of Finance, but was an independent entity. As Hobson had no previous experience in the Irish civil service, it is not overly surprising that he joined an office associated with Finance. Like External Affairs, it was a newly created department, there having been no need for such functions in Ireland under the Union with Great Britain.[19] The newness of Finance may have provided more scope for bringing in new blood. According to a former employee of the Stamping Department, some people who were recruited at its inception had been 'politically involved'.[20] Perhaps Hobson's old friends from his Dungannon Club days, P. S. O'Hegarty, Secretary of the Department of Posts and Telegraphs from 1922 to 1944, and Ernest Blythe, who served as Minister for Finance from September 1923 until March 1932, helped him to secure employment.

Deputy Director of Stamping was not, however, the position in a new Ireland that one would have predicted based on Hobson's earlier political career. Nonetheless, he held this position until his retirement in January 1948, even though his increasingly poor eyesight eventually made it difficult for him to supervise the output of the printing presses. Opportunities for further advancement were limited because he had been hired at the highest level within the technical (or industrial) grades of the civil service. According to a former member of Hobson's department, perhaps due to snobbery the technical grades were deemed inferior to the non-technical grades, and a transfer between the two was not made possible until the Stamping Department was restructured in the late 1970s.[21]

As a civil servant, Hobson built on his past employment experience in printing and publishing, but occasionally could indulge his interest in economic matters. For instance, he had the opportunity to serve as secretary to an inter-departmental committee on the sugar beet industry, compiling the committee's May 1933 report.[22] He also completed two government-funded editing projects, though he may have undertaken such work in an independent capacity.

Dublin Corporation commissioned him to edit *A Book of Dublin*, which first appeared in May 1929 and was then reprinted in June 1930.[23] Billed as an 'official handbook', this attractively illustrated volume presented the city of Dublin as historically and culturally significant and economically thriving. Presumably, potential tourists and investors were the target audience. The book, however, did not find favour with one reviewer in particular: Fr Timothy Corcoran, SJ, the editor of the *Catholic Bulletin*. He objected to the content of the volume, describing its two editions as 'manuals for the Ascendancy mind' that 'exuded in every page the drippings of deliquescent Protestantism'.[24]

Under the direction of a committee appointed by the Minister for Industry and Commerce, Patrick McGilligan, Hobson also edited the *Saorstát Éireann Official Handbook*, which aimed 'to give an account of the Irish Free State as it is to-day', as well as providing the historical background necessary for understanding modern Ireland.[25] The book was also a report on the achievements of the Cumann na nGaedheal government during the first decade of Irish independence. Unfortunately, the publication of the handbook was badly timed; it appeared in 1932, just as the electorate rejected William Cosgrave and Cumann na nGaedheal in favour of Éamon de Valera and Fianna Fáil.

Corcoran lambasted Hobson in gleeful purple prose. Edited by a Protestant and designed to provide an account of the first ten years of the Free State, the handbook was unlikely to find favour in the *Catholic Bulletin*, which reflected an extremist Catholic and an anti-Treatyite ethos. Corcoran objected to the book's cover as well as its contents. He referred to the cover design as 'Bulmer's blurb', describing it as 'an attempt to make Celtic traceries prance about as if they were cubist figures performing motley mummery to jazz music'. In his opinion, 'the Bulmer within' was even 'more objectionable' than the gaudy cover; he dismissed Hobson's introduction as a 'crude chunk of party propaganda' and gave mixed reviews to articles by individual contributors.[26]

Hobson and Corcoran may not have shared a taste in cover art or agreed on what aspects of Ireland to promote in government-funded publications, but they had one thing in common. Independent (or partially independent) Ireland was not turning out quite the way either of them wanted it to. For Hobson, Irish independence had proved a disappointment. When the Irish Free State was founded in 1922, he had anticipated 'a period of economic reconstruction' that would undo the effects of the Union between Britain and Ireland. Instead he witnessed what were, in his opinion, 'protracted and barren conflicts over verbal differences of politics which only the contestants, and not many of them, could understand, and these conflicts developed a fanatical bitterness which found its outlet in civil war'. He saw 'the high hopes, born of a national victory' get sucked into a quagmire of 'violence and folly'.[27] His concern for what he believed should be the new state's foremost priority – building up the economy

– led him to air his views on economic issues publically despite his position as a civil servant. In light of the poor economic conditions of the time, his employment in the Office of the Revenue Commissioners, and his early writings on economic nationalism in newspapers like the *Republic* and the *Peasant*, Hobson's interest and energy in raising awareness about ways to combat poverty, unemployment and emigration is not surprising.

Hobson praised the 1929 Shannon hydro-electric scheme, which harnessed the waters of the River Shannon to generate electricity, and pushed for it to be followed up by further bold steps to encourage Irish industry.[28] He advocated a policy of reforestation in order to provide Ireland with a native source of wood for the manufacturing industry, to generate much-needed employment in rural areas, and to preserve the Gaeltacht. In 1931 he privately published a 23-page pamphlet entitled *A National Forestry Policy*.[29] In this pamphlet he proposed 'the establishment of 525,000 acres of plantations within fifteen years', criticising the government's aim to plant 200,000 acres as too modest because it would not benefit the current generation socially and industrially.[30] He recommended the creation of a forestry authority, the development of 'a programme of land acquisition and planting on an adequate scale and for a definite and extended period', and a financial policy that 'would enable the work to proceed as planned and without interruption'.[31]

A critic in the *Dublin Magazine* lauded Hobson's 'far-reaching suggestions' as 'worthy of earnest consideration', but criticised him for ignoring the existence of forestry expertise within the Department of Agriculture. Instead Hobson had suggested 'the importation of trained technicians from abroad to advise on the utilisation of ... non-agricultural land'. The critic pointed out that when a 'distinguished German arboriculturist' who was unfamiliar with Irish conditions had served as an advisor on a plantation in Knockboy, Connemara, the results were disastrous.[32]

Hobson's advocacy of reforestation in the Gaeltacht stemmed from both cultural and economic concerns. In 1936 Hobson declared that 'the failure of successive Governments to attempt the economic reconstruction of the Gaeltacht [was] the most profoundly disappointing feature of the first fourteen years of Irish self-government.' In his view the economic renewal of the poverty-stricken Gaeltacht, 'which all our enthusiastic city Gaels have told us [was] essential for the survival of Irish language and culture', would do more to maintain the native language than 'superimposing Father O'Growney on the educational system of Archbishop Whately'.[33] Hobson argued that employment created through reforestation of the Gaeltacht would enable 'the people of the western counties ... to enjoy a good and an improving standard of life as the result of their own labours in the places where they live'. instead of having to migrate to another country as casual labourers or draw the dole 'to save them from destitution'.[34]

First Published about end of August 1905

Written by Bulmer Hobson

Dungannon Club Publications, No. 2. **PRICE ONE PENNY.**

TO THE WHOLE PEOPLE OF IRELAND
THE MANIFESTO
OF THE
DUNGANNON CLUB BELFAST

I. Ireland to-day.

Our position. Ireland stands to-day in the midst of the strong and powerful peoples weak and miserable, among the wealthy nations we are poor and beggarly, among the proud we cry with a weak voice faint-heartedly for that strong and independent national life that can only be won by strenuous effort and great sacrifice. We have but to let things drift, and continue in our old courses for another generation and the Irish Nation will have perished utterly; we have but to turn like men and take the helm into our own hands, and we can make it strong, and great and independent.

We can, if we will, build up a people self-contained, self-centered, self-reliant—a people not looking for the repeal of an English Act, nor for the permission of England to exist and develop to its highest and fullest capacity.

To-day we are uneducated, but our people must be taught: to-day our industries are paralised, and the people are leaving the land. They must be kept at home here in Ireland, industries must be started.

A complete commercial—a political and social reconstruction of the country is requisite—and has got to be undertaken by the men of Ireland now. It is a great work, but we will not step aside because of the greatness of it. IT CAN BE DONE IF THE PEOPLE WILL, AND IT MUST, OR THEY PERISH.

II. National Government.

English Rule. It is only with free political institutions that a people can develop its genius or its power; and so at the back of every evil that infests this land, over and above them all, and responsible for all, is the government of Ireland by England. England governs this country against the wishes of its people. Ethically her occupation of Ireland is immoral and indefensible—but John Bull is not worried with points of ethics or conscience. But so long as he governs this land against the will of its people, he has got to expect the utmost opposition from the people he insists on governing.

In the struggle between the two nations, our opponents have got an efficient weapon of attack in the form of their Government. We on the other hand have no organisation to oppose to their Government, so we must create one as speedily as may be. England may not recognise it as representative of the people, but her recognition is of little importance. A national organisation that is going to cope with injustice established for such a length of time and so

(1)

In the autumn of 1932 Hobson presented de Valera, the new president of the Executive Council, with a draft 'plan to break the economic depression in Saorstát Éireann and to relieve the government of the cost of maintaining the unemployed.'[35] Hobson, like many others, probably hoped that the new Fianna Fáil government would jumpstart the Irish economy. In addition, he may have wished to demonstrate a willingness to work with his new taskmasters. Hobson's plan involved the establishment of an Economic Recovery Commission, which would supervise and co-ordinate the work of two sub-commissions, one on Land Reclamation, Drainage and Forestry and the other on Housing and Town Planning. According to Hobson, de Valera said 'he entirely agreed with [the economic plan] and that it was just what he wanted to do – but he did nothing.'[36]

In September 1933 Hobson again wrote to de Valera about these economic proposals, asserting without any trace of modesty that 'after another year's close study I am still more completely satisfied that they are the best, if not the only real solution of the problem of unemployment here.' Hobson offered to meet with de Valera to answer any objections to his proposals that may have deterred the president from adopting them. Hobson had obviously circulated his memorandum to others because he explained in the letter that he had been asked to publish it, but he wanted to get de Valera's permission first. In conclusion, Hobson wrote: 'I hope you will believe that I only return to the subject from a desire to help in the solution of the most urgent problem which confronts the country.'[37] De Valera appears to have given Hobson permission to publish the memorandum anonymously. Hobson published a revised version, entitled *National Economic Recovery: An Outline Plan*, privately in 1934. It was reprinted by the Talbot Press the following year.[38]

This outline plan was not Hobson's first anonymous publication on economic issues. In 1933 he had published a pamphlet entitled *The New Querist*, which drew on the tradition of Church of Ireland bishop George Berkeley's eighteenth-century pamphlet *The Querist* by posing a series of nearly 200 economic queries for 'the consideration of the public'.[39] *The New Querist* reflects Hobson's belief that a change in monetary policy and government investment in projects like reforestation and housing could combat poverty, unemployment and emigration.

Berkeley was an advocate of self-sufficiency as one way of tackling Ireland's economic problems. In looking to Berkeley, Hobson was tapping into a tradition that was also being mined by Fianna Fáil. In an article tracing the direct and indirect influence of Berkeley's ideas on Fianna Fáil economic policy, William Murphy points out that Hobson drew on some of Berkeley's ideas, but for the most part used the bishop's 'structure and reputation' to convey some of Hobson's own ideas.[40] In particular, *The New Querist* reflects his interest in the social credit movement.

The founder of this movement was Major C. H. Douglas, a British engineer who published his theories of society in numerous articles, pamphlets and books. He came to public attention shortly after the First World War when some of his articles were published in a popular British avant-garde periodical called *New Age*. Douglas had 'a unique interpretation of the role of banks in issuing credit and creating money', believing 'that banks [could] create money for their own use or for loan simply by forming an account and crediting it with whatever amount they desire'. Douglas himself wrote that 'deposits are created, to a major extent, by purely book-keeping transactions on the part of the banking institutions.' As he saw it, if banks could create money by increasing the money supply, then governments could tap into this money supply for the public good.[41]

Hobson was intrigued with Douglas's ideas regarding the creation of money. In *The New Querist* he asked 'whether anything is scarce in this country except money?'[42] He suggested that the state should create money and spend it on wages to employ people to build much-needed houses, schools and roads, and to work on land drainage and reforestation projects. This in turn would provide people with an income that they could spend on goods, thus creating a demand for various commodities produced in Ireland. In his view, following such a plan would enable the Irish government to increase consumption and production in the home market, the only market over which it had any control.[43]

Hobson's interpretation of social credit was only one strand of his economic thinking; a second strand was similar to Keynesianism. He himself noted that critics dismissed his economic writings as 'merely an adaptation' of the ideas contained in John Maynard Keynes's 1936 book *The General Theory of Employment, Interest and Money*.[44] As a result of this influential book, government control of expenditure began to be seen as the way to provide full employment. What his critics failed to note was that Hobson's *New Querist* and *National Economic Recovery* actually pre-dated Keynes's book. In 1937 Hobson commented that 'the new trend in English economic thinking which has recently appeared is tremendously important. I am very pleased that I had published my proposals before Keynes' recantation.'[45] By 'recantation' Hobson meant Keynes's rejection of the then-dominant economic belief in non-interference with the free market.

Hobson's ideas were ahead of their time in a country where Department of Finance officials would not start to 'absorb and come to terms with Keynesian economics in an Irish context' until the later years of the Emergency, as the Second World War was known in neutral Ireland.[46] Thus, Hobson's economic pamphlets made little if any impact. In 1934 he admitted: 'I cannot say that my efforts have made any impression on our politicians, who seem to see all the facts except the relevant ones and have time to do everything except think.'[47] Despite being faced with such indifference, he kept writing and publishing his views.

In 1935 he established a small monthly paper called *Prosperity* to raise awareness about economic issues. The paper was published by the League against Poverty, which aimed to unite 'people of all parties, or of none, who wished to see the standards of economic life raised in Saorstát Éireann'.[48] Free copies were sent to prominent clerics.[49] Hobson served as editor of the paper, while Fred Johnson, the son of Tom Johnson, the former leader of the Labour party in the Dáil, worked as manager. Lord Monteagle, Frank Hugh O'Donnell and Dr Patrick McCartan provided funding for the publication.[50] The paper, which had an initial circulation of 300, published schemes for the economic reconstruction of Ireland and tapped into the Catholic social action movement by providing interpretations of the papal encyclicals on social issues, such as *Quadragesimo Anno* of 1931. Hobson wrote most of the articles under a variety of pseudonyms.[51]

Minister for Finance Seán MacEntee was so 'perturbed by the criticisms that were being levelled against his party's financial policy by the League against Poverty' that 'he requested that the Department of Justice identify the group behind it.' Garda Special Branch, which maintained dossiers on a number of organisations in the 1930s, delivered its report on the group on 23 April 1936.[52] Hobson is not mentioned in this report, suggesting that the investigation by the Gardaí found no evidence to link him with the League against Poverty, which they had deemed to be an organisation in name only.[53] Hobson, however, had gained considerable experience dodging police detectives back in his days as a Sinn Féin propagandist and member of the IRB.

In August 1936 the League against Poverty became the League for Social Justice, which was 'composed of people of all parties, or none, who wish to see the social and economic teaching of the papal encyclicals, given practical effect in Saorstát Éireann'.[54] Its 26-member council included Lord Monteagle, Fred Johnson, three clergymen, Fianna Fáil TD Seán Brady (a former member of the Dublin Fianna), and City Librarian of Dublin Roisín Walsh, among others.[55] Hobson's name does not appear on the list of council members. The League for Social Justice organised meetings to discuss Catholic social principles and published a series of pamphlets entitled *Towards a New Ireland*.[56]

In September 1936 *Prosperity* changed its name to *Social Justice*. The paper, however, folded in June 1937 after only 20 monthly issues.[57] As Hobson later noted, 'less than 100 people were sufficiently interested in the ideas it stood for to purchase it at the modest price of 2d. a copy.'[58]

Hobson's editorship of *Prosperity* brought him in touch with Mrs B. Berthon Waters, a writer on economic affairs, and the Rev. Edward Cahill, SJ, one of the founders of the Catholic Action movement in Ireland and Professor of Church History and Lecturer in Sociology at the Jesuit College in Milltown Park. Cahill and Waters were members of An Ríoghacht, a Catholic social action group established in 1926. It may seem odd that Hobson, a former Quaker, should team up with two Catholic social activists, but there were similarities in their views.[59] For instance, Catholic social thinking promoted the solidarity of community as an alternative to class struggle. Middle-class Hobson never had much time for class struggle. His Dungannon Clubs, which were part of the early Sinn Féin movement, had put what they saw as the interests of the nation before the divisive interests of class or religion.[60] In 1937 Hobson even admitted that 'personally I don't care if there are a lot of rich people so long as there are none left in involuntary poverty.'[61]

An Ríoghacht hoped to influence the social and economic policy of the Irish government by making a submission to the Commission on Banking, Currency and Credit, which met between 1934 and 1938. This commission, which was appointed by MacEntee, was directed to 'examine and report on the system in Saorstát Éireann of currency, banking, credit, public borrowing and lending' and 'to consider and report what changes, if any, are necessary or desirable to promote the social and economic welfare of the community and the interests of agriculture and industry'.[62] Hobson dismissed the commission as 'heavily loaded with partisans of the existing order'. Hobson, Waters and Cahill were keen to raise public awareness about the Banking Commission, so that matters 'of such vital importance to the whole community' would not be 'settled behind closed doors'.[63] Between July 1936 and October 1938 the trio tried to change the direction of the Banking Commission.[64]

In December 1936 Hobson, Cahill and Waters prepared a 16-page memorandum on behalf of the League for Social Justice, which they submitted to the commission on 14 January 1937. Unfortunately, it was delivered too late to be considered by the commission. Hobson then sent the memorandum to two economists in England in order to gain feedback. Although John G. Smith, Professor of Finance and Dean of the Faculty of Commerce at the University of Birmingham, and James E. Meade, a Fellow and Lecturer in Economics at Hertford College, Oxford, and future Nobel Laureate in Economics (1977), criticised certain parts of the document, they were generally positive. Cahill forwarded the economists' opinions to de Valera.[65] In addition, Cahill, Hobson and Waters sent de Valera a 'first and tentative draft of the form which a minority report might possibly take' in September 1937.[66] In writing their draft, the trio had had access to parts of the draft majority report,[67] which recommended maintaining the economic status quo, thus following the policy of the previous Cumann na nGaedheal government.

De Valera had suggested to his friend Eoin O'Keefe, who was a member of An Ríoghacht, that members of the commission who favoured a more progressive economic policy should submit a minority report. O'Keefe initially approached Alfred O'Rahilly, a member of the commission and Professor of Mathematical Physics at University College Cork, about preparing a minority report, but he was too busy. The job then fell to Hobson, Cahill and Waters.[68] Finín O'Driscoll has argued that de Valera, in instigating the production of a report, 'was attempting to ensure that the more radical element within Fianna Fáil could find solace in one of the minority reports and that those elements could not accuse him of losing the ideology of self-sufficiency that had brought Fianna Fáil to power.'[69]

The document written by Hobson, Cahill and Waters was presented as the Third Minority Report[70] in March 1938 by Peadar O'Loghlen, a Fianna Fáil politician from Ballyvaughan, Co. Clare, who had been appointed to the commission ostensibly to represent the interests of the rural community. O'Loghlen, though he had diligently attended meetings, had remained silent throughout the proceedings. It later emerged that he had been appointed not only as de Valera's watchdog,[71] but also 'to hold a watching brief for a group' within An Ríoghacht.[72] The Third Minority Report enraged MacEntee and the Secretary of the Department of Finance J. J. McElligott, neither of whom realised that a civil servant was partially responsible for the document. (Ironically, de Valera was more aware of Hobson's 'extracurricular activities' than the top men in Finance.) MacEntee and McElligott did not believe that O'Loghlen was the author and recognised that excerpts of the report were similar to passages in the anonymously published pamphlet *National Economic Recovery* and in two documents produced by the League for Social Justice, its submission to the Banking Commission and a pamphlet entitled *The Achill Island Tragedy*.[73]

The Third Minority Report also generated criticism from Fr Edward Coyne, SJ, an economist and future member of the Commission on Vocational Organisation. He was dismissive of Hobson's involvement, calling him a 'Quaker or Protestant' whose 'technique was well known': he 'gets a number of prominent or semi-prominent people to join forces and he then uses them as a means to propagate his fads'. Coyne viewed the scheme outlined in the report as 'quite untrue, most unwise, injurious to the encyclicals and would bring them into disrepute with educated Catholics, or would lead the uneducated to believe that the Third Minority Report really was a concrete remedy backed by the Pope'.[74]

The Third Minority Report disputed 'the validity of the link with sterling', the perceived need for a central bank, and the ability of 'the private sector to remedy unemployment or to provide any meaningful economic growth'. It recommended 'comprehensive government intervention in the provision of capital, capital development, and the provision of full employment', possibly through a state forestation policy.[75] The report reflects views put forward in Hobson's previous economic publications. Although de Valera praised the Third Minority Report, the production of which he had indirectly encouraged, the document made no impact on the existing policy.[76]

The contents of the Third Minority Report, and thus Hobson's ideas, later influenced the economic thought of Clann na Poblachta leader Seán MacBride.[77] In response to the British government's devaluation of sterling in September 1949, the cabinet of the Inter-Party government, of which MacBride was a member, would decide to establish a committee on devaluation the following month.

Hobson, by then in retirement, was appointed to the committee, but it does not appear to have functioned.[78] More recently, Des Gunning has suggested that the 'tone and attitude' of Hobson's economic writings 'anticipated current environmental "green" politics'.[79] For instance, Hobson's 'criticisms of the banks' dominance of the Irish economy were occasionally quoted by the Irish Green Party in the 1990s.'[80]

After his involvement with the production of the Third Minority Report, Hobson continued to work with Waters, writing pamphlets for the *Towards a New Ireland* series, which she edited.[81] This pamphlet series, which was published by the Irish People Co-Operative Society Ltd, supported 'a broadly-based policy of social and economic re-construction in Ireland appealing to all sections and interests in the life of the nation'.[82] In contrast to his own papers *Prosperity* and *Social Justice*, this pamphlet series claimed to have 'a wide circulation'.[83]

In addressing the need for economic renewal in the west of Ireland, Hobson's tone became increasingly sarcastic. In 1937 he noted:

> Perhaps when the last inhabitant of the Gaeltacht has departed for an English slum or a Scottish 'bothy' the Government will appoint a commission to report on the wealth which would be produced from the Irish Highlands. The report will be very interesting, but by then the absence of any available labour in the western desert will prevent its recommendations being carried out.[84]

In a review of Professor R. G. Stapledon's *The Hill Lands of Britain* Hobson praised the author's suggestions for developing and improving the productivity of highland areas, commenting that his work 'would be very highly prized in a rational society, and there is much that we in Ireland could profitably learn from him, if we had one here.'[85]

Hobson's remarks eventually landed him in hot water at work. As a civil servant he was prohibited from making political remarks in the public arena. However, at an An Ríoghacht meeting on 9 March 1938, Hobson commented on the issue of slum housing, proposing that:

> The government acting as a central bank should issue the money to local authorities for housing, and the money would be repaid out of the sale of the houses or rents from them. The number of houses built should depend on the natural limit imposed by materials and labour available, and not by the artificial limit of how local authorities could float loans.[86]

Press coverage of the meeting, which quoted Hobson's suggestions, provoked MacEntee to demand an explanation and apology from the rogue civil servant.

The disagreement between the civil servant and the government minister over what the former could or could not say in public begs a brief comparison of their respective political careers. Like Hobson, MacEntee was born and raised in Belfast and participated in the culturally nationalist Gaelic League and Ulster Literary Theatre. His father also supported Home Rule for Ireland. However, MacEntee, the younger of the two and a Catholic, did not join the advanced nationalist/republican organisations, such as Cumann na nGaedheal, the IRB, the Fianna and the Dungannon Clubs, in which Hobson had played a leading role in Belfast in the first decade of the twentieth century. In January 1914, while employed as assistant chief engineer at the Dundalk electricity works, MacEntee joined the Dundalk corps of the Irish Volunteers,[87] an organisation that Hobson was instrumental in setting up. The Easter Rising was a turning point for both men. Hobson's decision not to participate in the rebellion and his evasion of arrest effectively killed his rising political career.[88] In contrast, MacEntee's participation in the insurrection, for which he was not only imprisoned but also received a death sentence, from which he was later reprieved, helped to launch a political career first with Sinn Féin and then with Fianna Fáil that lasted until his retirement in 1969, the year of Hobson's death.[89] Thus Hobson's political career had ended just as MacEntee's was about to take off.

In responding to MacEntee's demand for an explanation and apology, Hobson defended his conduct. He explained that:

> In saying what I did I was endeavouring to make a contribution to the problem of slum clearance, on the necessity for which I thought there was complete unanimity of opinion among all classes and parties ... I thought the subject lay in a field of social effort which was completely outside politics, which civil servants could legitimately enter. I did not think I was contravening any regulation and did not intend to do so.

MacEntee, however, was not satisfied with this defence. In his view,

> it should have been perfectly clear to an officer of Mr Hobson's rank and responsibilities that his comments on what he conceives to be the government's duty in the matter of slum clearance and housing were distinctly of a political nature and that their public expression was a serious impropriety of [sic] Mr Hobson's part.

At MacEntee's insistence Hobson gave 'an unqualified undertaking' that he would not publicly comment on politics in future.[90]

Shortly afterwards in April 1938, Michael Deegan of the Land Commission complained that the League for Social Justice, which he had been told was founded by Hobson, had made comments regarding the forestry service. He lodged a protest and requested that the Revenue take steps to ensure 'that the rules which should guide civil servants in their public relations are observed'. In light of Hobson's recent 'undertaking' and an inability to attribute the offending comments on the forestry service to Hobson directly, no action was taken on this second occasion.[91]

In any case, by the late 1930s it had become increasingly difficult for Hobson to produce any writing for publication. In September 1937 he revealed that 'every time I agree to review a book fate intervenes and either I cannot see to read it or cannot get time to write about it.'[92] His failing eyesight eventually forced him to abandon writing economic propaganda and book reviews altogether.[93]

MacEntee does not appear to have held a grudge against Hobson as the minister approved a raise in the salary scale for the Deputy Director of Stamping in December 1938 to £500–£600.[94] Correspondence regarding the proposed revision of the salary scale provides insight into Hobson's performance as a civil servant:

> When he came to the Stamping Branch he was 41 years of age so that his first acquaintance with revenue principles and methods was made at an age when his mental outlook had already been formed. It is, therefore, only to be expected that he should be slow in adjusting himself to the ideas underlying revenue administration, and it is doubtful whether in fact this adjustment has ever fully taken place.[95]

Hobson's propensity for making public comments about economic matters may have been an example of his failure to adjust himself completely to the constraints of a civil service career.

In 1944, in light of new work undertaken since 1939 and Hobson having 'carried out his duties in a highly efficient manner', his salary was again raised, after a certain amount of debate, to £640 with the possibility of further increments. His supervisors, recognising that he was due to retire in four years time with only 23 years of pensionable service, recommended that he be placed on a new higher pay scale personal to him in order to ensure a better pension on his retirement in January 1948.[96] Such generosity may have been designed to provide recognition of his contributions to the struggle for Irish independence in the period 1900 to 1916, as well as his work for the Revenue since 1924.

Hobson spent most of his retirement living alone in Roundstone, Connemara where he had a house built overlooking the sea, his marriage, forged so romantically while on the run, having ended in separation around 1940–1.[97] Hobson lived in Roundstone until about 1963–4 when ill health forced him to move in with his daughter Camilla Mitchell and her family in Castleconnell, Co. Limerick.[98] In January 1969 he quipped to his son Declan that 'I have laughed at life and am ready to laugh at death.'[99] He died in August of that year, the same month in which rioting broke out on the streets of Derry and his native Belfast.

In 1968, a year before his death, Hobson complained that Irish political separatists had turned out to be economic unionists, content to settle for British policies that did not meet Irish needs.[100] His economic views were connected to his belief that a strong economy would lead to the eventual reunification of Ireland. He thought that the best way to bring unity was 'to make an Ireland so prosperous that Ulster cannot afford to stay out of it'.[101]

Both in the advanced nationalist propaganda of his youth and in the economic propaganda of his middle age, Hobson sought to combine idealism with pragmatism. In both cases his ideas only appealed to a minority audience. In his 1968 book *Ireland Yesterday and Tomorrow* he re-published some of his economic writings from the 1930s alongside his memoirs of his nationalist career, which were based on his Bureau of Military History witness statements. [102] This juxtaposition implies that he considered both periods of his life equally important. Perhaps he hoped that one day his economic ideas would gain mass appeal in the same way that a policy of passive resistance combined with guerrilla warfare, which he had advocated for many years prior to 1916, [103] garnered mass support after the great tragedy of his life, the Easter Rising.

Bulmer Hobson was a man who went his own way, acting in response to his own understanding of the truth. He was a rogue revolutionary who defied IRB orders when they ran counter to what he believed were the best interests of the Irish Volunteers and the nationalist movement in general. He favoured a policy of guerrilla warfare over insurrection because, in his view, it had more chance of military success. His commitment to the struggle for Irish independence could not be reconciled with the pacifist principles of his ancestral faith, so he resigned from the Religious Society of Friends. After independence, he continued to support the cultural life of Ireland through his involvement in such activities as book publishing and the foundation of the Gate Theatre. He also became a rogue civil servant who publicly criticised the economic policies of successive Irish governments. Advocating ideas stemming from his own versions of social credit and Keynesianism, Hobson suggested alternative economic policies for Ireland in a series of little-known publications. Always at the heart of his activism – and criticism – was an intense love of Ireland and a life-long commitment to improving his country culturally and economically.

12

THE MAKING OF IRISH REVOLUTIONARY ELITES
The case of Seán Lemass[1]

TOM GARVIN

Many years ago, in the late 1980s, I did some work on the social origins of Irish revolutionary elites, coming to the perhaps unsurprising conclusion that they were of lower-middle-class origin, coming commonly from families which had an agrarian agitational past, but whose combination of rather abstract radicalism and conservatism was classically lower middle class, as is common of revolutionary elites elsewhere in Europe and America.[2] Ethnic marginality (being Protestant or Jewish or of English, American or other foreign descent in the Irish case) sometimes fed nationalist fervour. In revisiting these ideas a few years ago, I did a book-length study of the life of Seán Lemass, who went on after the Irish revolution to become a key modernising leader of the country in the 50s and 60s of the twentieth century. To my surprise, I found that Lemass's own youth fitted these somewhat mechanical stereotypes rather well.

I

Making of a Jackeen

John Francis Lemass, later Jack to his childhood friends and family and ultimately public figure Seán Lemass, was born in Ballybrack, Co. Dublin on 15 July 1899. He was the third child and second son of the family. His elder brother by two years, Noel, was to be murdered viciously in 1923 after the Irish Civil War on the bleak and windswept Featherbed Mountain, south of Dublin city in Co. Wicklow. The killing was reportedly the work of men from Oriel House, the Irish Free State's Criminal Investigation Department, many of whom had been recruited from Michael Collins's notorious squad of hitmen. Jack thought in later life that Noel had been killed because he had been confused with his brother; he was to name his only son after his dead brother. At the time of the killing, Jack was in the Curragh prison camp, and was released on compassionate grounds because of the murder.[3] This compassion was ironically shown by the same Irish government whose nominal minions had committed the murder. A younger brother, Patrick, died in his teens, apparently of natural causes. The youngest brother, Frank, became an accountant and railway administrator and was to be a companion in careers and in politics after 1923. Another boy, Bernard, died in infancy. Jack's eldest sister was Alice, who became a medical doctor later; she was to die in mid-life of tuberculosis contracted in the line of duty. He also had two younger sisters, Claire and Mary Frances.

The children were, after the fashion of the time, born close together: eight children, all born between 1897 and 1914, a period of 17 years. John T. Lemass, the father, was a passionate follower of Charles Stewart Parnell, the charismatic nationalist leader. He had inherited a hatter's shop in Capel Street in inner Dublin, and was a modestly prosperous and well-known businessman; hence the rented summer house in then-rural and salubrious Ballybrack where Jack was born. Capel Street had once been the main street of the city, and still maintained something of that status as late as 1900, a status now more-or-less forgotten a century on as the city centre has moved east and south. Even then, the street was a relatively prosperous island in the ocean of the Dublin slumdom of that time. John's wife, Frances Phelan, came of a broadly similar background of skilled worker-cum-businessman, her father being a horticulturalist who worked in the Botanic Gardens in north Dublin city and also ran a florist's shop in Wicklow Street.[4]

The Phelan family had a Fenian background. In other words, Jack's father came of the radical but constitutionalist Parnellite tradition, while his mother came of the American-inspired insurrectionist Fenian or IRB tradition. This latter tradition can be best summarised by its unofficial American motto, 'Plenty of bucks for Dynamite, but not a cent for Blatherskite'. This duality may be a universal human phenomenon, as Patrick Leigh Fermor has suggested a weirdly similar dichotomy for modern Greece: Romios versus Hellene.[5] The Irish versions of these two tendencies (Fenian versus Parnellite or insurrectionist versus constitutionalist) were to fight it out between themselves inside young Jack's head. Eventually the Da won out, but it took time. Like many other republicans before him and since, Lemass had to come to terms with his twin inheritances of militarism and constitutionalism, and it took him over a decade to discard some of the wilder aspects of his republican formation. Some people thought that he never grew out of militant republicanism.

The family was characterised by a conflicted political tradition and an extraordinary work ethic and the young Jack Lemass learned early the virtues of patriotism along with hard work, skilled labour and systematic supervision of a workforce. It was said that the Christian Brothers in O'Connell Schools in North Richmond Street, Dublin, taught him the Irish four Rs: reading, writing, 'rithmetic and rebellion, but it is to be suspected that his family background also gave him a good grounding in Irish political history from a mixture of revolutionary and Parnellite viewpoints.

Young Jack grew up in, or on, Capel Street and although his father did take him on trips to different parts of the country, he remained very much a city boy all his life, with a fundamental disregard for rural attitudes and values. His Parnellite background may have soured him permanently on farmers and farmers' interests, although he never made such a point. As adolescents, he and Jimmy O'Dea, later to be the celebrated Dublin comedian, were best friends; a constant characteristic of Lemass all his life was a loyalty to his boyhood friends, to school friends and to old acquaintances who were uninvolved in political life. The two lads put their heads together at one stage and concocted a newspaper of sorts:

> The Lemass family had a hatter's shop almost opposite the O'Deas in Capel Street, which is how the two young friends first met, and one of their first youthful ventures together was to produce an entirely handwritten publication for distribution among their friends. The funny bits and the serial were written by Jim while Jack contributed the serious stuff.[6]

Later Jack and Jim did a fair amount of amateur acting, in a popular tradition that was still extant in a city always well known for producing actors and playwrights over the previous two centuries. Lemass played, at one stage, the part of Sir Lucius O'Trigger in Sheridan's *The Rivals*. Later on the pair kept up the friendship, and went on excursions, in particular to the seaside town of Skerries, Co. Dublin. Skerries was also where the Lemass family holidayed, and was, later on, to be a haunt of Lemass in his decades as a political leader. In 1924, Jim was to be Jack's best man at his marriage to Kathleen Hughes, in a very different Ireland.[7]

Jack's grandfather, also John Lemass, was from Co. Armagh in Ulster and was also a hatter and outfitter. He had been an enthusiastic member of the Land League of 1879–81, and a devout Parnellite.[8] The Land League, which had branches all over Ireland centred on a headquarters in Dublin, was an extraordinarily successful organisation, co-ordinating the rent strikes and boycotts carried out by hundreds of thousands of tenants. Instructions went down the line from headquarters in O'Connell Street, a very sturdy stone's throw from the Lemass shop in Capel Street, to the local branch secretaries. The Land League headquarters regulated the rules of shunning and boycotting, discouraged the use of Luddite tactics such as smashing labour-saving farm machinery, forbade open violence and advocated the naming of persons to be shunned. The League was essentially a mass membership political party on O'Connellite lines, and the immediate ancestor of a string of mass parties set up in nationalist Ireland over the following generation; it became a classic model in Ireland for the means by which the great numbers of the ordinary people of the country could be welded into one organisational weapon with a view to taking and wielding political power. Renamed the Irish National League in 1882, it dominated Irish popular politics for ten years after the triumphant successes of the Land League in the Land War of 1879–81. The League found itself acting not merely as an electoral committee, but as local law-giver, arbitrator, police and supreme court. For a while it came quite close to becoming a state within a state in British Ireland, and its example was one that was to inform directly the nascent underground Irish revolutionary state of 1919–22. That underground organisation similarly set up a state within a state, complete with postal system, land courts, general purpose courts, local government apparatus, parliament, army and even a police force of sorts. In fact, the land courts were a traditional form of local arbitration tribunal dating back to times even before the Land League and very probably based on the Whiteboy tradition of the eighteenth century.[9] Young Jack had political organisation and Parnellism in his blood.

Publicans and shopkeepers commonly provided the local leadership of the League, because, in general, such people had rather better educations than farmers and also because shops and pubs were, besides churches, the natural meeting places of country people. In a way, the pub became the centre of opposition to other sources of power, as landlords' agents and Catholic priests, as two sets of aspirant aristocrats, did not frequent them; it became the centre of a perpetual and rather popular opposition. The licensed trade was to gain considerable power in Ireland, a power which has not faded away completely even in the twenty-first century.

Eventually, the League was to split and collapse because of the embroilment of Parnell in a divorce case; in the subsequent general election of 1892, the rural areas of Ireland, with some significant exceptions, followed their priests in voting against the Protestant 'adulterer' and thereby set up an enduring and very powerful political myth of the noble leader pulled down by the ungrateful and bigoted mob, led by their anti-patriotic but all-powerful priests. Parnell died shortly afterwards, thereby intensifying the image of the betrayed tragic martyr. The myth of Parnell became grist to the mill of many Irish writers, including such very different ones as W. B. Yeats and James Joyce. By and large, Dublin and the other towns tended to stay loyal to the Uncrowned King of Ireland, and this reflected a classic town/country division among Irish nationalist opinion which was to linger on into the twentieth century and affect subsequent generations' politics in many often unrecognised ways.[10] Bourgeois and working-class Dublin became Parnellite in contrast to the mainly anti-Parnellite countryside whose farmers owed their property rights to Parnell's great movement; farmers were seen by Parnellite loyalists as priest-ridden ingrates. The Lemasses stayed staunchly Parnellite in the face of a massive anti-Parnellite farmers' vote, organised by priests.

Edward Mac Aonraoi, an old Gaelic Leaguer and civil servant who served under Lemass in later years, remarked in his old age on Lemass's resemblance to Parnell even in personal relationships. Like Parnell, Lemass, he commented, had few personal friends or acquaintances, and was possessed of 'the same inscrutability'. He did not know his civil servants, and kept his distance from them so as not to be accused of jobbery. He worked through his trusted Secretary of Department, John Leydon. Parnell, rather similarly, did not know his Members of Parliament.[11]

The eldest John Lemass was elected to Dublin City Council in 1885, and his son, Jack's father, continued in the same political tradition, but in a more quietly spoken and subdued fashion; he seems to have had a 'strong silent man' type of personality, quiet, but firm. Again, Seán Lemass echoed his family background rather well in his personality, rather self-contained and some-times rather stern, even forbidding and 'gruff'. However, he seems actually to have separated his public and private sides rather sharply, stepping easily from one role to the other; in private he could be genial and entertaining, as many witnesses attest.

This characteristic separation of one's life into two hermetically sealed worlds was a common enough feature of the social culture of the time in Irish cities and towns, and looked strange and almost off-putting to country people, with their communal way of life and disregard for privacy: the open half-door versus the closed hall door, or perhaps even Gemeinschaft versus Gesellschaft. Kevin Boland commented:

> My father [Gerald Boland] was joint honorary secretary of Fianna Fáil with Lemass and they worked very closely together. As it developed, however, Lemass became the headquarters man, my father the field man. Lemass had an abrupt manner – he didn't have the balance that was required for country people. He came to realise himself that he couldn't deal with the rural mind – it was too lackadaisical. My father had the patience for it – it took him three trips to get [Seán] Moylan [of North Cork IRA] to join [Fianna Fáil in 1926–7]. The thing was that if you identified a key IRA man in any one locality and got him to join, then you had a ready-made organisation that came along with him.[12]

Lemass himself, in answer to a question asked him about his republicanism by journalist Michael Mills in 1969, answered in terms of a strong Dublin Parnellite family tradition of electoral politics at an intensely local level, involving strong emotions and political passions of a kind which, as a child, he did not fully understand but which he certainly internalised subconsciously from the social environment around him:

Well, when you are talking about a Republican tradition you are talking in terms of the 1960s in relation to the 1900s. My father was always a strong Nationalist and my grandfather had been a Parnellite member of Dublin Corporation, for a year or so anyway. My father was active in the Irish Party in his early years. Indeed my earliest political experience at that time was when there was a by-election in the constituency in which we lived and the Irish Party had nominated a candidate of whom the local Nationalist Party supporters disapproved. I won't mention names because there are people of his family still alive, but in those days there was no such thing as a constituency convention to nominate a candidate. The Party leaders nominated a candidate and they nominated a candidate on this occasion who was generally regarded as not being the most suitable person for election to Parliament.

I remember the meeting being held in the back of my father's shop in Capel Street. Six or seven of the local traders were there. They were all strong Party supporters; and the long debate ended with the decision that for the first time in their lives they were going to vote against the Party, in support of an independent candidate who had been nominated to contest the seat against the Party candidate. They all went out of the shop in a group, like aristocrats going to the guillotine, with their faces set and their fists clenched, pale and drawn-looking, determined to do this thing which was a mortal sin for anyone involved in politics in those days. But they did it; they voted against the Party. That was in 1906 or 1907 and it is the earliest political experience I can remember. But it does represent the sort of political atmosphere in which I grew up. But there was not a Republican tradition in that sense. My father was still a strong member of the Irish Parliamentary Party after I joined the Volunteers.[13]

This 'earliest political experience' occurred when Lemass was seven or eight, when the Catholic Church understood a person to have reached the use of reason.

In the same interview he recalled how, having served as adjutant to Patrick Pearse in the GPO, he had been picked up by the police afterwards, but let go on account of his youth. After the fighting in Dublin ceased, involving much loss of life and the shelling of the city centre by British forces, 'the cops gave me a kick in the arse and sent me home to me Ma.' Lemass went home, to the Capel Street house a few yards away from the headquarters of the rebel Republic of Easter Week. He went on immediately to reminisce about this momentary filial rebellion in fond terms; there was no real generational or ideological division between old Parnellite and young Sinn Féiner; but the constitutional idiom in Irish political history had been momentarily and temporarily replaced by the insurrectionist one: 'When I got back home after [the] 1916 [Rising] I was very tired and I went to bed. I remember next morning my father came into the bedroom with a great big green white and orange celluloid button in his lapel, which was his way of telling me he had come over to our side.'[14] The approval of the older generation was still fondly remembered by the young rebel in his own old age.

II

The man from God knows where

Before 1916, Jack had, like many another in that generation, already changed his given name to a more patriotic Seán. He experimented briefly with a Gaelicised form of his surname, but wisely soon abandoned the attempt. After all, the name was at least not *English*. The Lemass family name seems to be Huguenot in origin, and was originally Lemaistre; at least that is both the family tradition and the folk opinion among his friends, colleagues and descendants in Dublin; it also is the opinion of MacLysaght's standard work on Irish surnames. The name was extant in Dublin and Carlow since the eighteenth century.[15] Lemass used to crack a family joke to the effect that they were all descended from French pirates. Physically he certainly looked somewhat un-Irish. There is a photograph of the young Lemass in Volunteer uniform dated around 1915 which resembles nothing more closely than pictures of young Italian conscripts fighting Austrian forces in the Alps at around that time.[16] His immediate ancestors came into Ireland from Scotland, and the hereditary skills of tailoring and millinery ran in the family for generations.

Presumably at some stage a Lemass converted to Catholicism, for Seán never regarded himself as anything other than a Catholic, although apparently one who became increasingly sceptical of religious belief systems as he grew older in body and colder of intellect. In a prison camp in 1920 he became unpopular, or at least distrusted, among northern Volunteers for refusing to go to mass or participate in a collective Rosary. He would stand apart and say out loud, apparently mocking the simple faith of his comrades, 'Oh God, if there is a God, save my soul, if I have a soul.'[17] His sceptical habit of mind extended to other realms of human concern, and he showed a marked ability all his life to change his mind when circumstances clearly demanded a rethink; in this his habits of mind differed from the fanatical and semi-religious political mentality that dominated the minds of so many young IRA men and Sinn Féiners of his era and later. Consistency, for him, was silly; you changed your mind when the evidence changed. His outlook was inherently empiricist and scientific. However, he always claimed an underlying consistency of general political outlook, while admitting a methodological agnosticism or eclecticism.

In 1914 and 1915, he did his Intermediate Certificate examination, emerging the second time with a very creditable string of honours in arithmetic, history, geometry, experimental science and French. He got passes in English, Latin and Irish. John Horgan points to his ability at mathematics: 'On the basis of his 1915 results he won a first-class exhibition in the mathematical group of subjects, worth £15. Three of his classmates did the same, affording the school a remarkable 40 per cent of the ten first-class exhibitions in the junior grade awarded in the country as a whole.'[18]

Despite his name change, there is rather little evidence of Lemass having any real interest in the Irish language or in the Gaelic League.[19] However, that did not prevent both Noel and Seán being swept up into the Irish Volunteers as very young men: Seán joined up, lying about his age, at age 15 and some months. Local circumstance seems again to have been the trigger, and Éamon de Valera a very early influence.

> I was fifteen when I joined. I was not, in fact, eligible for membership. There was a man named Pat Mullen employed in my father's shop. He was a very active Volunteer and he was always trying to persuade me to come along and join. I told him I didn't think I was old enough to join and he said – 'Well you look a great deal older than you are and this will be a white lie anyway.' So he brought me along and I was accepted as a member of the Volunteers. I was a member of A Company of the 3rd Battalion, commanded at that time by a man called Sheehan, one of those who did not fight in 1916. He was one of the Bulmer Hobson group who felt the Rising was a mistake. He was followed by the famous Joe O'Connor –'Holy Joe' as he was known.
>
> After I joined, de Valera was appointed the Battalion Commandant. The first time I saw de Valera was when he came down to a parade of our Company in York Street to address the Battalion. My impression of him was of a long, thin fellow with knee britches and a tweed hat. But he had, of course, enormous personal magnetism and the capacity to hold that crowd of Volunteers there at inordinate length as he always did. There was not a movement among the crowd until he had finished. It impressed me enormously, notwithstanding what I thought was his rather queer-looking appearance. [De Valera] had a theory, I remember, which even at that age I thought was a bit odd, about a tool which was to be capable of being used as a pike or as a trench digger. I must confess that I thought this was going a little bit far in bridging the gap in military technique. As far as I know, the tool never emerged. But, he had this simple approach to things: what have we to do? how can we do it? This was characteristic of him in politics later on. It was this capacity to talk to audiences in simple terms that gave him the tremendous influence he had. I have seen crowds of people standing in bitter cold and heavy rain while he talked for an hour-and-a-half or two hours about political matters in simple terms they could understand.[20]

De Valera, this strange man with the strange name, a name even stranger than Lemass, clearly had a huge impact on young Seán, a man who was later not to be easily influenced by other people; perhaps it was in part, as he suggested himself, because de Valera had a common touch and lacked the shyness that many detected in Lemass. Charles Haughey, his latter-day son-in-law, remarked that Lemass loved Dev 'with a kind of impatient fondness'.[21] When asked in 1969 who among Irish political figures had influenced him, Lemass had to repeat himself:

I find this hard to answer. I suppose the only one was de Valera, to whom I was personally committed all the time he was head of the Party and of the Government. Nobody, except de Valera, has ever influenced me to any extent; at least to the extent of making me change my outlook on an important matter. He was the only one who ever did … [Even when I was still very young] it would be de Valera. I had been associated with him before 1916, but not so much for a period afterwards. He was the one person who impressed me very much by the personal magnetism which he exercised to an extraordinary degree.[22]

Whether or not the Lemass brothers had much to do with the Gaelic League, Eoin MacNeill, joint founder of that cultural organisation and also Chief of Staff of the Irish Volunteers, had no trouble recognising the two young men on Easter Monday 1916, when he met them walking in the Dublin Mountains with Jimmy and Ken O'Dea, disappointed that the muster of the Volunteers planned for the previous day had been called off, as it happened, by MacNeill. MacNeill sadly told the lads that a Rising had gone ahead under the leadership of Patrick Pearse and James Connolly, and that public buildings in Dublin were being taken over by the Volunteers and the Citizen Army. This news galvanised the Lemass boys, presumably contrary to MacNeill's intentions, and they rushed off to join in what they apparently still half expected to be simply an ordinary parade, and found themselves engaged in a fully-fledged rebellion against the British authorities. Eventually Seán made his way to the General Post Office, and fought alongside Pearse, a man he hero-worshipped, being, as he remarked himself much later in the same connection, a very impressionable young man. Evidently, scepticism about Pearse's militarist romanticism set in fairly early on.[23]

Lemass made little of his exploits during Easter Week, but evidently the possibility of death in the fighting and even execution for treason afterward matured him very rapidly; he came to a realisation that something very big had happened and that he had almost unknowingly become part of a movement that would change Ireland for ever. His formal education effectively terminated at that point; his father, although he had come over to what was increasingly, and inaccurately, being termed the Sinn Féin cause, wanted his son to complete his education with a professional qualification in accountancy or the law. However, Lemass went to work part-time in his father's shop, proving to be quite innovative in his marketing strategies. Noel took a different course, staying in work while remaining a sleeper member of the Volunteer movement, an organisation that was rapidly evolving into what was later to be termed the Old IRA.

Lemass was not heavily involved in active service until quite late on in the Anglo-Irish conflict, unlike Noel, who seems to have been more involved. However, on 21 November 1920, Seán was involved in the systematic killing of British agents in Dublin by Michael Collins's 'squad' of hand-picked marksmen. The killings were in part a response to British successes in picking up or killing key

IRA men, plus the occasional innocent bystander shot by the authorities because of a confusion of names. Lemass's name is not on any list of named members of Collins's squad; there are at least 17 such names, as some people moved in and out of the dozen or so active members. Hence the sobriquet for the squad: 'the Twelve Apostles'. However, he was on active duty that day with his IRA battalion, so at a minimum it can be inferred that he did escort duty for one of the killers. A shroud of secrecy still hangs over the names of the perpetrators. Lemass himself fended off queries with curt remarks such as 'firing squads don't have reunions.' This itself sounds suspiciously like an admission; however, such a guarded admission would have heightened Lemass's political prestige and legitimacy in post-revolutionary Ireland. The men and women who had been 'out' in 1916–21 were admired. There is a persistent story, heard by myself as a young man, that Lemass was involved actively or passively in one of the killings on the south side of the city, that he handed his gun to a bystander, walked to a little-used workman's ferry, crossed the River Liffey and walked home. By this simple subterfuge, he walked through the police and military cordons. John Horgan has tracked this story down.[24]

My own doubts about his membership of the squad centre around the absence of his name from all of the known listings and the simple fact that, if he had been a member, it would have been rather unlikely for him to have chosen the anti-Treaty side in 1922; those close to Collins followed him, with some ambivalence, into the Free State. Again, Lemass said casually many years later that for him, Collins was a remote senior figure: 'I met him, but I did not know him. He was far above my rank in those days.'[25] Michael Mills told me that tears came to Lemass's eyes when, as an old man, he was asked about his involvement in the fighting of 1916–23; he desperately wanted it to be forgotten and forgiven.[26] There wasn't too much love lost between the squad members and ordinary Volunteers; the relationship seems to have resembled that between regular soldiers and guerrillas, or franc-tireurs as they were then known.

During the War of Independence, often called the 'Tan scrap' by veterans, Lemass was certainly hardened in his political purpose by the uncompromising and brutal acts of both sides in the struggle. When the Anglo-Irish Truce arrived in July 1921, he was by no means a die-hard purist, and seems to have wavered for a long time between the compromisers led by Collins and W. T. Cosgrave and the purists led by de Valera and Liam Lynch. In this, he was again like many another. In early 1922, he served briefly as an instructor for the new police force, the Garda Síochána, being set up by the Provisional Government. His leadership abilities had already been noticed. However, when his first pay cheque arrived, he noticed it was drawn on the Provisional Government rather than on the Government of the Irish Republic, and changed to the anti-Treaty side.[27]

This curious episode, displaying a legalism that was uncharacteristic of his later self, suggests that Lemass's republicanism was somewhat marginal. Perhaps he could not stay away from his beloved de Valera or from his pals in the Four Courts garrison; like many others, he went with his peer group, a natural thing to do at age 23. He was in the Four Courts throughout the bombardment of June 1922, and went on the run afterwards, having escaped from Free State custody with suspicious ease. Later he was picked up and interned in the Curragh Camp. He attempted to escape again and was badly beaten up by government soldiers.[28] The limits, or even the pointlessness, of political violence, were brought home to him by the Civil War that had followed the compromise Treaty settlement of 1922–3. The experience of being swept into violence by his peer group twice in ten years seems to have strengthened a natural self-sufficiency and determination not to be influenced decisively by anyone ever again.

III
Himself alone?

Lemass was commonly stereotyped as being a businessman manqué, and there is probably some truth in that proposition; certainly his business background imparted to him a respect for business, for enterprise and for buying and selling, innovation and efficiency which lasted all his life. He accepted implicitly the assumptions of private enterprise and the dynamism of capitalism, while having a radical streak in the form of respect for the worker, whom he saw as having a common interest with the employer rather than having a necessary class enmity. His daughter-in-law remembered his family background as one of niceness, but also a toughness and coldness.[29] Work was a pervasive ethic. Jack had something like a 'Joycean childhood', but certainly without the abject poverty of the actual Joyce family of that time: 'People would come in with fiddles etc. on a Sunday night, like a scene from *The Dead*; piano as well.'[30]

Despite his advocacy of state enterprise in later years, Lemass had an inborn preference for private enterprise; in Ireland, however, there was so little private enterprise he concluded that public enterprise would have to fill the gap, at least temporarily. There was also a solitary side to his character which manifested itself in a self-sufficiency, a privacy and a thoughtfulness that was almost academic in character: a certain monkishness. He told Michael Mills, in answer to a question about his not having proceeded to do law as his parents wished him to, in reality a question about his curtailed education in general:

I am not really able to answer this question. I don't know. I often thought when I was actively involved in political work dealing with the most contrary element in life, that's human beings, you know, that the ideal situation would to be a sort of research chemist up in the top back room of some university not dealing with human beings at all but dealing with inert materials and knowing that you could establish absolute truth in relation to these materials and not have any opinions about the truth. But this was merely a reaction from the experiences of those times [of 1916–23].[31]

He made a similar remark to Ken Whitaker, fantasising wistfully about being an atomic scientist or something of that sort.[32] James Ryan quoted him as reminiscing that, 'when at school the only thing I got real pleasure from was working out problems in Euclid, problems in mathematics.'[33] Again, he told his wife at one stage that if he had not become a politician he 'would have opted for the hermetic life and would have been perfectly happy to spend his days working out complex mathematical problems.'[34] He remarked to Seamus Brady, apparently in the early 60s, 'I would like to have been away from all worldly things like politics. To be in a hut in the mountains surrounded by books on mathematics and working out problems of physics. With such a life I could be very happy.'[35]

As Lemass suggested himself, these were probably the wistful daydreams of a rather workaholic man beset continually by pressing practical problems involving large numbers of powerful, articulate and sometimes aggressive people, like any busy public man. His most generous periods of isolation and leisure seem to have been granted to him as a guest of the British and later the Irish nations at two prison camps. In the British prison camp in Ballykinlar, Co. Down, in 1920–1 he was sometimes seen as stand-offish, always reading, particularly in economics. In the Irish government's prison camp at the Curragh in 1922–3, he seems to have hit the books more seriously, the camp serving, as such camps often had before and would serve again, as universities for guerrillas trying to think their way out of their political quandaries. He had books sent in regularly from outside, and devoured them. He was sometimes twitted because of this unusual studiousness, and also on account of his unusual demeanour and appearance. He was nicknamed, because of his dark complexion, 'the Jewman', or teased because of his toothbrush moustache as 'Charlie Chaplin'.[36] Constance Markievicz referred to him as 'Mephistopheles', presumably because of his dark complexion, brown eyes, sleek black hair and pencil moustache.[37] He also had a wolfish grin and an occasionally ferocious sense of humour.

However, he was mainly remembered as sitting in a corner ploughing through books sent in from outside dealing mainly with economics and history; Horgan suggests that his real intellectual and emotional formation occurred around this period in the Curragh. His appearance was always immaculate; to be well dressed was to keep up one's own morale and that of others around one, was his openly expressed attitude.[38] He was seen as a serious young fellow, even something of what a later generation might describe as an 'anorak'. One comrade remembered: 'In Tintown [Curragh Camp] all the lads were larking around. Lemass would be sitting in a corner reading books on economics. Known as "the little Jewman". Soldiers guarding them were paid on Wednesdays: he'd take money off them at cards.'[39]

Although a nervous speaker as a young man, Lemass persevered, and was to become one of the most incisive, aggressive and well-prepared public speakers of his generation, who could destroy an ill-prepared opponent with a devastating, almost brutal, well-informed and cutting remark. He had an extraordinary memory, like many of the top administrators of twentieth-century Ireland; Michael Collins, John Leydon, John Garvin and Garret FitzGerald come to mind among others. Lemass is seen by some as having been a man with a mission. Liam Skinner, a biographer who veered toward the hagiographic but who was well-informed, claimed that Lemass saw himself from early on as having a vocation to pull Ireland into the modern world: 'As a Minister, he was guided by the unshakable conviction that the work he was doing was peculiarly his – because he had deliberately fitted himself for it – and that he could do it better than anyone else.'[40]

However, he did have firm friends, in particular Kathleen Hughes, who wrote to him from 1916 until their marriage in 1924. The two families had known each other from Skerries holidays in pre-war days. Kathleen described herself as being of a placid, non-worrying disposition, certainly a qualification for being Lemass's 'best pal', as several people described the relationship. Kathleen was very religious and, also unlike Seán, could write a good letter in Irish. Haughey remembered that Lemass 'adored her'.[41] The Hugheses were a moderate constitutional nationalist family, and Kathleen's father, a buyer for Arnott's fashionable department store, did not really approve of young Lemass, and was, if anything, a bit pro-British.[42] 'That boy is always on the run; he'll never be able to make a home for you' was his perception of the 25-year-old ex-gunman.[43] Kathleen seems to have had a huge stabilising influence on Lemass, and certainly accepted his part-time domesticity and the fact that he had a job which demanded his attention almost literally 24 hours a day. But then, she was already familiar with his non-stop work habits. He turned into a devoted family man and father, often going home for lunch during working hours, a common practice in the small city that Dublin was at that time.

Lemass also held on to his school friends into later life, and, characteristically, observed a rather strict separation between his professional colleagues and his personal friendships. He was known for his loyalty to old friends, a loyalty that survived his rise to national and international fame in later years. Kevin Boland pointed to the importance for Lemass of his old comrades in the Four Courts during the crisis of June 1922, many of them fierce republicans with a somewhat shaky relationship to the reigning constitutional order, even in its de Valeran form. Lemass's real legitimacy in their eyes was his national and military record, not his democratic status as Taoiseach of an illegitimate 'Free State government' as the IRA continued to term it:

> The Four Courts Garrison remained the core of Lemass's strength (organisation) in Dublin, until they began to disappear. There was an annual mass for the Four Courts Garrison in Dublin Castle and one year [in the early 1960s Seán Lemass's son] Noel Lemass went down and told the secretary, 'Skinner' Reilly, that he was there to represent the Taoiseach. Reilly said fiercely: 'You're not here to represent the Taoiseach. You're here to represent your father. There's no-one here to represent the Taoiseach.'[44]

One interviewer in 1953 commented on Lemass's personality; his pipe always beside him in the office, in an ashtray made of an aircraft engine piston, 'kindliness of light brown eyes set in innumerable crows' feet, warm voice'.[45] De Valera, with whom Lemass had been politically close all their adult lives, admitted at one stage that he had never quite been able to size up his younger colleague.[46] In part this was due to de Valera's lack of any interest in economics, or any real grasp of economic issues. Lemass, on the other hand, had a passionate obsession with economic development as the only real key to Ireland's historical and social problems and shared little of de Valera's interest in culture or the Irish language. Whitaker remembered in the 1990s:

> In 1956–57 Seán Francis Lemass was laid up and inactive for some months; [I] went to see him in hospital. 'Dev wants me to use this time to brush up on my Irish. But I'd prefer it if you sent me some books on economics' [he said] – he got Sayers on banking, stuff on development economics, and by Lewis, the Jamaican. He had been reading about the US division of powers.[47]

Michael Hayes, admittedly a biased observer, commented years later on de Valera's lack of interest in what anyone else had to say. Furthermore, 'he never at any point in his career up to [retirement in] 1959 showed any close acquaintance with the hard realities and details of any Irish financial or economic problem.'[48] The relationship between de Valera and Lemass was to be an odd, and perhaps classic, mixture of friendship, mutual fondness and intellectual and temperamental distance, a mutual dependence pact which each tacitly observed. To me, this writer, the working partnership was not unlike the classic partnership between the rock and the wild man, the yogi and the commissar or Don Quixote and Sancho Panza: that between the dreamer and the practical man, each utterly dependent on the other, and each aware of the fact that he could not operate without the other.

In the 1960s, Hayes described the relationship in acerbic, but rather shrewd, terms. Free State leaders like Kevin O'Higgins had assumed that de Valera would fade out of politics because of the dreamlike unreality of his political position and style in the late 1920s and early 1930s.

That was their great mistake. He was capable of lasting much longer and I think for that Lemass deserves great credit, much more than he has ever got. Lemass did what Kevin O'Higgins refused to allow, what J. J. [Walsh] tried to do. He supplied the bread and butter argument while de Valera supplied Kathleen ní Houlihan with green robes.[49]

MICHAEL LAFFAN
A select bibliography

CLARA CULLEN

1968
'The development of Sinn Féin' (MA thesis, University College Dublin).

1969
'1919 Dáil RIP', *Public Affairs: The Monthly Review of the Institute of Public Administration* i, pp 16–17.

1970
'The Sinn Féin party, 1916–1921', *Capuchin Annual* xxxvii, pp 227–35.

1971
'The unification of Sinn Féin in 1917', *Irish Historical Studies* xvii:67, pp 353–79.

1973
'The question of French security in British policy towards France and Germany, 1918–1925' (PhD thesis, University of Cambridge).

1979
'New variations on an old theme: recent works on Irish history, 1914–1922', *Stair: Journal of the History Teachers' Association of Ireland* ii, pp 11–13.

1982
'Violence and terror in twentieth-century Ireland: IRB and IRA', in Wolfgang J. Mommsen and Gerhard Hirschfeld (eds), *Social Protest, Violence and Terror in Nineteenth- and Twentieth- Century Europe* (London: Macmillan in association with Berg for the German Historical Institute), pp 155–74. [Also published in a German translation in Wolfgang J. Mommsen und Gerhard Hirschfeld (eds), *Sozialprotest, Gewalt, Terror: Gewaltanwendung durch Politische und Gesellschaftliche*

Randgruppen im 19. und 20. Jahrhundert (Stuttgart: Klett-Cotta, 1982), pp 182–206; and reprinted in Richard M. Golden (ed.), *Social History of Western Civilization, Vol. II: Readings from the Seventeenth Century to the Present* (New York: St Martin's Press, 1988), pp 255–71].

1983

The Partition of Ireland 1911–1925 (Dundalk: Dundalgan Press for the Historical Association of Ireland).

1984

'Two Irish states', *Ireland: Dependence and Independence, The Crane Bag* viii:1, pp 26–37.

1985

'"Labour must wait": Ireland's conservative revolution', in P. J. Corish (ed.), *Radicals, Rebels and Establishments* (Belfast: Appletree Press), pp 203–22.

1988

'Introduction', in Michael Laffan (ed.), *The Burden of German History 1919–1945: Essays for the Goethe Institute* (London: Methuen), pp ix–xii.

'Weimar and Versailles: German foreign policy, 1919–33', in Laffan (ed.), *The Burden of German History 1919–1945*, pp 81–102.

1989

'John Redmond (1856–1918) and Home Rule', in Ciaran Brady (ed.), *Worsted in the Game: Losers in Irish History* (Dublin: Lilliput Press in association with RTÉ), pp 133–42.

1991

'Insular attitudes: the revisionists and their critics', in Máirín Ní Dhonnchadha and Theo Dorgan (eds), *Revising the Rising* (Derry: Field Day), pp 106–21.

1994

'Sinn Féin from dual monarchy to the first Dáil', in Brian Farrell (ed.) *The Creation of the Dáil* (Dublin: Blackwater Press in association with RTÉ), pp 15–29.

1997

'The sacred memory: religion, revisionists and the Easter Rising', in Judith Devlin and Ronan Fanning (eds), *Religion and Rebellion: Historical Studies XX* (Dublin: UCD Press), pp 174–91.

1998

'The ballot and the bullet: the political and military struggle for Irish independence, 1916–1921', in *[Proceedings of the] International Symposium for the March
1st Independence Movement* (Seoul: [*s.n.*]), pp 335–40.

1999

The Resurrection of Ireland: The Sinn Féin Party 1916–1923 (Cambridge: Cambridge
University Press).

'Sinn Féin', in W. J. McCormack (ed.), *The Blackwell Companion to Modern Irish
Culture* (Oxford: Blackwell), pp 535–7.

2003

'Conscription crisis', in Brian Lalor (ed.), *The Encyclopaedia of Ireland* (Dublin:
Gill and Macmillan), p. 232.

'German plot', in Lalor (ed.), *Encyclopaedia of Ireland*, p. 436.

2004

'Civil war', in James S. Donnelly Jr, Karl S. Bottigheimer, Mary E. Daly, James E.
Doan and David W. Miller (eds), *Encyclopedia of Irish History and Culture* (2
vols, Detroit MI; London: Macmillan Reference USA), i, pp 91–4.

'The emergence of the "Two Irelands", 1912–25', *History Ireland* xii:4 (2004), pp 440–4.

'Home Rule movement and the Irish Parliamentary Party: 1891 to 1918', in
Donnelly *et al.* (eds), *Encyclopedia of Irish History and Culture*, i, pp 302–6.

'Republicanism in the revolutionary decade: the triumph and containment of
militarism, 1912–23', in Maurice J. Bric and John Coakley (eds), *From Political
Violence to Negotiated Settlement: The Winding Path to Peace in Twentieth-
Century Ireland* (Dublin: UCD Press), pp 49–61.

'Sinn Féin movement and party to 1922', in Donnelly *et al.* (eds), *Encyclopedia of
Irish History and Culture*, ii, pp 660–2.

2005

'The making of a revolutionary: Casement and the Volunteers, 1913–14', in Mary
E. Daly (ed.), *Roger Casement in Irish and World History* (Dublin: Royal Irish
Academy), pp 64–73.

2006

'The decade of the Rising: F. X. Martin on 1916', in Howard B. Clarke and J. R. S. Phillips
(eds), *Ireland, England and the Continent in the Middle Ages and Beyond: Essays in
Memory of a Turbulent Friar, F. X. Martin, OSA* (Dublin: UCD Press), pp 325–32.

2007

'Easter Week and the historians', in Mary E. Daly and Margaret O'Callaghan (eds), *1916 in 1966: Commemorating the Easter Rising* (Dublin: Royal Irish Academy), pp 323–42.

2008

'Cumann na nGaedheal', in *Fine Gael: A History* ([Dublin]: Fine Gael), pp 6–8.

2009

'Casement, Sir Roger David (1864–1916)', in James McGuire and James Quinn (eds), *Dictionary of Irish Biography* (9 vols, Cambridge: Cambridge University Press), iv, pp 277–86.

'Griffith, Arthur Joseph (1871–1922)', in McGuire and Quinn (eds), *Dictionary of Irish Biography*, ii, pp 402–6.

'Redmond, John Edward (1856–1918)', in McGuire and Quinn (eds), *Dictionary of Irish Biography*, viii, pp 411–8.

'Williams, (Thomas) Desmond (1921–87)', in McGuire and Quinn (eds), *Dictionary of Irish Biography*, ix, pp 947–9.

2012

'1912 and all that', in *Revolutionary States: Home Rule & Modern Ireland* (Dublin: Dublin City Gallery The Hugh Lane), pp 65–8.

'Cádaveres ilustres: el entierro de los héroes nacionalistas Irlandeses', in Ludger Mees (ed.), *La Celebración de la Nación: Simbolos, Mitos y Lugares de Memoria* (Granada: Comares), pp 47–61.

'In the shadow of the national question', in Paul Daly, Rónán O'Brien and Paul Rouse (eds), *Making the Difference? The Irish Labour Party, 1912–2012* (Cork: Collins Press), pp 32–42.

2014

Judging W. T. Cosgrave: The Foundation of the Irish State (Dublin: Royal Irish Academy).

2015

'Bloomsyear: Ireland in 1904', in Anne Fogarty and Fran O'Rourke (eds), *Voices on Joyce* (Dublin: UCD Press), pp 25–35.

'The history of history in UCD. Section 2: after independence', in *The History Review: Journal of the UCD History Society* xvii (2015), pp 25–56, forthcoming.

2016

'Arthur Griffith', in Eugenio Biagini and Dan Mulhall (eds), *The Shaping of Modern Ireland: A Centenary Reappraisal* (Manchester: Manchester University Press), forthcoming.

'Eamon de Valera', in Oliver Janz and Nicholas Apostolopoulos (eds), *1914–1918-Online: International Encyclopedia of the First World War*, 1914–1918-online.net, forthcoming.

'Sinn Féin and the rise of advanced nationalism', in John Crowley, Donal Ó Drisceoil, Mike Murphy (eds), *Atlas of the Irish Revolution* (Cork: Cork University Press), forthcoming.

'Sinn Féin/Dáil Éireann', in Crowley *et al.* (eds), *Atlas of the Irish Revolution*, forthcoming.

NOTES

Introduction

1   Peter Hart, 'Definition: defining the Irish revolution', in Joost Agusteijn (ed.), *The Irish Revolution, 1913–23* (Basingstoke, 2002), p. 30.

2   R. F. Foster, *Vivid Faces: The Revolutionary Generation in Ireland, 1890–1923* (London, 2014), p. xvii.

Michael Laffan, Portrait of a historian

1   Some of the information in this piece is based on an interview with Michael Laffan conducted by the author in February 2011. A copy of the interview has been preserved by the author and will be deposited with UCD Archives.

2   'Dedicated army officer and family man', *Irish Times*, 19 Sept. 2009.

3   James Grant, *Under the Red Dragon: A Novel* (London, 1872); G. A. Henty, *In the Reign of Terror* (London, 1888); Rear-Admiral E. R. G. R. Evans, *To Sweep the Spanish Main* (London, [1930]).

4   William Lee, SJ, quoted in Louis McRedmond, *To the Greater Glory: A History of the Irish Jesuits* (Dublin, 1991), p. 302.

5   Donal McCartney, *UCD: A National Idea: The History of University College, Dublin* (Dublin, 1999), p. 218.

6   Tom Garvin, 'The strange death of clerical politics in University College, Dublin', *Irish University Review* xxviii:2 (autumn–winter 1998), p. 310.

7   F. H. Hinsley *et al.*, *British Intelligence in the Second World War*, (4 vols, London, 1979–90).

8   Michael Laffan, 'The question of French security in British policy towards France and Germany, 1918–1925' (PhD thesis, University of Cambridge, 1973).

9   On this debate see Ciaran Brady (ed.), *Interpreting Irish History: The Debate on Historical Revisionism* (Dublin, 1994).

10   Michael Laffan, 'Two Irish states', *The Crane Bag* viii:1: *Ireland: Dependence and Independence* (Oct. 1984), p. 26.

11   Ibid., p. 36.

12   Brendan Bradshaw, 'Nationalism and historical scholarship in modern Ireland', *Irish Historical Studies* xxvi:104 (Nov. 1989), pp 329–51.

13   Kevin Whelan, 'The recent writing of Irish history', *UCD History Review* (1991), p. 30.

14   Seamus Deane, 'Remembering the Irish future', *The Crane Bag* viii:1: *Ireland: Dependence and Independence*, pp 81–92; 'Wherever green is read', in Máirín Ní Dhonnchadha and Theo Dorgan (eds), *Revising the Rising* (Derry, 1991), pp 91–105.

15   Michael Laffan, 'Insular attitudes: the revisionists and their critics', in Ní Dhonnchadha and Dorgan (eds), *Revising the Rising*, p. 106.

16   Herbert Butterfield, *The Whig Interpretation of History* (London, 1931).

17   Oliver MacDonagh, *Ireland* (Englewood Cliffs NJ, 1968), p. 100.

18   Michael Laffan, *The Resurrection of Ireland: The Sinn Féin Party, 1916–23* (Cambridge, 1999), p. 462.

19   Michael Laffan, 'The sacred memory: religion, revisionists and the Easter Rising', in Judith Devlin and Ronan Fanning (eds), *Religion and Rebellion: Papers Read before the 22nd Irish Conference of Historians, Held at University College Dublin, 18–22 May 1995* (Dublin, 1997).

20   James McGuire and James Quinn (eds), *Dictionary of Irish Biography* (9 vols, Cambridge, 2009).

21   Micheal Laffan, *Judging W. T. Cosgrave: The Foundation of the Irish State* (Dublin, 2014).

1

'Voteless Alas': Suffragist protest and the census of Ireland in 1911

1   In preparing this chapter I have been encouraged, or directed towards valuable census entries, by Catherine Cox, Catriona Crowe, Leeann Lane, Mary McAuliffe and Paul Rouse. In particular, however, I want to thank Nicole Jackson, who generously alerted me to several suffragist census entries that I would otherwise have missed.

2   Cliona Murphy, *The Women's Suffrage Movement and Irish Society in the Early Twentieth Century* (London, 1989), p. 36.

3   The digitisation of the 1911 census of Britain has allowed Jill Liddington and Elizabeth Crawford to conduct a similar exercise. See Jill Liddington and Elizabeth Crawford, '"Women do not count, neither shall they be counted": suffrage, citizenship and the battle for the 1911 census', *History Workshop Journal* lxxi:1 (2011), pp 98–127.

4   Martin Pugh, *The March of Women* (Oxford, 2000), pp 171–223.

5   Carmel Quinlan, *Genteel Revolutionaries: Anna and Thomas Haslam and the Irish Women's Movement* (Cork, 2002), p. 169.

6   Diane Urquhart, *Women in Ulster Politics 1890–1940: A History Not Yet Told* (Dublin, 2000), p. 11.

7   James Cousins and Margaret Cousins, *We Two Together* (Madras, 1950), p. 178.

8   Ibid., p. 202.

9   June Purvis, *Emmeline Pankhurst: A Biography* (London, 2002), p. 97.

10   Liddington and Crawford, 'Women do not count, neither shall they be counted', p. 111.

11   *Freeman's Journal*, 7 Feb., 22 Mar. 1911.

12   Edward Higgs, 'The statistical Big Bang of 1911: ideology, technological innovation and the production of medical statistics', *Social History of Medicine* ix:3 (1996), pp 409–26.

13   Liddington and Crawford, 'Women do not count, neither shall they be counted', pp 110–14; Ian White, 'No vote – no census: an account of some of the events of 1910–1911', *Population Trends* cxlii (winter 2010), pp 33–51.

14   *Freeman's Journal*, 15 Mar. 1911; Murphy, *The Women's Suffrage Movement and Irish Society*, p. 35.

15   IWSLGA minutes, 9 Mar. 1911, nationalarchives.ie/topics/DWSA/DWSA8.pdf (accessed 1 July 2011).

16   *Irish Times*, 30 Mar. 1911; *Freeman's Journal*, 30 Mar. 1911.

17   *Irish Times*, 3 Apr. 1911.

18   Ibid., 1 Apr. 1911.

19   Purvis, *Emmeline Pankhurst*, p. 159.

20   *Freeman's Journal*, 3 Apr. 1911.

21   *Irish Times*, 3 Apr. 1911.

22   Ibid.

23   *Census of Ireland, 1911: General Report* (1913), p. xvii.

24   Rosemary Cullen Owens, *Smashing Times: A History of the Irish Women's Suffrage Movement 1889–1922* (Dublin, 1984), p. 42.

25   Census return, 16 Rathmines Rd, census.nationalarchives.ie/reels/nai000143840/ (all of the census returns that follow were viewed on the National Archives of Ireland's census website during July 2011).

26   Census return, 61.2 Harcourt St, census.nationalarchives.ie/reels/naio00187048/; Census return, 46 Landsdowne Rd, census.nationalarchives.ie/reels/naio00125708/.

27   Census return, 9 Back Sea View, Warrenpoint, census.nationalarchives.ie/reels/naio02281640/; Census return, 56.2 Belmont Rd, census.nationalarchives.ie/reels/naio02204132/.

28   Murphy, *The Women's Suffrage Movement and Irish Society*, p. 25.

29   Ibid., p. 19.

30   Census return, 1 Lovers Walk, Cork, census.nationalarchives.ie/reels/naio01854891/; Census return, 1 Drishane, Castlehaven, census.nationalarchives.ie/reels/naio02022267/.

31   Mary Clancy, 'Women of the west: campaigning for the vote in early twentieth-century Galway, *c*.1911–*c*.1915', in Louise Ryan and Margaret Ward (eds), *Irish Women and the Vote: Becoming Citizens* (Dublin, 2007), p. 48.

32   Census return, 49 Fairhill Rd, census.nationalarchives.ie/reels/naio03934073/; Census return, 13 Townparks, census.nationalarchives.ie/reels/naio02383783/; Census return, 7 Tievegarriff, census.nationalarchives.ie/reels/naio02382925/; Census return, 16 Newtownsmith, census.nationalarchives.ie/reels/naio03933463/.

33   Census return, 10 George St, census.nationalarchives.ie/reels/naio02759893/.

34   Susan M. Parkes, 'A danger to the men? Women in Trinity College Dublin in the first decade, 1904–1914', in Judith Harford and Claire Rush (eds), *Have Women Made a Difference? Women in Irish Universities, 1850–2010* (Oxford, 2010), p. 63.

35   Census return, 12 Palmerston Rd, census.nationalarchives.ie/reels/naio00142936/.

36   Judith Harford, *The Opening of University Education to Women in Ireland* (Dublin, 2008), pp 135–6.

37   Census return, 16 Rathmines Rd, census.nationalarchives.ie/reels/naio00143840/.

38   Census return, 55 Terenure Rd, census.nationalarchives.ie/reels/naio00147729/.

39   Census return, 14 Mulgrave St, census.nationalarchives.ie/reels/naio02756734/.

40   Margaret Ward, *Hanna Sheehy Skeffington: A Life* (Dublin, 1997), p. 47; see also Quinlan, *Genteel Revolutionaries*, p. 168.

41   Helen Morony to Hanna Sheehy Skeffington, 14 Dec. 1912, NLI, Sheehy Skeffington papers, MS 41,180/3; Des Ryan, 'Women's suffrage associations in Limerick, 1912–1914', *The Old Limerick Journal* (winter 1993), p. 41.

42   William Murphy, 'Suffragettes and the transformation of political imprisonment in Ireland, 1912–1914', in Ryan and Ward (eds), *Irish Women and the Vote*, pp 114–35.

43   Census return, 16 St Edward's Terrace, census.nationalarchives.ie/reels/naio00147599/; Census return, 20 Lower Baggot St, census.nationalarchives.ie/reels/naio00214816/.

44   Edward Higgs, 'Women, occupation and work in the nineteenth-century censuses', *History Workshop* xxiii (spring 1987), pp 59–80. In Britain, women could become enumerators from 1891 but this was not the case in Ireland.

45   Liddington and Crawford, 'Women do not count, neither shall they be counted', p. 121.

46   Violet Jameson to Hanna Sheehy Skeffington, 26 Oct. 1911, NLI, Sheehy Skeffington papers, MS 41,180/1.

47   *Irish Citizen*, 24 May 1913.

48   Census return, 33 Sutton South, Howth, census.nationalarchives.ie/reels/naio00023428/; Census return, 2 Winton Rd, census.nationalarchives.ie/reels/naio00145415/.

49   Census return, 122.4 St Stephen's Green, census.nationalarchives.ie/reels/naio00193627/.

50   Hanna Sheehy Skeffington to Francis Sheehy Skeffington, 28 July, 5 Aug. 1912, NLI, Sheehy Skeffington papers, MS 40,466 (5).

51   Margaret Ward, '"Suffrage first, above all else!" An account of the Irish suffrage movement', *Feminist Review* x (1982), pp 21–36; Beth McKillen, 'Irish feminism and national separatism 1914–1923', *Éire-Ireland* xvii:3 (1981), pp 2–67 and *Éire-Ireland* xvii:4 (1982), pp 72–90; Murphy, *The Women's Suffrage Movement and Irish Society*, pp 5, 41–6.

52   Leeann Lane, 'Rosamond Jacob: nationalism and suffrage', in Ryan and Ward (eds), *Irish Women and the Vote*, p. 176.

53   Census return, 16 Newtown Rd, census.nationalarchives.ie/reels/nai003500225/.

54   Census return, 66 Knockrea, Cork, census.nationalarchives.ie/reels/nai001896413/.

55   *Freeman's Journal*, 4 Apr. 1911.

56   Interestingly, some of the suffragettes of Birmingham spent the night at the Gaelic League Hall. Ibid.

57   Hanna Sheehy Skeffington, 'Reminisences of an Irish suffragette', in Rosemary Cullen Owens, *Votes for Women* (Dublin, 1975), p. 26.

58   Cousins and Cousins, *We Two Together*, p. 202.

59   Census return, 35 Strand Rd, census.nationalarchives.ie/reels/nai000120393/.

60   Census return, 11 Grosvenor Pl., census.nationalarchives.ie/reels/nai000149717/.

61   *Irish Times*, 7 Jan. 1911; Ibid., 3 Apr. 1911.

62   W. J. Lowe and E. L. Malcolm, 'The domestication of the Royal Irish Constabulary, 1836–1922', *Irish Economic and Social History* xix (1992), pp 27–48.

63   Census return, 17.3 Lower Sherrard St, census.nationalarchives.ie/reels/nai000076096/ .

64   Census return, 3.1 Cliff Terrace, census.nationalarchives.ie/reels/nai000248882/.

65   Census return, 39 Raglan Rd, census.nationalarchives.ie/reels/nai000126622/.

66   Census return, 15 Highfield Rd, census.nationalarchives.ie/reels/nai000146779/.

67   Census return, 54.2 Willowbank St, census.nationalarchives.ie/reels/nai001403437/.

68   Leeann Lane, *Rosamond Jacob: Third Person Singular* (Dublin, 2010), pp 55–7, 83–4.

69   Census return, 17 Parnell St, census.nationalarchives.ie/reels/nai003499390/.

70   Census return, 16.1 Sandymount Ave, census.nationalarchives.ie/reels/nai000117041/.

71   *Freeman's Journal*, 6 Apr. 1911.

72   Census return, 11 Sandford Rd, census.nationalarchives.ie/reels/nai000144714/.

73   Census return, 21 Annesley Park, census.nationalarchives.ie/reels/nai000135902/; Census return, 23 Sandhurst Drive, census.nationalarchives.ie/reels/nai001486544/.

74   Census return, 2 Woosley St, census.nationalarchives.ie/reels/nai001489628/.

75   Census return, 10 Park Drive, census.nationalarchives.ie/reels/nai000143168/.

76   Census return, 2.3 Lower Leeson St, census.nationalarchives.ie/reels/nai000188013/.

77   Ward, *Hanna Sheehy Skeffington*, p. 49; Senia Pašeta, *Irish Nationalist Women 1900–1918* (Cambridge, 2013), pp 71–2.

78   *Irish Times*, 7 Apr. 1911; *Freeman's Journal*, 7 Apr. 1911.

79   Murphy, *The Women's Suffrage Movement and Irish Society*, pp 182–3.

80   Census return, 23 Northumberland Rd, census.nationalarchives.ie/reels/nai000127296/.

81   Census return, 15 Sherrard St, census.nationalarchives.ie/reels/nai000076088/.

82   Census return, 21 Simmonscourt Rd, census.nationalarchives.ie/reels/nai000113154/.

83   Census return, 35 Skegoniel Ave, census.nationalarchives.ie/reels/nai001424269/.

84   Census return, 27 Dartmouth Square, census.nationalarchives.ie/reels/nai000137861/.

85   Census return, 32 Hollybank Ave, census.nationalarchives.ie/reels/nai000139102/.

86   Ward, *Hanna Sheehy Skeffington*, p. 74.

87   Liddington and Crawford, 'Women do not count, neither shall they be counted', pp 101–3.

88   Ibid., p. 99.

89   IWSLGA minutes, 9 Mar. 1911, nationalarchives.ie/topics/DWSA/DWSA8.pdf (accessed 1 July 2011).

90 Purvis, *Emmeline Pankhurst*, p. 159.

91 Leif Jerram, *Streetlife: The Untold History of Europe's Twentieth Century* (Oxford, 2011), pp 111–4.

92 *Freeman's Journal*, 1 Apr. 1911.

93 *Irish Times*, 30 Mar. 1911; *Freeman's Journal*, 30 Mar. 1911.

94 Sheehy Skeffington, 'Reminisences of an Irish suffragette', p. 26.

95 This search uncovered 47 women who evaded, refused, protested or were identified as suffragist in the returns.

96 Census return, 80 Bryansburn, Bangor, census.nationalarchives.ie/reels/nai002288883/; Urquhart, *Women in Ulster Politics 1890–1940*, pp 16–17, 26–8, 177–8.

97 Census return, 101 Agincourt Ave, census.nationalarchives.ie/reels/nai001464376/.

98 Jennifer Fitzgerald, '"The Queen's girl": Helen Waddell and women at Queen's University Belfast, 1908–1920', in Harford and Rush (eds), *Have Women Made a Difference?*, pp 80–1.

99 Census return, Aghogan, Co. Tyrone, census.nationalarchives.ie/reels/nai003385200/. Nugent's return gives her rank or profession as 'suffragette', although this may have been added by someone else as there appear to be some discrepancies in the handwriting on this form.

100 Liddington and Crawford, 'Women do not count, neither shall they be counted', p. 120.

101 The class-bound nature of the movement has been noted regularly in the historiography. See, for example, Murphy, *The Women's Suffrage Movement and Irish Society*, p.10 and Cullen Owens, *Smashing Times*, pp 47–8.

102 Census return, 1 Marlborough Park, census.nationalarchives.ie/reels/nai001493897/.

103 Census return, 12 Brighton Square, census.nationalarchives.ie/reels/nai000145920/.

104 Census return, 23 Maryville Park, census.nationalarchives.ie/reels/nai001494130/.

105 Murphy, *The Women's Suffrage Movement and Irish Society*, p. 17.

106 Ward, *Hanna Sheehy Skeffington*, p. 117.

107 W. E. Vaughan and A. J. Fitzpatrick (eds), *Irish Historical Statistics: Population 1821–1971* (Dublin, 1978), pp 66–8.

108 *Census of Ireland for the Year 1911: Preliminary Report with Abstract of the Enumerators' Summaries* (1911), p. 3.

109 *Freeman's Journal*, 6 Apr. 1911.

110 Ibid.

111 Liddington and Crawford also stress the importance of bearing in mind that 'Edwardian women possessed multiple identities.' See Liddington and Crawford, 'Women do not count, neither shall they be counted', p. 120.

2

Sport and war: The 1915 All-Ireland hurling championship

1 This chapter has been written in the knowledge that Michael's interest in sport might best be described as non-existent. Nonetheless, hope springs eternal that a belated conversion might still be possible.

2 From Seamus Redmond, 'The Hurler's Prayer', quoted in John Phelan, *In the Shadow of the Goalpost* (Laois, 2004), p. 563.

3 The county was officially known as Queen's County but on 13 December 1903 a decision of the GAA Central Council directed that for GAA matters the county be known as Leix. A similar decision was made to rename King's County as Offaly, *Cumann Lúthchleas Gaedheal Árd Chómhairle Miontúiriscí, 1899–1925*, Central Council minutes, 13 Dec. 1903, GAA Museum and Archives.

4   See Paul Rouse, 'Sport and Ireland in 1881', in Alan Bairner (ed.), *Sport and the Irish: Histories, Identities, Issues* (Dublin, 2005).

5   See Paul Rouse, 'Empires of sport: Enniscorthy, 1880–1920', in Colm Tóibín (ed.), *Enniscorthy: A History* (Wexford, 2010), pp 333–68.

6   Eric Hobsbawm, *Nations and Nationalism since 1780: Programme, Myth, Reality* (Cambridge, 1990), p. 143.

7   See, for example, J. A. Mangan, *Physical Education and Sport* (Oxford, 1973); Thomas Hughes, *Tom Brown's Schooldays* (London, 1857); J. A. Mangan, *Athleticism in the Victorian and Edwardian Public School* (London, 2000); John Lowerson, *Sport and the English Middle Classes 1870–1914* (Manchester, 1993); J. A. Mangan (ed.), *Reformers, Sport, Modernizers: Middle-Class Revolutionaries* (London, 2002).

8   See Rouse, 'Sport and Ireland in 1881'.

9   *The Shamrock*, 8 July 1882.

10   R. M. Peter, *The Irish Football Annual* (Dublin, 1880), p. 79.

11   Cusack has been the subject of two full biographies: Marcus de Búrca, *Michael Cusack and the GAA* (Dublin, 1989) and Liam P. Ó Caithnia, *Micheál Ó Cíosóg* (Galway, 1982). The most recent scholarship on Cusack includes Seán McNamara, *The Man from Carron* (Clare, 2005); Paul Rouse, 'Michael Cusack: sportsman and journalist', in Mike Cronin, William Murphy and Paul Rouse (eds), *The Gaelic Athletic Association: 1884–2009* (Dublin, 2009); and Dónal MacAnallen, 'Michael Cusack and the revival of Gaelic games in Ulster', *Irish Historical Studies* xxxvii:14 (May 2010), pp 23–47.

12   W. F. Mandle, *The Gaelic Athletic Association and Irish Nationalist Politics 1884–1924* (Dublin, 1987), p. 24.

13   See, for example, Mike Cronin, Mark Duncan and Paul Rouse, *The GAA: A People's History* (Cork, 2009).

14   Tim Carey, *Croke Park: A History* (Dublin, 2004), pp 42–95.

15   *Cumann Lúthchleas Gaedheal Árd Chómhairle Miontúiriscí, 1899–1925*, Central Council minutes, 2 June 1912, GAA Museum and Archives.

16   When Ireland played England in a rugby international in Cork in 1904 the attendance reached 12,000 and the Irish Rugby Football Union developed Lansdowne Road as a venue for international rugby and regularly drew crowds of more than 10,000 to matches. Crowds attending soccer matches were also increasing through this period. In 1904 a crowd of 6,000 attended the Leinster Cup final in Dublin. Attendances at soccer games in Dublin were much lower than those in Belfast where up to 20,000 people were estimated at a match between city rivals, Linfield and Belfast Celtic. By the eve of the First World War, 21,000 people were attending the Irish Cup final. All of this placed Ireland firmly in line with the phenomenon of the dramatic increase in attendances at sporting events in Britain. There, attendances at Football League matches, for example, reached 40,000 on occasion and enjoyed an average attendance at 32 FA Cup ties in 1913 of 20,600. See Mandle, *The Gaelic Athletic Association*, p. 151; Malachy Clerkin and Gerard Siggins, *Lansdowne Road* (Dublin, 2010), pp 96–100; and Neal Garnham, *Association Football and Society in Pre-Partition Ireland* (Belfast, 2004), p. 115, 129.

17   See, for example, Richard Holt, *Sport and the British: A Modern History* (Oxford, 1989). See also Neil Wigglesworth, *The Evolution of English Sport* (London, 1996); Neil Tranter, *Sport, Economy and Society in Britain, 1750–1914* (Cambridge, 1998); Dennis Brailsford, *British Sport: A Social History* (Cambridge, 1992); Bairner (ed.), *Sport and the Irish*; and Mike Huggins, *The Victorians and Sport* (London, 2007).

18   Wilkie Collins, *Man and Wife* (London, 1870), p. 207.

19   Eric Halladay, 'Of pride and prejudice: the amateur question in English nineteenth-century rowing', *The International Journal of the History of Sport* iv:1 (1987), pp 39–55.

20 For a brilliant exposition of the relationship between the GAA and amateurism, see Dónal MacAnallen, '"The Greatest Amateur Association in the world"? The GAA and amateurism', in Cronin, Duncan and Murphy (eds), *The Gaelic Athletic Association*, pp 157–82.

21 Clare GAA Circular re. Hurling Championship semi-final for the Championship of Munster, Ennis, July 1914, Clare County Museum; Circular letter asking people of Leix to contribute to the training fund, 29 Aug. 1914, GAA Museum and Archive, GAA/Laois/2.

22 *Limerick Leader*, 4 Feb. 1914.

23 Ibid.

24 See for example *Cork Weekly Examiner*, 6 Feb. 1915; *Limerick Leader*, 9 Oct. 1914; *Mayo News*, 12 May 1917.

25 *Limerick Leader*, 12 Oct. 1914.

26 *Clare Champion*, 24 Oct. 1914.

27 Ibid., 17, 24 Oct. 1914.

28 Ibid., 24 Oct. 1914.

29 Tomás Mac Conmara, '"Tip and slashin" – Clare's hurling victories of 1914', *Clare Association Yearbook, 2006*. Later, two men involved in the preparation of the Clare team for this success – Stephen Clune and Jim Ó Hehir – wrote to the GAA asking that they too should receive All-Ireland medals for their part in the success. Their request was denied.

30 *Clare Champion*, 10 Sept. 1914.

31 Ibid., 24 Oct. 1914.

32 Ibid., 10 Sept. 1914.

33 MacAnallen, 'The Greatest Amateur Association in the world', p. 165.

34 *Clare Champion*, 22 Aug. 1914.

35 Ibid., 3 Oct. 1914.

36 Mac Conmara, 'Tip and slashin'.

37 This section of the chapter is hugely indebted to the work of Mark Reynolds at the GAA Museum and Archives, especially with the John J. Higgins collection.

38 Anonymous letter to the Leix County Secretary, *c.* Oct. 1914, GAA Museum and Archives, GAA/Laois/74.

39 Letter from M. J. Sheridan and John J. Higgins, Honorary Secretaries to the Training Fund Sub-Committee, to each of the officers of the county committee and to club secretaries, 6 Mar. 1914, GAA Museum and Archives, GAA/Laois/1(2).

40 Circular letter asking for contributions to the training fund, 29 Aug.1914, GAA Museum and Archives, GAA/Laois/2.

41 See, for example, misc. subscriptions, GAA Museum and Archives, GAA/Laois/5–44.

42 Receipt card, Sept. 1914, GAA Museum and Archives, GAA/Laois/5.

43 See, for example, misc. subscriptions, GAA Museum and Archives, GAA/Laois/5–44.

44 E. Fitzgerald to John J. Higgins, 25 Nov. 1914, on Wynn's headed notepaper, GAA Museum and Archives, GAA/Laois/ 88.

45 James F. O'Crowley to John J. Higgins, 6 Oct. 1914, GAA Museum and Archives, GAA/Laois/89. On his notepaper, O'Crowley styled himself as 'J. F. O'Crowley, One of the original seven at founding of GAA 1884'. This was untrue. O'Crowley had not attended the first meeting of the GAA, though he had been involved in the GAA from at least 1886 and had been commissioned to make the medals for the first All-Ireland championships.

46 Phelan, *In the Shadow of the Goalpost*, p. 18.

47 Robert O'Keefe to John J. Higgins, 7 Sept. 1914, GAA Museum and Archives, GAA/Laois/4.

48 E. P. McEvoy to John J. Higgins, 22 Oct. 1914, GAA Museum and Archives, GAA/Laois/4.

49 Schedule on amounts needed to pay substitute workers, *n.d.* GAA Museum and Archives, GAA/Laois /45.

50   J. Quigley to John J. Higgins, 19 Sept. 1914, GAA Museum and Archives, GAA/Laois /59.

51   Mrs Lalor to John J. Higgins, 29 Oct., 30 Nov. 1914, GAA Museum and Archives, GAA/Laois /68–9.

52   See Arnold Mahon, 'An analysis of the development of sport in Laois/Queen's County within the context of the period 1910–1920' (MA thesis, University College Dublin, 2007).

53   Ballygeeghan went on to win five championships in a row between 1914 and 1918. See Phelan, *In the Shadow of the Goalpost*.

54   Robert O'Keefe to John J. Higgins, 18 Nov. 1914, GAA Museum and Archives, GAA/Laois/178.

55   Ballygeeghan and Kilcotton were the powerhouses of the Laois team. They had met in the 1915 Laois county final and the match had ended in a draw. Ballygeeghan had come up from junior level in 1914 to immediately win that year's Laois championship and their rivalry with the established force of Kilcotton was rather intense. To ensure that all players were available, Fr Kearney had decided that the replay would not be played until after the All-Ireland final against Cork. In all, there were eight changes from the team defeated the previous year by Clare. The Laois team comprised six players from the Ballygeeghan club, with the remainder from Kilcotton, Rathdowney, Rapla and Abbeyleix, *Sport*, 23 Oct. 1915. All through the 1915 championship O'Keefe was engaged in a confidential exchange of letters with members of the county committee who were provided with his views on team selection and preparation. See misc. correspondence, GAA Museum and Archives, GAA/Laois/165–75.

56   *Sport*, 30 Oct. 1915.

57   Letter from John Finlay, 22 Mar. 1915, GAA Museum and Archives, GAA/Laois/96.

58   *Sport*, 23 Oct. 1915.

59   Notes on training methods, *c.* 1914, GAA Museum and Archives, GAA/Laois/ 73.

60   P. Daly to John J. Higgins, 11 Oct. 1915, GAA Museum and Archives, GAA/Laois /91.

61   Letter from Fr J. J. Kearney, 11 Oct. 1915, GAA Museum and Archives, GAA/Laois/97.

62   *Sport*, 23 Oct. 1915.

63   Teddy Fennelly, *One Hundred Years of GAA in Laois* (Laois, 1984), p. 31.

64   Jim Doyle to Fr J. J. Kearney, 1 Oct. 1915 and Dick 'Drug' Walsh to John J. Higgins, 15 Oct. 1915, GAA Museum and Archives, GAA/Laois/94–5.

65   'Notes for players previous to match', *n.d.*, GAA Museum and Archives, GAA/Laois/71.

66   *Irish Independent*, 1 Sept. 1976.

67   It remained one of the quirks of the championship that the matches did not always run as smoothly as might be expected. Because of the delay in finishing the Munster championship, the Munster Council of the GAA had nominated Clare to play the Connacht champions, Galway, in the All-Ireland semi-final. Then, when Cork duly beat Clare in the Munster championship, it was they who progressed to play the All-Ireland final.

68   Robert O'Keefe to John J. Higgins, 27 Sept. 1915, GAA Museum and Archives, GAA/Laois/156.

69   *Sport*, 30 Oct. 1915.

70   Ibid.

71   Interview with John Lawless, GAA Oral History Project. John Lawless was born in January 1911. He was raised in Kyle, Abbeyleix, which bordered the parish of Ballacolla. He worked on the Hamilton estate in Moyne as did his father. He played hurling for Kyle and later for Abbeyleix, and also made hurleys. This file and all the other material held in the GAA Oral History Project were transferred to the GAA Museum and Archives in 2014.

72   See, for example, Joe McDonald, 18 North Main Street, Naas, to John J. Higgins, 10 Apr. 1915, GAA Museum and Archives, GAA/Laois/1915.

73   Joseph McDonald to John J. Higgins, 20 Oct. 1915, GAA Museum and Archives, GAA/ Laois/103.

74   William McDonald to John J. Higgins, 10 Aug. 1916, GAA Museum and Archives, GAA/ Laois/112.

75   Robert O'Keefe to John J. Higgins, 19 Oct. 1915, GAA Museum and Archives, GAA/ Laois/169.

76   *Village*, 15 July 2005; Phelan, *In the Shadow of the Goalpost*, p. 352.

77   *Sport*, 30 Oct. 1915.

78   *Irish Independent*, 22 Oct. 1915.

79   Ibid., 25 Oct. 1915.

80   Anon., *125 Years of Laois GAA* (Laois, 2009), p. 23.

81   *Irish Independent*, 25 Oct. 1915.

82   *Irish Times*, 25 Nov. 2011.

83   *Sport*, 30 Oct. 1915.

84   Ibid.

85   *Irish Independent*, 25 Oct. 1915.

86   *Sport*, 30 Oct. 1915.

87   Interview with John Lawless, GAA Oral History Project. Various songs were written in honour of the team. See Phelan, *In the Shadow of the Goalpost, passim*.

88   Algernon Coote to John Drennan, 26 Oct. 1915, GAA Museum and Archives, GAA/ Laois/106. See also Patrick F. Meehan, *The Members of Parliament for Laois & Offaly (Queen's and King's Counties) 1801–1918* (Laois, 1972), p. 65.

89   Telegraph from Meehan to John Drennan, 28 Oct. 1915, GAA Museum and Archives, GAA/ Laois/108.

90   *Sport*, 30 Oct. 1915.

91   Robert O'Keefe to John J. Higgins, 23 May 1915, GAA Museum and Archives, GAA/ Laois/154.

92   Misc. correspondence, 1915, 1916 and 1917, GAA Museum and Archives, GAA/Laois/135–7.

93   Robert O'Keefe to John J. Higgins, 28 Oct. 1915, GAA Museum and Archives, GAA/ Laois/107.

94   See, for example, *Leinster Leader*, 30 Oct. 1915.

95   See, for example, *Sport*, 30 Oct. 1915.

96   *Gaelic Athlete*, 12 June 1915.

97   *Irish Times*, 25 Oct. 1915.

98   Ibid., 19, 23 Oct. 1915. The paper published its report of this incident on two separate occasions.

99   Mandle, *The Gaelic Athletic Association*, p. 105.

100 *Cumann Lúthchleas Gaedheal Árd Chómhairle Miontúiriscí, 1899–1925, 1901 Annual Convention*, GAA Museum and Archives.

101 Paul Rouse, 'The politics of culture and sport in Ireland: a history of the GAA ban on foreign games, 1884–1971. Part one: 1884–1921', *International Journal of the History of Sport* x:3 (1993), pp 333–60.

102 At a meeting of the GAA clubs of the Enniscorthy district in November 1912, for example, Boggan and Kehoe argued passionately against the practice of GAA teams togging out in licensed premises. Boggan argued that 'no true Gael should touch intoxicating drink nor make a dressing room of a licensed premises.' A local priest, Fr Murphy, told the members of the Gaelic League in Enniscorthy that they should be involved with Gaelic games and not with 'the games of the foreigner' or 'athletic souperism'. In an attempt to confront such 'souperism'

on every front, the Enniscorthy Gaelic Athletic Tennis Club was established in 1914 and was a huge success in its first year. Although not officially a part of the GAA, members of the Association were its leading lights, including Michael De Lacey, a schoolteacher who later fought in the 1916 Rising. *Enniscorthy Echo*, 30 Nov. 1912; *Irish Times*, 17 May 1914; *Enniscorthy Echo*, 18 July 1914, 13 Mar. 1915.

103   *Irish Times*, 17 Mar. 1914.

104   Rouse, 'The politics of culture and sport in Ireland'.

105   Robert O'Keefe, 18 Dec. 1914, GAA Museum and Archives, GAA/Laois/180.

106   *Gaelic Athlete*, 14 Nov. 1914.

107   *Clonmel Chronicle*, 24 Mar. 1915.

108   *Clare Champion*, 29 Jan. 1916.

109   *National Volunteer*, 15 May 1915.

110   *Gaelic Athlete*, 27 Dec. 1913.

111   *Limerick Leader*, 3 Apr. 1914.

112   William Murphy, 'The GAA during the Irish revolution, 1913–23', in Cronin, Duncan and Murphy (eds), *The Gaelic Athletic Association*, p. 70.

113   Misc. notes, 1914. NLI, J. J. O'Conell papers, MS 22,114.

114   This section of the chapter owes much to Murphy's excellent article 'The GAA during the Irish revolution, 1913–23'.

115   Tom Johnstone, *Orange, Green and Khaki: The Story of the Irish Regiments in the Great War, 1914–1918* (Dublin, 1992), p. 89; Paul Maguire, *Follow Them Up from Carlow: Carlow's Lost Generation* (Naas, 2002), p. 89.

116   *Irish Independent*, 17 Sept. 1914.

117   *Sunday Independent*, 16 Aug. 1914.

118   *Irish Independent*, 15 Sept. 1914.

119   Ibid., 24 Feb. 1915.

120   *Cork Examiner*, 7 Aug. 1914.

121   *Limerick Leader*, 14 Aug., 14 Sept. 1914.

122   *Gaelic Athlete*, 24 Apr. 1915.

123   *Kilkenny Journal*, 10 Mar. 1915.

124   *Enniscorthy Echo*, 28 Nov. 1914.

125   Ibid.; *Cumann Lúthchleas Gaedheal Árd Chómhairle Miontúiriscí, 1899–1925*, Central Council minutes, 3 Oct. 1914, GAA Museum and Archives.

126   Thomas Doyle, BMH WS 1,041, p. 2. See also Robert Brennan, *Allegiance* (Dublin, 1950), pp 34–5, 51.

127   *Enniscorthy Echo*, 24 Oct. 1914.

128   Anon., *Sixty Glorious Years: The Authentic Story of the GAA* (Dublin, 1946), p. 66.

129   *Cork Examiner*, 12 June 1917.

130   *Cork Weekly Examiner*, 9 June 1917.

131   *Clare Champion*, 22 Jan. 1916.

132   Ibid.

133   *Tipperary Star,* 23 Oct. 1914.

134   Daniel McCarthy, *Ireland's Banner County: Clare from the Fall of Parnell to the Great War 1890–1918* (Ennis, 2002), p. 106.

135   Jim Cronin, *Munster GAA Story* (Ennis, 1984), p. 103.

136   *Cork Weekly Examiner*, 16 June 1917.

137   *Gaelic Athlete*, 19 Dec. 1914.

138   Seán Kierse, *History of Smith O'Brien GAA Club, Killaloe 1886–1987* (Killaloe, 1991), p. 139

139 Tom O'Donoghue, *The Arravale Rovers Story: The GAA in the Parish of Tipperary* (Tipperary, 1995), p. 104.

140 *Leinster Leader*, 6 Nov. 1915.

141 *Clare Champion*, 3 July 1915.

142 *Enniscorthy Echo*, 24 Oct. 1914.

143 *Irish Times*, 3 Aug. 1915; *Leitrim Observor*, 7 Aug. 1915.

144 *National Volunteer*, 8 May 1915.

145 *Irish Times*, 29 Apr. 1915.

146 Ibid., 26 June 1914.

147 *Gaelic Athlete*, 27 Mar. 1915.

148 Ibid., 3 Apr. 1915.

149 Ibid., 13 Mar. 1915.

150 Ernie O'Malley, *On Another Man's Wound* (Dublin, 1936), pp 62–3.

3 Michael Keogh: Recruiting sergeant for Casement's Irish Brigade

1 Most of these articles are in the possession of the Keogh family, Dublin. A number of them appeared in the *Sunday Chronicle* in December 1952.

2 Interview with Michael Keogh's son, Kevin, and daughter-in-law, Mary, Dublin (31 Jan. 2008).

3 UCDA, Michael McKeogh papers, p.128. Michael Keogh used 'McKeogh' and 'Kehoe' as variants on his name.

4 Interview with Kevin and Mary Keogh, Dublin (31 Jan. 2008).

5 Jeffrey Dudgeon, *Roger Casement: The Black Diaries with a Study of His Background, Sexuality and Irish Political Life* (Belfast, 2002), p. 452.

6 As a British consul, Casement's investigations and reports exposed appalling human-rights abuses of the natives of the Congo in central Africa, under Leopold II of Belgium, and of the natives of the Putumayo in South America.

7 Robert Monteith, *Casement's Last Adventure* (2nd edn, Dublin, 1953), pp 107, 80, 89–90.

8 Dudgeon, *Roger Casement: The Black Diaries*, p. 452.

9 Brian Maye (ed.), *With Casement's Irish Brigade* (Drogheda, 2010), p. 1.

10 Ibid., pp 1–4.

11 Ibid., p. 5.

12 Originally, Zouave was the name given to some infantry regiments in the French army. The Papal Zouaves were formed to defend the Papal States in the late 1850s as the Italian unification movement sought to incorporate the states into a united Italy.

13 *Irish Times*, 17 Oct. 1983.

14 Michael Keogh wrote a number of newspaper articles from the 1920s to the 1950s. Some of these have survived in the papers to which the author has had access; some are inaccessible for various reasons. This particular article has no evidence on it of where it was published but bears the date of July 1952. Most of his articles seem to have been published in a British paper called the *Sunday Chronicle*. This title disappeared in 1955 when it was merged with the *Empire News*. See Maye (ed.), *With Casement's Irish Brigade*, p. v.

15 Ferdinand Maximilian Joseph (1832–67) was a member of the Austrian imperial Habsburg family. With the backing of Napoleon III of France and a group of Mexican monarchists, he was proclaimed Maximilian I of Mexico in 1864. He was overthrown by Mexican republicans and executed in 1867.

16 Maye (ed.), *With Casement's Irish Brigade*, p. ix.

17   Ibid., pp ix–x.

18   Ibid., p. x.

19   Ibid., p. 35.

20   As Monteith's reference to 'other attractions' suggests, Keogh had developed a relationship with a German woman.

21   For a recent summary of Casement's time in Germany, see Séamus Ó Síocháin, *Roger Casement: Imperialist, Rebel, Revolutionary* (Dublin, 2008), pp 408–38.

22   John MacBride (1865–1916) had emigrated to South Africa where he raised the Irish Transvaal Brigade to fight the British when the Boer War broke out in 1899. Most members were Irish or Irish-American miners living in the Transvaal.

23   Monteith, *Casement's Last Adventure*, p. 93.

24   Andreas Roth, '"The German soldier is not tactful": Sir Roger Casement and the Irish Brigade in Germany during the First World War', *The Irish Sword* xix:78 (winter 1995), p. 329.

25   Ibid., p. 330.

26   Ibid.

27   For the details of the full agreement, see Maye (ed.), *With Casement's Irish Brigade*, chapter 5 *passim*.

28   Roth, 'The German soldier is not tactful', p. 330.

29   Dudgeon, *Roger Casement: The Black Diaries*, p. 450. Belgian neutrality was guaranteed in 1839 by five European powers: Britain, France, Prussia, Austria and Russia. When the Germans invaded Belgium en route to France in early August 1914, Britain used this violation of Belgian neutrality as the reason for declaring war on Germany. War for the defence of 'little Catholic Belgium' was an effective British recruiting slogan, especially in Ireland.

30   Reinhard Doerries, *Prelude to the Easter Rising: Sir Roger Casement in Imperial Germany* (London, 2000), pp 9–12, 14.

31   Monteith, *Casement's Last Adventure*, p. 131.

32   See John Borgonovo, *Informers and the 'Anti-Sinn Féin Society': The Intelligence War in Cork City 1920–21* (Dublin, 2007), pp 76–7.

33   See Maye (ed.), *With Casement's Irish Brigade*, appendix 3.

34   The story of Michael Keogh's life from 1911 to 1922, and particularly his time in Germany from 1914 to 1919, told in his own words, can be found in ibid., pp 7–179.

35   Interview with Kevin and Mary Keogh, Dublin (31 Jan. 2008).

36   'Abstract of service R985 Cpl Michael Kehoe', Military Archives, Cathal Brugha Barracks. I am grateful to archivist Lisa Dolan for drawing this source to my attention.

37   In the possession of Kevin Keogh senior, Dublin.

38   Interview with Kevin and Mary Keogh, Dublin (31 Jan. 2008).

39   Information supplied by Michael Keogh's grandson, Kevin, son of Kevin Keogh (6 Nov. 2011). Kevin Keogh junior has done extensive research on his grandfather's life and is preparing a website which will cover all aspects of it.

40   In the possession of Kevin Keogh senior, Dublin.

41   Interview with Kevin and Mary Keogh, Dublin (31 Jan. 2008).

42   Monteith, *Casement's Last Adventure*, pp 120–1.

43   For biographical details on Quinlisk, see Maye (ed.), *With Casement's Irish Brigade*, pp 73–4. He had two articles published under the title 'The German Irish Brigade: diary of Casement's lieutenant' in the British magazine *Land and Water*, 6 Nov. 1919, pp 18–20 and 13 Nov. 1919, pp 16–17.

44   Maye (ed.), *With Casement's Irish Brigade*, pp ix–x.

45   Ibid., pp 37–8.

46   Ibid., p. 77.

47   For John Devoy see Terry Golway, *Irish Rebel: John Devoy and America's Fight for Ireland's Freedom* (New York, 1988).

48   B. L. Reid, *The Lives of Roger Casement* (New Haven CT and London, 1976), pp. 307–8.

49   See Maye (ed.), *With Casement's Irish Brigade*, p. 42, 77

50   Ibid., p. 39.

51   Ibid., p. 151.

52   Ibid., p. 68.

53   Ibid., pp 3–4.

54   Ibid., pp 118–21.

4
A souring of friendships?: Internal divisions in the leadership of the Irish Parliamentary Party in the aftermath of the Easter Rising

1   I would like to extend my sincere thanks to Michael Laffan who first cultivated and encouraged my interest in the history of the Irish Parliamentary Party. I was privileged to be one among many scholars to whom he has given generously both his time and his expertise. Furthermore, I owe my thanks to Diarmaid Ferriter and John Coakley for their supervision and encouragement of my research at University College Dublin. I gratefully acknowledge the funding of the Irish Research Council for the Humanities and Social Sciences who funded the research upon which this work is based.

2   The Irish party had split in December 1890 over the question of Charles Stewart Parnell's continued leadership of the movement following his involvement in the O'Shea divorce case. Philip Bull's, 'The United Irish League and the re-union of the Irish Parliamentary Party, 1898–1900', *Irish Historical Studies* xxvi:101 (May 1988) is an excellent study of the party's reunification.

3   Michael Wheatley, 'John Redmond and federalism in 1910', *Irish Historical Studies* xxxii:127 (May 2001), p. 343.

4   Healy had been expelled from the parliamentary party by December 1900 and a bitter and public battle between Dillon and O'Brien led to the latter's withdrawal from public life in November 1903. A brief rapprochement was arrived at in January 1908. The entrances and exits of O'Brien and Healy from the party between 1908 and 1909 are summarised in Frank Callanan, *T. M. Healy* (Cork, 1996), pp 456–9.

5   *Freeman's Journal*, 21 Sept. 1914.

6   John T. Donovan to John Redmond, 7 Feb. 1917, NLI, Redmond papers, MS 15,185.

7   See Stephen Gwynn, *John Redmond's Last Years* (London, 1919), pp 130–1.

8   On Redmond's contribution to the war effort and his work on recruitment, the most comprehensive account can be found in Joseph P. Finnan, *John Redmond and Irish Unity, 1912–1918* (New York, 2004), p. 78 *et seq.*

9   Dillon to O'Connor, 1 Mar. 1915, TCD, Dillon papers, MS 6741/239.

10   Two important sources on this subject are Edward MacLysaght, 'Some memoires of the Irish Convention 1917–1918', *Capuchin Annual* (1968), pp 345–50 and R. B. McDowell, *The Irish Convention, 1917–18* (London, 1970).

11   For just two examples, see F. S. L. Lyons, 'The passing of the Irish Parliamentary Party (1916–1918)', pp 95–106 and Maureen Wall, 'Partition: the Ulster question (1916–1926)', p. 79, both in Desmond Williams (ed.), *The Irish Struggle, 1916–1926* (London, 1966).

12   In particular, see F. S. L. Lyons, *John Dillon: A Biography* (London, 1968), pp 372–80.

13   It should not be assumed that this distinction between the London and Dublin men of the leadership was absolute. Redmond, and even O'Connor, visited Ireland frequently during the war. However, only Dillon and Devlin possessed an acute and detailed comprehension of the shifting nature of grassroots Irish politics in these years, particularly in Dublin, where the strength of advanced nationalism was growing.

14   Chief Secretary George Wyndham's 1903 Land Act, which emanated from the consensus arrived at the Mansion House conference, largely settled the Irish land question, which had dominated the Irish policies of Conservative and Liberal governments alike from the 1870s onwards. For a highly comprehensive if one-sided insight into this earlier period in the party's history, William O'Brien's, *An Olive Branch in Ireland and Its History* (London, 1910), pp 126–290 is a valuable contemporary account. On the origins of the phrase 'conference plus business', see Joseph V. O'Brien, *William O'Brien and the Course of Irish Politics, 1881–1918* (Berkeley CA, 1976), p. 184.

15   Both Redmond and O'Brien had been expressly proposed as tenant representatives in the letter that prompted the conference. See John Shawe-Taylor (open letter of 2 Sept. 1902), in O'Brien, *Olive Branch*, p. 140.

16   On this, see O'Brien, *William O'Brien*, pp 151–9.

17   See 'Mr Devlin's memo', 20 Feb. 1914, NLI, Redmond papers, MS 15,181/3. Devlin was the last to consent to this. On his conversion, see A. C. Hepburn, *Catholic Belfast and Nationalist Ireland in the Era of Joe Devlin, 1871–1934* (Oxford, 2008), pp 148–9.

18   A good summary of the details of this can be found in Denis Gwynn, *The Life of Redmond* (London, 1932), pp 338–41.

19   A reference to Clan na Gael, the American wing of Irish physical force republicanism. In 1900, Clan na Gael been reformed under the leadership of the veteran Fenian John Devoy and thereafter played a leading role in financing Irish republicanism in the advent of the 1916 Rising.

20   Dillon to Redmond, 23 Apr. 1916, NLI, Redmond papers, MS 15,182/22.

21   Significantly, on 6 March, an Irish journalist working in Chicago had written to Redmond giving a detailed information of a planned 'rising', although his expected date of summer 1917 represented a dangerous miscalculation. Bernard McGillian to Redmond, 6 Mar. 1916, TCD, Dillon papers, MS 6749/609.

22   A letter discussing all the different conduits of information between Dublin and London and their respective demerits is Dillon to Redmond, 2 May 1916, NLI, Redmond papers, MS 15,182/22.

23   Dillon observed that he had not actually heard from Devlin since 'Monday week' [16 Apr. 1916] in a letter to T. P. O'Connor dated 'Tuesday evening', 2 May 1916, TCD, Dillon papers, MS 6741/302.

24   Hepburn, *Catholic Belfast*, p. 175.

25   On 2 May alone, Dillon noted Devlin's absence and expected arrival in no less than three communications now in the NLI, Redmond papers, MS 15,182/22.

26   Dillon to O'Connor, 2 May 1916, TCD, Dillon papers, MS 6741/302.

27   Redmond to Dillon, 4 May 1916, TCD, Dillon papers, MS 6749/622. Devlin was already in Dublin by the time this letter was written. In addition, this letter would not have reached Dillon for at least another day as it was hand delivered by Annie O'Brien, a secretary in the United Irish League offices on O'Connell Street. This information is recorded in a note on the envelope.

28   Hepburn, *Catholic Belfast*, p. 175; Dillon to Redmond, 8.15 [p.m.], 2 May 1916, NLI, Redmond papers, MS 15,182/22.

29   As late as 17 May, Dillon exclaimed to O'Connor that 'this house has been over-run by all

sorts and conditions seeking for release of prisoners or laying before me details of hardships and outrages.' During the Rising, soldiers had also been a frequent presence at Dillon's house at 2 North Great George's Street and actually played a crucial role in getting communications in and out of the city after the postal system had been crippled by the seizure and destruction of the General Post Office. Dillon to O'Connor, 17 May 1916, TCD, Dillon papers, MS 6741/307 and Dillon to Redmond, 30 Apr. [1916], NLI, Redmond papers, MS 15,182/22.

30   See Dillon to Redmond, 8.15 [p.m.], 2 May 1916, NLI, Redmond papers, MS 15,182/22.

31   Gwynn, *Life of Redmond*, p. 97. See also Dermot Meleady, *Redmond: The Parnellite* (Cork, 2008), pp 77–8, 316.

32   See Bessie O'Connor to Redmond, 1 Mar. 1917, NLI, Redmond papers, MS 15,215/2/B, giving details of O'Connor's marital and legal status. O'Connor's first biographer is more discrete in his treatment of his subject's relationship with Mrs Crawford, referring to it as a 'sympathetic companionship' and stating that the couple lived 'near one another', Hamilton Fyfe, *T. P. O'Connor* (London, 1934), pp 200–1.

33   *Hansard 5 (Commons)*, lxxxi, 2512 (27 Apr. 1916).

34   Lyons, *Dillon*, p. 373.

35   *Hansard 4 (Commons)*, xx, 591–3 (20 Mar. 1902). For Dillon's own defence of his actions, see Dillon to Redmond, 22 Mar. 1902, NLI, Redmond papers, MS 15,182/3/B.

36   *Hansard 5 (Commons)*, lxxxii, 631–2 (10 May 1916).

37   Redmond's disbelief and naivety over the happenings in Ireland are summed up in Redmond to Dillon, 4 May 1916, TCD, Dillon papers, MS 6749/622.

38   *Hansard 5 (Commons)*, lxxxii, 632 (10 May 1916). Sheehy Skeffington, along with two other civilians, was unlawfully executed by Captain John Bowen-Colthurst at Portobello Barracks, Rathmines, Dublin on 26 April 1916. On the charge of murder, Bowen-Colthurst was subsequently found guilty but insane by military court-martial. Roger Casement was initially judged by British authorities and, it would appear from this source, also by John Dillon, to have been the mastermind behind the Rising.

39   John Redmond, 'Memorandum of an interview with Asquith', 3 May 1916, quoted in Gwynn, *Life of Redmond*, p. 480.

40   Redmond to Dillon, 4 May 1916, TCD, Dillon papers, MS 6749/622.

41   Lyons, *Dillon*, pp 379–80. The four in question were Éamonn Ceannt, Con Colbert, Michael Mallin, and Seán Heuston. Of these, only Ceannt had been a signatory.

42   Quoted in Gwynn, *Life of Redmond*, p. 481.

43   As stated by Wall, 'Partition: the Ulster question (1916–1926)', p. 79.

44   *Hansard 5 (Commons)*, lxxxii, 37 (3 May 1916).

45   Ibid.

46   P. H. Pearse, Tom Clarke, and Thomas MacDonagh were the first to be executed. Including Casement, the final number executed was 16.

47   Redmond to Dillon, 3 May 1916, TCD, Dillon papers, MS 6749/620.

48   Dillon to Redmond, 7 May 1916, NLI, Redmond papers, MS 15,182/22. See also Lyons, *Dillon*, p. 379.

49   On Dillon's attitude towards Connolly's socialism, see Lyons, *Dillon*, p. 335; for comments on Kent as a murderer, see Dillon to Redmond, 7 May 1916, NLI, Redmond papers, MS 15,182/22. Lyons mistakenly implies that the 'Kent' referred to in Dillon's letter was Éamonn Ceannt. Details from the trials of both men confirm that Dillon was in fact referring to Kent rather than Ceannt. See Lyons, *Dillon*, pp 379–80. For transcripts and commentaries of the trials of Éamonn Ceannt and Thomas Kent see Brian Barton, *From Behind Closed Doors: Secret Court Martial Records of the 1916 Easter Rising* (Belfast, 2002), pp 181–97 and 251–66 respectively.

50   Dillon to Redmond, 7 May 1916, NLI, Redmond papers, MS 15,182/22.

51   *Hansard 5 (Commons)*, lxxxii, 945 (11 May 1916).

52   Dillon to O'Connor, 1 Mar. 1915, TCD, Dillon papers, MS 6741/239.

53   Sir Lawrence Parsons raised the 16th (Irish) Division and commanded it up to 5 December 1915, shortly before it was moved into action on the Western Front.

54   Dillon to O'Connor, 1 Mar. 1915, TCD, Dillon papers, MS 6741/239.

55   Dillon to O'Connor, 20 May 1916, TCD, Dillon papers, MS 6741/310.

56   Lyons, *Dillon*, p. 423.

57   Ibid., pp 423–4.

58   See Philip Bull, 'O'Brien, William', in James McGuire and James Quinn (eds), *Dictionary of Irish Biography* (Cambridge, 2009) (accessed online 9 Dec. 2009). Significantly, the *Freeman's Journal* joined in the campaign against O'Brien and conciliation, see Felix M. Larkin, 'Two gentlemen of the *Freeman*: Thomas Sexton, W. H. Brayden and the *Freeman's Journal*, 1892–1916', in Ciara Breathnach and Catherine Lawless (eds), *Visual, Material and Print Culture in Nineteenth-Century Ireland* (Dublin, 2010), pp 216–7.

59   This shift was exemplified by the rejection of the Irish Council Bill in 1907, which Redmond referred to as a 'half-measure'. See Gwynn, *Life of Redmond*, p. 148.

60   For a more complete analysis of the conference see Conor Mulvagh, '"Amicable in tone yet fruitless in result": politicians, press and public and the Buckingham Palace Conference, 1914', *History Studies: University of Limerick History Society Journal* viii (2007), pp 77–92.

61   H. H. Asquith to Venetia Stanley, 22 July 1914 [102], in H. H. Asquith, *Letters to Venetia Stanley*, Michael and Eleanor Brock (eds), (Oxford, 1982), p. 109.

62   Gwynn, *Life of Redmond*, p. 343.

63   It is recorded that James Craig similarly offered his hand to Dillon when the conference broke up. John Hostettler, *Sir Edward Carson: A Dream Too Far* (Chichester, 1997), p. 213, and Lyons, *Dillon*, p. 353.

64   Lloyd George's memorandum of an interview with Dillon conducted in November of 1913 is illuminating in tracing Dillon's reasoning for conceding to the principle of temporary exclusion for Ulster. Lloyd George, 'Interview with Mr John Dillon, at No. 11 Downing St.', 17 Nov. 1913, Parl. Arch., Lloyd George papers, LG/C/20/2/4.

65   Lyons, *Dillon*, p. 387.

66   Gwynn, *Life of Redmond*, p. 505 and Denis Gwynn, *The History of Partition (1912–1925)* (Dublin, 1950), p. 150. On the 1909 budget debacle, see Gwynn, *Life of Redmond*, pp 162–4.

67   While it is only an indication of the depth of their friendship, O'Connor was making plans to go to the theatre with Lloyd George in the middle of June 1916 while negotiations on the Irish question were at a delicate stage. O'Connor to Lloyd George, 19 June 1916, Parl. Arch., Lloyd George papers, LG/D/14/3/15.

68   L. W. Brady, *T. P. O'Connor and the Liverpool Irish* (London, 1983), p. 231.

69   Ibid., p. 233.

70   See in particular O'Connor to Lloyd George, 7 June 1916, Parl. Arch., Lloyd George papers, LG/D/14/2/17 and O'Connor to Lloyd George, 16 June 1916, Parl. Arch., Lloyd George papers, LG/D/14/3/5.

71   Lyons, *Dillon*, p. 408.

72   See Devlin's memorandum of this interview, marked 'secret', 15 May 1916, NLI, Redmond papers, MS 15,181/3.

73   Devlin, memorandum of interview with Lord Northcliffe, 15 May 1916 (Secret), NLI, Redmond papers, MS 15,181/3.

74   O'Connor to Dillon, 18 May 1916, TCD, Dillon papers, MS 6741/308.

75 Ibid.

76 R. F. Foster, *Modern Ireland, 1600–1972* (London, 1988), p. 486.

77 It is not strictly fair to label Redmond as a 'London man'. He spent an increasing amount of time in Aughavannagh in South Wicklow during the war years. However, rural Wicklow could not provide the same level of insight into the rapid changes in public mood available to Dillon, who spent the majority of his time in Dublin.

78 Hepburn, *Catholic Belfast*, p. 176.

79 Eamon Phoenix, *Northern Nationalism: Nationalist Politics, Partition and the Catholic Minority in Northern Ireland, 1890–1940* (Belfast, 1994), p. 22. Lloyd George's assurances to Carson (29 May 1916) are reproduced in Gwynn, *History of Partition*, p. 149.

80 O'Connor to Dillon, 19 May 1916, TCD, Dillon papers, MS 6741/309.

81 Hepburn, *Catholic Belfast*, p. 178.

82 A full breakdown of the voting in the Ulster Convention is contained in Hepburn, *Catholic Belfast*, p. 179. R. B. McDowell earlier gave the caveat that, of the 270 delegates from Fermanagh, Tyrone, and Derry city, an overwhelming 183 (68 per cent of those delegates) voted against the proposals. McDowell, *Irish Convention*, pp 53–4.

83 Dillon to O'Connor, 20 May 1916, TCD, Dillon papers, MS 6741/310. This letter cuts off abruptly, but it continues in a fragment labelled MS 6741/333, in which Dillon lists some of his grievances around the actions of the government.

84 Dillon to O'Connor, 27 May 1916, TCD, Dillon papers, MS 6741/311.

85 Dillon to O'Connor, 28 June 1916, quoted in Lyons, *Dillon*, p. 398.

86 On O'Connor's impressions of Dublin during a brief visit to attend a party meeting there, see Brady, *O'Connor*, p. 232.

87 See Gwynn, *History of Partition*, p. 156.

88 Hepburn, *Catholic Belfast*, pp 180–1.

89 Asquith to Redmond, 28 July 1916, quoted in Gwynn, *Life of Redmond*, pp 522–3.

90 The diary of Frances Stevenson confirms that Lloyd George viewed the convention more as a means of allowing 'peace to reign for a few months' rather than a means of 'ultimately solving the Irish puzzle': diary entry for 19 May 1917, in Frances Stevenson, *Lloyd George, a Diary*, A. J. P. Taylor (ed.), (London, 1971), p. 158.

91 Redmond to Lloyd George, 17 May 1917, quoted in Finnan, *Redmond*, p. 218. William O'Brien's faction and the Dublin and Cork trades councils also abstained. On the level of abstentions, see Lyons, *Dillon*, p. 418. For a full list of the Convention's delegates, see *Report of the Proceedings of the Irish Convention* (London, 1918) [Cd 9019], pp. 52–3.

92 See Dillon's memorandum on the proposed basis for an Irish Convention, reproduced in Lyons, *Dillon*, p. 417.

93 Ibid., p. 416.

94 Dillon to O'Connor, 1 June 1917, quoted in ibid., p. 419.

95 On the position of the *Freeman's Journal* by this point, see Larkin, 'Two gentlemen of the *Freeman*', p. 220.

96 On the evolution of Midleton's proposals, see McDowell, *Irish Convention*, pp 129–134.

97 Ibid., pp 134–5.

98 Ibid., p. 146.

99 On the schism of Dillon and O'Donnell from Redmond over the Midleton scheme, see McDowell, *Irish Convention*, p. 149.

100 On the interesting course taken by Gwynn from 1915–19, see Patrick Maume, 'Gwynn, Stephen Lucius', in McGuire and Quinn (eds), *Dictionary of Irish Biography* (accessed online 22 June 2010).

101 S. Gwynn to Redmond, 17 Nov. 1917, quoted in McDowell, *Irish Convention*, pp 135–6.

102 Michael Laffan, *The Partition of Ireland, 1911–1925* (Dundalk, 1983), p. 56.

103 Redmond to Dillon, 26 Feb. 1918, TCD, Dillon papers, MS 6749/669.

104 Ibid.

105 Michael Wheatley, *Nationalism and the Irish Party: Provincial Ireland 1910–1916* (Oxford, 2005), p. 79.

106 For Devlin's personal loyalty to Redmond as well as Dillon as he withdrew support from Redmond at the Convention, see Devlin to Dillon, 20 Dec. 1917, TCD, Dillon papers, MS 6730/184.

5
Painting pictures and telling tales:
The scholarly and popular portrayal of Patrick Pearse, 1916–27

1   While the fact that Patrick Pearse (1879–1916) had a squint in his left eye may explain the abundance of photographs in profile, there are many other images of him during his lifetime which are not used as often as those in profile. Born 10 November 1879 to an English father and Irish mother, Pearse was a writer, educationalist, and revolutionary. He joined the Gaelic League at the age of 16, and later edited the newspaper *An Claidheamh Soluis*. A keen Irish speaker and writer (prose, poetry and drama), he founded St Enda's, a bilingual school, in Rathfarnham in 1908 having already qualified as a barrister in 1900. In 1914 he was sworn into the Irish Republican Brotherhood and was also a member of the Irish Volunteers. By 1915 he was a member of the IRB's secret Military Council, the core group that began planning for a rising. Pearse read the Proclamation of the Republic from the GPO on 24 April 1916 and formally surrendered to Brigadier General Lowe on 29 April 1916. He was 36 years of age when he was executed on 3 May 1916.

2   Roisín Higgins, 'Remembering and forgetting P. H. Pearse', in Roisín Higgins and Regina Uí Chollatáin (eds), *The Life and After-Life of P. H. Pearse* (Dublin, 2009), p. 138.

3   Jonathan Githens-Mazer, *Myths and Memories of the Easter Rising: Cultural and Political Nationalism in Ireland* (Dublin and Portland OR, 2006), p. 213.

4   Lucien Febvre, 'History and psychology', in Peter Burke (ed.), *A New Kind of History: From the Writings of Febvre* (London, 1973), p. 4.

5   Desmond Ryan, *The Man Called Pearse* (Dublin, 1923; 1st edn, 1919), p. 1.

6   'Coilin' [Seán MacGiollarnáth], *Patrick H. Pearse: A Sketch of His Life* (Dublin, 1917), p. 2. Curiously, the equation of a psychological duality within Pearse with the timing and outcome of the Rising is also proposed, much later, in Seán Farrell Moran, *Patrick Pearse and the Politics of Redemption: The Mind of the Easter Rising 1916* (Washington DC, 1994), p. 3: 'Patrick Pearse was exactly the right man at exactly the right moment in his country's history ... the solution Pearse sought and found for his own life was the same solution that changed Irish history – the Easter Rising of 1916.'

7   M. J. Hannan, *Irish Leaders of 1916 – Who Are They?* (Butte MT, 1920), p. 1, quoted in Joost Augusteijn, *Patrick Pearse: The Making of a Revolutionary* (London, 2010), p. 325.

8   Other biographies and detailed studies of Pearse outside the timeframe of this chapter include but are not limited to the posthumous publication of Pearse's autobiography edited by Mary Brigid Pearse, *The Home Life of Patrick Pearse* (Dublin, 1935); Seamus Ó Searcaigh, *Padraic Mac Piarais* (Dublin, 1938); Hedley McCay, *Patrick Pearse: A New Biography* (Cork, 1966); Proinsias McAonghusa and Liam Ó Réagáin (eds), *The Best of Pearse* (Cork, 1967); Raymond Porter, *P. H. Pearse* (New York, 1973); Ruth Dudley Edwards, *Patrick Pearse: The Triumph of Failure*

(London, 1977); Brian P. Murphy, *Patrick Pearse and the Lost Republican Ideal* (Dublin, 1991); Moran, *Patrick Pearse and the Politics of Redemption*; Elaine Sisson, *Pearse's Patriots: St Enda's and the Cult of Boyhood* (Cork, 2004); Brendan Walsh, *The Pedagogy of Protest: The Educational Life and Work of Patrick H. Pearse* (Oxford, 2007). On the Rising and commemoration see Mary E. Daly and Margaret O'Callaghan (eds), *1916 in 1966: Commemorating the Easter Rising* (Dublin, 2007), Higgins and Uí Chollatáin (eds), *The Life and After-Life of P. H. Pearse*, Augusteijn, *Patrick Pearse: The Making of a Revolutionary*, Róisín Ní Ghairbhí and Eugene McNulty (eds), *Patrick Pearse: Collected Plays / Drámaí an Phiarsaigh* (Sallins, 2013), and Brian Cowley, *Patrick Pearse: A Life in Pictures* (Cork, 2013). See Augusteijn, *Patrick Pearse: The Making of a Revolutionary*, p. 325 and chapter 6 for further analysis of publications on Pearse outside Ireland during this period.

9   Ryan, *The Man Called Pearse*. He quotes his own work in *Remembering Sion: A Chronicle of Storm and Quiet* (London, 1934), p. 141.

10   Louis N. Le Roux, *The Life of Patrick Pearse*, Desmond Ryan (trans.), (Dublin, 1932), p. 38.

11   Ibid., p. 210.

12   'Coilin', *Patrick H. Pearse: A Sketch of His Life*, p. 15.

13   In the short story 'Brigid of the Songs', the main character Brigid is a singer who carries and upholds the knowledge and traditions from generations before her but the judges of the feis at which she competes do not recognise this and favour a younger woman for the prize. In typical Pearse fashion, Brigid overcomes hardship and adversary and as she is awarded the prize in Dublin, dies, and in doing so wins, as the priest says, a greater reward.

14   James Hayes, *Patrick Pearse: Storyteller* (Dublin, 1919), p. 73, 79.

15   Pearse's play *The Singer* (originally due to be staged before the Rising) can also be viewed as overtly political in how it examines the morality of rebellion through the characters of MacDara and the schoolteacher Maoilsheachlainn. See also Ní Ghairbhí and McNulty (eds), *Patrick Pearse: Collected Plays / Drámaí an Phiarsaigh* for further analysis of the plays of Pearse.

16   James Moran in *Staging the Easter Rising: 1916 as Theatre* (Cork, 2005), p. 27, makes the broader point that '*The Singer* reveals that breaking with British sovereignty could also mark a moment at which conventional sexual attitudes and orthodoxies would be re-examined and rethought.' Augusteijn examines the sexual and religious orientations in *The Singer* in the first two chapters of *Patrick Pearse: The Making of a Revolutionary*.

17   Le Roux, *The Life of Patrick Pearse*, pp 200–1.

18   Desmond Ryan, *The Rising: The Complete Story of Easter Week* (Dublin, 1949), p. 111.

19   Ryan, *The Man Called Pearse*, p. 103.

20   Cúchulainn is a mythological hero with exceptional strength who appears in the Ulster Cycle. Pearse frequently used Cúchulainn's image to show superb sportsmanship, physical strength and the ideal male revolutionary to his students at St Enda's. Indeed, Oliver Sheppard's bronze statue of Cúchulainn sits in the General Post Office in Dublin as a memorial to the 1916 Rising.

21   See Moran, *Staging the Easter Rising*, chapter 2, for a more in-depth analysis.

22   William Irwin Thompson, *The Imagination of an Insurrection: Dublin, Easter 1916 – a Study of an Ideological Movement* (New York, 1967).

23   Cathaoir Ó Braonáin, 'Padraic H Pearse', in *Poets of the Insurrection* (Dublin, 1918), p. 57. This volume examines poetry by Pearse, McDonagh, Plunkett and Seán MacEntee.

24   Martin Daly [Stephen MacKenna], *Memories of the Dead – Some Impressions* (Dublin, 1916), p. 17. This representation of Pearse comprises Thompson's whole argument in *The Imagination of an Insurrection*.

25   Ibid., p.18.

26   Anon., *The Poets of 1916: With Lives and Notes* (Dublin, 1931), p. 5.

27   Francis P. Jones, *History of the Sinn Féin Movement and the Irish Rebellion* (New York, 1919), p. 153. It is interesting to note that a comprehensive analysis of the educational, political and sociological theories which Pearse expanded in *The Murder Machine* in particular – progressive and left-wing in their approach and unlike the portraiture of Pearse generally painted – did not occur until 1980 with the publication of Séamus Ó Buachalla, *A Significant Irish Educationalist: The Educational Writings of P. H. Pearse* (Dublin and Cork, 1980). The gap long evident in Irish historiography has, in part, been filled with Elaine Sisson's 2004 study of St Enda's and the cult of boyhood and Brendan Walsh's 2007 in-depth analysis in *The Pedagogy of Protest*.

28   *Irish Independent*, 4 May 1916; see also 26–29 Apr. and 1–3, 10 May 1916.

29   *Irish Times* quoted in Tim Pat Coogan, *Ireland in the Twentieth Century* (London, 2003), p. 60. See also *Irish Times*, 22, 28–29 Apr., 1 May 1916. W. Alison Phillips also took this moral stance on the Rising in *The Revolution in Ireland 1906–1923* (London, 1926).

30   Frank Thornton, BMH WS, quoted in Coogan, *Ireland in the Twentieth Century*, p. 60.

31   *Irish Catholic*, May 1916, quoted in A. Raftery, *The Teachings of Padraig Pearse* (Dublin, 1966), p.7.

32   *Daily News*, 10 May 1916.

33   The Fenian O'Donovan Rossa died in America and was burried at Glasnevin Cemetery in Dublin on 1 August 1915. One of the most important aspects of his funeral was that the Irish Citizen Army, the IRB and the Volunteers were all present. Ruth Dudley Edwards in her biography of Pearse states that 'it was Pearse's greatest test and he rose to the occasion, with a speech which was his masterpiece.' Dudley Edwards, *Patrick Pearse: The Triumph of Failure*, p. 236. Pearse's oration is often quoted, in particular: 'They have left us our Fenian dead, and while Ireland holds these graves, Ireland unfree shall never be at peace.'

34   Augusteijn, *Patrick Pearse: The Making of a Revolutionary*, p. 323.

35   Edith Somerville to Col. John Somerville, 24 Nov. 1917, quoted in Peter Hart, *The IRA at War 1916–1923* (Oxford and New York, 2003), p. 110.

36   W. B. Yeats to Lady Gregory, 11 May 1916, *The Letters of W. B. Yeats*, Allen Wade (ed.), (London, 1954), p. 612.

37   Nora Connolly, *The Irish Rebellion of 1916 or the Unbroken Tradition* (New York, 1918), p. 175.

38   Plunkett to the moderate Irish-American James Byrne, 14 June 1916, quoted in Trevor West, *Horace Plunket: Co-Operation and Polictics, an Irish Biography* (Washington DC, 1986), p. 152.

39   James Stephens, *The Insurrection in Dublin* (London, 1992; 1st edn, 1916), p. 57. See also Eimar O'Duffy, *The Wasted Island* (Dublin, 1919) for a personal account of Pearse.

40   Stephens, *The Insurrection in Dublin*, pp 90–1.

41   The authors based much of their narrative on the assumption that the Rising was wholly German-based as did L. G. Redmond-Howard in *Six Days of the Irish Republic: A Narrative and Critical Account of the Latest Phase of Irish Politics* (Dublin and London, 1916).

42   W. B. Wells and Nicholas Marlowe, *A History of the Irish Rebellion of 1916* (Dublin and London, 1916), p. 948, 66.

43   Ibid., p. 72.

44   For the full text of the Proclamation see E. Curtis and R. B. McDowell (eds.) *Irish Historical Documents 1172–1922* (London, 1943) or R. F. Foster, *Modern Ireland: 1600–1972* (London, 1989), appendix 1.

45   Wells and Marlowe, *A History of the Irish Rebellion of 1916*, p. 217.

46   Stephens, *The Insurrection in Dublin*, p. 111.

47   F. A. MacKenzie, *Irish Rebellion: What Happened and Why* (London, 1916), preface, and Padraic Colum and Mary Colum, *The Irish Rebellion of 1916 and Its Martyrs* (New York, 1916),

p. 269, 281. Both of these are cited and analysed in Augusteijn, *Patrick Pearse: The Making of a Revolutionary*, chapter 6.

48   Jones, *History of the Sinn Féin Movement*, p. 152.

49   Padraic Colum and Edward J. O'Brien, *Poems of the Revolutionary Brotherhood* (Boston, 1916), p. xiii and xxv. Colum and O'Brien print eight of Pearse's poems from *Suantraidhe agus Goltraidhe* (1912) including 'Naked I saw thee', published under the title 'Ideal'. They also published poems by Thomas MacDonagh, Joseph Mary Plunkett and Sir Roger Casement, thus branding them as 'revolutionary' poets, a line that was to be echoed by historians F. S. L. Lyons and Roy Foster in later years.

50   Anon., *The Sinn Féin Leaders of 1916: With Fourteen Illustrations and Complete Lists of Deportees, Casualties, etc.* (Dublin, 1917), pp 6–7.

51   McCay, *Patrick Pearse: A New Biography*, p. 5

52   Augusteijn, *Patrick Pearse: The Making of a Revolutionary*, p. 328. This point is expanded upon in this chapter even though Augusteijn admits that 'in general it is clear that all parties referred to him irrespective of their political colour.'

53   William Michael Murphy, *The Parnell Myth and Irish Politics 1891–1956* (New York, 1981), p.157.

54   See Diarmaid Ferriter, *Judging Dev: A Reassessment of the Life and Legacy of Éamon de Valera* (Dublin, 2007) for further analysis of de Valera.

55   Augusteijn, *Patrick Pearse: The Making of a Revolutionary*, p. 236.

56   See Patrick Pearse, 'Peace and the Gael' (Dec.1915) in which he rationalises the need for war as a way to break tyranny, and that few 'fight for the good thing'. Ireland is placed within the context of the war in Europe and here Pearse views the Irish as being exploited and ensalved like the Poles, a fate which is worse than suffering war. He also proclaims the oft-quoted phrase 'war is a terrible thing, but war is not an evil thing. It is the things that make war necessary that are evil.' Pearse, 'Peace and the Gael', in *Political Writings and Speeches* (Dublin, 1924), pp 213–18.

57   Éamon de Valera, election speech in East Clare, June 1917, *Speeches and Statements of Éamon de Valera 1917–1973*, Maurice Moynihan (ed.), (Dublin, 1946), p.6.

58   The Treaty debates took place from December 1921 to January 1922. On 7 January 1922, the Dáil ratified the Treaty by a small majority of seven seats.

59   Moran, *Staging the Easter Rising*, p. 42.

60   Henry Patterson, *The Politics of Illusion: Republicanism and Socialism in Modern Ireland* (London, 1989), p.12.

61   'Arguments against the Treaty', NLI LO P117, Leaflet 14, item EPH B221.

62   'Means to an end', NLI LO P117, Leaflet 7, item EPH B217. See also items 24–38.

63   P. H. Pearse, *The Spiritual Nation* (Dublin, 1922; 1st edn, 1916), in *Collected Works of Padraic H. Pearse: Political Writings and Speeches* (Dublin and London, 1922), preface, p. 294.

64   'Liberty of the person inviolable: the political faith of Tone and Pearse', NLI LO P117, item 20 also EPH C101.

65   Lionel Pilkington, *Theatre and the State in Twentieth-Century Ireland: Cultivating the People* (London and New York, 2001), pp 86–7.

66   Michael Laffan, *The Partition of Ireland 1911–1925* (Dundalk, 1983), p. 117.

67   Martin Mansergh, *The Legacy of History for Making Peace in Ireland* (Cork, 2003), p. 240.

68   Diarmaid Ferriter, '"A figurative scramble for the bones of the patriot dead": commemorating the Rising, 1922–65', in Daly and O'Callaghan (eds), *1916 in 1966*, p. 200.

69   *Irish Times*, 30 Apr. 1926.

70   Cosgrave at the fourth annual convention of Cumann na nGaedheal, *Irish Times*, 12 May 1926.

71   *Bowman: Sunday: 8.30*, RTÉ Radio, 1, 5 Dec. 2010.

72   W. T. Cosgrave, *Policy of the Cumann na nGaedheal Party* (Dublin, 1927).

73   *An Phoblacht*, 2 Apr. 1926.

74   A. E. [George Russell], 'Ireland past and future: a survey from many angles', in William G. Fitzgerald (ed.), *The Voice of Ireland: A Survey of the Race and Nation from all Angles by the Foremost Leaders at Home and Abroad* (Dublin, 1924), pp 86–92.

75   W. T. Cosgrave, 'At the bend of the way: the last milestone on our "Via Dolorosa"', in Fitzgerald (ed.), *The Voice of Ireland*, pp 64–70.

76   This shadowing of Pearse on the stage was to be in direct contrast with his portrayal in the plays *The Roads* and *The Priest* that Margaret Pearse sanctioned in the 1930s.

77   Seán O'Casey, *Three Plays: Juno and The Paycock; The Shadow of a Gunamn; The Plough and the Stars* (London, 1980); *The Plough and the Stars*, Act II, p. 178.

78   O'Casey, *The Plough and the Stars*, Act II, p. 169, 178, 204.

79   Peter Thompson, 'The Plough and the superstars', *In Dublin*, 2 Mar. 1989, p. 17.

80   Christopher Morash, *A History of Irish Theatre 1601–2000* (Cambridge, 2002), p. 170. It is worth noting that Blythe was the Abbey's paymaster at this time.

81   *Irish Independent*, 15 Feb. 1926.

82   Interestingly, W. B. Yeats also wrote a play in which a revolutionary from the GPO comes into contact with a mother who is portrayed very differently from the typical 'nationalist' mother such as Margaret Pearse. While *The Dreaming of the Bones* was written in 1917 it was not staged in the Abbey until 1931 when the production coincided – and contrasted – with Fianna Fáil's use of 1916 propaganda in connection with the 1932 general election.

83   Hart, *The IRA at War 1916–1923*, p. 4, 105.

84   Moran, *Staging the Easter Rising*, p. 51.

85   James Quinn, 'Laying the ghosts: Patrick Pearse and the reproach of history', in Higgins and Uí Chollatáin (eds), *The Life and After-Life of P. H. Pearse*, p. 110.

86   Election leaflet, 'Who are the war makers?', in O'Kennedy-Brindley Ltd. Advertising, *Making History: The Story of a Remarkable Campaign* (Dublin, 1927).

87   Cumann na nGaedheal election propaganda, Saoránac pamphlet, NLI, LO P106, item 22. Note how the Irish fada is omitted as part of the word play and rhyming.

88   Cosgrave, *Policy of Cumann na nGaedheal*. It is interesting to note that by the 1932 elections Cosgrave's declaration of Cumann na nGaedheal's policy was very careful not to mention the Rising, Northern Ireland, the question of partition, or Pearse.

89   Éamon de Valera in an interview in April 1926, quoted in Uinseann MacEoin (ed.), *Survivors: The Story of Ireland's Struggle as Told through Some of Her Outstanding Living People* (Dublin, 1980), p. 52.

90   *Fianna Fáil (Republican Party): Córú, Constitution 1934–35* (Dublin, [1934?]).

91   Brian Harvey, *Cosgrave's Coalition* (London 1980; 1st edn, 1978), pp 144–5.

92   Augusteijn, *Patrick Pearse: The Making of a Revolutionary*, p. 326. Augusteijn mistakenly refers to the station as RTÉ.

93   There has been, of late, a broader view of Pearse. For example the bibliographies of published works and unpublished works in Lindsay Dowling, 'Music, Pádraig Pearse and Scoil Éanna 1908–1916' (MA thesis, National University of Ireland, Maynooth, 2005) and Augusteijn, *Patrick Pearse: The Making of a Revolutionary* illustrate the trend towards a more inclusive and, indeed, European view of Pearse.

94   Arthur Koestler, *Darkness at Noon* (reprint edn, London, 1978; 1st edn 1940), p. 41.

95   Higgins, 'Remembering and forgetting P. H. Pearse', p. 137.

96   Dudley Edwards borrowed the phrase from Desmond Ryan.

97   As mentioned earlier, it is generally accepted that O'Casey's character The Figure at the

Window in *The Plough and the Stars* is based on Pearse, and certainly, the voice and what it speaks of has elements of some of Pearse's speeches. In the end, though, it is a lone voice whose words achieve nothing.

98 Moran, *Staging the Easter Rising*, p. 123.

6

Physical force within the bounds of political constraints: GHQ's role in the War of Independence

1   I am forever grateful to Michael Laffan for giving me the opportunity to continue my research and providing invaluable support and encouragement throughout my studies.

2   In this chapter the term 'Volunteers' is used to describe members of both the Irish Volunteers and the Irish Republican Army.

3   Margery Forester, *Michael Collins: The Lost Leader* (London, 1972), pp 73–4.

4   Florence O'Donoghue, 'Re-organisation of the Irish Volunteers, 1916–1917', *Capuchin Annual* (1967), p. 385.

5   Maryann Gialanella Valiulis, *Portrait of a Revolutionary: General Richard Mulcahy and the Founding of the Irish Free State* (Dublin, 1992), p. 45.

6   Ibid.

7   Ibid.

8   Maryann Gialanella Valiulis, *Almost a Rebellion: The Irish Army Mutiny of 1924* (Cork, 1985), p. 16.

9   Valiulis, *Portrait of a Revolutionary*, p. 44

10   P. S. O'Hegarty, *The Victory of Sinn Féin* (Dublin, 1998), p. 124.

11   Ibid.

12   'Typed manuscript of a memoir written by Seán Ó Murthuile, relating to the period from the rise of Sinn Féin to the "Army Mutiny" and ensuing inquiry', UCDA, Richard Mulcahy papers, P7a/209, p. 62.

13   James Mackay, *Michael Collins: A Life* (Edinburgh, 1996), p. 84.

14   Richard Mulcahy, 'Autobiography (unpublished): 1916–1918 and the IRA', UCDA, Richard Mulcahy papers, P7b/139, p. 5.

15   Richard Mulcahy, 'Volunteers Executive', UCDA, Richard Mulcahy papers, P7b/200, p. 4.

16   Ibid., p. 9

17   Ibid., p. 12

18   'Establishment of GHQ', UCDA, Richard Mulcahy tapes, P7/26A.

19   Richard Mulcahy, 'Volunteers Convention', UCDA, Richard Mulcahy papers, P7b/200, p. 15.

20   Mulcahy, 'Volunteers Executive', p. 9.

21   Ibid.

22   Valiulis, *Portrait of a Revolutionary*, pp 28–31.

23   Richard Mulcahy, 'Conscription and the General Headquarters Staff', *Capuchin Annual* (1968), p. 386.

24   'Justification for the War for Independence', UCDA, Richard Mulcahy tapes, P7/7B.

25   O'Donoghue, 'Re-organisation of the Irish Volunteers', p. 384.

26   Mulcahy, 'Volunteers Executive', p. 11.

27   Michael Hopkinson, *The Irish War of Independence* (Dublin, 2002), p. 25.

28   Richard Mulcahy, 'Lecture on Collins at Grosvenor Hotel, 29.10.63', UCDA, Richard Mulcahy papers, P7/D/66, p. 13; see also 'GHQ and Mulcahy's position', UCDA, Richard Mulcahy tapes, P7/7A.

29   Valiulis, *Portrait of a Revolutionary*, p. 47.

30   Ibid., p. 40.

31   Ibid., p. 36.

32   Ibid., p. 41.

33   Richard Mulcahy, 'Question of the Chief of Staff position', UCDA, Richard Mulcahy papers, P7/D/96, pp 8–9.

34   Mulcahy, 'Lecture on Collins at Grosvenor Hotel, 29.10.63', p. 12.

35   Valiulis, *Portrait of a Revolutionary*, pp 38–9.

36   'Account of Séamus Robinson's part in the War of Independence', NLI, Frank Gallagher papers, MS 21,265, p. 19; see also Séamus Robinson, BMH WS1721, p. 19.

37   Dan Breen, *My Fight for Irish Freedom* (Dublin, 1989; 1st edn, 1924), p. 41.

38   Joost Augusteijn, *From Public Defiance to Guerrilla Warfare: The Experience of Ordinary Volunteers in the Irish War of Independence 1916–21* (Dublin, 1996), pp 87–9.

39   Michael T. Foy, *Michael Collins's Intelligence War: The Struggle between the British and the IRA, 1919–1921* (London, 2006), p. 24.

40   M. L. R. Smith, *Fighting for Ireland? The Military Strategy of the Irish Republican Movement* (London, 1995), p. 35.

41   Robert Taber, *The War of the Flea: Guerrilla Warfare Theory and Practice* (New York, 1965), p. 130.

42   Forester, *Michael Collins*, p. 59.

43   Valiulis, *Portrait of a Revolutionary*, p. 47.

44   Smith, *Fighting for Ireland?*, p. 36.

45   Augusteijn, *From Public Defiance to Guerrilla Warfare*, p. 270.

46   O'Donoghue, 'Re-organisation of the Irish Volunteers', p. 385.

47   S. E. Finer, *The Man on Horseback: The Role of the Military in Politics* (London, 1962), p. 17.

48   Richard Mulcahy, 'The Irish Volunteers Convention 27 October 1917', *Capuchin Annual* (1967), p. 409.

49   Richard Mulcahy, 'The position in Dublin', UCDA, Richard Mulcahy papers, P7/A/47, p. 1.

50   Richard Mulcahy, 'Staff Memo: The War as a Whole, 24/3/21', UCDA, Richard Mulcahy papers, P7/A/17, pp 2–3.

51   Pádraig Yeates, *A City in Turmoil: Dublin 1919–21* (Dublin, 2012), p. ix.

52   Valiulis, *Portrait of a Revolutionary*, p. 253.

53   Richard Mulcahy, 'Lecture on Collins by Mulcahy to members of the Donegalmen's Association, 11.12.64', UCDA, Richard Mulcahy papers, P7/D/66.

54   Yeates, *A City in Turmoil*, pp 188–203.

55   Peter Hart (ed.), *British Intelligence in Ireland, 1920–21: The Final Reports* (Cork, 2002), pp 3–5.

56   Peter Hart, *Mick: The Real Michael Collins* (London, 2005), p. 220.

57   Ibid., p. 219.

58   T. Ryle Dwyer, *The Squad and the Intelligence Operations of Michael Collins 1919–1921* (Cork, 2005), pp 36–7.

59   Foy, *Michael Collins's Intelligence War*, p. 24.

60   Mulcahy, 'Lecture on Collins to the Donegalmen's Association, 11.12.64', UCDA, Richard Mulcahy papers, P7/D/66, p. 16C.

61   Richard Mulcahy, 'Two-part critique of Piaras Béaslaí's biography on Collins', UCDA, Richard Mulcahy papers , P7/D/67, part 2, p. 55.

62   Tom Barry, *Guerilla Days in Ireland* (Dublin, 1981; 1st edn, 1949), p. 185.

7
Violence against women during the Irish War of Independence, 1919–21

1   Charles Townshend, *Easter 1916: The Irish Rebellion* (London, 2005); Fearghal McGarry, *The Rising: Ireland, Easter 1916* (Oxford, 2010).

2   This archive is currently being released on a phased basis and is available online at militaryarchives.ie/collections/online-collections/military-service-pensions-collection.

3   Eithne Coyle, 'A history of Cumann na mBan', *An Phoblacht*, 8, 15 Apr. 1933; Margaret Buckley, *Jangle of Keys* (Dublin, 1938); Kathleen Clarke, *Revolutionary Woman*, Helen Litton (ed.), (Dublin, 1991); John Borgonovo (ed.), *Florence and Josephine O'Donoghue's War of Independence: A Destiny that Shapes Our Ends* (Dublin, 2006).

4   P. L., 'Cumann na mBan in rebel Cork', in *Rebel Cork's Fighting Story, 1916–21: Told by the Men Who Made It* (Cork, 2009; 1st edn, 1947), pp 274–7; R. M. Fox, 'How the women helped', in *Dublin's Fighting Story, 1916–21: Told by the Men Who Made It* (Cork, 2009; 1st edn, 1947), pp 395–406; Granuaile, 'In the fight with Cumann na mBan', in *Kerry's Fighting Story, 1916–21: Told by the Men Who Made It* (Cork, 2009; 1st edn, 1947), pp 327–34; S. B., 'The Honourable Mary Spring Rice', and Madge Daly, 'Gallant Cumann na mBan of Limerick', both in *Limerick's Fighting Story, 1916–21: Told by the Men Who Made It* (Cork, 2009; 1st edn, 1947), pp 304–6 and 361–70.

5   Gerda Lerner, 'Placing women in history: definitions and challenges', *Feminist Studies* iii:1–2 (autumn 1975), p. 5, 14.

6   Margaret Ward, *Maud Gonne: Ireland's Joan of Arc* (London, 1990); Maria Luddy, *Hanna Sheehy Skeffington* (Dundalk, 1995); Margaret Ward, *Hanna Sheehy Skeffington: A Life* (Cork, 1997); Anne Marreco, *The Rebel Countess: The Life and Times of Constance Markievicz* (London, 1967); Anne Haverty, *Constance Markievicz: Irish Revolutionary* (London, 1988).

7   Michael Brennan, *The War in Clare, 1911–1921: Personal Memoirs of the Irish War of Independence* (Dublin 1980), p. 40; Kathleen Keyes McDonnell, *There Is a Bridge at Bandon: A Personal Account of the Irish War of Independence* (Bandon, 1972), p 117, 128, quoted in Louise Ryan, 'Splendidly silent: representing Irish republican women, 1919–23', in Ann-Marie Gallagher *et al.* (eds), *Re-Presenting the Past: Women and History* (Harlow, 2002), pp. 36–7.

8   Ryan, 'Splendidly silent', pp 36–40.

9   Margaret Ward, *Unmanageable Revolutionaries: Women in Irish Nationalism* (Kerry, 1983); Aideen Sheehan, 'Cumann na mBan: policies and activities', in David Fitzpatrick (ed.), *Revolution? Ireland, 1917–1923* (Dublin, 1990), pp 88–97; Roger Sawyer, *'We are but Women': Women in Ireland's History* (London, 1993); Sinéad McCoole, *No Ordinary Women: Irish Female Activists in the Revolutionary Years, 1900–1923* (Dublin, 2003).

10   Marie Coleman, *County Longford and the Irish Revolution, 1910–1923* (Dublin, 2003), pp 179–90.

11   Cal McCarthy, *Cumann na mBan and the Irish Revolution* (Cork, 2007; 2nd edn, 2014); Ann Matthews, *Renegades: Irish Republican Women, 1900–1922* (Dublin and Cork, 2010); Margaret Ó hÓgartaigh, *Kathleen Lynn: Irishwoman, Patriot, Doctor* (Dublin, 2006); John Cowell, *A Noontide Blazing: Brigid Lyons Thornton, Rebel, Soldier, Doctor* (Dublin, 2005).

12   Jason Knirck, *Women of the Dáil: Gender, Republicanism and the Anglo-Irish Treaty* (Dublin, 2006); Joanne Mooney Eichacker, *Irish Republican Women in America: Lecture Tours, 1916–1925* (Dublin, 2003).

13   Peter Hart, 'A new revolutionary history', in Peter Hart, *The IRA at War, 1916–1923* (Oxford, 2003), p. 10, 28.

14   Peter Hart, *The IRA and Its Enemies: Violence and Community in Cork, 1916–1923* (Oxford,

1998), pp 248, 300, 308–10, Michael Hopkinson, *The Irish War of Independence* (Dublin, 2002), pp 110–11.

15 Fearghal McGarry, *Eoin O'Duffy: A Self-Made Hero* (Oxford, 2005), pp 65–6.

16 Terence Dooley, *The Plight of the Monaghan Protestants, 1912–1926* (Dublin, 2000), pp 44–5.

17 IRA General Order no. 12, 9 Nov. 1920, quoted in Richard (Dickie) Willis and John (Jackie) Bolster, BMH WS 808.

18 McGarry, *Eoin O'Duffy*, pp 65–6; Dooley, *The Plight of the Monaghan Protestants*, pp 44–5.

19 Census return, census.nationalarchives.ie/pages/1911/Monaghan/Sheskin/Aghanamee-na/812306/ (accessed 30 July 2014). I am grateful to Drs Fearghal McGarry and Daithí Ó Corráin for their advice on this issue.

20 Peter Hart, 'The Protestant experience of revolution in southern Ireland', in Hart, *The IRA at War, 1916–1923*, pp 223–40.

21 Seán Healy, BMH WS 1,643.

22 Michael Collins, BMH WS 1,301.

23 D. M. Leeson, *The Black and Tans: British Police and Auxiliaries in the Irish War of Independence* (Oxford, 2011), pp 51–62.

24 Jane Leonard, '"English dogs" or "poor devils"? The dead of Bloody Sunday morning', in David Fitzpatrick (ed.), *Terror in Ireland, 1916–1923* (Dublin, 2012), p. 139.

25 Leeson, *Black and Tans*, p. 178.

26 Ibid., pp 46, 176–8; Coleman, *County Longford and the Irish Revolution*, p. 120.

27 Elisabeth Jean Wood, 'Variation in sexual violence during war', *Politics and Society* xxxiv:3 (Sept. 2006), p. 308, 335, n. 3. Some scholars do not accept this distinction; in the case of French women accused of collaboration with the Nazis, Tal Nitsán considers 'the shaving of their hair, closely related to femininity and sexuality' as 'an act of sexual violence', Tal Nitsán, 'The body that writes: reflections on the process of writing about wartime rape avoidance in the Israeli-Palestinian conflict', in Raphaëlle Branche and Fabrice Virgili (eds), *Rape in Wartime* (Basingstoke, 2012), p. 160.

28 Elizabeth D. Henieman, 'Introduction: the history of sexual violence in conflict zones', in Elizabeth D. Heineman (ed.), *Sexual Violence in Conflict Zones: From the Ancient World to the Era of Human Rights* (Philadelphia PA, 2011), p. 9.

29 Labour Party, *Report of the Labour Commission to Ireland* (London, 1922), pp 80–1. This commission, established by the British Labour Party in response to concerns about Crown force actions in Ireland, and led by Labour's chief whip Arthur Henderson, visited Ireland in late 1920 'to inquire into the whole question of "reprisals" and violence in Ireland'.

30 Cait [Kate] O'Callaghan, BMH WS 688.

31 Michael Kilroy, BMH WS 1,162.

32 Marie Coleman, *The Irish Revolution, 1916–1923* (London, 2013), p. 93.

33 Dispute exists as to whether or not the Pearson women actually witnessed this event: Alan Stanley, *I Met Murder on the Way: The Story of the Pearsons of Coolacrease* (Carlow, 2005), pp 79–80; Paddy Heaney and Pat Muldowney, 'The true story of the events at Coolacrease', in Paddy Heaney et al. (eds), *Coolacrease: The True Story of the Pearson Executions – An Incident in the Irish War of Independence* (Millstreet, 2008), pp 51–4.

34 On Bloody Sunday, 21 November 1920, a total of 41 people were killed, including: 13 British personnel, mostly intelligence agents, who were shot dead by Michael Collins's 'Squad'; 14 civilians attending a football match at Croke Park who died when the Black and Tans opened fire at the venue; and three senior IRA prisoners who died in suspicious circumstances in Dublin Castle. Coleman, *Irish Revolution*, pp 92–3; Leonard, '"English dogs" or "poor devils"?', pp 107–8.

35 Leeson, *Black and Tans*, p. ix.

36   James Maloney, BMH WS 1,525.

37   Michael Rock, BMH WS 1,398.

38   Anne Dolan, 'The British culture of paramilitary violence in the Irish War of Independence', in Robert Gerwarth and John Horne (eds), *War in Peace: Paramilitary Violence in Europe after the Great War* (Oxford, 2012), p. 208.

39   Wood, 'Variation in sexual violence during war', p. 308.

40   Labour Party, *Report of the Labour Commission to Ireland*, pp 28–9.

41   Eunan O'Halpin, 'Counting terror: Bloody Sunday and *The Dead of the Irish Revolution*', in Fitzpatrick (ed.), *Terror in Ireland, 1916–1923*, p. 148.

42   'Proceedings of a Court of Inquiry assembled at Dundrum on the 23rd December 1920 by order of Lieut. Colonel R. H. G. Wilson, Commanding Troops, Tipperary, for the purpose of investigating and reporting upon the circumstances under which MISS KATE MAHER met her death at Dundrum on the 21st December 1920', J. B. Houghton, Deputy Adjutant General, to the Commander, 6th Division, 15 July 1921, TNA, WO 35/155B. I am indebted to Dr Anne Dolan for drawing this case to my attention and furnishing me with the source material relating to it.

43   R. Wilson, O/C troops, South Riding, Tipperary, to Headquarters, 16th Infantry Brigade, Fermoy, 7 Jan. 1921, TNA, WO 35/155B.

44   The *Irish Bulletin*'s coverage of these cases is examined in detail by Louise Ryan in her article '"Drunken Tans": representations of sex and violence in the Anglo-Irish War', *Feminist Review* lxvi (autumn 2000), pp 88–91.

45   Erskine Childers, *Military Rule in Ireland* (Dublin, 1920), pp 8–12.

46   The American Commission on Conditions in Ireland was an eight-member commission established in 1920 to draw international attention to the situation in Ireland during the War of Independence. It took evidence from a range of witnesses and while its report *Evidence on Conditions in Ireland*, which was published in July 1921, was too late to have much effect the hearings of evidence raised consciousness in the USA about the disturbed state of Ireland. See Francis M. Carroll, *American Opinion and the Irish Question, 1910–1923* (Dublin, 1978), pp 162–70.

47   The WILPF was established in The Hague in 1915 'to study, make known and eliminate the causes of war', wilpfinternational.org/about-us/history/. Robinson, a British Labour Party activist and suffragist who opposed the First World War, was one of its founders, and led a delegation to Ireland to investigate violence there during the War of Independence, Leah Leneman, 'Robinson [*née* Wilkie], Annot Erskine [Annie] (1874–1925)', in *Oxford Dictionary of National Biography*, oxforddnb.com/view/article/48529?docPos=1 (accessed 28 July 2014).

48   American Commission on Conditions in Ireland, *Evidence on Conditions in Ireland* (Washington DC, 1921), pp 382, 564, 600, 749–51.

49   bureauofmilitaryhistory.ie.

50   Seamus Fitzgerald, BMH WS 1,737.

51   George F. H. Berkeley, BMH WS 994.

52   Frank Henderson, BMH WS 821.

53   Sarah Benton, 'Women disarmed: the militarization of politics in Ireland, 1913–23', *Feminist Review* l (summer 1995), p. 165.

54   Leeson, *Black and Tans*, p. 180.

55   Ryan, 'Drunken Tans', p. 74. See also Matthews, *Renegades*, pp 266–82.

56   Gemma Clark, *Everyday Violence in the Irish Civil War* (Cambridge, 2014), p. 192.

57   'Statement of atrocities on Women in Ireland, Made and Signed by Mrs Hanna Sheehy-Skeffington', NLI, ILB 330 P3.

58   T. K. Wilson, *Frontiers of Violence: Conflict and Identity in Ulster and Upper Silesia, 1918–1922* (Oxford, 2010), p. 5.

59   The B-Specials were a part-time, armed and paid section of the Ulster Special Constabulary, which was formed to quell violence in Ulster in 1920. Many B-Specials were UVF members and the force had a reputation for sectarian attacks on Catholics.

60   Wilson, *Frontiers of Violence*, pp 76–7, 168–71.

61   Robert Lynch, 'Explaining the Altnaveigh massacre', *Éire-Ireland* liv:3 and 4 (fall/winter 2010), pp 184–210.

62   Lindsey Earner-Byrne's recent study of a rape of a women in Co. Westmeath during the Civil War in January 1923 by men 'calling themselves Republicans' highlights how the general breakdown of law and order created turmoil in which crimes were often carried out under the guise of political action, making it impossible to ascribe a political motive or otherwise. See Lindsey Earner-Byrne, 'The rape of Mary M.: a microhistory of sexual violence and moral redemption in 1920s Ireland', *Journal of the History of Sexuality* xxiv:1 (Jan. 2015), pp. 75–98.

63   Sir Edward Carson (1854–1935), leader of the Ulster Unionist Party, 1910–21.

64   *Hansard, 5 (Lords)*, li, 465–6 (13 July 1922); Wilson, *Frontiers of Violence*, pp 120–1; R. B. McDowell, *Crisis and Decline: The Fate of the Southern Unionists* (Dublin, 1997), p. 133.

65   Clark, *Everyday Violence in the Irish Civil War*, pp 187–9.

66   Ibid., p. 201.

67   *Hansard, 5 (Commons)*, clvi, 1027–8 (11 July 1922).

68   Wood, 'Variation in sexual violence during war', pp 311–14; Benton, 'Women disarmed', p. 150.

69   Wood, 'Variation in sexual violence', pp 307, 313–17; Nitsán, 'The body that writes', pp 153–68.

70   Robert Gerwarth, 'Sexual and nonsexual violence against "politicized women" in central Europe after the Great War', in Heineman (ed.), *Sexual Violence in Conflict Zones*, pp 122–36.

71   Wilson, *Frontiers of Violence*, p. 166.

72   Wood, 'Variation in sexual violence', p. 330.

73   Unless otherwise stated, the analysis in this section is based on a detailed examination of various explanations for the variation in sexual violence suggested by Elisabeth Jean Wood, Wood, 'Variation in sexual violence', pp 321–30.

74   Charles Townshend, *The British Campaign in Ireland, 1919–1921: The Development of Political and Military Policies* (Oxford, 1975), pp 149–50; Leeson, *Black and Tans*, p. 217.

75   Hart, *The IRA at War*, pp 122–4.

76   Ross O'Mahony, 'The sack of Balbriggan and tit-for-tat terror', in Fitzpatrick (ed.), *Terror in Ireland, 1916–1923*, pp 58–74.

77   Joanna Bourke, *Rape: A History from 1860 to the Present* (London, 2007), pp 363–4.

78   Clive Emsley, *Soldier, Sailor, Beggarman, Thief: Crime and the British Armed Services since 1914* (Oxford, 2013), pp 124–5.

79   Clark, *Everyday Violence in the Irish Civil War*, p. 192.

80   Bourke, *Rape*, p. 372.

81   Maria Luddy, *Prostitution and Irish Society, 1800–1940* (Cambridge, 2007), pp 61–70.

82   Leeson, *Black and Tans*, pp 29–30.

83   Clark, *Everyday Violence in the Irish Civil War*, p. 22.

84   Diarmaid Ferriter, *Occasions of Sin: Sex and Society in Modern Ireland* (London, 2009), p. 93. This opinion is endorsed by Gemma Clark, see Clark, *Everyday Violence in the Irish Civil War*, p. 186.

85   I am grateful to a number of scholars who made valuable comments on versions of this paper that were delivered at a conference on 'Dangerous Women' in Queen's University Belfast in March 2013 and at the annual meeting of the American Conference for Irish Studies and Canadian Association of Irish Studies at University College Dublin in June 2014.

8
'Spies and informers beware ...'

1   Proceedings of a court of inquiry in lieu of inquest on Bridget Walpole, 7 Mar. 1921, TNA, WO 35/159B.

2   Proceedings of a court of inquiry in lieu of inquest on Patrick Sheehan and John Sullivan, memo on the file cover, 30 June 1921, TNA, WO 35/159B. Also referred to in this manner in a summary of cases, courts of inquiry in lieu of inquest, civilians Sept. 1920–May 1921, 6 July 1921, TNA, WO 35/162, and in the case of Patrick D'Arcy, TNA, WO 35/147B.

3   Proceedings of a court of inquiry in lieu of inquest on Bridget Walpole, 7 Mar. 1921, TNA, WO 35/159B.

4   General Order no. 20, 20 Apr. 1921, referred to 'All cases of persons killed by the British and marked by them as spies "executed by the IRA" shall be speedily investigated and reported on.' General Orders, new series, Ernie O'Malley's copy, TCD, EPB, Denis Johnston papers, OLS JOH 122 no. 2.

5   A notice posted in South Tipperary in October 1919 reminded that 'there must be no informers in this generation'. *Weekly Irish Times*, 4 Oct. 1919.

6   See Eunan O'Halpin and Daithí Ó Corráin, *The Dead of the Irish Revolution* (forthcoming, 2016).

7   'When do you notice a pin least? When it is in a pin cushion! When do you notice an individual murder least? When it is one of a series of related murders.' Agatha Christie, *The A.B.C. Murders* (London, 1936), p. 237.

8   See for example Peter Hart, *The IRA and Its Enemies: Violence and Community in Cork, 1916–1923* (Oxford, 1998) and John Borgonovo, *Spies, Informers and the 'Anti-Sinn Féin society': The Intelligence War in Cork City, 1920–1921* (Dublin, 2007).

9   According to General Order no. 20, issued 20 Apr. 1921, 'a convicted spy shall not be executed until his conviction and sentence have been ratified by the Brigade Commandant concerned.' UCDA, Richard Mulcahy papers, P7/A/45.

10   Brighid O'Mullane, BMH WS 450.

11   Ibid.

12   Ibid.

13   See for example General Order no. 13, Women Spies, issued 9 Nov. 1920, General Orders, new series, Ernie O'Malley's copy, TCD, EPB, Denis Johnston papers, OLS JOH 122 no. 2.

14   Michael Collins quoted in Kenneth Griffith and Timothy O'Grady, *Ireland's Unfinished Revolution: An Oral History* (2nd edn, Boulder CO, 1999), p. 171.

15   *Irish Times*, 22 Nov. 1922.

16   *Weekly Irish Times*, 24 Mar. 1923; General Order no. 12, 14 Nov. 1922, UCDA, Ernie O'Malley papers, P17a/20.

17   *Weekly Irish Times*, 28 Apr. 1923.

18   *Irish Times*, 17 Oct. 1924.

19   Margaret D'Arcy Daly to James Everett, 25 Sept. 1948, UCDA, Richard Mulcahy papers, P7b/124 (18). She referred to the death taking place in 1920 in her letter, but her brother was shot in June 1921. The case was investigated at the time and again in 1948–9.

20   See for example Lloyd George's use of the example of the labelled bodies in response to a letter from the Bishop of Chelmsford which had been signed by him and 19 other leaders of various religious denominations in Great Britain complaining about the state of Ireland. *Manchester Guardian*, 20 Apr. 1921.

21   Speech by Lloyd George at the Guildhall banquet, 9 Nov. 1920, quoted in Mark Pottle (ed.),

Champion Redoubtable – The Diaries and Letters of Violet Bonham Carter, 1914–1945 (London, 1998), p. 117.

22   See for example Micheál Ó Suilleabháin's complaints about his own 'dilapidated fowling piece', the 'few badly-armed youths' he had for back-up, and the fact that he had often only two cartridges for the shotgun he kept together with an elastic cord. Micheál Ó Suilleabháin, *Where Mountainy Men Have Sown* (Tralee, 1965), pp 55–6.

23   Proceedings of a court of inquiry in lieu of inquest on Hugh Duffy, 4 Apr. 1921, TNA, WO 35/149A.

24   Proceedings of a court of inquiry in lieu of inquest on an unknown man, 4 July 1921, TNA, WO 35/161A.

25   Proceedings of a court of inquiry in lieu of inquest on Martin Scanlon, 10 May 1921, TNA, WO 35/159B. Scanlon was killed in Kilrooskey, Co. Roscommon; proceedings of a court of inquiry in lieu of inquest on William Good, 29 Mar. 1921, TNA, WO 35/149B. Good died between Bandon and Timoleague, Co. Cork. His father had been killed earlier the same month.

26   Proceedings of a court of inquiry in lieu of inquest on William Elliott, 24 Jan. 1921, TNA, WO 35/149B. Elliott was shot in Ballinalee, Co. Longford on the same night as William Charters.

27   Proceedings of a court of inquiry in lieu of inquest on Kate Carroll, 16–17 Apr. 1921, TNA, WO 35/147B. She died near Scotstown, Co. Monaghan; proceedings of a court of inquiry in lieu of inquest on Michael Coen, 2 Apr. 1921, TNA, WO 35/147A. Coen was shot near Ballyhaunis, Co. Mayo.

28   Alan Stanley, *I Met Murder on the Way: The Story of the Pearsons of Coolacrease* (Carlow, 2005); Philip O'Connor (ed.), *Coolacrease: The True Story of the Pearson Executions, an Incident in the Irish War of Independence* (Cork, 2008). The debate intensified following articles by Eoghan Harris in the *Sunday Independent* in 2005 and the broadcast of 'Guns and neighbours: the murder of the Pearson family at Coolacrease' in the 'Hidden History' series, RTÉ, 23 Oct. 2007.

29   'To members of the IRA', publicity leaflet, Col. C. S. Foulkes, TNA, CO 904/168. The handbill included the following disapproval of guerrilla warfare and its methods: 'War between white men should be carried out in a sportsmanlike manner, and not like fights between savage tribes.'

30   Seen in the response to the publication of Gerard Murphy's *The Year of Disappearances: Political Killings in Cork, 1921–1922* (Dublin, 2010).

31   The majority of examples are taken from over 1,500 courts of inquiry in lieu of inquest held in the National Archives, London, TNA, WO 35/145–WO 35/163.

32   Quoted in Wilfrid Ewart, *A Journey in Ireland 1921*, Paul Bew and Patrick Maume (eds), (2nd edn, Dublin, 2008), p. 23.

33   Proceedings of a court of inquiry in lieu of inquest on Thomas Cunningham, 20 June 1921, TNA, WO 35/148. Cunningham was shot in Belmont, Co. Offaly.

34   John Cosgrove, said to be a well-known Sinn Féiner, was shot in reprisal for the deaths of Hugh O'Hanlon and James Smith, both believed to have been shot by the IRA in Camlough, Co. Armagh on 7 June 1921. John McCoy, BMH WS 492.

35   Proceedings of a court of inquiry in lieu of inquest on John Cosgrove, 15 June 1921, TNA, WO 35/148; proceedings of a court of inquiry in lieu of inquest on Philip Dunne, 18 June 1921, TNA, WO 35/149B. Dunne was shot in Kilmeague, Co. Kildare, after attempting to fight off his attackers. His body was not labelled.

36   Proceedings of a court of inquiry in lieu of inquest on Thomas Byrne, 8 Apr. 1921, TNA, WO 35/147A. Byrne, sometimes cited as Beirne, was shot in Drumlish, Co. Longford.

37   Proceedings of a court of inquiry in lieu of inquest on Denis Donovan, 30 Mar. 1921, TNA, WO 35/149A. Donovan was shot in Bandon, Co. Cork.

38   Proceedings of a court of inquiry in lieu of inquest on John Gilligan, 8 Apr. 1921, TNA, WO 35/149B. Gilligan was shot in Loughglinn, Co. Roscommon.

39   Proceedings of a court of inquiry in lieu of inquest on William Elliott, 24 Jan. 1921, TNA, WO 35/149B.

40   Proceedings of a court of inquiry in lieu of inquest on Michael Coen, 2 Apr. 1921, TNA, WO 35/147A.

41   Proceedings of a court of inquiry in lieu of inquest on Kate Carroll, 16–17 Apr. 1921, TNA, WO 35/147B.

42   Proceedings of a court of inquiry in lieu of inquest on Thomas Byrne, 8 Apr. 1921, TNA, WO 35/147A.

43   Proceedings of a court of inquiry in lieu of inquest on John Good, 12 Mar. 1921, TNA, WO 35/149B. Good's son, William, was killed and labelled shortly after returning home for his father's funeral. See proceedings of a court of inquiry in lieu of inquest on William Good, 29 Mar. 1921, TNA, WO 35/149B.

44   Memo by Macready on file, proceedings of a court of inquiry in lieu of inquest on John Good, 12 Mar. 1921, TNA, WO 35/149B.

45   Proceedings of a court of inquiry in lieu of inquest on Martin Daly, 21 Mar. 1921, TNA, WO 35/147B.

46   Patrick Broady or Briody, a shoemaker from Cavan, was reported to have been 'murdered on the public road', *Irish Times*, 25 May 1921. Crosby Boyle was also found dead on the 'public road' in Co. Tipperary, *Irish Times*, 16 June 1921.

47   Proceedings of a court of inquiry in lieu of inquest on John Sheehan, 24 Mar. 1921, TNA, WO 35/159B. Sheehan had been taken from his home near Kanturk, Co. Cork.

48   Proceedings of a court of inquiry in lieu of inquest on John Doran, 13 Jan. 1921, TNA, WO 35/149A. Doran was shot in the yard of his home near Camlough, Co. Armagh. Accounts vary as to whether he was killed by the IRA or by Crown forces; proceedings of a court of inquiry in lieu of inquest on Thomas Walker, 16 Apr. 1921, TNA, WO 35/159B. Walker died in a quarry near his home in Ballinfull, Co. Sligo.

49   Proceedings of a court of inquiry in lieu of inquest on John Sheehan, 24 Mar. 1921, TNA, WO 35/159B.

50   Proceedings of a court of inquiry in lieu of inquest on John Wymes, 8 Apr. 1921, TNA, WO 35/159B. Wymes was shot on the same night as John Gilligan in Loughglinn, Co. Roscommon.

51   Proceedings of a court of inquiry in lieu of inquest on John Fitzgerald, 7 June 1921, TNA, WO 35/149B. Fitzgerald was shot on Ballybeggan racecourse, near Tralee, Co. Kerry.

52   A sheet of paper with the word 'spy' on it was found in an empty house near the body of Sgt Thomas McGrath in March 1923. *Weekly Irish Times*, 10 Mar. 1923.

53   *Irish Times*, 26 Mar. 1921.

54   *Manchester Guardian*, 10 May 1921. McGawley was also reported as McAuley and McGauley.

55   Intelligence Dept. to OCs all Battalions, 10 Mar. 1921, UCDA, Ernie O'Malley papers, P17a/105. Lists, names reported to be under suspicion, are regularly found in both the Richard Mulcahy and Ernie O'Malley papers. In O'Malley's collection, these lists continue through the Civil War. See for example 'List of Lady Spies, Touts & Searchers', UCDA, Ernie O'Malley papers, P17a/34.

56   Monthly intelligence report for East Limerick Brigade for July 1921, 29 July 1921, UCDA, Richard Mulcahy papers, P7a/8.

57   Brigid Ní B[unclear] to unknown, 16 Oct. 1922, UCDA, Ernie O'Malley papers, P17a/73.

58   Patrick Corrigan to Rev. Livingstone, 27 Dec. 1965, Monaghan County Museum, Marron papers, 6D1–10.

59   Chief of Staff to Brigade Commandant, Kilkenny, 1 June 1921, UCDA, Richard Mulcahy papers, P7/A/19(2).

60 Chief of Staff to Adjutant General, 29 July 1921, UCDA, Richard Mulcahy papers, P7/A/22(280).

61 Statement of service by William Corcoran, 11 May 1943, UCDA, Seán Mac Eoin papers, P151/1175(2); statement by Andrew Donlon, *n.d.*, UCDA, Seán Mac Eoin papers, P151/1185(6); statement by Michael Cullen, *n.d.*, UCDA, Seán Mac Eoin papers, P151/1177(3); statement by William Smith, *n.d.*, UCDA, Seán Mac Eoin papers, p151/1269(7); statement by William Smith, *n.d.*, UCDA, Seán Mac Eoin papers, p151/1269(4).

62 Quoted in Griffith and O'Grady, *Ireland's Unfinished Revolution: An Oral History*, pp 190–2.

63 Ewart, *A Journey in Ireland 1921*, p. 128.

64 Proceedings of a court of inquiry in lieu of inquest on James and Thomas Skelton, 22 Mar. 1921, TNA, WO 35/159B.

65 Proceedings of a court of inquiry in lieu of inquest on Patrick and John Watters, 20 June 1921, TNA, WO 35/160. The Watters brothers may have been killed in reprisal for the shooting of Constable William Campbell, but it was also suspected by the court of inquiry that they had been killed by the IRA for refusing to carry out assigned duties.

66 Proceedings of a court of inquiry in lieu of inquest on John Good, 12 Mar. 1921, TNA, WO 35/149B; proceedings of a court of inquiry in lieu of inquest on William Good, 29 Mar. 1921, TNA, WO 35/149B.

67 Proceedings of a court of inquiry in lieu of inquest on Patrick Sheehan and John Sullivan, 4 July 1921, TNA, WO 35/159B.

68 Proceedings of a court of inquiry in lieu of inquest on William Elliott, 24 Jan. 1921, TNA, WO 35/149B; proceedings of a court of inquiry in lieu of inquest on William Charters, 28 Jan. 1921, TNA, WO 35/147A.

69 Proceedings of a court of inquiry in lieu of inquest on John Gilligan, 8 Apr. 1921, TNA, WO 35/149B; proceedings of a court of inquiry in lieu of inquest on John Wymes, 8 Apr. 1921, TNA, WO 35/159B.

70 Proceedings of a court of inquiry in lieu of inquest on Thomas and Michael Waldron, 9 July 1921, TNA, WO 35/159B.

71 Proceedings of a court of inquiry in lieu of inquest on Patrick and John Watters, 20 June 1921, TNA, WO 35/160; proceedings of a court of inquiry in lieu of inquest on John Buckley, 30 June 1921, TNA, WO 35/147A.

72 Tadhg Crowe of the 3rd Tipperary Brigade IRA recorded his interpretation of Buckley's death in his Bureau of Military History statement: '... a party of police in civilian clothes called again at Maloney's of Gurthdrum. This time they took out one of the workmen, John Buckley, and shot him. To make it look like the work of the IRA they put a label "Spies and informers beware" on the dead body. Buckley was a member of my company in Solohead and there was no doubt about his integrity.' BMH WS 1658.

73 Proceedings of a court of inquiry in lieu of inquest on William Doran, 31 Jan. 1921, TNA, WO 35/149A.

74 Proceedings of a court of inquiry in lieu of inquest on Thomas and Michael Waldron, 9 July 1921, TNA, WO 35/159B.

75 Proceedings of a court of inquiry in lieu of inquest on William Charters, 28 Jan. 1921, TNA, WO 35/147A.

76 *Irish Times*, 16 June 1921. Boyle was also referred to as Francis Crossley Boyle.

77 Ibid.

9
'Have we been playing at Republicanism?':
The Treaty, the Pact Election and the Civil War in Co. Galway

1   I wish to acknowledge the permission of Manchester University Press to reproduce some of the material in this article. For a broader discussion on the topic see Úna Newell, *The West Must Wait: County Galway and the Irish Free State 1922–32* (Manchester, 2015).

2   Quoted in *Tuam Herald*, 7 Jan. 1922.

3   The Anglo-Irish Treaty, signed in London on 6 December 1921, confirmed dominion status on 26 counties of Ireland. The settlement marked a significant advancement on earlier offers of Home Rule, but it failed to secure an Irish republic. After weeks of debate the proposed agreement was approved by the Dáil by the narrow majority of 64 votes to 57 on 7 January 1922.

4   *Connacht Tribune*, 4 Feb. 1922.

5   *East Galway Democrat*, 14 Jan. 1922.

6   Professor Joseph Whelehan: teacher. He was elected (uncontested) for Galway in May 1921 when the county became a single electoral constituency.

7   *Tuam Herald*, 18 Mar. 1922; *Dáil Éireann Treaty Deb.*, 93 (21 Dec. 1921).

8   Liam Mellows: clerk in Dublin in 1905. Son of a British army sergeant, he joined Fianna Éireann in 1909 and the IRB in 1912, and was full-time organiser for the Irish Volunteers in County Galway in 1914–15. The radicalisation of the Galway Volunteers, particularly in East Galway, is synonymous with the name of Mellows who led the local insurrection in Easter 1916. However, the tradition of agrarian crime and unrest in the west and the incessant hunger for land division and land redistribution all helped dictate the pattern of the Galway rebellion. Mellows was elected (uncontested) for Sinn Féin in East Galway in December 1918. In America (where he escaped to after the Rising) he worked on the *Gaelic American* and assisted de Valera's tour in 1919–20. After his arrival back in Dublin, he acted as IRA Director of Purchases in 1921 and was returned (uncontested) for the Galway constituency. Despite losing his seat at the pact election, 1922, he was appointed Minister for Defence in the republican government. After the surrender of the Four Courts anti-Treaty garrison, he was imprisoned in Mountjoy jail. He was executed on 8 December 1922 by the Provisional Government in reprisal for the killing of Seán Hales TD.

9   Brian Cusack: medical doctor, founding member of the Irish Volunteers in Galway and member of the IRB. He was elected as a Sinn Féin deputy for North Galway in December 1918 and was returned (uncontested) for Galway in May 1921. A War of Independence veteran, he spent most of the Civil War period in the Curragh internment camp.

10   Frank Fahy: teacher, general secretary of the Gaelic League, Sinn Féin and Irish Volunteer veteran, and a student at King's Inns, Dublin. He served as second in command to Ned Daly in the Four Courts area during the Easter Rising. He spent terms in several British jails and was released in June 1917. He was elected as a Sinn Féin deputy for South Galway in December 1918. Active during the War of Independence, he was returned (uncontested) for Galway in May 1921. He later became a Fianna Fáil TD and was Ceann Comhairle of the Dáil from 1932 to 1951.

11   *Dáil Éireann Treaty Deb.*, 195 (3 Jan. 1922).

12   J. J. Lee, *Ireland 1912–1985: Politics and Society* (Cambridge, 1989), p. 67; John M. Regan, *Myth and the Irish State: Historical Problems and Other Essays* (Kildare, 2013), pp 1–38, 43, 89.

13   *Dáil Éireann Treaty Deb.*, 338 (7 Jan. 1922). De Valera used the oasis metaphor in a letter to John Hagan, Rector of the Irish College in Rome, on 13 January 1922. See Dermot Keogh, *The Vatican, the Bishops and Irish Politics, 1919–1939* (Cambridge, 1986), p. 82.

14   Patrick Hogan: solicitor, farmer, vice-president of the Irish Farmers' Union and member of Sinn Féin. In 1920 he was arrested and interned in Ballykinlar, Co. Down, where he remained until the truce. He became TD for Galway (uncontested) in May 1921. He served as Minister for Agriculture from 1922 to 1932. The successful enactment of the 1923 Land Act during a period of political and social conflict was testament to his ability as a minister. He died in a car accident in Aughrim, Co. Galway in July 1936. Reacting to the news of his death W. T. Cosgrave announced: 'Our best man is gone.' *Irish Independent*, 16 July 1936.

15   *Dáil Éireann Treaty Deb.*, 63 (20 Dec. 1921).

16   Ibid., 196 (3 Jan. 1922). Some pro-Treaty supporters, Collins in particular, argued that the Treaty be accepted as a stepping stone towards the ultimate attainment of complete independence in the fullness of time.

17   Quoted in *Tuam Herald*, 4 Mar. 1922.

18   F. S. L. Lyons, 'The meaning of independence', in Brian Farrell (ed.), *The Irish Parliamentary Tradition* (Dublin, 1973), p. 229.

19   *Dáil Éireann Treaty Deb.*, 253 (4 Jan. 1922).

20   Ibid., 197 (3 Jan. 1922).

21   Ibid.

22   Ibid., 229 (4 Jan. 1922).

23   See Lee, *Ireland 1912–1985*, p. 67, for his interpretation of this argument.

24   *Dáil Éireann Treaty Deb.*, 231 (4 Jan. 1922).

25   Land congestion, economic degradation, and the festering poverty of the west remained unresolved. In February 1922, the local press carried reports of famine-like conditions in the region. Year after year parts of Connemara, in particular, lurked on the borderland of want and distress, depending on perennial relief measures to stave off starvation. While the overall situation could not be accurately described as a general 'famine', there were many cases of acute distress in the west of Ireland. For further details on local levels of deprivation see Newell, *The West Must Wait*, chapter 4.

26   *Dáil Éireann Treaty Deb.*, 252 (4 Jan. 1922).

27   Ibid., 196 (3 Jan. 1922). Fahy, a scholar of the law, accused the press of concealing the truth and making false representations.

28   *Tuam Herald*, 25 Feb. 1922.

29   *Dáil Éireann Treaty Deb.*, 61 (20 Dec. 1921).

30   George Nicholls: solicitor, founding member of the Galway branch of the Irish Volunteers in December 1913, first president of the Thomas Ashe Sinn Féin Club in Galway city and chairman of Galway County Council (1920–5). He was arrested on the morning of the local rebellion in 1916 along with other Volunteer organisers including Padraig Ó Máille. Interned in Britain, he was released in December 1916. He was elected (uncontested) for Sinn Féin in Galway in May 1921.

31   *Dáil Éireann Treaty Deb.*, 198 (3 Jan. 1922).

32   Padraig Ó Máille: farmer, Gaelic League organiser and Sinn Féin activist. A prominent member of the Irish Volunteers, he was arrested on the morning of the Galway rebellion in 1916. He was interned in Wandsworth prison, Frongoch and Reading jail and released in December 1916. He was elected as a Sinn Féin deputy for Connemara in December 1918 and was returned (uncontested) for Galway in May 1921. A charismatic War of Independence veteran, he was shot and wounded on 7 December 1922 outside the Ormond Hotel in Dublin by republican forces during the Civil War. His travelling companion and fellow pro-Treaty deputy Seán Hales was killed in the attack.

33   *Dáil Éireann Treaty Deb.*, 140 (22 Dec. 1921).

34   *Galway Observer*, 15 Apr. 1922.

35   *Connacht Tribune*, 21 Jan. 1922.

36   *Dáil Éireann Treaty Deb.*, 92–3 (21 Dec. 1921).

37   *East Galway Democrat*, 25 Feb. 1922.

38   Minutes of Galway County Council, 30 Dec. 1921, Galway County Council Archives, Galway CC Minute Books, GC1/3.

39   *Tuam Herald*, 31 Dec. 1921.

40   Ibid., 18 Feb. 1922.

41   *East Galway Democrat*, 14 Jan. 1922.

42   *Dáil Éireann Treaty Deb.*, 21 (19 Dec. 1921); *Dáil Éireann Private Sessions*, 161 (15 Dec. 1921). For further details on de Valera's compromise proposal see, for example, 'The Anglo-Irish Treaty and Mr de Valera's alternative' (Dublin, 1924), NAI, DT, S9302/A; Lee, *Ireland 1912–1985*, p. 51; Jeffrey Prager, *Building Democracy in Ireland: Political Order and Cultural Integration in a Newly Independent Nation* (Cambridge, 1986), p. 63; F. S. L. Lyons, 'The great debate', in Farrell (ed.), *The Irish Parliamentary Tradition*, pp 249–52. For another discussion on de Valera's policy of external association and Griffith's belief in a dual monarchy see Michael Laffan, *The Resurrection of Ireland: The Sinn Féin Party, 1916–1923* (Cambridge, 1999), p. 425.

43   Éamon de Valera, 'The alternative to the Treaty', 1923, NAI, DT, S9302/A.

44   *Connacht Tribune*, 4 Feb. 1922.

45   Ibid.

46   The 2nd and 4th Western Divisions of the IRA declared against the Treaty. The 1st Western Division supported it.

47   *Connacht Tribune*, 15 Apr. 1922.

48   Ibid., 8 Apr. 1922.

49   Ibid., 1 Apr. 1922.

50   Ibid., 6 May 1922. Here one cannot help but to think of the Free State propaganda poster 'This is where he was in 1921', NLI, Ephemera collection, POL/1920–30/9; or see Laffan, *The Resurrection of Ireland*, p. 415. Father Michael Griffin was killed in Galway in November 1920. The disappearance of the young curate sparked a heated exchange between Bishop Thomas O'Dea of Galway and the Chief Secretary for Ireland, Sir Hamar Greenwood. Speaking in the House of Commons, Greenwood had rejected any responsibility for the disappearance of Griffin stating: 'I do not believe that this priest has been kidnapped by any armed forces of the Crown. It is obviously such a stupid thing that no member of the forces of the Crown would do it.' O'Dea's reply to the Chief Secretary, after the recovery of the curate's body, lacked the customary prudent reserve of the bishop. 'This murder', he wrote, 'marks a new departure in the campaign, indicating, it would appear, the beginning of an attack on the Church and religion … It is the belief of all in Galway that Father Griffin was shot by Government forces. The people of Ireland do not shoot their priests.' O'Dea to Greenwood, 25 Nov. 1920, Galway Diocesan Archives, Thomas O'Dea papers, Box 31/7. See also *Connacht Tribune*, 20, 27 Nov. 1920.

51   *Galway Observer*, 8 Apr. 1922.

52   Michael Hopkinson, *Green against Green: The Irish Civil War* (2nd edn, Dublin, 2004), p. 63.

53   *Connacht Tribune*, 8 Apr. 1922.

54   *Galway Observer*, 15 Apr. 1922.

55   Nationally, of the 58 anti-Treaty Sinn Féin candidates who stood for election, 36 were elected and 22 were defeated. Pro-Treaty Sinn Féin, on the other hand, returned 58 of its 65 candidates. Michael Gallagher (ed.), *Irish Elections 1922–44: Results and Analysis* (Limerick, 2003), p. 18.

56   Ibid., p. 14. Between August 1923 and September 1927 Galway consistently registered the lowest percentage electoral turnout in all the contested constituencies until it was replaced at

the foot of the national poll by the Dublin North, Dublin South, Dublin County and Kildare constituencies in February 1932. However, the flawed and inflated nature of the electoral register, both at national and local level, meant that the turnout figures for Galway were artificially low. For instance, in 1923 Galway recorded a figure of 7,977 more people on the register than existed in the adult population. In 1927, the electoral register recorded a surplus of 3,696 voters. In 1932, it recorded a deficit of 7,720. For a further discussion on the fundamental problems with the electoral register see Richard Sinnott, *Irish Voters Decide: Voting Behaviour in Elections and Referendums Since 1918* (Manchester, 1995), pp 84–7.

57   The Representation of the People Act, 1918, extended the voting franchise in Ireland to all adult males of 21 years and granted it for the first time to women aged over 30 who were themselves householders or else married to a householder. Nationally, the Act generated a threefold increase in the number of people eligible to vote. In County Galway, the electorate increased from 29,625 in 1911 to 82,276 in 1918. In 1923, the August general election was the first to be fought on a universal adult suffrage when modifications to the electoral law extended the franchise rights to women between the ages of 21 and 30.

58   Michael Gallagher, 'The pact general election of 1922', *Irish Historical Studies* xxi:84 (Sept. 1979), p. 421.

59   Here the use of the word 'muzzle', in a political context, imitates that employed by Arthur Griffith during the Treaty debates when he criticised his detractors' attempts to try to silence or suppress the voice of the people: 'The Irish people will not be deceived ... Some of you will try to muzzle it; but that voice will be heard, and it will pierce through ... Distrust the people, muzzle the people, where then is gone self-determination for the people?' *Dáil Éireann Treaty Deb.*, 341 (7 Jan. 1922).

60   *Connacht Tribune*, 15 Apr. 1922.

61   *Galway Observer*, 15 Apr. 1922.

62   *East Galway Democrat*, 6 May 1922.

63   *Connacht Tribune*, 8 Apr. 1922.

64   *Tuam Herald*, 27 May 1922.

65   *Galway Observer*, 17 June 1922.

66   *East Galway Democrat*, 17 June 1922.

67   For further details on this incident see *Connacht Tribune*, 27 May, 3 June 1922; NAI, Department of Justice, H5/313; John Cunningham, 'The "Soviet at Galway" and the downfall of Dunkellin', *Cathair Na Mart: Journal of the Westport Historical Society* x (1990), pp 115–23.

68   *Connacht Tribune*, 10 June 1922.

69   For additional information on the Sligo-East Mayo contest, reports of intimidation, the alleged kidnapping of personation officers acting for the two independent candidates, and the two sides' different degrees of commitment to the pact, see Michael Farry, *The Aftermath of Revolution: Sligo 1921–23* (Dublin, 2000), pp 64–74.

70   Letter to the editor by Martin Egan, Galway Executive member of the Irish Farmers' Union, explaining the decision of the Co. Galway farmers not to nominate candidates for the coming election. *Connacht Tribune*, 10 June 1922.

71   *Census of Ireland, 1926, Vol II: Occupations* (Dublin, 1927), pp 20–1.

72   *Galway Observer*, 17 June 1922.

73   Repudiating the authority of the Dáil, a group of anti-Treaty IRA radicals, including Rory O'Connor, Ernie O'Malley and Liam Mellows, had seized the Four Courts building in Dublin on 14 April 1922 and established a republican military headquarters.

74   *Connacht Tribune*, 15 Apr. 1922.

75   Ibid., 24 June 1922.

76   In an attempt to stifle the separatist movement, and, in part, in response to the stand-off over conscription, a large proportion of the Sinn Féin leadership was arrested on the night of 17–18 May 1918 under allegations of treasonable contact with Germany.

77   For more details on Mellows's social policy and his activities in Galway in 1916, see Úna Newell, 'The rising of the moon: Galway 1916', *Journal of the Galway Archaeological and Historical Society* lviii (2006), pp 114–35; Fergus Campbell, *Land and Revolution: Nationalist Politics in the West of Ireland 1892–1921* (Oxford, 2005), chapter 5.

78   For an expansion of this theory see 'The count at Galway', *Connacht Tribune*, 24 June 1922.

79   Gallagher (ed.), *Irish Elections 1922–44*, p. 15.

80   Hopkinson, *Green against Green*, p. 158.

81   *Connacht Tribune*, 8 July 1922.

82   Ibid.

83   Hopkinson, *Green against Green*, p. 63, 150.

84   *Connacht Tribune*, 29 July 1922. The bridge was repaired in October 1922, but other bridges around Tuam were also destroyed.

85   Minutes of Galway Urban District Council, 6 July 1922, Galway City Council Archives, Galway UDC Minute Books, GA3/8/116.

86   Quoted in *Connacht Tribune*, 29 July 1922. The letter was sent by boat from Roundstone.

87   See, for instance, Erhard Rumpf and A. C. Hepburn, *Nationalism and Socialism in Twentieth-Century Ireland* (Liverpool, 1977), pp 61–2; Peter Pyne, 'The third Sinn Féin party: 1923–26', *Economic and Social Review* i:2 (1969–70), pp 229–42.

88   For a further discussion on the effect these imprisonments had, particularly on the families of those belonging to the small farming class, see, for example, Gilbert Morrissey, O/C Athenry Battalion Irish Volunteers, BMH WS 1,138, 25 June 1953.

89   In east Galway agrarian agitation shaped the nature of civil war violence, but across the county the land question was unfinished business. For a discussion on the overlap between nationalism and the desire for land redistribution see Newell, *The West Must Wait*, chapter 3; Campbell, *Land and Revolution*, chapter 6; Tony Varley, 'Agrarian crime and social control: Sinn Féin and the land question in the west of Ireland in 1920', in Ciaran McCullagh, Mike Tomlinson and Tony Varley (eds.), *Whose Law and Order? Aspects of Crime and Social Control in Irish Society* (Belfast, 1988), pp 54–75; Varley, 'Irish land reform and the west between the wars', *Journal of the Galway Archaeological and Historical Society* 56 (2004), pp 213–32.

90   Hopkinson, *Green against Green*, p. 219.

91   Ibid.

92   Report on condition of the Western Command, 14 Mar. 1923, UCDA, Moss Twomey papers, P69/30 (222–3).

93   Minutes of Divisional Council, 2nd Western Division, 21 Oct. 1923, UCDA, Moss Twomey papers, P69/104 (112).

94   General report on the 2nd Western Division, 30 Sept. 1924, UCDA, Moss Twomey papers, P69/104 (7).

95   Report on the Council Meeting, 2nd Western Division, 21 Dec. 1923, UCDA, Moss Twomey papers, P69/104 (108).

96   Hopkinson, *Green against Green*, p. 212.

97   Gallagher (ed.), *Irish Elections 1922–44*, p. 14, 45.

98   For communications between the Chief of Staff and O/C of the Western Divisions see UCDA, Moss Twomey papers, P69/34.

99   Eunan O'Halpin, *Defending Ireland: The Irish State and Its Enemies Since 1922* (Oxford, 1999), p. 39.

10

'Always in danger of finding myself with nothing at all': The military service pensions and the battle for material survival, 1925–55

1   M. A. Hopkinson, 'Barry, Thomas Bernadine ("Tom")', in James McGuire and James Quinn (eds), *Dictionary of Irish Biography* (9 vols, Cambridge, 2009), I, pp 349–51.

2   Tom Barry, *Guerrilla Days in Ireland* (Dublin, 1949).

3   Hopkinson, 'Tom Barry', p. 350

4   Barry to Military Service Registration Board, Dec. 1938, MA, IE/MSPC/MSP34REF57456: Thomas Barry.

5   Barry to Military Service Registration Board, 27 Dec. 1938, MA IE/MSPC/MSP34REF57456: Thomas Barry.

6   Extract from Tom Barry's sworn evidence [*n.d.*], MA IE/MSPC/MSP34REF57456: Thomas Barry.

7   Barry to Military Service Registration Board, 29 Jan. 1940, MA IE/MSPC/MSP34REF57456: Thomas Barry.

8   Quirke to Secretary, Military Service Pensions Board, 2 Feb. 1940, MA IE/MSPC/MSP34REF57456: Thomas Barry.

9   De Valera to Referee, Military Service Pensions Board, 2 Mar. 1940, MA IE/MSPC/MSP34REF57456: Thomas Barry.

10   F. Begley to Secretary, Military Service Pensions Board, 18 April 1940, MA IE/MSPC/MSP34REF57456: Thomas Barry.

11   Assessment Board to Tom Barry, 15 July 1940, MA IE/MSPC/MSP34REF57456: Thomas Barry.

12   The files are held in the Military Archives, Cathal Brugha Barracks, Rathmines, Dublin.

13   'The Army Pensions Acts, 1923–1953: summary of legislation and files created', Apr. 2009 and 'The Military Service Pensions Collection: origins, scope and content', Apr. 2009, MA, MSPC, 4.

14   'The Army Pensions Acts', MA, MSPC, 4.

15   Ibid.

16   Ibid.

17   Ibid.

18   Mary Malone to Minister for Defence, 5 May 1925, MA, IE/MA/MSPC/ID315: Michael Malone.

19   Secretary of Department of Defence to Director of Army Intelligence, Col M. Costello, 11 May 1925, MA, IE/MA/MSPC/ID315: Michael Malone.

20   M. A. Hopkinson, 'Breen, Daniel ("Dan")', in McGuire and Quinn (eds), *Dictionary of Irish Biography*, I, pp 796–7.

21   Dan Breen, *My Fight for Irish Freedom* (Dublin, 1924) was Breen's account of his War of Independence experiences.

22   Costello to Secretary, Department of Defence, 20 May 1925, MA, IE/MA/MSPC/ID315: Michael Malone.

23   William O'Brien to Richard Mulcahy, 6 Feb. 1924, MA, IE/MA/MSPC/ID178: James Connolly.

24   Secretary of Department of Defence to Army Finance Office, 8 Feb. 1924, MA, IE/MA/MSPC/ID178: James Connolly.

25   Account of interview conducted with Lily Connolly by Sergeant James Murphy, 15 Feb. 1924, MA, IE/MA/MSPC/ID178: James Connolly.

26   Memo from J. J. Hogan, army finance officer, to Department of Defence containing

amended Award Certificate for Lily Connolly, 7 July 1937. IE/MA/MSPC/ID178: James Connolly, Dec. 1938.

27   Nora Connolly O'Brien to 'Seamus', 9 July 1941, MA, IE/MA/MSPC/ID178: James Connolly.

28   Kathleen Clarke to Judge Thomas O'Donnell, 20 May 1941, MA, IE/MA/MSPC/ID178: James Connolly.

29   Assessment Board to Nora Connolly O'Brien, 19 Oct. 1941, MA, IE/MA/MSPC/ID178: James Connolly.

30   C. Gifford Wilson to T. Hennessy TD, 21 June 1930, MA, IE/MA/MSPC/ID34: Thomas Mac-Donagh.

31   Donagh MacDonagh to Department of Defence, 26 Oct. 1936, MA, IE/MA/MSPC/ID34: Thomas MacDonagh.

32   Donagh MacDonagh to Éamon de Valera, 16 Jan. 1936, MA, IE/MA/MSPC/ID34: Thomas MacDonagh.

33   Fr 'A' to Seán MacEntee, 10 Feb. 1937, MA, IE/MA/MSPC/ID34: Thomas MacDonagh.

34   Bridget Hourican, 'MacDonagh, Donagh', in McGuire and Quinn (eds), *Dictionary of Irish Biography*, V, pp 916–7.

35   'The Military Service Pensions Collection', MA, MSPC, 4.

36   Edmund Hogan, 'James Hogan: a biographical sketch', in Donnchadh Ó Corráin (ed.), *James Hogan: Revolutionary, Historian, Political Scientist* (Cork, 2001), pp 1–34.

37   James Hogan to Assessment Board, 15 Mar. 1944, MA, IE/MA/MSPC/MSP34/REF1985: James Hogan.

38   Oscar Traynor to Secretary, Department of Defence, 4 May 1945, MA, IE/MA/MSPC/MSP34/REF1985: James Hogan.

39   Assessment Board to James Hogan, 19 Sept. 1945, MA, IE/MA/MSPC/MSP34/REF1985: James Hogan.

40   Annie Maher to Board of Assessors, 17 Nov. 1937, MA, IE/MA/MSPC/MSP34/REF23572: William Maher.

41   Note for Advisory Committee, 21 Jan. 1942, MA, IE/MA/MSPC/MSP34/REF23572: William Maher.

42   Secretary of Department of Defence to William Maher, 9 Apr. 1942, MA, IE/MA/MSPC/MSP34/REF23572: William Maher.

43   John Maher to Office of the Referee, 22 Oct. 1956, MA, IE/MA/MSPC/MSP34/REF23572: William Maher.

44   Office of Referee note of 11 Sept. 1957, MA, IE/MA/MSPC/MSP34/REF23572: William Maher.

45   John Maher to Office of the Referee, 24 June 1958 and reply of 16 July 1958, MA, IE/MA/MSPC/MSP34/REF23572: William Maher.

46   John Maher to Secretary, Department of Defence, 22 Aug. 1958, MA, IE/MA/MSPC/MSP34/REF23572: William Maher.

47   Secretary, Department of Defence to John Maher, 6 Sept. 1958, MA, IE/MA/MSPC/MSP34/REF23572: William Maher.

48   Denis Doran to R. Corish TD, Mayor of Wexford, Jan. 1942, MA, IE/MA/MSP34REF 24224: Denis Doran.

49   Attorney General to Secretary, Department of Defence, 2 Feb. 1940, MA, IE/MA/MSP34REF 24224: Denis Doran.

50   L. M. Fitzgerald, Department of Finance, to J. O'Connell, 20 May 1942, MA, IE/MA/MSP34REF 24224: Denis Doran.

51   Denis Doran to Secretary, Department of Defence, 17 Oct. 1942, MA, IE/MA/MSP34REF 24224: Denis Doran.

52   Patrick Wade to Department of Finance, 25 Oct. 1946, MA, IE/ /MA/MSPC/MSP34REF56199: Patrick Wade.

53   John Guiney, note of 4 Apr. 1940, MA, IE/MA/MSPC/MSPREF63404: John Guiney.

54   Katie Walsh to Office of Referee, 25 Oct. 1940, MA, IE/MA/MSPC/MSP34REF25857: Katie Walsh.

55   Note of Advisory Committee, 16 Oct. 1941, MA, IE/MA/MSPC/MSP34REF25857: Katie Walsh.

56   Scollan to Office of the Referee, 29 May 1938, MA, IE/MA/MSPC/MSP34REF463: John Joseph Scollan.

57   Sworn statement of Scollan made before the Advisory Committee on 22 Oct. 1935; Scollan to Office of the Referee, 30 Nov. 1936 and 29 May 1938, MA, IE/MA/MSPC/MSP34REF463: John Joseph Scollan.

58   Margaret Murphy to Secretary, Department of Defence, 28 Jan. 1933, MA, IE/MA/MSPC/ Departmental Records/8262: John Murphy.

59   Report on John Murphy by Thomas Mackham, 2 May 1933, MA, IE/MA/MSPC/Departmental Records/8262: John Murphy.

60   Ibid.

61   Lucy Byrne to Secretary, Department of Defence, 10 May 1946, MA, IE/MSPC/MSPF/ MSP24/4055: Patrick Byrne.

11
From rogue revolutionary to rogue civil servant: The resurrection of Bulmer Hobson

1   This chapter expands on and revises some of the material contained in chapter 9 of my monograph, *Bulmer Hobson and the Nationalist Movement in Twentieth-Century Ireland*, which was published by Manchester University Press in 2009. I would like to acknowledge the receipt of funding from the former Irish Research Council for the Humanities and Social Sciences, which made some of the research for this chapter possible.

2   For a detailed discussion of Hobson's nationalist career, see Marnie Hay, *Bulmer Hobson and the Nationalist Movement in Twentieth-Century Ireland* (Manchester, 2009); Marnie Hay, 'Bulmer Hobson: the rise and fall of an Irish nationalist, 1900–16' (PhD thesis, University College Dublin, 2004). I would like to thank Professor Michael Laffan for his adept and genial supervision of this thesis.

3   See Marnie Hay, 'The foundation and development of Na Fianna Éireann, 1909–16', *Irish Historical Studies* xxxvi:141 (May 2008), pp 53–71.

4   See Marnie Hay, 'Kidnapped: Bulmer Hobson, the IRB and the 1916 Easter Rising', *Canadian Journal of Irish Studies* xxxv:1 (spring 2009), pp 53–60; Marnie Hay, 'The mysterious "disappearance" of Bulmer Hobson', *Studies* xcviii:390 (summer 2009), pp 185–95.

5   Hay, *Bulmer Hobson and the Nationalist Movement*, pp 201–3.

6   Bulmer Hobson, *Ireland Yesterday and Tomorrow* (Tralee, 1968), p. 112.

7   His father Benjamin Hobson Jr was a commercial traveller from outside Lurgan, Co. Armagh, who identified himself politically as a Gladstonian Home Ruler. Hobson's mother Mary Ann Bulmer was a suffragist and amateur archaeologist from Darlington, Co. Durham in England. For more detail on the Hobson family, see Hay, *Bulmer Hobson and the Nationalist Movement*, pp 6–11.

8   For a discussion of Hobson's influences and involvement in nationalist organisations in Belfast, see chapters 1–3 of Hay, *Bulmer Hobson and the Nationalist Movement*.

9   Claire Hobson (née Gregan), BMH WS, BMH WS 685; parish marriage register, Rathfarnham, NLI, microfilm no. P8972; Mary Ann Bulmer Hobson, 'Bulmer family chronicle from before

1050 to 1936', NLI, MS 5220; Obituary of Mrs Claire Hobson, *Irish Independent*, 24 Feb. 1958.

10   In the 1901 census Hobson is recorded as an 18-year-old apprentice printer while the 1911 census lists him as a 28-year-old journalist, census.nationalarchives.ie/pages/1901/Antrim/ Clifton_Ward_Belfast/Hopefield_Avenue/1004537/;census.nationalarchives.ie/pages/1911/Down/ Holywood_Urban/Ballycultra/232384/(accessed online 11 Jan. 2011).

11   *Thom's Directory* first listed Hobson at the Mill House in 1920.

12   Quidnunc, 'An Irishman's diary', *Irish Times*, 26 Feb. 1958.

13   Hay, *Bulmer Hobson and the Nationalist Movement*, pp 219–20.

14   Quidnunc, 'An Irishman's diary'.

15   Christopher Shepard, 'A liberalisation of Irish social policy? Women's organisations and the campaign for women police in Ireland, 1915–57', *Irish Historical Studies* xxxvi:144 (Nov. 2009), p. 579; Roger Mitchell to Marnie Hay, 21 Jan. 2011 (email in possession of author).

16   P. Ó Ceallaigh to S. Ó Muimhneacháin, 7 June 1944, in remuneration of higher posts in Stamping Branch, NAI, Dept. of Finance, FIN/E2/1/39; Ronan Fanning, *The Irish Department of Finance 1922–58* (Dublin, 1978), p. 39.

17   In February 1923 the Irish government announced its plans to set up the Office of the Revenue Commissioners. By April 1923 the office was established. Seán Réamonn, *History of the Revenue Commissioners* (Dublin, 1981), pp 56–8; Paddy Ryan (ed.), *Revenue over the Years* (Dublin, 1998), pp 8–11; conversions with Paddy Ryan, (now former) Assistant Principal, Communications Branch, Office of the Revenue Commissions (25, 29 Aug. 2006).

18   Telephone conversation with Cormac O'Callaghan (20 Sept. 2006). Mr O'Callaghan joined the Stamping Department as an Assistant Stamper in 1947 and later rose to the position of Director of Stamping.

19   Basil Chubb, *The Government and Politics of Ireland* (3rd edn, London, 1992), p. 230.

20   Telephone conversation with Cormac O'Callaghan (20 Sept. 2006).

21   Ibid.

22   Bulmer Hobson, 'Report of the Inter-Departmental Committee on the Sugar Beet Industry', May 1933, NLI, Bulmer Hobson papers, MS 13,172.

23   See Bulmer Hobson (ed.), *A Book of Dublin* (2nd edn, Dublin, 1930).

24   Molua (Fr Timothy Corcoran, SJ), 'The last pose of Bulmer', *Catholic Bulletin* (Apr. 1932), p. 273.

25   Bulmer Hobson (ed.), *Saorstát Éireann Official Handbook* (Dublin, 1932), p. 15.

26   Molua, 'The last pose of Bulmer', pp 274–9.

27   Hobson, *Ireland Yesterday and Tomorrow*, p. 111.

28   Bulmer Hobson, *A National Forestry Policy* (Dublin, 1931), p. 4.

29   See ibid., pp 1–23. Tom Garvin has countered Hobson's reasons for reforestation. Garvin argues that 'the real [nationalist] desire for reforestation was rooted in aesthetics and restorationism rather than in economic calculation,' adding that the replacement of Irish trees, which had been chopped down and shipped to Britain in the eighteenth century, 'would be a very impressive physical symbol of the undoing of the conquest'. *Nationalist Revolutionaries in Ireland, 1858–1928* (Dublin, 2005), p.135.

30   Review of *A National Forestry Policy*, *Dublin Magazine* (Apr.–June 1933), p. 91.

31   Hobson, *A National Forestry Policy*, p. 15.

32   Review of *A National Forestry Policy*, p. 92.

33   Bulmer Hobson, 'Forestry and the Gaeltacht', *Ireland To-Day* (Aug. 1936), p. 33. Fr Eugene O'Growney was the author of the standard Irish language textbooks used in the early twentieth century, while Church of Ireland archbishop Richard Whately played a leading role in the establishment of the Irish national school system in the nineteenth century.

34   Ibid., p. 34.

35   Bulmer Hobson's draft economic recovery plan, NLI, Hobson papers, MS 13,172.

36   Comment written on Hobson's draft economic recovery plan, NLI, Hobson papers, MS 13,172.

37   Hobson to de Valera, 23 Sept. 1933, NLI, Hobson papers, MS 13,172.

38   See Bulmer Hobson, *National Economic Recovery: An Outline Plan* (Dublin, 1935). This pamphlet is reprinted in Hobson, *Ireland Yesterday and Tomorrow*, pp 128–70.

39   *The New Querist* is reprinted in Hobson, *Ireland Yesterday and Tomorrow*, pp 115–27.

40   William Murphy, 'Cogging Berkeley?: *The Querist* and the rhetoric of Fianna Fáil's economic policy', *Irish Economic and Social History* xxxii (2005), p. 63, 76.

41   Edward Bell, *Social Classes and Social Credit in Alberta* (Montreal, 1993), pp 37, 42–4.

42   Hobson, *The New Querist*, reprinted in Hobson, *Ireland Yesterday and Tomorrow*, p. 116.

43   Ibid., p. 123.

44   Ibid., p. 128.

45   Hobson to William Glynn, 4 June 1937, NAI, DT, S12293.

46   Fanning, *The Irish Department of Finance*, p. 357.

47   Hobson to Dr William Maloney, 31 July 1934, NLI, Joseph McGarrity papers, MS 17,604 (2).

48   Bulmer Hobson, 'The League against Poverty', *Prosperity* (Nov. 1935), p. 1.

49   Garda Special Branch report, NAI, Dept. of Justice, JUS/8/436.

50   Finín O'Driscoll, 'Social Catholicism and the social question in independent Ireland: the challenge to the fiscal system', in Mike Cronin and John M. Regan (eds), *Ireland: The Politics of Independence, 1922–49* (London, 2000), p. 134. Francis Spring Rice, 4th Baron Monteagle of Brandon, was an uncle of the Hon. Mary Spring Rice, who had joined Hobson in playing central roles in the 1914 Howth gun-running. Industrialist Frank Hugh O'Donnell was the owner of a men's clothing company, founder of the Federation of Irish Manufacturers and a future senator. Patrick McCartan was a medical doctor and politician from Carrickmore, Co. Tyrone who had been a nationalist associate of Hobson's since their days in the Dungannon Clubs. thepeerage.com/p35899.htm#i358984 (accessed online 8 July 2014); Bridget Hourican, 'Rice, Mary Ellen Spring' and Marie Coleman, 'McCartan, Patrick' in James McGuire and James Quinn (eds), *Dictionary of Irish Biography* (Cambridge, 2009) (accessed online 8 July 2014); 'Nominated for the Senate – Frank Hugh O'Donnell', *Irish Press*, 18 Mar. 1938; and oireachtas.ie/members-hist/default.asp (accessed online 8 July 2014).

51   These pseudonyms included Rigel, Aldebaran, X, Altair and Corvus. Cathal O'Shannon, William Glynn, B. Berthon Waters, Olive Gibson and Dr Eamon O'Hogan were among the other contributors. The bound copy of *Prosperity/Social Justice* in the Special Collections Department of the University College Dublin Library was annotated by Hobson, who listed the authors of most of the articles in the paper.

52   O'Driscoll, 'Social Catholicism', p. 135.

53   Garda Special Branch report, NAI, Dept. of Justice, JUS/8/436.

54   Bulmer Hobson, 'The manifesto of the League for Social Justice', *Prosperity* (Aug. 1936), p. 74.

55   *Social Justice* (Nov. 1936), p. 104. For Brady's Fianna connection, see Pauric J. Dempsey, 'Brady, Seán Ernest', in McGuire and Quinn (eds), *Dictionary of Irish Biography* (accessed online 7 Feb. 2011).

56   Maurice Curtis, 'Catholic action as an organised campaign in Ireland, 1921–1947' (PhD thesis, University College Dublin, 2000), p. 291; Hobson to Edward Cahill, 6 June 1936, IJA, Cahill papers.

57   In the June 1937 issue of *Social Justice* Hobson announced that the paper was going to 'suspend publication during the summer months' (p. 1). He never revived it.

58   Note in Hobson's handwriting written on a bound copy of *Prosperity/Social Justice* in the Special Collections Department of the University College Dublin Library.

59   Hobson reported that he resigned from the Society of Friends in 1914 because participation in an openly militant organisation like the Irish Volunteers was inconsistent with the pacifist principles of the Quaker faith. Hobson, *Ireland Yesterday and Tomorrow*, p. 1. The records of the Society of Friends, however, list his resignation date as 14 Octtober 1915, HLRSFI, Gen. File 69/2. Hobson may have resigned informally in 1914, but the Lisburn Monthly Meeting later requested written confirmation of his resignation.

60   See Bulmer Hobson, *To the Whole People of Ireland: The Manifesto of the Dungannon Club* (Belfast, 1905), p. 7.

61   Hobson to William Glynn, 4 June 1937, NAI, DT, S12293.

62   *Commission of Inquiry into Banking, Currency and Credit – Reports and Minutes of Evidence* (Dublin, 1938). For a discussion of the commission, see Tom Feeney, *Seán MacEntee: A Political Life* (Dublin, 2009), pp 79–92.

63   Hobson, *Ireland Yesterday and Tomorrow*, p. 171.

64   O'Driscoll, 'Social Catholicism', p. 135.

65   Ibid., pp 135–6.

66   Cahill to de Valera, 8 Sept. 1937, NAI, DT, S12293.

67   Ibid.

68   J. Anthony Gaughan, *Alfred O'Rahilly, II: Public Figure* (Dublin, 1989), pp 312–13; Enda Delaney, 'Fr Denis Fahey, CSSp, and Maria Duce, 1945–1954' (MA thesis, National University of Ireland, Maynooth, 1993), p. 31.

69   O'Driscoll, 'Social Catholicism', p. 136.

70   Hobson, *Ireland Yesterday and Tomorrow*, p. 171; Delaney, 'Denis Fahey', p. 29. 'Draft for a report – Banking Commission 1938' is reprinted in Hobson, *Ireland Yesterday and Tomorrow*, pp 172–243.

71   O'Driscoll, 'Social Catholicism', p. 133.

72   Gaughan, *Alfred O'Rahilly*, p. 310.

73   Annotated copy of the Third Minority Report, NAI, Dept. of Finance, FIN/F009/0018/38.

74   Edward Coyne to Provincial, 1 Sept. 1938, IJA, Coyne papers, quoted in Curtis, 'Catholic action as an organised campaign in Ireland', p. 309.

75   Eithne MacDermott, *Clann na Poblachta* (Cork, 1998), p. 61.

76   Delaney, 'Denis Fahey', p. 31.

77   MacDermott, *Clann na Poblachta*, p. 61.

78   Gaughan, *Alfred O'Rahilly*, pp 387–8. The committee consisted of 'the Taoiseach and ministers for finance, industry and commerce, agriculture and external affairs, officials from their respective departments, the governor of the Central Bank, three professors of economics, Bulmer Hobson and a nominee of the Irish Banks' Standing Committee' (p. 388).

79   Des Gunning, 'Bulmer Hobson, "the most dangerous man in Ireland"', *History Ireland* (spring 2002), p. 5.

80   Patrick Maume, 'Hobson, (John) Bulmer', in McGuire and Quinn (eds), *Dictionary of Irish Biography* (accessed online 12 Jan. 2011).

81   Hobson and Waters co-wrote the first pamphlet in the series, which was entitled *Forging New Links of the Empire*. His other contributions to the series included *Invisible Empire*, *Afforestation*, *National Monetary Policy*, and *Full Home Market*. See Waters to Hobson, 21 May 1948, NLI, Hobson papers, MS 13,161 (9).

82   Flyer for the *Towards a New Ireland* pamphlet series, HLRSFI, William Glynn papers.

83   Hobson, *Ireland Yesterday and Tomorrow*, p. 171.

84   Bulmer Hobson, review of R. G. Stapledon, *The Hill Lands of Britain*, *Ireland To-Day* (Oct. 1937), p. 84.

85   Ibid.

86   *Irish Independent*, 10 Mar. 1938.

87   Deirdre McMahon, 'MacEntee, Seán (John) Francis', in McGuire and Quinn (eds), *Dictionary of Irish Biography* (accessed online 12 Jan. 2011).

88   Bulmer Hobson, statement to Joseph McGarrity, Apr. 1933, NLI, McGarrity papers, MS 17,453.

89   MacMahon, 'MacEntee, Seán (John) Francis'.

90   Correspondence regarding statements made by Bulmer Hobson at a meeting of An Ríoghacht, NAI, Dept. of Finance, FIN/E109/17/38.

91   Ibid.

92   Hobson to Mr Sheehy, 21 Sept. 1937, NLI, James L. O'Donovan papers, MS 21,987/vi.

93   Hobson, *Ireland Yesterday and Tomorrow*, p. 114. Fanciful folklore within the Revenue alleged that Hobson's 'eyesight was impaired as a result of injuries received during the 1916 rising'. Paddy Ryan, 'The old stamping ground', *An Rabhchán* (Feb. 1995), pp 10–11. Hobson himself stated that he had had 'persistent' 'eye trouble' since the age of 17. Seán Ó Lúing, 'Talking to Bulmer Hobson', *Irish Times*, 6 May 1961.

94   Seán MacEntee to William O'Brien, 17 Dec. 1938, in remuneration of higher posts in Stamping Branch, NAI, Dept. of Finance, FIN/E2/1/39.

95   Note for chairman, Nov. 1938, in remuneration of higher posts in Stamping Branch, NAI, Dept. of Finance, FIN/E2/1/39.

96   Office of the Revenue Commissioners to Secretary, Dept. of Finance, 24 Jan. 1944, in remuneration of higher posts in Stamping Branch, NAI, Dept. of Finance, FIN/E2/1/39.

97   Roger Mitchell to Marnie Hay, 9 June 2012 (email in possession of author). Commenting on the sudden death of Claire Hobson in Dublin in 1958, an *Irish Times* columnist recalled not only her 'humour, tolerance, and an insatiable, but always kindly curiosity', but also her 'sound judgement' in relation to literature and theatre. Quidnunc, 'An Irishman's Diary'.

98   Roger Mitchell to Marnie Hay, 9 June 2012 (email in possession of author); Hay, *Bulmer Hobson and the Nationalist Movement*, pp 229–30.

99   Bulmer Hobson to Declan Hobson, 26 Jan. 1969. I would like to thank Hobson's grandson Roger Mitchell for providing me with a copy of this letter.

100   Hobson, *Ireland Yesterday and Tomorrow*, p. 112.

101   Ibid., p. 91.

102   Hobson provided the Bureau of Military History with 16 separate witness statements relating to various nationalist organisations and associates.

103   See Bulmer Hobson, *Defensive Warfare: A Handbook for Irish Nationalists* (Belfast, 1909).

12

The making of Irish revolutionary elites: The case of Seán Lemass

1   This chapter is a reworked and rethought version of an argument first offered in my *Judging Lemass*, published by Royal Irish Academy, Dublin, 2009. I am grateful to the Institute for Irish Studies, University of Liverpool, for their comments on a draft of this article at the Conference of the Society for the Study of Nineteenth-Century Ireland, 30 June and 1 July, 2011.

2   Tom Garvin, *Nationalist Revolutionaries in Ireland 1858–1928* (Oxford, 1987).

3   Interview with Peggy O'Brien (Nov. 1994), John Horgan Archive (JHA), in my private possession.

4   Michael O'Sullivan, *Seán Lemass: A Biography* (Dublin, 1994), pp 2–3.

5   Patrick Leigh Fermor, *Roumeli* (London, 1966).

6   Philip P. Ryan, *Jimmy O'Dea: The Pride of the Coombe* (Dublin, 1990), pp 27–8.

7   John Horgan, *Seán Lemass: The Enigmatic Patriot* (Dublin, 1993), p. 32.

8   Ibid., pp 4–7.

9   Tom Garvin, *1922: The Birth of Irish Democracy* (Dublin, 1996), pp 63–91; Tom Garvin, 'Defenders, ribbonmen and others: underground political networks in pre-famine Ireland', *Past and Present* xcvi (Aug. 1982), pp 133–55.

10   Tom Garvin, *The Evolution of Irish Nationalist Politics* (Dublin, 1981), pp 69–88.

11   Edward Mac Aonraoi to Todd Andrews, 6 Mar. 1980, UCDA, C. S. Andrews papers, P91/158; on Parnell and his MPs, I am indebted to Art Cosgrave, conversations, 1980s.

12   Interview with Kevin Boland (24 Nov. 1994), JHA.

13   *Irish Press*, 20 Jan. 1969.

14   Ibid.

15   Edward MacLysaght, *The Surnames of Ireland* (Dublin, 1973), p. 193.

16   See the dust jacket of O'Sullivan, *Seán Lemass: A Biography*.

17   Horgan, *Seán Lemass*, p. 20.

18   Ibid., p. 9.

19   Conversations with Alvin Sanford Cohan, University of Georgia (1969–70).

20   *Irish Press*, 20 Jan. 1969.

21   Interview with Charles Haughey (24 Oct. 1994), JHA.

22   *Irish Press*, 29 Jan. 1969.

23   Ibid.

24   John Horgan gives the best account. See Horgan, *Seán Lemass*, pp 17–18. A similar, autobiographical account of his *own* use of the ferry on Bloody Sunday is supplied by Charles Dalton in his *With the Dublin Brigade* (London, 1929), pp 106–8. This fact makes the entire story look a little folkloric.

25   *Irish Press*, 29 Jan. 1969.

26   Interview with Michael Mills (16 Jan. 2008).

27   Horgan, *Seán Lemass*, p. 22.

28   Ibid., p 26.

29   Interview with Eileen Lemass (3 Dec. 2008).

30   Interview with Maureen Haughey (27 Feb. 1995), JHA.

31   *Irish Press*, 21 Jan. 1969.

32   Interview with T. K. Whitaker (4 Apr. 2008).

33   Interview with James Ryan (6 Dec. 1968), JHA.

34   O'Sullivan, *Seán Lemass: A Biography*, p. 191.

35   NAI, DT, S16,663 B/61.

36   Horgan, *Seán Lemass*, p. 26.

37   Interview with Kevin Boland (24 Nov. 1994), JHA.

38   Horgan, *Seán Lemass*, pp 26–7; C. S. Andrews, *Dublin Made Me* (Dublin, 1979), p. 222.

39   Interview with unnamed source (31 Aug. 1993), JHA.

40   Liam Skinner, unpublished biography of Seán Lemass, UCDA, P161, pp 1–2.

41   Interview with Charles Haughey (24 Oct. 1994), JHA.

42   *Irish Press*, 7 Feb. 1969.

43   *Irish Independent*, 12 May 1971.

44   Interview with Kevin Boland (24 Nov. 1994), JHA.

45   *Times Pictorial*, 4 Apr. 1953.

46   Garvin, *Judging Lemass*, p. 178.

47   Interview with T. K. Whitaker (1994), JHA. The books referred to are likely to have been Richard Sidney Sayers, *Modern Banking* (1st edn, London, 1938) and either *The Principles of Economic Planning* (1949) or *The Theory of Economic Growth* (1955) by St Lucia-born economist William Arthur Lewis.

48   UCDA, Michael Hayes papers, P53/303/235–507.

49   UCDA, Michael Hayes papers, P53/304/225.

INDEX